BTRIPP BOOKS

BOOK REVIEWS FROM

2016

BY BRENDAN TRIPP

These reviews originally appeared on the
"BTRIPP'S BOOKS" book review blog:
http://btripp-books.livejournal.com/

Copyright © 2017 by Brendan Tripp

ISBN 978-1-57353-416-1

An Eschaton Book

Front cover photo courtesy Kenn W. Kiser via morguefile.com.
Back cover photo courtesy Sebastian Santana via morguefile.com.

PREFACE

From 1993 through 2004, I ran the *first* manifestation of Eschaton Books (now in its third revival). Initially started as a vehicle to publish my poetry, it soon became evident that the market for poetry is vanishingly small, and in 1994 we "pivoted" into being a metaphysical press.

In this time, I was largely a one-man shop, doing everything from editorial to shipping, which was a huge time commitment, and I typically worked 14 hour days, 7 days a week to keep things moving. I bring up all this here because, despite having been a life-long avid reader, during this period I had precious little time for reading, and what reading I *did* get done was largely reviewing book submissions. However, I never stopped *buying* books, which began to stack up in prodigious "to be read" piles.

When Eschaton went out of business in 2004 (in a not unusual denouement for a small press – we had a distributor who ended up never paying us, while selling through all our stock), I found myself with a lot of reading to catch up on, and a need to keep my writing chops sharp. So, I began to pen little reviews of what I was reading, and post those on the web.

As the years went by, this became "a thing" that I was doing, and, for a while, I was targeting a fairly aggressive goal of getting at least 72 non-fiction books read per year. By 2015, this had resulted in my having read and reviewed 700 books over that 12-year span.

In recent years (since the upswing in print-on-demand publishing), I have had numerous acquaintances suggest that I put out my reviews as books. I was, at first, rather hesitant on the concept (as, after all, the material was free to read on the web), but I eventually figured that if various people thought it was a good idea, I might as well give it a shot.

While I could have started at the beginning, I decided that those were less representative of the whole, so opted to begin with the most recent ones and work backwards, resulting in ten volumes released in 2016, with the reviews from 2004-6 in one book, and then annual collections through 2015.

This is the eleventh of these collections, and features 63 reviews. Obviously, this a lot thicker volume than some of its predecessors, as my per-review word count has definitely crept up over time ... from around 500 words when I first started writing these, to sometimes in excess of 3,000 words if I'm really getting into it.

As I've mentioned previously, there were a couple of people who were interested in helping sell these who were encouraging me to go to a "flat rate" per volume, which I was initially resistant to. While the print-on-demand tech is wonderful, the costs are fairly high per copy, and there had to be "enough meat on the bone" to make it into the wider wholesale markets (such as when a bookstore orders in a copy), so I had to pick a cover price that would cover that, or not be able to sell through those channels.

After messing around with the numbers, I picked the rather odd $15.97 as the price ... it's "sort of" numerologically derived, being both a prime number, and a part of the famed Fibonacci sequence ... which is both less than what most of the books had been priced (at the quarter-per-review rate I'd first come up with), and enough for even the longer page-count volumes to get into "extended distribution".

As noted in previous intros, I do not write classic reviews, but more a telling of my personal interaction with a particular book. This means that I talk about where and how I got the book, how it relates to other things I've read, what sort of reactions it triggered in me (and why), and how one can get a copy if it sounds appealing. When reading a biography of Hunter S. Thompson (see page 135), I noted some similarity in my style of reviewing to how his "journalistic style" was being described ... but I'm not sure if I'm ready to try to assume the mantle of "Gonzo". Needless to say, if the reader is devoted to "standard" book reviewing styles, this might be an irritation ... however, it does make these reviews somewhat idiosyncratic to me, resulting in a collection that is something of a "my encounters with books" sort of deal, which will, hopefully, be of interest to many readers.

- Brendan Tripp

CONTENTS

v - Preface

vii - Contents

1 - Saturday, January 9, 2016
Now, how did THAT happen?
The Rapture of the Nerds: A tale of the singularity, posthumanity, and awkward social situations
by Cory Doctorow & Charles Stross

5 - Friday, January 29, 2016
Long ago ...
Marilyn & Me: A Photographer's Memories
by Lawrence Schiller

7 - Saturday, January 30, 2016
Thinking yourself well ...
Cure: A Journey into the Science of Mind Over Body
by Jo Marchant

11 - Sunday, January 31, 2016
But wait, there's more ...
How Enlightenment Changes Your Brain: The New Science of Transformation
by Andrew Newberg, MD & Mark Robert Waldman

15 - Saturday, February 20, 2016
Customer Service, new style ...
Hug Your Haters: How to Embrace Complaints and Keep Your Customers
by Jay Baer

19 - Sunday, February 21, 2016
A certain glow ...
The Age of Radiance: The Epic Rise and Dramatic Fall of the Atomic Era
by Craig Nelson

23 - Sunday, March 13, 2016

Too much of a good thing?
**Less Medicine, More Health:
7 Assumptions That Drive Too Much Medical Care**
by Dr. H. Gilbert Welch

28 - Monday, March 14, 2016

*This stuff has been kicking around
a lot longer than you think ...*
The Magic of Believing
by Claude M. Bristol

31 - Thursday, March 17, 2016

Getting visible ...
**It's Not Who You Know, It's Who Knows YOU!
A Practical Business Guide to Raising Your Profits
By Raising Your Profile**
by David Avrin

34 - Friday, March 18, 2016

"... Messing With My Mind!"
Influence: The Psychology of Persuasion
by Robert B. Cialdini

38 - Saturday, March 26, 2016

A different side ...
Love Is the Cure: On Life, Loss, and the End of AIDS
by Elton John

42 - Tuesday, March 29, 2016

More like 53 skills in 11 groupings ...
**The Art of People: 11 Simple People Skills
That Will Get You Everything You Want**
by Dave Kerpen

46 - Saturday, April 9, 2016

Turning threats into opportunities ...
**The Upside: The 7 Strategies
for Turning Big Threats Into Growth Breakthroughs**
by Adrian J. Slywotzky

51 - Sunday, April 10, 2016

A writing class with Mr. King ...
On Writing: A Memoir of the Craft
by Steven King

56 - Monday, April 11, 2016

A blast from the past ...
If it Ain't Broke...Break It!: And Other Unconventional Wisdom for a Changing Business World
by Robert J. Kriegel

61 - Tuesday, April 12, 2016

Banking on your unconscious mind ...
Success is Not an Accident: The Mental Bank Concept
by John G. Kappas, Ph.D.

65 - Saturday, April 23, 2016

Going up against the "Democrat-Media Complex" ...
**Righteous Indignation:
Excuse Me While I Save the World!**
by Andrew Brietbart

70 - Sunday, April 24, 2016

Glad THAT'S over with ...
Gödel, Escher, Bach: An Eternal Golden Braid
by Douglas R. Hofstadter

74 - Thursday, May 26, 2016

One of the greats ...
Auguste Escoffier: Memories of My Life
by Auguste Escoffier

78 - Friday, May 27, 2016

"All day on channel nine"?
Listen To This
by Alex Ross

81 - Saturday, May 28, 2016

From one tormented moment ... to the next
An Unquiet Mind: A Memoir of Moods and Madness
by Kay Redfield Jamison

84 - Sunday, May 29, 2016

From "funnel" to "radar" ...
**The Invisible Sale: How to Build
a Digitally Powered Marketing and Sales System
to Better Prospect, Qualify and Close Leads**
by Tom Martin

88 - Friday, June 10, 2016

War is Hell ...
**On Killing: The Psychological Cost
of Learning to Kill in War and Society**
by Lt. Col. Dave Grossman

93 - Monday, June 13, 2016

Preaching to the choir ...
God Is Not Great: How Religion Poisons Everything
by Christopher Hitchens

99 - Tuesday, June 14, 2016

Stuff you probably didn't know ...
**We the People: The Modern-Day Figures
Who Have Reshaped and Affirmed
the Founding Fathers' Vision of America**
by Juan Williams

105 - Saturday, June 18, 2016

Another play ...
Arms & The Man
by George Bernard Shaw

108 - Sunday, June 19, 2016

The tyranny of good intentions?
**The Third Industrial Revolution: How Lateral Power
Is Transforming Energy, the Economy, and the World**
by Jeremy Rifkin

111 - Tuesday, June 21, 2016

Looking for Emmanuel Goldstein?
**The Joy of Hate: How to Triumph over Whiners
in the Age of Phony Outrage**
by Greg Gutfeld

116 - Wednesday, June 22, 2016

Memories ... tasty, tasty memories ...
**Talking with My Mouth Full:
My Life as a Professional Eater**
by Gail Simmons

120 - Thursday, June 30, 2016

Unless It Comes with a Comfy Chair ...
**The Simple Beauty of the Unexpected:
A Natural Philosopher's Quest for Trout
and the Meaning of Everything**
by Marcelo Gleiser

125 - Wednesday, July 6, 2016

An excellent introduction ...
**Living in Blue Sky Mind:
Basic Buddhist Teachings for a Happy Life**
by Richard Gentei Diedrichs

129 - Thursday, July 7, 2016

Managing emotions within negotiations ...
Beyond Reason: Using Emotions as You Negotiate
by Roger Fisher & Daniel Shapiro

133 - Tuesday, July 12, 2016

"Souls of Poets dead and gone ..."
Lyric Poems
by John Keats

135 - Wednesday, July 13, 2016

When the going gets weird ...
**Outlaw Journalist:
The Life and Times of Hunter S. Thompson**
by William McKeen

138 - Saturday, July 23, 2016

You really should read this one ...
**The Conscience of a Libertarian: Empowering the
Citizen Revolution with God, Guns, Gold and Tax Cuts**
by Wayne Allyn Root

144 - Sunday, July 24, 2016

Why religion?
Breaking the Spell: Religion as a Natural Phenomenon
by Daniel C. Dennett

149 - Tuesday, August 2, 2016

Training camp for the emotional side ...
**Emotional Agility: Get Unstuck, Embrace Change,
and Thrive in Work and Life**
by Susan David, PhD.

154 - Wednesday, August 3, 2016

Once upon a time, there was a ...
The Decision Maker: Unlock the Potential of Everyone in Your Organization, One Decision at a Time
by Dennis Bakke

157 - Sunday, August 7, 2016

Observing culinary history ...
Steal the Menu: A Memoir of Forty Years in Food
by Raymond Sokolov

162 - Monday, August 8, 2016

My choice is "nope!" ...
Choice Point: Align Your Purpose
by Harry Massey & David R. Hamilton, Ph.D.

165 - Sunday, August 21, 2016

How does that work, again?
Darwin's Devices: What Evolving Robots Can Teach Us About the History of Life and the Future of Technology
by John Long

169 - Monday, August 22, 2016

The Odd Couple ...
Love & War: Twenty Years, Three Presidents, Two Daughters and One Louisiana Home
by Mary Matalin & James Carville

174 - Saturday, September 3, 2016

An amazing look at an icon ...
Pure Goldwater
by John W. Dean & Barry M. Goldwater Jr.

179 - Sunday, September 4, 2016

Originally nothing. Where is dust?
Don't-Know Mind: The Spirit of Korean Zen
by Richard Shrobe

182 - Friday, September 9, 2016

A lucky tale ...
Captive: My Time as a Prisoner of the Taliban
by Jere Van Dyk

185 - Saturday, September 10, 2016

A snapshot ...
JFK Jr., George, & Me: A Memoir
by Matt Berman

188 - Sunday, September 11, 2016

The "Pathfinder of the Seas" ...
**Tracks in the Sea: Matthew Fontaine Maury
and the Mapping of the Oceans**
by Chester G. Hearn

193 - Saturday, September 17, 2016

Useful and Transcendent ...
**Golden Gate:
The Life and Times of America's Greatest Bridge**
by Kevin Starr

198 - Monday, September 19, 2016

Fair & Balanced ...
Roger Ailes: Off Camera
by Zev Chafets

203 - Friday, September 30, 2016

Must be crazy ...
**Sane New World:
A User's Guide to the Normal-Crazy Mind**
by Ruby Wax

207 - Saturday, October 1, 2016

No cure for meaninglessness ...
The Power of Meaning: Crafting a Life That Matters
by Emily Esfahani Smith

213 - Saturday, October 8, 2016

... if I sang out of tune
**Friendfluence:
The Surprising Ways Friends Make Us Who We Are**
by Carlin Flora

218 - Saturday, October 15, 2016

"You can't handle the truth!", or something ...
Lost Ancient Technology Of Peru And Bolivia
by Brien Foerster

222 - Sunday, October 16, 2016

The right side of the airwaves ...
Rush Limbaugh: An Army of One
by Zev Chafets

226 - Monday, November 14, 2016

Mission Implausible ...
Dark Mission: The Secret History of NASA
by Richard C. Hoagland & Mike Bara

230 - Tuesday, November 15, 2016

Saling away ...
The Art of the Sale: Learning from the Masters About the Business of Life
by Philip Delves Broughton

234 - Wednesday, November 30, 2016

Calls you out by name ...
See a Little Light: The Trail of Rage and Melody
by Bob Mould & Michael Azerrad

238 - Saturday, December 3, 2016

Learning to Stop Worrying and Love the Bomb?
Thinking Beyond the Unthinkable: Harnessing Doom from the Cold War to the Age of Terror
by Jonathan Stevenson

241 - Sunday, December 4, 2016

So many scammers ...
Beggars, Cheats, & Forgers: a History of Frauds Through the Ages
by David Thomas

245 - Wednesday, December 28, 2016

Complicated Abe ...
Lincoln Unbound: How an Ambitious Young Railsplitter Saved the American Dream --and How We Can Do It Again
by Rich Lowry

248 - Thursday, December 29, 2016

Awesome book ...
The Fifth Agreement: A Practical Guide to Self-Mastery
by don Miguel Ruiz & don Jose Ruiz

253 - Friday, December 30, 2016

"not mandatory"
Keep It Pithy: Useful Observations in a Tough World
by Bill O'Reilly

256 - Saturday, December 31, 2016

"everyday is silent and grey"
Autobiography
by Morrissey

261 - **QR Code Links**

279 - **Contents - Alphabetical By Author**

287 - **Contents - Alphabetical By Title**

Saturday, January 9, 2016[1]

Now, how did THAT happen?

Well, this was an interesting way to start off the new year. As regular readers know, I have read nearly *no* fiction over the past couple 12-15 years (I can think of maybe 4 titles out of over 700+ books read in that span), and, generally speaking, don't even *look* at a book if it says "a novel" on the cover. So, I was *totally* blind-sided by Cory Doctorow and Charles Stross' The Rapture of the Nerds: A tale of the singularity, posthumanity, and awkward social situations[2], which I recently picked up at the dollar store. There was nothing in the sub-title that made me think this was fiction (although, in reflection, I suppose "awkward social situations" would be a somewhat touchy thing for a non-fiction book), and I had *no idea* that Doctorow was a scifi author (I was familiar with him as a blogger and tech writer, a voice of the Electronic Frontier Foundation, and advocate for "open source" software and Creative Commons licensing). So, I launched into this thinking it was going to be somewhat similar to my recently-reviewed Our Grandchildren Redesigned[3], with a somewhat different spin (encompassing those *"awkward social situations"*). But, no. Not that certain *aspects* of related futurisms aren't thickly woven through the book, but it's a *story* and very much in the Douglas Adams / Terry Pratchett mold (I have no idea if this is Doctorow's regular mode, but I was frequently reminded of those authors when reading this – even when they weren't being directly referenced).

I must admit, *part* of me wanted to stop reading with that "ooh, ick – *cooties!*" reaction (fiction is, after all, something of a Jedi Mind Trick to get you infected with the author's fantasies, and I *hate* being manipulated like that), but I figured (as it was a pretty quick read – I'm amazed how much the pages fly by in fiction as opposed to the stuff I usually read) that since it was not an *uninteresting* read (I walked away with at least one "that's a fascinating concept" data point), I'd press on.

Unfortunately, as I've noted before, I have *very* little experience in reviewing fiction … most of the habits I've built up in non-fiction would no doubt be decried as "spoilers", so *please*, if this is an issue for you (and I know from reading the boards over on LibraryThing, there are a LOT of people who get their panties in a wad over the most minimal details being revealed about a novel), just stop reading here and skip down to the end of the review.

Of course, one of those habits is sticking in little slips of paper as bookmarks to get me back to particularly interesting concepts, nice turns of phrase, or significant bits of exposition to flesh out my review. I did manage to stick *three* of these in here, one early on for a notable rant that I found amusing: *"Jesus Buddha humping the corpse of Oliver Cromwell …"* – amusing, if not particularly *enlightening* in this context. As I noted above, there was at least one blatant nod to Douglas Adams here: *"Hyperspace bypasses, Vogon poetry, the heat death of the universe: none of these things feature in the extraordinary situation now pertaining to the end of the world …"*, and I've probably missed numerous other shout-outs (oh, there are Dalek references and Ayn Rand as well). One thing that I'm quite familiar with is the virtual world of Second Life (where I worked in my last full-time job), and there is "Your Second Life" in the book, one quote relating to this that I found hilarious was this snippet: *"Architectural hubris is cheap as air in the cloud."* (given that in the waning days of my tenure in SL, I built this[4] Speer-like bit of "architectural hubris", and I can only imagine what would be possible given near-infinite computing power!

Anyway, to the story outline … the main character is Huw Jones, a Welsh fellow (initially) who is stubbornly clinging on to a "reality-based" lifestyle in an age when significant chunks of the race (including his parents) have "uploaded themselves into the cloud" (something discussed in that book I linked to above) and are living in a virtual reality based on planetary matter reduced to "computronium", which is formed into Dyson spheres. Here's a chunk of descriptive text:

> The cloud – the diffuse swarm of solar-powered nano-computers hat the singularity built from the bones of the inner solar system (Earth aside) – consists of quadrillions of chunks of raw quantum computing power, each of them powerful enough to run a shard in which thousands of human-scale minds can thrive (or a handful of superhuman ones). Entire small moons and planets were consumed back in the day …
>
> From the outside, from a terrestrial embodied point of view, the cloud looks like a single entity, a monolithic slab of smartmatter thinking with the mysterious and esoteric thoughts of an uploaded syncitium of futurist minds, disembodied think-states floating in an abstract neurological void.
>
> But on the inside, the cloud consists of a myriad of shards separated by light-speed communications links, the homes of hordes of bickering beings who cling to their own individuality as tightly as any mud-grubbing neophobe. …

Huw is *such* a "neophobe" that he lives without electricity, and spends much of his time hand-making ceramics. However, he ends up going to a party at an acquaintance's place, and everything goes to heck. He wakes up and finds he's acquired a glowing bio-hazard tattoo (an official warning device), which he has to keep hidden, as he's been called to *jury duty* in a court in North Africa where extreme technologies are considered – his voice nominally being needed *as* a neophobe.

Now, while the story unfolds in a reasonably straight line, much of the detail is quite convoluted. Despite Huw's lifestyle, even those who have *not* "uploaded" have a lot of options, including changing their sexes seemingly on a whim, so a character "Bonnie", goes from female to male to female to male throughout the book, and Huw spends much of this in a female form. It appears that the whole pretense of the trial is a sham, set up to get Huw in the presence of a particular entity, which manifests as a whistle-like thing that hops down Huw's throat. This is an "ambassador" of some galactic super cloud entity, which has inexplicably chosen *him* (her?) as the representative of the various manifestations of humanity.

Oh, on the way to the final trial, Huw is captured by some strange Fundy cult in the American south, interfaces with a very odd counter-cult, and gets exposed to a massive ant culture … all on the way to having his/her awareness uploaded against his/her will into the cloud (which he previously described, in the case of his parents, as their "suicide" as the physical brain, etc. gets dematerialized in the process of uploading its encoded information).

Once uploaded he is set into a training phase, and has two years of "subjective time" to learn how to operate in the cloud. Huw – the central one – uses this time to re-create his home in Wales and throw pots. However, there are *hundreds of thousands* of other "instances", with the version 639,219 being her main opponent in parts of the book (referred to as the number, as Huw refuses to call her "Huw") - one who had actually spent those two years learning to be an expert in life in the cloud. Oh, and most of the jurors get a teapot with a genie inside it … Huw's genie is a major factor in helping (sort of) Huw in his/her struggles with 639,219.

Eventually, Huw is set to be tested by the Authority – the galactic entity:

> "It calls itself the Authority. It claims it represents a hive-intelligence merged from about 2^{16} intelligent species from the oldest part of the galaxy. It claims that there were once about four orders of magnitude more such species, but the rest were wiped out in vicious, galactic resource wars that only ended with the merger of the remaining combatants into a single entity. Now it patrols the galaxy to ensure that any species that attempt transcendence are fit to join it. If it finds a species wanting, **pfft!** It takes care of them before they get to be a problem".

Or, in a later discussion:

> It's not about integrating Earth into the cloud, or about some stupid squabble over aesthetics: if the galactic federation finds us Guilty of Being a Potential Nuisance, we don't get a second chance.

Huw's cloud-based Mother is a character who becomes significant once he's uploaded, but his Dad (or a projection of something like his Dad) ends up being the foil (judge?) with whom he has to work a "world building kit", the results of which will tell the Authority whether or not humanity makes the cut. Huw thinks he's still finishing things up when his Dad says *"The objective of the exercise was to procure a representative sample of moves, played by a proficient emissary, and we've now delivered that."*, to which Huw rather desperately responds: *"You mean that was it?"* … and his Dad explains:

> "Son, do you know how long you were in there?" His dad raises an eyebrow. "You spent nearly a million subjective days shoving around sims, and so did the other billion instances of you that came through the door. If a trillion subjective years isn't enough for –"

Leading up to the (rather anti-climactic, given all the chaos preceding it) revelation that Huw/humanity passed the test. Some loose ends get tied up, a lot of others are left hanging, and the book just sort of ends.

OK, safe to come back in if you were waiting for the spoilers to stop.

As I mentioned, I got The Rapture of the Nerds[5] (in the hardcover edition) at the dollar store less than a month ago, so copies might well still be bouncing around that channel. It is still in print in a paperback (and ebook) edition, and at least one web site seems to have the entire book online (thanks to Doctorow's very liberal view of copyright). Used copies of this are available via the on-line new/used vendors for as little a 1¢ (plus shipping) for a "very good" copy.

I must admit that parts of this messed with my mind in a very Philip K. Dick way, so, while I found it an *enjoyable* read, I also found it somewhat *disturbing*, but I just don't "do fiction" these days, and I'm pretty sure somebody used to hosting other people's fantasies on their brain systems wouldn't have the same reactions. As it reminded me of the works of a number of authors I quite liked in my fiction-reading past, I guess I'm pretty safe in recommending it, especially as it's quite reasonably available.

Notes:

1. http://btripp-books.livejournal.com/179356.html
2. http://amzn.to/1kos7qF
3. http://btripp-books.livejournal.com/176509.html
4. https://goo.gl/SkePKM
5. http://amzn.to/1kos7qF

Friday, January 29, 2016[1]

Long ago ...

Sometimes books have a very brief trip from store shelf to the to-be-reviewed pile, and this is one of them ... my having just run into it at the dollar store a scant ten days ago. I guess what pushed Lawrence Schiller's Marilyn & Me: A Photographer's Memories[2] through my reading pipeline was that it was small, short, and not a particularly taxing subject (compared to some of the other stuff I've been reading of late), so it offered something easy and distracting. What more can you ask for a buck?

Frankly, this is a very brief look into the past ... it's scarcely over a hundred pages, it's a small-format book, and has many pages (17?) of photographs, mostly from shoots described in the book. The author, still extant, is turning 80 this year, and he's evidently working on putting out "memories" of points in his career while he can still connect with them. He notes that he doesn't *have* "notes" from back then (1960-62), so this is from his recall from a half a century on. This leads to a less detailed telling, but one with an almost dream-like arc.

The book starts out in 1960 when the author was a 23-year-old photographer ... but hardly a novice, having done considerable work for various of the top magazines at the time. He had been assigned by *Look* to photograph Marilyn Monroe on the set of a film she was doing, and was being shown around the studio by one of their publicists when he first met Marilyn. At this point, she was already in her mid-30's and seemed amused to be working with a press photographer so much younger than her, being both playful and open with Schiller.

One of the things that he recalls was the "business" side of Marilyn ... she, for instance, insisted on being able to approve all shots, and could be very picky about what she thought was OK, too much muscle tone in a leg, the wrong angle on the hair, the eyes not being just right, and it would get a red X on the proof sheet. Oh, yes ... and this was back in the *real film* days – Schiller carried multiple cameras around with him, loaded with both color and B&W film, which he personally took back to his darkroom to process and print. So there were delays involved, ones that he tried to minimize by getting the contact sheets (kids: that's where the strips of film were shot directly onto the photo paper, creating 8x10's with many small images on them) done as soon as possible, and back to Marilyn.

He did notice, however, that Marilyn, even using a pro magnifier, was rejecting shots because she really couldn't see the details ... he eventually printed enlarged versions on large sheets, and found that she was rejecting far fewer images.

Another thing about that side of her that he returns to a number of times is her insecurity, if not anger, about being paid as little as she was compared to other actresses. She even insisted, on one set of images, that the magazines could only use them if they had *nothing* about Elizabeth Taylor in the issue.

One film that he was on set for involved a scene where Marilyn was swimming nude in a pool, and one of the places Schiller was looking to sell the more revealing images was *Playboy* (with Marilyn's approval). He has a record of his correspondence with Hugh Hefner, some of which is reproduced here – offering a fascinating window into the dynamics of the early days of that magazine (Hef had a great idea for a front and back cover shoot, which never got done).

Much of Marilyn & Me[3] is like that, a look at what seems like a long-ago era, with vignettes of the movie studios (and assorted actors, and ancillary staff), the photographers of the time (he teamed up with some for a couple of projects here – back in the days of film, exclusivity drove up the price of images significantly), and Los Angeles of the era.

Schiller was there right at the end ... he had swung by Marilyn's house soon after Fox had re-started *Something's Got To Give*, and he was going to drop off some prints to her, and see if what her publicist had said on the phone to him (about how the Playboy deal was off) was true (Marilyn said that *"she wasn't authorized to make that call"*). That was Saturday morning, the next day she was dead.

As noted above, there are a number of photographs in this, as you would expect, but far fewer than one might anticipate. Most, naturally, are of Marilyn, but there's one of the author, a few of Marilyn with co-stars on set, a couple "newsy" ones following her death (including a very poignant one of Joe DiMaggio and his son), and the cover of *Life* that he scored with a portrait shot for a memorial issue. It's hardly a "photo book", but it has just enough of those images to give a visual counterpart to the narrative.

Again, I found Marilyn & Me[4] less than two weeks ago at the dollar store, so it might well still be kicking around those channels at this point. It's still in print (in a very nice deckle-edge hardcover and an ebook edition), so might be out there in the brick & mortar stores. The on-line big boys have it, of course, at a bit of a discount, and there are some copies via the new/used vendors as well (but, oddly, not in the penny-plus-shipping range yet). Having been a child of the 60's, a lot of the ambient detail of this book was quite nostalgic (especially the old-style photography stuff) ... it certainly is an interesting look into a world that one is *familiar* with, on the surface, but one that wasn't easy to access. The author had that access, and opens up that world to the reader.

Notes:

1. http://btripp-books.livejournal.com/179485.html

2-4. http://amzn.to/1Kr1Z5w

Saturday, January 30, 2016[1]

Thinking yourself well ...

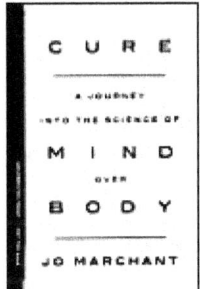

This is another of those "Early Reviewer" books from LibraryThing.com ... and it seems that, after years of reviewing there, I've gotten into a relationship with the LTER "almighty algorithm", where if I request a science book, the odds are pretty good that I'm going to get that one sent to me. This came out as part of the November batch, so if I had gotten around to reading it right away, I would have actually been "early", as this just came out a couple a weeks ago (not necessarily a "feature" in the LTER program, which frequently gets books as something of an afterthought from the publishers, sometimes considerably later than their release date).

Anyway, Jo Marchant's Cure: A Journey into the Science of Mind Over Body[2] is a look at how, as exemplified in a wide number of research studies, the mind affects the body – often in ways that are quite counterintuitive. Part of this is the by-now familiar issue with placebos. It's a major irritation (embarrassment?) for the pharmaceutical industry that absolutely neutral placebo pills in double-blind studies will perform as well as, or in many cases *better* than the drugs being tested. This is where the book starts off.

It is amazing what's in the literature about this ... I'm cherry-picking three examples to describe here .. first, there was *one kid* with severe autism that, almost inexplicably, got notably better following a procedure involving running a tube down to his stomach. The doctors tried to sort out all the possible factors, and eventually identified a hormone the kid had been given that was designed to increase digestive enzymes. The child's parents were *begging* the doctors to keep giving the kid the hormone, which they did for a few doses, but then stopped as it was an "off label" use. However, by this time word of the "results" had spread through the whole autism community, and hundreds of families were clamoring for access to the prescription. Eventually a strict double-blind test was set up, with half the patients getting the hormone and half getting a saline shot. What this showed was that there was *no* difference in improvement between the two ... however, *both* showed a 30% improvement on the autism test scale. Another illustration here was an Italian researcher who has set up a lab high up in the Alps, where he's testing effects of altitude sickness ... here subjects are asked to exercise while their blood, etc. is being monitored. The division here is then between a group that's given oxygen, and another that's just breathing air through a mask. The group that only *thought* they were getting oxygen showed similar changes in prostaglandin levels and vasodilation ... although (obviously) the actual oxygen levels in their bloodstream stayed the same. Most remarkable, though, is the material on *fake surgeries*, where subjects either got an actual procedure or a detailed "play acting" of one. The procedure was *"vertebroplasty, which injects medical cement into the fractured bone to strengthen it"* (in the spine) and the researchers had 131 patients at 11 medical centers, with the patients aware that they had only a 50/50 chance of getting the actual procedure. What was amazing here is that, even with *surgery* there was no significant difference between the results of the two groups – both sets of patients reported in follow-ups having their pain reduced by almost half. The story focuses on one lady, who was nearly crippled from a fall, who walked out of the hospital after the sham procedure, reported feeling vastly better, and resumed her previous activities (including golf!) afterwards.

The author then goes into a chapter on Pavlovian-style conditioning, which shows that the mind (& body) can be "tricked" into responding (because of other external cues) as though actual medications were being used. One patient ended up having her dosage effectively halved over the course of a year by utilizing cod liver oil and rose perfume as accompaniments to her actual drugs, which led her immune system to *act like it was getting the drugs* even when she was just being exposed to the taste/scent cues. As bizarre as this sounds, it's not really all that much different from having one's mouth water at the *thought* of biting into a lemon, or having one's gut go all acrophobic when seeing a vertiginous video scene.

Another fascinating bit here was in studies of exercise and fatigue ... looking for a way to improve the performance of athletes ... one set of researchers noted:

> *Obviously, there is a physical limit to what the body can achieve. But rather than responding directly to tired muscles ... the brain acts in advance of this limit, making us feel tired and forcing us to stop exercising well before any peripheral signs of damage occur. In other words, fatigue isn't a physical event, but a <u>sensation</u> or <u>emotion</u>, invented by the brain to prevent catastrophic harm.*

One area that Marchant looks into is that of pain management ... she paints some really gruesome pictures of the work needed for burn victims (many wounded soldiers), and how toxic the drugs can be. She points out:

> *... the U.S. ... makes up less than 5% of the global population but consumes 80% of the world's supply of opioid prescription drugs. By 2012 15,000 Americans were dying each year from prescription pill overdoses, more than from heroin and cocaine combined.*

... with the CDC calling painkiller addiction "the worst drug epidemic in U.S. History". As an alternative to the painkiller drugs, several centers are using Virtual Reality systems which cut pain scores by 35%, and can reduce pain ratings as much as 40% on top of patients drug doses. Needless to say, I found this interesting as my last full-time job was working with a "metaverse developer", creating projects in Second Life. The author says *"there is relatively little research interest in non-pharmacological methods to help people deal with pain"*, and cites a Stanford researcher's view:

> *... that part of the reason for the lack of enthusiasm is economic. Pain relief is a billion-dollar market, and drug companies have no incentive to fund tri-*

> *als that would reduce patient's dependence on their products ... And neither have medical insurers, because if medical costs come down, so do their profits ... "there's no intervening industry that has the interest in pushing {non-pharmacological methods}*

She notes that this might be about to change, with the acquisition by Facebook of Oculus, whose "Rift" provides Virtual Reality immersion for somewhere around $350 rather than the $90,000 that some of the hospital systems run.

There is a *lot* of stuff in here ... mindfulness, biofeedback, even an extensive look at Lourdes ... however, at the end she veers into areas that she holds *don't* have any effect, Reiki, Homeopathy, "aura cleansing", faith healing, all of which she notes score no better than placebo results (of course, those are enough for many). However, those "touchy-feely" approaches might be appreciated just because they *are* high-contact:

> *a health science researcher at the Mayo Clinic ... wants to help doctors take account of how patients feel, instead of relying solely on physical tests. That's tough to do in a rushed appointment. "In modern medicine doctors usually only have one-to-three minutes of any given clinical visit with a patient that are unaccounted for ..."*

Yet, she further notes that only 0.2% of the $30 billion NIH budget goes to testing mind-body therapies. This is in relation to these rather horrific data points (pardon the large quote):

> *But the main threats facing us now are not acute infection, easily cured with a pill, but chronic, stress-related conditions for which drugs are not nearly as effective. We've seen that in many cases, painkillers and antidepressants may not work much better than placebo. The top ten highest grossing drugs in the U.S. help only between 1 in 25 and 1 in 4 of the people who take them; statins may benefit as few as 1 in 50.*
>
> *Meanwhile, medical interventions are causing harm that dwarfs any damage done by alternative treatments. In 2015, an analysis of psychiatric drug trials published in the <u>British Medical Journal</u> concluded that these drugs are responsible for more than half a million deaths in the Western world each year, in return for minimal benefits. Meanwhile, medical errors in hospital are estimated to cause more than 400,000 deaths per year in the U.S. alone – making it the third leading cause of death after heart disease and cancer – with another 4-6 million cases of serious harm.*

Again, I've really only been able to skim the surface of the material that's in Cure[3], and while not all of it is as gripping as the bits highlighted above, it's an real eye-opener.

As noted, at this writing this has been out less than two weeks, so it should certainly be available at your local bookstore (if you still *have* a local bookstore) ... otherwise, the on-line guys have it at a substantial (40% off of cover) discount. The book has both strengths and weaknesses largely based on the wide array of specific topics addressed ... it's a bit of a fire-hose of info, without much of it really having a resolved state when the author moves on to the next thing, and I don't think she is able to weave the multiple threads into a whole. It *is* a font of fascinating stuff that's happening out there, and if you're interested in this sort of thing, you may well want to check it out.

Notes:

1. http://btripp-books.livejournal.com/179750.html

2-3. http://amzn.to/1MDQ9EE

Sunday, January 31, 2016[1]

But wait, there's more ...

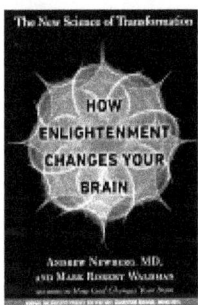

Well, this is a bit of an unusual case, a LTER – Library-Thing.com "Early Review" program – book that is actually *early* enough that I've gotten it read and am cranking out the review *well* in advance of its official release date (mid-March). The book, too, is a bit unusual, being co-authored by an MBA coach and a doctor who's the head of research in "integrative medicine" at a university hospital, writing about spiritual stuff. Actually, by the *end* of the book it's not as odd a mix (I'll hold off on *that* commentary until further into this) as it would seem up front, but, still ...

Andrew Newberg, MD and Mark Robert Waldman's How Enlightenment Changes Your Brain: The New Science of Transformation[2] is evidently a follow-up to their *How God Changes Your Brain*, and it appears that they're both (they collaborated on several titles, but have a number of others separately) big into the "biology of belief" (or various similar spins on that concept). Frankly, I'm *very* glad I hadn't looked into their publishing history before I read the book, because it probably would have put me off of this from the start (as their titles sound *awfully* "preachy"). However, it goes a long way to explaining the vague disconnect that I was having with the book (which is notably *not* "preachy", although it goes to great lengths to be "inclusive" of various – especially the major monotheisms – traditions). Needless to say, I would have preferred this to been a "non-religious" look at the topic, and felt the authors weren't really trying to "go there" ... but I guess that's just me.

That gripe out of the way, I ended up with *way* more little bookmarks than usual in this ... meaning that I found a lot of notable points. The book is somewhat anchored in the authors' personal stories, with bits like *"As I reflected on the problem of how my own brain – my own mind – was trying to find truth, I found myself becoming more contemplative."*. They make a distinction between "small e" *enlightenment*, and "big E" *Enlightenment*, and these weave back and forth through the book, and everything is structured in a "Spectrum of Human Awareness", which goes Level 1 – Instinctual, Level 2 – Habitual, Level 3 – Intentional, Level 4 – Creative, Level 5 – Self-Reflective, and Level 6 – Transformational, which moves from "biological awareness" to "everyday consciousness" to "spiritual awareness", with levels 2-4 being where we find ourselves most of time.

Despite my kvetching above, the authors do have a chapter "Enlightenment Without God", so they address the issue, but it still seems like a bit of a stretch for the authors. They note:

> Since our main purpose in writing this book is to show the neurological evidence that personal transformation is available to everyone, we want to address Enlightenment through the eyes of a disbeliever.

> The past decade has seen a dramatic rise in atheism, and religious affiliation is at its lowest point in American history. In fact, over forty-six million Americans publicly declare themselves nonreligious. That's 20 percent of the adult population, with nearly a 60 percent drop-out rate for those who are younger than 30.

Interestingly, most of what's presented in this chapter are quotes from interviews with an array of "non-religious" interviewees, which then pivots into discussing *drugs*. I think a pro-religious bias hangs over this chapter particularly, as though the authors can't really *connect* with a non-religious world view, and imply that atheists need psychedelics to have enlightenment experiences!

The book is split into three sections, "The Roots of Enlightenment", "The Paths Towards Enlightenment", and "Moving Toward Enlightenment" with chapters covering various subjects from "What Enlightenment Feels Like" to "Channeling Supernatural Entities" (*yeah*, I know). As you can tell from that last bit, they poke around in a lot of neighborhoods which many might not consider particularly "enlightenment" oriented. However, they keep the neuroscience end of things up, and generally will happily hook *anybody* (Pentecostals speaking in tongues, mediums talking to the dead, Buddhist monks adept at meditation, Sufis doing *dhikr*, etc.) up to a brain scan. Here's their description of the process:

> We devised an experiment using single photo emission computed tomography (SPECT) to measure different regions of the brain. When certain areas become more active, there is increased blood flow, and if that occurs in the frontal lobe, for instance, your decision-making skills make increase. If it occurs in the parietal lobe, your conscious awareness of yourself may increase. If it occurs in the amygdala, you might feel suddenly fearful, and if it occurs in the thalamus, we believe that the event you are experiencing will feel more real and intense.
> To do a SPECT scan we start by placing a small intravenous catheter in your arm. Then when you are performing a particular activity – {such as} entering a trance state – we inject a small amount of a radioactive tracer that quickly travels to the most active areas of your brain. These tracers are generally considered quite harmless since the several nanograms of material are so small. Importantly, once the tracer gets to the active part of the brain, it stays there. So after you've completed the activity (for example, prayer or psychography) we want to measure … we'll take you down the hall to our SPECT camera and literally take a picture of what your brain was doing at that moment.

One of the things I found slightly irritating here is how they sort of dismiss some practices, while getting all enthusiastic about others. While they are very positive about a number of religious forms (discussed in detail – along with commentary on what is happening in the brains of the practitioners), they do note:

> Evidence suggests that no matter what you think Enlightenment might be, the actual experience is usually very different from anything you could imagine. At some level you must be willing to accept whatever the experience brings. In most religions, this is referred to as surrender, or giving your will over to some higher authority or power. This requires faith, perseverance, and devotion.
>
> But giving up old beliefs involves risk. So religion poses a double bind: traditions demand that you adhere to the specific tenets of the organization, but Enlightenment involves transcending them. This partly explains why new religions typically are established by people who felt enlightened by their spiritual endeavors, and it also explains why the orthodoxy will persecute them. And when your beliefs are transformed, it appears to be neurologically impossible to return to the old ones.

They go into various elements about "belief", and this bit stood out:

> Our brains do not like ambiguity – a cognitive function called "uncertainty bias" … regulated by the same frontal and parietal regions that are involved in Enlightenment experiences. In other words, when you decrease your frontal lobe activity … your sense of certainty decreases. This makes it easier for the brain to engage in belief-changing activities. But when the brain activity returns to normal after the experience, it reestablishes the sense of certainty of your new, enlightened beliefs in a powerful way.

I don't know why, but I found the last section of the book, which attempts to walk the reader through *practices* for attaining "enlightenment", somewhat bizarre … additionally, this is in fairly direct opposition to their statement: "Enlightenment isn't a *practice*, it's an emergent experience that can be triggered when the brain transitions from one stage of consciousness to the next." They have set up a framework for the reader to experiment with various approaches (from reciting a particular prayer, or chanting a specific phrase, to staring at a blank piece of paper, and others) which has five steps: Desire, Prepare, Engage, Surrender, and Reflect. The way they frame these, however, sounds awfully "cultish" to me, such as *"you must genuinely desire insight and change"* and *"you must completely surrender and immerse yourself in the ritual experience"*. Perhaps it's my "deep agnosticism" and distrust of religions that makes this part as uncomfortable as it was for me, but much of the material in this last part of the book had me asking "what's a neuroscientist doing telling me to intone Arabic phrases while swaying back and forth?".

This brings me back to a point in the opening paragraph above. As I've noted in other³ reviews, I really feel *used* when I get to the end of a book to find it's been, on some level, a long-form promo for a service by the author. And, in what I *thought* was going to be a "companion website" with additional information, there it was – a pitch for an "information product" on 5 CDs – which claims to be *"based on a new model of human consciousness that Consolidates Over 31,000 Studies ..."* and *"shows you how to tap into progressively higher states of brain activity and awareness where problems are easier to solve and goals are easier to reach"*. Talk about an "aha!" moment. At least it's "reasonably priced" compared to a lot of stuff in that market.

As noted, How Enlightenment Changes Your Brain⁴ doesn't come out for a while ... so if this all sounds like something you want to get into, you're going to have to wait a couple of months. Needless to say, I was deeply ambivalent on this book, with it repeatedly veering into zones where I'm thinking it's campaigning for the Templeton Prize*⁵, to the whole "shill for the program" bit. This, of course, being set against the very interesting *science* involved. However, I'll freely admit that these sorts of things bug me *far more* than most people, so you might be all gung-ho for this and end up spending your afternoons happily chanting *allah-hu* on the way to shifting the relative activity of assorted brain regions.

Notes:

1. http://btripp-books.livejournal.com/180156.html
2. http://amzn.to/1Rs5qAr
3. http://btripp-books.livejournal.com/149630.html
4. http://amzn.to/1Rs5qAr
5. https://goo.gl/a1RRpy

Saturday, February 20, 2016[1]

Customer Service, new style ...

As readers keeping score on this stuff will know, I've reviewed a couple of Jay Baer's books before (here[2] and here[3]), so when I got wind of his new one, Hug Your Haters: How to Embrace Complaints and Keep Your Customers[4], I shot off a note to the good folks at Portfolio/Penguin and requested a review copy. This is interesting in that it's a very narrow-focus book – as you might guess, about customer service – based on a research project that Jay had initiated with Edison Research, which Tom Webster (of that firm) notes in his Foreword as being based on two questions:

• How has the proliferation of social media, review sites, and other online fora changed consumer expectations of what "good customer service" really means?
• When interactions between brands and humans are played out on a public stage, how must brands "perform" in order to satisfy not only the customer but the customer's audience?

Frankly, the answers to these ended up going in a direction that Jay had not expected, with the results boiling down to two closely linked realities: "Answering complaints increases customer advocacy across all customer service channels. ... Conversely, not answering complaints decreases customer advocacy across all customer service channels.", which then leads to "The Hug Your Haters success equation": **Answer every complaint, in every channel, every time.** Simple, right? Well, off the bat he notes "It takes cultural alignment, resource allocation, speed, a thick skin, and an unwavering belief that complaints are an opportunity."

The study involved was not huge, but was large enough to be "a statistically valid cross-section of ages, incomes, racial makeups, and technology aptitudes", I note this because the material in the book tends to circle back to the same set of example companies, ones that I suspect were the topic of the response research. These range from small operations to major internationals, so there's certainly a range of scope involved (one gal, from a 13-unit pizza chain handling all the interactions, vs. whole departments in big companies).

I also kept finding bits to stick bookmarks in for here (a dozen or more), so a lot of this may be quoting from the text. This also has a lot of humor involved, and I found myself literally "laughing out loud" at a few of them (and I was "live tweeting" parts of this as I was reading). One of these was the story about Dave Kerpen (another author I've reviewed previously), who personally responds to every one-star review he gets on Amazon, apologizes, and "offers to refund money spent, plus money for the pain and suffering of having read the book" – as a reader of a lot of books, I've certainly encountered reads that would have qualified for the extra refund!

One of the key points as to why this book is important is that, for many companies, *"a 5 percent increase in customer retention can boost profits by 25 to 85 percent"*, and while most organizations have a pretty good grasp on how much *acquiring* new customers costs, few have a solid idea of how many are becoming disaffected and ending up as ex-customers. In a move similar to Kerpen's strategy, the gal from the pizza chain regularly provides gift certificates to individuals leaving complaints on sites like Yelp. This is elaborated here:

> *So few companies hug their haters today that those that make this commitment are almost automatically differentiated and noteworthy when compared to their competitors. ... In today's world, meaningful differences between businesses are rarely rooted in price or product, but instead in customer experience.*

"Haters" are defined in two main categories, "offstage haters" who complain in private, and "onstage haters" who complain in public, with the former connecting via email and phone (and possibly letter), with the latter utilizing social media, review sites, etc. (another "LOL" moment came in the suggestion involving something of a "complaint cafe" which would feature old-style desk phones that would provide one, *"trembling with aggrieved frustration, the nearly extinct sensation of slamming a real handset into its cradle"*). There's an age trend here, with older consumers tending to use "offstage" approaches. Interestingly, the more tech one has the more likely one is going to be a "frequent complainer" – 84% of which have a smartphone, and 94% have a Facebook account (and 43% use it daily). Of course, this raises the somewhat existential issue of what *is* a "complaint" ... something that one is going to take the time to craft an e-mail complaint about might be a lot more serious than a bit of snark tossed off on Twitter.

Another concept introduced here is the "Hatrix" (which I noted could be construed as a "Matrix" knock-off, good performances in hockey, or some more-hostile relative of Harry Potter character Bellatrix ... depending on how you wanted to pronounce it), an infographic of which is supposedly available for download on the book's companion site (http://HugYourHaters.com), although I wasn't able to find it there. This deals primarily with response time and expectation on different channels ... where nearly 90% of complaints aired via email or phone expected a response, only around 50% of on-line complainers expected a response, *however* of those who did, nearly 40% expected that response within *60 minutes* ... versus the 63% of responses that come within 24 hours. There's a ton of data that's been teased out of these surveys, way too varied to even touch on here, but I guess all that's laid out in that infographic.

An additional idea that's put forth here is that "customer service is a spectator sport" ... as all those "on-stage" complaints are out in public, and your company's response is being seen by way more than the individual making the complaint. One of the dangers in this game is the big "meh" category, those customers, ex-customers, or potential customers who don't *care* enough to get involved, but are interested enough to pay attention to how you're treating the ones who *are* complaining. This is complicated because of costs involved:

> Handling a customer interaction in social media costs less than one dollar, on average, compared to two and a half to five dollars for an e-mail interaction, and more than six dollars to provide telephone customer service.
>
> Every time a customer wants to interact with your business and selects an onstage channel instead of an offstage channel, the stakes are raised because the interaction is public. That's the challenge. But if you save five dollars every time a customer chooses to interact publicly, isn't it worth it to handle your business out in the open?

Again, Hug Your Haters[5] is chock full of stories about good and bad (and *really* bad) customer service … but, generally speaking, each needs a lot more backstory than makes sense to include in this review. However, there was *another* "LOL" moment here that is related to one of these stories, so I'll sketch it out to you. In this instance, a florist provided really crappy product for a special event. The recipient complained with a detailed (albeit not hostile) email, to which the florist responded a rather curt *"Don't ever contact us again."*, and when the customer escalated all this info up into social media channels, the florist began making threatening phone calls. The author notes: *"Yes, you should answer customer complaints, but, for the record, stalking customers and threatening them with bodily harm is not part of the Hug Your Haters success formula."* (!) This is part of the "5 Obstacles" section which provides ways of looking at one's corporate culture and customer service team to make sure things work smoothly (and not counterproductively). Another "wake up" factoid that's provided here is that business spends WAY more on "getting customers" than "keeping customers", with $500 *billion* spent globally on marketing, versus only $9 billion on customer service. Often companies *think* they're doing "customer service" but are actually doing "marketing research" … the author notes a post-stay survey by a hotel in Las Vegas (which he got into trying to complain about something), which involved 50+ pages of questions, with only a comment field at the very end to actually *complain*.

Now, regular readers of these reviews will know that I'm not a big fan of mnemonic acronyms, but Jay introduces a couple here, one for dealing with offstage haters, and one for onstage haters. First there is "HOURS" for the offstage haters, which is derived from *"Be Human, Use One Channel, Unify Your Data, and Resolve the Issue with Speed"*, then, for the onstage haters, "FEARS" which comes from *"Find All Mentions, Display Empathy, Answer Publicly, Reply Only Once, Switch Channels"*. I'm not sure these would help *me* remember this, but "your mileage may vary". He has a chapter based on each of these, with more details involved.

Finally, there's a thing in the Afterword that I thought I'd pass along … it's the "three most important things" the author learned while writing the book (and, again, the results of the research went off in a completely different direction than he'd anticipated when starting the project):

> 1. Customer service is more complicated that ever, but the formula for success is knowable and achievable.

> 2. Interacting with your customers, especially when they're upset, is 100 percent worth the effort.
>
> 3. You need to answer every complaint, in every channel, every time.

I really appreciate books that do what Jay does in the appendix – putting in an "executive summary" of the book, hitting the high points in just 6-7 pages. It's always nice to be able to go back to something for a "refresher" and not have to start at the front!

As noted, [Hug Your Haters][6] is (at this writing) still not released (although it's only got about two weeks to go), so you can either go to the online big boys and pre-order it, or order it directly from the companion web site, where you'll get "bonuses" to sweeten the deal. I really enjoyed this book for the stories, for the humor, and for the fascinating info ... if you have any interest in business (or human behavior), you'll probably get a lot out of it too.

Notes:

1. http://btripp-books.livejournal.com/180438.html
2. http://btripp-books.livejournal.com/108780.html
3. http://btripp-books.livejournal.com/145689.html
4-6. http://amzn.to/1PvkJqb

Sunday, February 21, 2016[1]

A certain glow ...

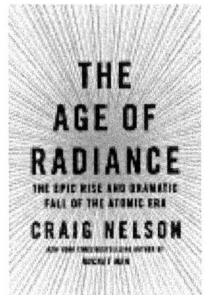

As I have previously noted, I rely on the dollar store for an on-going injection of *serendipity* in my to-be-read piles, connecting me with interesting titles that I might not otherwise have considered. However, every now and again, I'll hit something there which is clearly "something that I'd have picked up anyway", and this is an example of this later group. Craig Nelson's The Age of Radiance: The Epic Rise and Dramatic Fall of the Atomic Era[2] is the sort of thing I'd have snagged to increase my knowledge in a particular area, and so it's a "win" getting it for a buck!

While *interesting* and *informative*, this is also a bit of an odd book ... tracing an arc from the early days of discovery of radioactive elements straight on through the Fukushima disaster ... which means this is a relatively new title (it came out not quite two years ago at this point). The author is a publishing industry pro, with a number of notable books to his credit. This might explain one of the things I found uncomfortable here ... in many reviews I've *wished* that somebody had applied a firmer editorial hand to a book ... here, I get the feeling that a lot of *opinions* of the author have been relegated to something like a snide comment hiding in a cough. Although the book only has a few places where an "anti-nuclear" vibe rises to the surface, I get the feeling that this might have had a prior iteration that verged into a bit of polemic that got scrubbed from the final version. Again, this is just the sense I got in reading through this, but it makes me wonder if the book as it stands is how it was initially envisioned by the author.

Also, for a *science* book, this is remarkably well written, with nearly *poetic* descriptions of everything from an individual's facial hair to the environs of an improvised laboratory. While evidently extraordinarily well researched, it presents a tale of discovery which is engaging in the telling, rarely drifting off into dry regurgitation of historical factoids. The book is in four sections, essentially pre-WW2, WW2, the Cold War, and civilian Nuclear.

It begins with a chapter centering on the Curies and how the first concepts on radioactive materials were developed. However, the story isn't just a lab-bench journal, but looks at the personal background of Marie Curie, from when she was a governess of a Polish family, whose son wished to, but was forbade to marry her ... hardly the standard Science textbook material. However, lest you think this veers too much into biographies of the main players, it is counter-balanced with *fascinating* items like the route that Uranium-238 takes to end up as Lead-206. I have been back-and-forth on whether I should block-quote that whole piece for you here, but it's fifteen steps, with various isotopes of Uranium, Thorium, Protactinium, Radium, Radon, Polonium, Bismuth, and Lead, involved ... including their half lifes, ranging from U-238's 4.5 *billion* year half life to Po-214's minuscule 0.164 *microsecond* half life (and on to stable Pb-206) ... which seemed a bit excessive.

The next chapter looks at Enrico Fermi, who Carl Sagan noted (after rattling off 16 specifics) *"It's hard to think of another physicist of the twentieth centu-*

ry who's had so many things named after him.", and like the Curies, there is a lot of background material here as well. The "gathering storm" in Europe is a major factor in the first part of the book, and one of the stories about Fermi was how he and his family arranged things to depart from mainland Europe (to England then to the U.S.) directly following his trip to Stockholm to accept the Nobel Prize in 1938. Others were not so lucky to get out early. The next chapter shifts the focus to Budapest, with Leo Szilard, Otto Han, and Lise Meitner, the latter ending up needing to be all but "abducted" by Niels Bohr to get her safely to Copenhagen.

The second section of the book is several chapters detailing the war-time development of atomic science, featuring familiar names such as Robert Oppenheimer, Edward Teller, Ernest Lawrence, and John von Neumann, and perhaps less-known names such as Colonel Leslie Groves, who was the military's main contact with the scientists ... first looking at the events leading up to the breakthrough sustained reaction under University of Chicago's Stagg Field, December 2, 1942, then the "Manhattan Project" leading to the development of atomic bombs our at Los Alamos, New Mexico. One of the sub-themes in this part was the infiltration of Soviet spies, especially physicist Klaus Fuchs, in the very heart of the U.S. atomic program. One interesting side note here is the suggestion that the only reason Fuchs had the access he had was that Teller was unwilling to work on some of his assigned projects, and Fuchs was brought in to supplement him. This may have saved the U.S.S.R. a decade or more in their development of nuclear weapons.

One point raised here was that the U.S. did what Germany failed to do ... one of the physicists suggested that the Nazis were unlikely to succeed with atomic science because they kept most of the scientists in separate locations, where all the top players in the Allied program were in isolation off in Los Alamos. Also, it's noted that the U.S. spent *billions* on developing multiple approaches to obtaining advanced radioactive materials, with major research centers in several locations ... essentially trying *every* option rather than picking *one* ... which also led to being able to provide key ingredients to the bombs when it got to that point.

Another thing the author notes is that the atomic attacks on Hiroshima and Nagasaki were, while certainly *horrific*, far less so than the fire bomb attack on Tokyo several months before, in which over 100,000 Japanese died. In terms of attacking *targets*, Hiroshima and Nagasaki could have been destroyed by similar fire bomb attacks. This sets up one of the books "subtle" messages, that nuclear weapons are not particularly *practical*, and that the entire atomic arms race was more a psychological conflict than a military one.

The next section is all about the Cold War, and how both sides kept ratcheting up the stakes. Actually, it turns out that, at least early on, the Soviets had a very minimal atomic arsenal. They were aware that we were running spy flights over their territory, so kept most of their missiles on flatbed trucks that could be re-located to look like there were a lot more of them than was actually the case! However, there was a lot of paranoia on both sides of the conflict, and where the U.S. had about 400 atomic bombs in 1950 (realistically enough to destroy the Soviet Union), by 1955 that number was up to 2,280 (which turns out to be 20x what the USSR had at that time), and by

1967 the U.S. nuclear arsenal was up to a staggering 32,500 weapons.

The madness (as ironically spelled out as actual acronyms MAD – *Mutual Assured Destruction* and NUTS – *Nuclear Utilization Target Selection*) evident in that spiral of expansion, is paralleled with things, only coming to light *now*, that are almost comic, if they weren't so *serious* ... a remarkable example detailed here deals with the "secret unlock codes", which in numerous movies and TV shows were closely guarded parts of the nuclear launch sequence, which, in reality, were set to "00000000" – with an item on the launch checklist being *"ensure that no digits other than zero had inadvertently been dialed into the panel"*! The author also paints the famed RAND Corporation think-tank (founded by Air Force Generals Hap Arnold and Curtis LeMay) as something out of *Dr. Strangelove* (which he also credits with being closer to the reality of how things were in the 50's and 60's than anybody wants to admit) with items like:

> *In 1961, RAND created the Single Integrated Operational Plan or SIOP-62, a revision of Massive Retaliation/Sunday Punch, as it would release the whole of the American nuclear arsenal if the country was provoked. One billion people would eventually die from fire and radiation, with 285 million in the ellipsoidal target from China to Eastern Europe perishing in the initial blast.*

All of this almost came into play in 1962, with the U.S. and the Soviets coming close to realizing MAD.

The final section of the book is primarily about nuclear power – or, more precisely, nuclear power *disasters* (Nelson is seemingly no fan of even the *concept* of nuclear power), with chapters on Three Mile Island, Chernobyl, and Fukushima, with an odd look at Regan's "Star Wars" in the middle of that (in which the author notes:

> *Today America continues to spend $55 billion a year on atomic weapons that have never and will never be used. Cutting this arsenal in half would save $80 billion over the next ten years, and even then the Pentagon would have fourteen times as many warheads as the nearest competitor, China.*)

The stories of the three well-known nuclear disasters are pretty bizarre, largely in how much they're based on serious human stupidity (one gets the feeling from this that Homer Simpson is a fairly accurate representative of the industry), and have some deeply disturbing parts to them. One factoid that really stood out was this: *"Chernobyl was merely the fourteenth most lethal nuclear accident in USSR history, with the other thirteen kept classified until the empire fell."*. Whuh? It appears that we only *know* about Chernobyl because it spread a cloud of radiation across all of Europe ... but there were *thirteen* worse accidents? That's not a nice thing to think about.

Needless to say, a book that starts with the first discoveries of radiating materials, and ends up with the near-evacuation of Tokyo (because nobody checked local fishing lore about the historical certainty of tsunamis where they built the nuclear power plant), is not a simple read, but, as noted above, the writing is engaging, the information quite illuminating, and one comes out of it feeling as though one has actually *learned* something. I am glad that The Age of Radiance[3] did not end up floating off into polemics against all things nuclear, although by the end, you can sort of tell that the author "is against it" (he summarily dismisses the safe, small, and recycling GenIV reactors – despite that India is in full development mode on these). If this sounds like something you'd like to get, it's available – still in print in hardcover, paperback, and ebook versions – plus the new/used guys have "very good" copies of the hardcover for as little as 1¢ (plus $3.99 shipping). I've not seen any more copies at the dollar store since I picked this up (last November), so you've probably missed the $1 deal ... but I'm glad I got this, and you'd probably be happy with it as well.

Notes:

1. http://btripp-books.livejournal.com/180682.html

2-3. http://amzn.to/1WQZDEc

Sunday, March 13, 2016[1]

Too much of a good thing?

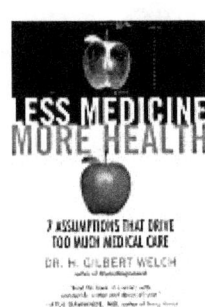

This is another of those "Early Reviewer" books from LibraryThing.com ... which has recently been connecting me with a number of books in related areas. Unfortunately, a lot of these[2] have only been so-so (well, let me drop the caveat in here that *most* of the books that I end up getting through LTER aren't exactly items that I went *looking* for, but clicked on them on the monthly request list because they "sounded interesting enough", so going in on these I'm rarely in a "can't wait to read it" mode, and not particularly predisposed to an enthusiastic reaction). While this was, indeed, *interesting enough* it also only netted *three* of my little bookmarks, meaning that there wasn't a whole lot "jumping off the page" for me to reference. Of course, this is a somewhat unfair way to preface my review of Dr. H. Gilbert Welch's Less Medicine, More Health: 7 Assumptions That Drive Too Much Medical Care[3].

Those of you who follow these reviews over on my main blog will realize, I've been through *a lot* of "medical care" over the last half year or so, and thereby the material here should be pretty much "on target" for me ... but somehow this wasn't necessarily the case. The author is a medical doctor who is both a professor at the School of Medicine at Dartmouth, and an internist with the V.A. (most of his stories in the book come from that work). His main area of research has been in the area of cancer screening, and has published books about that, as well as a controversial study in 2012 that indicated that the wide-spread use of mammography was having no appreciable effect of breast cancer death rates. This book essentially is an expansion of the focus of his previous titles, *Overdiagnosed* and *Should I Get Tested For Cancer?*, moving into general cultural assumptions about medical care.

Since I don't have a lot of bookmarks here to build a narrative with, I think it might be useful to just run through what these "7 Assumptions" are, and then go into some detail on those:

> Assumption #1: All Risks Can Be Lowered
> Assumption #2: It's Always Better To Fix The Problem
> Assumption #3: Sooner Is Always Better
> Assumption #4: It Never Hurts To Get More Information
> Assumption #5: Action Is Always Better Than Inaction
> Assumption #6: Newer Is Always Better
> Assumption #7: It's All About Avoiding Death

Now, presented with that list of propositions, I suspect that most folks would be in agreement all the way down the list ... which is, I assume, why Welch wrote this book, as, point-for-point, he presents arguments against each. He actually pairs a "disturbing truth" with each assumption in the chapter headings, and these go:

> D.T. #1: Risks can't always be lowered – and trying creates risks of its own.
> D.T. #2: Trying to eliminate a problem can be more dangerous than managing one.
> D.T. #3: Early diagnosis can needlessly turn people into patients.
> D.T. #4: Data overload can scare patients and distract your doctor from what's important.
> D.T. #5: Action is not reliably the "right" choice.
> D.T. #6: New interventions are typically not well tested and often being judged ineffective (even harmful).
> D.T. #7: A fixation on preventing death diminishes life.

All of my little bookmarks are from the middle of the book – in Assumptions #2-4 – so I'm going to let those "disturbing truths" stand on their own as an indication of what's covered in the other chapters, and zoom in to the bits that caught my fancy while reading this.

The most *memorable* part of this for me was from the third chapter ... where Welch splits different types of cancer out into different "critters" ... each with a different progression. I was trying to figure a way of communicating this to you briefly, but I'm going to have to break down and type out a few paragraphs to get you what's the essence of this (sorry about that!):

> Let's start with the benefit of cancer screening. It's an important benefit: avoiding a cancer death. At the same time, it's equally important to acknowledge that screening doesn't avoid most cancer deaths. People who are regularly screened still can die from the cancer being screened for. Every randomized trial of screening has shown this. It's not the patient's fault. It's not the doctor's fault. It's not the screening test's fault. Instead it reflects the dynamics of cancer.
> When I was in medical school, I was taught that anything labeled "cancer" would inexorably progress. Once a cell had the DNA derangement of cancer, it was only a matter of time until the cancer spread throughout the body. And it was only a matter of time until it killed the patient.
> But we now recognize the world of cancer is much more diverse. At one extreme, autopsies have shown that many of us have small cancers that never bother us during life – particularly cancers of the prostate, breast, and thyroid gland. At the other extreme, screening programs have shown that early cancer detection doesn't help everyone; many go on to die from cancer despite early detection. These observations bring us to a new conceptual model of cancer – and to turtles, rabbits, and birds.

> It's a barnyard pen of cancers. The goal is not to let any of the animals escape the pen to become deadly. But the turtles aren't going anywhere anyway. They are the indolent, nonlethal cancers. The rabbits are ready to hop out at any time. They are the potentially lethal cancers, cancers that might be stopped by early treatment. Then there are the birds. Quite simply: they are already gone. They are the most aggressive cancers, the ones that have already spread by the time they are detectable, the ones that are beyond cure.
>
> Screening can only help with the rabbits. The turtles don't need help; the birds can't be helped. The turtles create the problem of overdiagnosis ..., the birds create the problem of limited benefit.

The author goes into a lot of data about these various groups, but one particularly caught my eye – it was a 30-year study of 50,000 patients looking at a specific cancer. Half these subjects were systematically screened for this cancer, and half were not. At the end of 30 years, most had died. Of the screened group, 2% died of the cancer, while the non-screened group had a 3% death rate of that cancer – a 33% reduction. That's great, right? Well, it depends. The mortality rate for both groups was *"exactly the same"* year-in-year-out, with the rate at the end of 30 years being 71% in both groups – *"Screening didn't help people live longer. Not even a little bit."* ... pretty sobering if one's hoping that having that test is going to improve your longevity.

The next thing I want to bring to your attention is from the second chapter ... the one about "fixing the problem". Welch backgrounds this with a discussion about the "two broad categories of medical research" evidence-based (randomized trials), and observational. He notes that EBR has been mocked by some, inviting researchers such as Welch to review the effectiveness of parachutes by using randomized controlled trials. He counters this with a look at how, indeed, some trials are not ideal, including:

> One of the pharmaceutical industry's favorite strategies is to study the effect of a drug on the few patients who have severe disease, find some benefit, and then hope that doctors extrapolate the benefit to many patients with a less severe forms of the disease. It's a cleaver strategy: it's like testing parachutes on the few people who jump out of airplanes and then selling them as protection against falls to the many people who walk downstairs. Severely ill patients always stand to benefit more from intervention than those who are less severely ill ... Yet the harms of intervention are roughly equivalent in the two groups. So the net effect of intervention regularly looks better in the severely ill.

The last thing I have marked to bring up is from the information chapter, which has a central story regarding a critique of the opening of an "Information Age" exhibit at the Smithsonian, that Welsh had kept handy for decades:

> Data, information, useful knowledge, wisdom … that's a good vocabulary. Good enough for me to keep the article around for a quarter century. I might tweak the definitions a bit for clinical medicine. Data would be the measure of lung impedence. They would only become information if they reliably told us about the likelihood that the patient would develop a clinical problem (shortness of breath) – a problem that might lead to a hospitalization. The information would become useful knowledge only if we had a course of action that reliably lowered that likelihood. Wisdom requires balancing the benefits and harms of that action – and knowing how the patient values the carious outcomes – to arrive at a decision about what to do.
>
> Just because you have data doesn't mean you have information. Having information doesn't mean you have useful knowledge. And wisdom – well, that's a whole new ball game.
>
> …
>
> The central question of this chapter is whether obtaining more clinical data on individuals with medial problems reliably leads to useful knowledge. The short answer is: no. The natural follow-up question is whether there is any reason – other than cost – not to obtain more clinical data. The short answer is: yes. More clinical data not only can create anxiety for patients, they can also initiate cascades that lead to unneeded medical care.

While the author is, obviously, "flying in the face of" the "common knowledge" about medicine, he's hardly "against it" like the anti-vaxxers and other neo-Luddites out there … but he is saying it's become way too easy for even basic medical care to *cascade* into complicated, intrusive, expensive, and potentially *unneeded* care. And, of course, the way our (U.S.) medical system is set up – nobody gets *paid* for letting a condition simply "run its course" as the body heals itself (or doesn't), so there are systemic financial pressures to act on things that might have better outcomes with *inaction*.

There is a lot of info in Less Medicine, More Health[4], with the author describing numerous studies, etc. supporting his assorted points. And, as noted above, he's not averse to admitting the other side has supporting material as well, so it's a much more "balanced" look than one might expect for something going so jarringly against the "assumptions" of modern medical care. He personalizes this with a lot of stories from his own clinical work (mainly in the V.A.), illustrating points with what had happened to various patients he'd encountered. The book, however, doesn't have much of a "story arc", as it is a detailed look into these relatively thorny issues, so it's hardly "a beach read" (for most folks, at least), but given the universal applicability of medical care, this might have some interest even to the fiction readers out there.

This is brand new (just hitting the shelves a week or so back at this writing), so it should be at least *available* via your local brick-and-mortar book vendor, but the on-line big boys have it at about 20% off of cover, and, oddly, some of the new/used guys have it *new* for about half off (plus shipping). While interesting, and applicable to everybody still breathing, I don't think I can call this an "all and sundry" recommendation, as you *really* have to be into this stuff to get the most out of reading it.

Notes:

1. http://btripp-books.livejournal.com/180905.html
2. http://btripp-books.livejournal.com/179750.html
3-4. http://amzn.to/245KFyW

Monday, March 14, 2016[1]

This stuff has been kicking around a lot longer than you think ...

I frequently have mentioned the little book marks (real little, they typically are about 1/8"x1/2" – torn from a register receipt that I'd "prepped" by folding to the needed length) that I put in my books while reading. Most of these are to highlight pages where interesting stuff is happening to regurgitate in these reviews, but others are for my own reference, often to other books. When "the system is working as it should", I'll note the book being referenced, look it up on Amazon, and either pick up a copy if I'm feeling so inclined, or drop it into a wishlist until I can get a used copy for cheap. Well, this is one of those "other books". At this point I'm not sure what book I read about *this* book in (it's been a while since I've read this sort of woo-woo stuff), but it was evidently in one of those "Law of Attraction" things, which referred back to some foundational predecessors of *The Secret*, etc. This was a bit of a "pig in a poke", as a 1¢ used copy ... and I ended up with a 1969-vintage mass-market paperback edition (there are evidently far more recent ones out there) of Claude M. Bristol's 1948 The Magic of Believing[2].

I suppose it's easy to think that the whole "attraction" racket is new, but as Mitch Horowitz outlined in his One Simple Idea[3], and to a certain extent in Occult America[4], there have been variations of this stuff floating around for *ages* ... so it shouldn't be particularly surprising to have this sort of material dating back to the end of WW2 (when this was composed).

Of course, *because* it dates from that long ago, there's a LOT of stuff in here which is "different planet" oriented (a world before cell phones, before computers, heck, before *TV*). It also is yet another reminder of how fleeting fame can be (as anciently noted by Marcus Aurelius[5]), as many of the "celebrities" the author name-checks in here have not maintained name recognition down the decades, leaving the modern reader at a loss for the context that the author, 70-some years ago, assumes these names carry with them.

One of the stark "different world" aspects here is how the author, a "hard-headed journalist" who started his writing career as a correspondent for the Army's *Stars and Stripes* in World War One (and ended up as an *investment banker*), was a very public advocate for this "believing" stuff. One of the sub-themes here is how the author was expecting the whole spiritual aspect to life becoming a major *scientific* area. When he was writing this was back when J.B. Rhine[6] was running a Parapsychology lab at Duke university, and many other major institutions had similar programs. It's interesting that advances made in *physics* in the wake of the WW2 nuclear program seems to have totally shifted the balance to the physical/easily-measurable sciences and away from the "mystical", pretty much burying the sort of thing that The Magic of Believing[7] is dealing with for many decades. An example of this is here:

> However, great investigators and thinkers of the world, including many famous scientists, are in the open today, freely discussing the subject and giving the results of their experiments. The late Charles P. Steinmetz, famous engineer of the General Electric Company, shortly before his death declared: "The most important advance in the next fifty years will be in the realm of the spiritual – dealing with the spirit – thought." Dr. Robert Gault, while professor of Psychology at Northwestern University, was credited with the statement: "We are at the threshold of our knowledge of the latent psychic powers of man."

Again, the author does not seem to be any sort of "flake", just a standard hard-boiled businessman of his time, yet he's totally into this "newage" type of approach ... using it as a tool the way that his current corporate-world descendants might implement TQM, Agile, or Six Sigma. This doesn't make the "sound" of his pronouncements any less odd in that context, as, while what he says in the book could have been penned *yesterday* by some totally off-the-deep-end "believer", this is an *established investment banker / journalist* coming up with passages like:

> However, most of the sustained and continuing manifestations come as result of belief. It is through this belief with its strange power that miracles happen and that peculiar phenomena occur for which there appears to be no known explanation. I refer now to deep-seated belief – a firm and positive conviction that goes through every fiber of your being – when you believe it "heart and soul," as the saying goes. Call it a phase of emotion, a spiritual force, a type of electrical vibration – anything you please, but that's the force that brings outstanding results, sets the law of attraction into operation, and enables sustained thought to correlate with its object. This belief changes the tempo of the mind or thought-frequency, and, like a huge magnet, draws the subconscious forces into play, changing your whole aura and affecting everything about you – and often people and objects at great distances. It brings into your individual sphere of life results that are sometimes startling – often results you never dreamed possible.

One of the interesting features here is that this isn't just "philosophy" - the author charts out specific *exercises* as well. One of which is "the mirror technique" ... which I wish Bristol had written out as a side-bar or something (did they even do "sidebars" back in 1948? I'd think they'd have been challenging to typeset before computers), as he sort of rolls through various examples of using it. In short, it's looking at yourself in the mirror, and:

> *... look into the very depths of your eyes, tell yourself that you are going to get what you want – name it aloud so you can see your lips move and you can hear the words uttered. ... You can augment this by writing with soap on the face of the mirror any slogans or key words you wish, so long as they are the key to what you have previously visualized and want to see in reality.*

He recommends that if you're an executive or sales manager, and want to "put more push into your entire organization", you should teach your employees this technique and "see that they use it". He goes on from this to discuss "the power of the eyes", and "that if you act the part you will become that part", with using the mirror to "rehearse" that act.

I would typically do this earlier in a review, but I think a chapter listing could be useful to get the gist of what's in here:

    I. How I came to Tap the Power of Belief
    II. Mind-Stuff Experiments
    III. What the Subconscious Is
    IV. Suggestion Is Power
    V. The Art of Mental Pictures
    VI. The Mirror Technique for Releasing the Subconscious
    VII. How to Project Your Thoughts
    VIII. Woman and the Science of Belief
    IX. Belief Makes Things Happen

In the "project your thoughts" chapter, he goes into detail on telepathy, including several pages reproducing an article by Dr. Rhine in full. Needless to say, from the perspective of a "physics dominated" culture – where (even in business) "if you can't measure it, it doesn't exist" – it sounds very strange having this sort of material coming from the likes of Mr. Bristol. Somewhat similarly, the chapter on how women can use these techniques (!) sounds bizarre from a modern perspective ... although the author is writing from a post- "Rosie the Riveter" renaissance of women in the workforce, the tenor here is that most women wouldn't consider that they *could* use these mental exercises, and need to be *told* that they can! Like the old Virginia Slims cigarette tag line put it ... things have "come a long way".

Anyway, The Magic of Believing[8] is an interesting read, and I'm guessing that some of the exercises that Bristol recommends are likely to be reasonably effective. While I picked this up used, you can also find on-line versions for free download ... and a more recent pressing of the mass-market paperback I got appears to still be in print – so you could even get it *new*. If you're interested in "The Secret" and related "law of attraction" stuff, you should probably pick this up, as it's no doubt among the "source documents" for those things.

Notes:
1. http://btripp-books.livejournal.com/181243.html
2. http://amzn.to/21sVtVy
3. http://btripp-books.livejournal.com/154464.html
4. http://btripp-books.livejournal.com/81115.html
5. http://btripp-books.livejournal.com/178849.html
6. http://btripp-books.livejournal.com/18661.html
7-8. http://amzn.to/21sVtVy

Thursday, March 17, 2016[1]

Getting visible ...

Soooo ... I hate it when I sit down to write a review and discover that I'd put in exactly *zero* little bookmarks to lead me back to choice bits in the text ... and I just discovered that this is one of those cases. I'm rather confused by this, as the lack of bookmarks is frequently the effect of my not productively interfacing with the book, yet I had found this one engaging, entertaining, and reasonably informative ... but, obviously, never felt moved to stick a marker in there. Odd.

Anyway, I'd run into some mention of David Avrin's It's Not Who You Know, It's Who Knows YOU! A Practical Business Guide to Raising Your Profits By Raising Your Profile[2] somewhere on-line (I don't recall where, but I do remember trying to track down his publisher – unsuccessfully – to request a review copy ... they've not got much of an on-line presence, and are "coincidentally" located in the same small Colorado town as the author, so I'm guessing this was, essentially, self-published). I ended up looking over on Amazon and was able to score a very good copy of the hardcover (signed, even!) from the new/used vendors for well under a buck (plus shipping).

The author presents himself as "The Visibility Coach" (http://visibilitycoach.com), with a focus on marketing and strategic branding. The format of the book is a lot of 1-3 page topics (70, if my count is right), grouped in three main sections: Your Brand, Creating Awareness, and The Pitch ... each closing with a "The Visibility Coach says:" banner with some pithy comment on the preceding section (with *every one* of these including his *logo*, which I found irritating in its incessant repeating, yet forgivable in the context of a "personal branding" screed).

What I found *especially* confusing in my not having marked anything here is the realization that I've already *used* references to material in other contexts! One would think that I'd have targeted those for later use – guess I was breezing through this too fast to "stop and mark the proses" *{sorry about that}*. Of course, in my defense, a large collection of individual bits, loosely assembled into a few thematic sections, doesn't build much of a narrative arc ... so a lot of the "good bits" just flew by, and I was into the next part before realizing that the last one was choice.

This leaves me in a position to do some "cherry picking" via a scan-through of the text ... not ideal, but *hey*. I guess I'll start with the above-noted bit that I already used. I was posting in my main blog[3] about the re-release of one of my old poetry collections, and was contemplating the market (or lack thereof) for all my emo navel-gazing. This refers to Avrin's piece on what he calls the *"Sesame Street Strategy"*, which starts out talking about the career decline of Donny Osmond, moves into the disastrous mid-stream moves of *Maxim* magazine (when they sought to change *with* their initial readers, rather than target a particular "self-replicating market"), and eventually ends up on Sesame Street:

> In fact, if you have a self-replicating market, you can often continue to offer products and services to each new batch of customers that comes along. I call this the <u>Sesame Street Strategy</u>. How is it that Sesame Street has stayed on the air for more than 40 years? Because every year there is a new crop of five-year-old children (gleaned from the ranks of last year's four-year-olds) hungry for learning and entertainment. Companies ... {addressing this market} ... continue to grow and thrive because kids inexplicably seem to keep being born and growing up – needing to learn stuff. Who knew?

The author uses this to pose the question if your business has to keep changing to chase after your existing customers, or if you have a new batch of target customers coming in the door as your previous ones move on.

Of course, the topic of "visibility" keeps coming up, in slightly different contexts. In the wonderfully titled "Schtick Out" piece Avrin notes:

> To become top-of-mind, you need to craft or highlight something about yourself, your message, or your business that is readily and easily identifiable with you – and <u>only</u> you. When you hear someone say, "Yah, it's been done," it's usually not a very subtle reminder that there is nothing special in copying someone else. So here's the question: What do you do, that only you do?

He lists a number of examples, from the chocolate chip cookies featured at Doubletree Hotels, to the political snark of Ann Coulter. About half the book later, he revisits this with a personal example, which, while approaching *obnoxious* on one level, is also brilliant for the reasons he details in "See and Be Seen":

> Some years back, I was attending a conference with my colleagues at the National Speakers Association and having fun zipping around the convention hotel on a Segway scooter. The Segway was brand new at the time and caused a lot of buzz. As I rounded a corner, I passed a woman who said, "Hey, I remember you!" "That's the point!" I said with a smile as I zoomed past.
> For a time, the Segway was my schtick. I used to bring it along as my signature at conferences and conventions around the world. It was a great way to meet far more people than I normally would at such a large event. ...
> More important, I always knew that I could call any of the hundreds or even thousands of fellow attendees in the weeks that followed and say, "I was the guy on the Segway." People would instant-

> ly recall who I was and the conversation was a breeze from there. If I'm going to call myself the Visibility Coach, I better be visible!
> My question for you then is: "What are you doing to be noticed and remembered by your prospects?" ...
> What are *you* doing to be seen and remembered? How are you ensuring your top-of-mind status with your clients and prospects?

He does note that most folks don't need to "find some hokey stunt to draw attention to yourself", but suggests that most could find "a distinctive hook or activity that dovetails nicely into who you are or what you do".

This isn't just "philosophies" of visibility, however, as there are several sections with direct coaching and practical advice. I especially found the "Good TV" part of interest, as "doing media" can be such a disaster if it's not handled well. This part was especially useful:

> Here's the key to a good media interview: Most reporters don't know the subject nearly as well as the guest. So when a reporter asks you something, answer it briefly and transition into what you really went there to talk about. You can expertly move past the often irrelevant or less important question by simply employing transitional phrases. ...
> {he gives several examples}
> Then go on to say what you came there to say, and do it with passion, regardless of the questions asked. If the reporter has something else in mind, don't worry – they'll jump in. Get on the edge of your seat and advocate for your position, organization, product, or crusade, and do it as if you only have one minute to make your case (because that's likely all you *do* have), and keep talking!

He goes on to point out that answering the questions is not what makes "good TV" – it's presenting a coherent message in a passionate, engaging way.

This "updated version" of It's Not Who You Know, It's Who Knows YOU![4] has only been out a couple of years, but appears to be out of print (the author's site points over to Amazon, and they only have the ebook version, plus copies through the new/used aftermarket vendors), so will be unlikely to be on the shelves of your local bookstore. If I had one general caveat to pass along about this, it would be that it's more for *businesses* than *individuals*, although, obviously from the examples given above, much of the material is applicable to both. I found much of this very useful ... and you might too.

Notes:
1. http://btripp-books.livejournal.com/181379.html
2. http://amzn.to/1YmDVss
3. http://btripp.livejournal.com/1233371.html
4. http://amzn.to/1YmDVss

Friday, March 18, 2016[1]

"... Messing With My Mind!"

In the reading that I do, I will frequently come across books referenced in other books, which are variously praised and recommended. I have, unfortunately, developed a fairly cynical view of "highly recommended" books, because, frankly, so many of them are "meh" at best. This one is an exception to that rule ... Robert B. Cialdini's much-lauded Influence: The Psychology of Persuasion[2] is a truly exceptional book, and I'm very pleased to have made the effort (OMG – I paid *retail* ... or at least Amazon's discounted version thereof) to get it.

I think the power of this book comes from the combination of efforts that Dr. Cialdini put into researching it, not only in the classic college laboratory setting with student volunteers, but also going out in the field, with his becoming a participant observer:

> ... Participant observation is a research approach in which the researcher becomes a spy of sorts. With disguised identity and intent, the investigator infiltrates the setting of interest and becomes a full-fledged participant in the group to be studied. So when I wanted to learn about the compliance tactics of encyclopedia (or vacuum-cleaner, or portrait-photography, or dance-lesson) sales organizations, I would answer a newspaper ad for sales trainees and have them teach me their methods. Using similar but not identical approaches, I was able to penetrate advertising, public-relations, and fund-raising agencies to examine their techniques. Much of the evidence presented in this book, then, comes from my experience posing as a compliance professional, or aspiring professional, in a large variety of organizations dedicated to getting us to say yes.
>
> One aspect of what I learned in this three-year period of participant observation was most instructive. Although there are thousands of different tactics that compliance practitioners employ to produce yes, the majority fall within six basic categories. Each of these categories is governed by a fundamental psychological principle that directs human behavior and, in so doing, gives the tactics their power. This book is organized around these six principles, one to a chapter. The principles – consistency, reciprocation, social proof, authority, liking, and scarcity – are each discussed in terms of their function in society and in terms of how their enormous force can be commissioned by a compliance professional who deftly incorporates them into requests for purchases, donations, concessions, votes, assent, etc.

What he found in his research is both fascinating and *scary*. I have a very low tolerance to "being manipulated", so I was being quite reactive to a lot of the stories in here ... on one hand hating those applying these techniques, and on the other hand being amazed that so many people are thoughtlessly taken in by them. These range from the mild (the quote by the character "Face" from the old *The A-Team* TV show comes to mind: *"That's not even a real smile. It's just a bunch of teeth messing with my mind!"*), to the truly horrific (the classic Milgram Study, and similar).

One of the things that I really liked, structurally, in the book was the inclusion of a "How To Say No" section in each chapter – allowing the reader to walk away from each technique with a framework for not being influenced by it (or not as much as one might be), and a "Reader Report" which features a story sent in by somebody on one side or another of the influence game illustrating the principle at hand in that chapter. These both provide a pattern in the information, but also shift the frame a bit, leading to a more nuanced view of these techniques in action. Another thing I found quite endearing was the author's "catch phrase", as it were, of *Click, whirr!*, indicating where "*Click*, and the appropriate tape is activated; *whirr* and out rolls the standard sequence of behaviors." ... except for when it's *not* the appropriate reaction – the initial instance of this was dealing with turkeys (who acted maternally to anything making the "cheep cheep" call of baby turkeys – even if the sound was coming from a stuffed predator that would have been viciously attacked otherwise), or robins (who would territorially defend against anything with red breast feathers, but ignore perfect replicas of competitors *without* that one triggering element), but Cialdini generalizes that out to any pre-programmed behaviors ... including ones we exhibit: *"there are many situations in which human behavior does not work in a mechanical, tape-activated way, what is astonishing is how often it does"*.

The book is chock-full of amazing cases ... things that one would think couldn't *possibly* be real, but there's solid research on these. An example is (in the "consistency" chapter) how agreeing to a small step will prime you for a major step later ... in this study, experimenters had gone through suburban neighborhoods asking people to take a small (3" square) sign saying "be a safe driver", and nearly everybody did. Two weeks later, other experimenters came through both the original neighborhoods and a set of "control" neighborhoods that hadn't been asked to take the small sign. These were now requesting to put a very large, unattractive "drive carefully" sign in the subjects' front lawns. As one might expect, in the control group, most – 83% – said no, but in the group that had previously taken the tiny sign, an amazing 76% agreed to let the billboard be installed in front of their homes! It appears that simply acceding to the minor request *changed the view these people had of themselves* into something that "consistency" forced them to also agree to the later unreasonable request. The author warns:

> ... be very careful about agreeing to trivial requests. Such an agreement can not only increase our compliance with very similar, much large requests, it can also make us more willing to perform a variety of larger favors that are only remotely connected to the little one we did earlier. It's this second, general kind of influ-

> ence concealed within small commitments that scares me. ... It scares me enough that I am rarely willing to sign a petition anymore, even for a position I support. Such an action has the potential to influence not only my future behavior but also my self-image in ways I may not want. And once a person's self-image is altered, all sorts of subtle advantages become available to someone who wants to exploit that new image.

He goes on to discuss, in detail, Chinese-run POW camps in the Korean War. There were constant pressures to make concessions (writing essays to win a piece of fruit or a few cigarettes) that would then provide the basis of further expansions on themes the Communists wanted expressed, moving in tiny increments from one self-image to a new one that could be exploited for propaganda, etc. Similarly he notes how Amway tries to have its reps get the *customer* to fill out the order form ... leading them to be more convinced that they wanted what they were ordering.

One of the useful things in the "social proof" chapter is spun out of the studies around the notorious Kitty Genovese murder, where dozens of witnesses saw the (long drawn out) attack, but no one *did* anything, even calling the police ... each assuming "somebody else" was helping. The author recommends, if one is in an emergency situation, singling out *one* person in the environment and *specifically* asking for help ... this breaks through the "pluralistic ignorance effect" and spurs individuals into action. Cialdini describes an accident he had been in, where, just like in the research, nobody was stopping to help ... he realized what was happening and directly addressed drivers cruising by to call the police, etc. Also in this chapter there is one of the hardest-to-believe studies ... the pattern of suicides that follow stories of suicides in the media – which apparently *trigger* additional suicides: *"within two months after every front-page suicide story, an average of fifty-eight more people than usual killed themselves"* – a pretty shocking statistic, which is made creepier by the analysis that the follow-up suicides were predictably among people *similar* in age, sex, race, etc., to the initial death ... and really disturbingly: *"the average number of people killed in a fatal crash of a commercial airliner is more than three times greater if the crash happened one week after a front-page suicide story than if it happened one week before"*! The author finds this sufficient horrific that he notes:

> Evidently, the principle of social proof is so wide-ranging and powerful that its domain extends to the fundamental decision for life or death. ... A glance at the graphs documenting the undeniable increase in traffic and air fatalities following publicized suicides, especially those involving murder, is enough to cause concern for one's safety.

He goes on to note that homicides have similar patterns of increase following news of killings (like those don't happen on a daily basis in places like Chicago!), and he then takes an extensive look at the mass suicides in Guyana, and how Jim Jones was able to control the People's Temple faithful to the extent that they'd kill themselves at his command.

In the "liking" chapter, there are all sorts of things in play, attractiveness, similarity, and even blatantly insincere compliments. One study of Canadian federal elections found that attractive candidates got 2.5x the votes of unattractive candidates ... although, when surveyed, three quarters of the voters outright denied this happening, with only 14% even being open to the possibility. Lots of salesmen do "cold reads" for any clues of attitudes and interests of their prey ... and fabricate stories that correspond to those as a way of connecting. I guess the guy in a recent commercial for a shaving system is dead on, where he's in a waiting area for a job interview with a bunch of other candidates, and notices that the portraits of the company's leadership all feature bald/shaved heads ... he bolts out, gets shaving gear, and comes back as the only one among the hopefuls that now *looks* like the company's guy. As far as compliments, *"Positive comments produced just as much liking for the flatterer when they were untrue as when they were true."*, and *"this was the case even though the men fully realized that the flatterer stood to gain from their liking him"* ... giving support to the strategy of one featured car salesman who sent out 13,000 cards to his contact list *every month* with the simple message "I like you!" on seasonably-themed cards. Also in this chapter are looks at integration failures, good cop / bad cop interrogation dynamics, and how TV weather people get *blamed* (and sometimes attacked) for the weather.

Aside from the Milgram material in the "authority" section, there are some factors looked at that also give one pause ... like how an actor who has played a doctor on TV can be effectively used to push products with his "medical" expertise (Robert Young / "Marcus Welby" for Sanka for example), or how clothes/cars/accessories can stand in for actual achievement. Another tactic familiar to everyone is the "scarcity" approach, from on-going "going out of business" sales (there was one luggage shop on Michigan Avenue here which had been "going out of business" for at least a decade before the building was eventually torn down), to the holiday toy scam of creating a demand that goes unfilled at the end of the year, only to be made widely available ("but you *promised!*") a month or so later (although that latter story is actually in the "consistency" chapter).

Obviously, there is a whole lot in Influence[3], and I've only been able to skim through some of the highlights here. This is such an eye-opener that it's definitely one of those "all and sundry" recommendations ... you *need* to read this!

It's currently available in both paperback and ebook editions, and I suspect that you'd be able to find this at most bigger brick-and-mortar book stores. The on-line big boys, however, have it for a whopping 44% off at this writing, making it as cheap to get that way as picking up a used copy (plus shipping). Again, this is well worth your time, and is even something that I wish they'd make required reading in the schools.

Notes:

1. http://btripp-books.livejournal.com/181759.html

2-3. http://amzn.to/21EOHfE

Saturday, March 26, 2016[1]

A different side ...

As regular readers of this space know, I find a lot of quite interesting books at dollar stores, the rather random nature of what shows up where in that channel lending a signature serendipity to my to-be-read piles. One thing I have discovered is that there is no systematic distribution of individual titles (i.e., four copies to every store in a particular area), with some books only being at one location, and a different "mix" in different regions. Because of this, I always look forward to checking out the Dollar Trees when I'm out of town, and a week or so back I was attending a demo at my elder daughter's college, and made a point to check out the one near our hotel. I found a couple of promising titles there, one of them being Love Is the Cure: On Life, Loss, and the End of AIDS[2] by famed rock & roll legend Elton John.

I was a big fan of the author in the 70's, certainly from 1971's *Madman Across The Water* (which still is one of our "road trip" CDs), and was thrilled to get so see him a few years back, when I was trying to shift gears to a bartending career (I was working temp at a big event Allstate was doing down in Millennium Park, where he was the headliner). I had, however, sort of drifted away musically over the past couple of decades, so hadn't been "following" him much, and by the time this book picks up (in 1985), he was pretty much off my radar, aside, of course, for the mega-hits (like cuts from *The Lion King*) that were hard to avoid.

The book starts with the author flipping through a magazine in a doctor's office, and seeing an article about Ryan White, an Indiana teen who had hemophilia, and had contracted HIV via a clotting agent used to treat his disease. Reading this article set John on a trajectory that led to both his sobriety and the founding of the Elton John AIDS Foundation.

This is an intensely personal tale, but it is, ultimately, more a missive from the head of the EJAF[3] than strictly being an autobiographical piece. On one level, John is nearly perfectly positioned to tell the story of HIV/AIDS, as he was in the thick of the "gay community" in the years that it was being ravaged by the disease. At several points, he mentions that it's pretty much a miracle that *he* didn't get AIDS, as so many of his friends (he cites some really atrocious body counts), succumbed to it. He also got to see (as he attempted to help Ryan White, and other victims around the country) how spotty the care was, when there was *any*, and this sparked him to want to do something.

However, before he could be effective helping *others*, he needed to get his act together. A couple of months after Ryan's funeral, John had something of an intervention with his boyfriend at the time, which resulted in him finally deciding that he needed to get help. At this point he was dealing with a wide array of addictive behaviors, involving cocaine, alcohol, food, and sex. He notes:

> *What made matters harder was that there were even few rehab facilities that were willing to treat multiple problems at once. Dual diagnosis was discouraged, for reasons I still do not agree with. Most treatment centers expected you to go to one facility to be treated for your eating disorder before you went to another for your drug addiction, and then yet another for alcoholism. That wasn't acceptable to me. I felt very strongly at the time (and I still do) that all of my problems had the same root cause, and that I couldn't treat one without treating them all. Luckily, we found a place in Chicago that would take me in and treat all my addictions at once ...*
> *Six weeks after I entered the program {in July}, I was released. It was September 1990. I returned to London ...*

I was fascinated by the parallels, as I went into a sobriety program in July of 1985 (in Chicago), and got out six weeks later ... and, like John, have been "clean and sober" since.

A few months after his release he relocated to Atlanta, and was involved with assisting HIV service groups there, but in the fall of 1992 Elizabeth Taylor asked him to participate in a HIV/AIDS fundraiser that her foundation was doing at Madison Square Garden in NYC, and this inspired him to start up his own foundation, specifically focused on AIDS. One of the primary elements contributing to the success of the EJAF was from the realization:

> *... very early on, we made a key decision: our job would be to raise the money, and we would build partnerships to get it into the right hands. With the help of experts on our board ... this is how we would proceed.*
> *We did an extensive search and were lucky – extraordinarily lucky – to find the National Community AIDS Partnership. ... What {was} understood in those early years was essential: with so many separate organizations providing their own services to their own regions, we needed something that would help us respond to the crisis in a truly coordinated and strategic way. ...*
> *The goal of the partnership wasn't just to collect money and distribute it; it was to mobilize social service organizations that already existed, that already had infrastructure, and to turn their attention to HIV/AIDS.*

John, his associates, and media friends were called upon to help encourage congress to accelerate both assistance to those effected by the disease, but also to the core research looking for a cure. Aside from the main foundation in the US, John also opened up a sister operation in the UK, which is responsible not only for programs there, but around the world. As horrific as the situation was in America, where AIDS patients were frequently shunned and made pariahs, the stories the author relates about the situation in Africa are remarkable in their savagery:

> In 2009, South Africa's Medical Research Council conducted a study surveying the extent of the rape crisis {largely driving the HIV/AIDS epidemic there}. Researchers found that one-quarter of the men interviewed admitted to raping someone. Another study found that more than 60 percent of boys over the age of eleven believed that "sex is a male's natural entitlement and forcing a girl to have sex does not constitute a rape nor an act of violence."
>
> If a society doesn't think there's anything wrong with rape, then anybody who speaks out against it will be stigmatized. One rape survivor in South Africa told the international relief organization Médecins Sans Frontières, "People laugh at me and say, 'Oh, you will get HIV/AIDS now.' These are my neighbors and people who live around me. They don't seem to think the men that raped me did anything wrong."

To at least attempt to address this systematic cultural depravity, the EJAF along with Médecins Sans Frontières and a number of local organizations, have started a 24/7 acute care and support center in outskirts of Cape Town. He also discusses issues in Thailand, programs in the Ukraine, projects in Haiti, and in America's deep south (portions of which seem to be indistinguishable from Third World hell-holes). While the Clinton's organization has been involved in HIV programs, it was G.W. Bush whose administration actually pushed through serious governmental involvement in the AIDS crisis, announcing, in his 2003 State of the Union address, the initiative known as PEPFAR – the President's Emergency Plan for AIDS Relief. This initially was slated to devote $15 billion from 2003 to 2008, and was renewed in 2008 at nearly triple that, $48 billion. Needless to say, this was a shock to John (and probably most of the AIDS community) and he eventually had a chance to talk with Bush when Elton John was awarded the lifetime achievement Kennedy Center Honors in 2004, he says:

> I remember having the greatest conversation with him. He was warm, charming, and very complimentary, not only about my music but also about the work of my foundation. He knew all about what we were doing, and he was endlessly knowledgeable about HIV/AIDS as well.

John is considerably less charitable with the Catholic Church, and specifically Pope John Paul II, and (to a slightly lesser extent) Pope Benedict XVI, both of whom issued official proclamations claiming that condoms are ineffective at preventing the spread of AIDS – dooming thousands to horrible deaths in Africa and Latin America.

One of the most interesting things discussed here is how *preventable* AIDS is. John compares it to various other diseases:

> *Consider the difference between AIDS and cancer. If you were able to treat everybody with cancer on the planet, if you could give everyone the best, most cutting-edge treatment possible, other people would still get cancer. And, sadly, a lot of those who received treatment would still die. ... But, at this point, if all AIDS research were to suddenly stop, if we were never able to make another discovery in our understanding of the HIV virus, we could still beat it. We could save the life of nearly every HIV-positive person and prevent all future infections. ... In 2011, researchers funded by the U.S. Government made a miraculous discovery: people living with HIV who receive treatment are up to 96 percent less likely to pass on the virus to a sexual partner. In other words, current treatments are so effective that they reduce the presence of the HIV virus in an infected person's body to almost nil. ... That means treatment is also prevention.*

John follows this up with a look at what it would take to get there ... dollar by dollar. *"We know how to end AIDS, and we know what it would cost: an additional $5 to $7 billion each year from now until 2020, and not very much more than we're spending today beyond that."* To put that number in context, he trots out some interesting figures ... Americans spend *$16.9 billion on chocolate* per year, in the first quarter of 2012 Apple made profits of $13 billion, and "a handful of Wall Street banks" in 2010 paid out a whopping $20.8 billion *in bonuses* to employees and executives. He also does some math voodoo to compare the US national budget to something that one could wrap one's mind around ... if the budget had $3,700 in the checking account, would you spare $5 to $7 *"to save millions upon millions of lives"*? Or, put another way, for *"a rounding error in the federal budget – the United States could single-handedly end AIDS".*

Love Is The Cure[4] (I'm sure Robert Smith would agree ... had to get that in here somewhere) is still in print, but having hit the dollar stores, the on-line after-market has "like new" used copies for as little as a penny (plus shipping). Elton John has done a masterful job at pleading his case (again, this is largely a thesis by him as head of the EJAF), while providing enough "inside story" on his amazing life to keep it "juicier" than a book from a NGO would likely be. It initially came out in 2012, so is fading a bit on the "today's headlines" side of things, but as a history of AIDS, and what has been done to battle it, and what *could* be done to battle it, it stands pretty solidly on its own.

This is one that I pretty much would recommend "to all and sundry", as it's a topic that everybody should at least be conversant with, and given that it can be found for a minimal investment (although regular sales go to support EJAF, if you don't mind shelling out a few more bucks), you should consider picking up a copy.

Notes:
1. http://btripp-books.livejournal.com/181767.html
2. http://amzn.to/1U8DZ0f
3. http://ejaf.org/
4. http://amzn.to/1U8DZ0f

Tuesday, March 29, 2016[1]

More like 53 skills in 11 groupings ...

It's a funny thing. This is the *third* of Dave Kerpen's books that I've reviewed, and they've *all* come into my hands as prizes for "live Tweeting" during one of his presentations! I got Likeable Business[2] and Likeable Social Media[3] at a talk he was giving at one of the old "Big Frontier" events, and got his brand-new The Art of People: 11 Simple People Skills That Will Get You Everything You Want[4] for the volume of Tweets I was generating during a recent webinar he was doing. I don't know if Kerpen gives out so many promo copies that this isn't unusual in terms of *his* book distribution, but it really sort of stands out in *my* acquisition stream (it could be like that – in Jay Baer's recent book[5] he writes about Kerpen's policy for one-star review he gets on Amazon to apologize and *"offers to refund money spent, plus money for the pain and suffering of having read the book"*!).

This *is* a bit of a strange duck, however ... with its structure being one of its strong points ... if sort of masking its avowed intent as expressed in the subtitle *11 Simple People Skills That Will Get You Everything You Want* (there I go again, having problems with a subtitle). I was about half-way through the book when I began to wonder when we were going to learn about these 11 "skills" ... having not really registered that the book was set up in 11 sections (each having 4-6 small – the book's only 250 or so pages long – chapters looking at particular "skills" ... I guess going with *"53 Simple People Skills"* would have had less shelf appeal in sounding somewhat overwhelming).

To give you an idea of the arc of the book, here are the titles for those 11 sections:

1. *Understanding Yourself and Understanding People*
2. *Meeting the Right People*
3. *Reading People*
4. *Connecting with People*
5. *Influencing People*
6. *Changing People's Minds*
7. *Teaching People*
8. *Leading People*
9. *Resolving Conflict with People*
10. *Inspiring People*
11. *Keeping People Happy*

Needless to say, while those are broad-stroke "skills", they're not very specific (or actionable), so there's the 53 individual topics to deal with. Each of these run 3-4 pages, and conclude with a "FAST" (First Action Steps to Take) section, with three or four suggestions for taking action on the specific topic. This structure makes what could have been a bit of a brow-beating something more like a simple walk-though of bite-size ideas.

Now, I'm really going to try to not "go negative" here, but there were several points where I was seriously questioning what he was doing in some of the sections ... from trotting out some long-since-debunked "saws" popular with "personal development" speakers (like the "93 percent of communication is non-verbal" meme, which I was able to find – in a couple of minutes *on my phone* while reading in the park – that the primary researcher of the study Kerpen cites here had very specifically noted was taken *grossly* out of context and was not generalizable beyond the extremely narrow scope of the study ... why doesn't anybody ever check these things?), to starting the book with a section dismissing the Myers-Briggs categories in favor of the "Enneagram" model (which is, of course, submitted in its watered-down "newspaper horoscope" later-day form popular with corporate trainers, rather than the complete system propagated by Gurdgieff and Ouspensky with essential complexities such as "shock points", etc.[6]). What I found especially confusing was that from starting the book with this salvo (and dedicating 12 pages to an appendix for an assessment you can do to find "your enneagram type") this never came up again ... making me wonder if the author had a business relationship with, or at least owed a big favor to, the guy whose organization is promoted as a resource for enneagram info!

The other thing that one might find unexpected in a book purporting to impart skills, is that this is largely structured as a series of personal stories illustrating how the author encountered, learned from, overcame, etc., things related to the various individual "skills" (the 53 specific ones) ... making this less of a "manual" and more of a tale of "how Dave learned about this stuff" (and how he'd suggest you work on these). While this certainly makes The Art of People[7] a more breezy read, it also makes it a whole less *direct* than it might have been (and you know how little I connect with "teaching stories").

These gripes aside, there is quite a lot of very good material in here, some of it I found immediately of use (despite being an Enneagram Type 5: "Striving to be Detached" – meaning that my main "people skill" is trying to avoid having to deal with 'em!). One of these came in a very early chapter titled "How to Understand Someone Better Than You Do Your Friends (in Just Three Minutes)", which talks about a conference where the speaker was attempting to do just that for the audience. He gave, in sequence, three questions for each to pose to somebody next to them, with a minute each to get both responses. As I tend to have a hard time *caring* what's important to other people, I found this fascinating. The questions were:

> "What is the most exciting thing you're working on right now?",
> "If you had enough money to retire and then some, what would you be doing?", and
> "What is your favorite charity organization to support and why?"

What is probably most telling about this is Kerpen's note that:

> Although Steven and I exchanged a few emails after the event, it's been over two years since that first and only conversation I had with him. But

> *here's the really interesting thing: It's been over two years, yet I still recall with ease the content of that conversation. I still know more about Steven after three minutes over two years ago than I do about most of my casual friends from high school, college, and work.*

He goes on to suggest a list of 10 questions, and in the FAST section recommends picking 3 of them and using them as ice breakers at one's next social setting ... I just might take him up on the suggestion.

I found the next chapter, "Be Interested Instead of Interesting" of use as well (as I do tend to "bloviate", in O'Reilly's terminology), this is condensed into a bullet point (or, in the book, a free-standing quote on its own page) as *"The secret to getting people to adore you is to shut up and listen."*, even to the point of deflecting courtesy questions from the other person and making it "their turn" to speak again. This is followed up in subsequent chapter with:

> *Listen to understand, authentically try to connect deeply with people, help them feel less lonely, and you will find yourself far more able to influence them.*

... in which Kerpen stresses the "authenticity" part (which, sadly, brings *my* cynical mind the classic quote of Jean Giraudoux: *"The secret of success is sincerity. Once you can fake that you've got it made."*). These concepts come up later in the context of the aforementioned non-verbal communication (not 93%, but a useful thing to keep in mind), and in concepts like "mirroring" (where you parrot back wordings used by the person you're speaking with in terms like "I hear you saying", and similar). On this latter point the author says:

> *People in general don't want advice even when they ask for it. They just want to feel heard. As you practice and get good at mirroring, you will help people feel heard, and they will love you for it. Focus on really emphasizing the "feeling words" you hear as well; mirroring feelings is much more valuable than mirroring thoughts.*

Again, there is a LOT of interesting items in here, including "validation", "simple keys to networking" (develop a "signature style" – Kerpen has owned 29 pairs of *orange shoes*, making him stand out in pretty much any crowd), how to "help people come up with *your* idea", acting with confidence, making "the ask" (it's amazing how often the actual "ask" doesn't happen), build teams of advisors and accountability coaches, using the phenomena of "mirror neurons" to do what are essentially Jedi Mind Tricks on audiences (project what you want to have them mirror), using LinkedIn to connect with people you might not be otherwise able to (and using it to introduce other people to folks you think they should know), and even "Be Unoriginal". This last one leads into the second appendix, where Kerpen presents *fourteen pages* of quotes, and a link to a site he's set up with even more ... which he recommends using in talks, meetings, and even social media postings, which he justifies with:

> *There truly is very little original thought left out there, so why shouldn't we take advantage of the brilliant minds of the past and borrow the words they used to convey ideas and inspire others?*

One other thing he suggests that I had some resonance with was the suggestion to start sending out actual, physical, thank-you cards. He starts this chapter talking about a "barely legible" card he'd gotten from the CEO of a big company that he'd interviewed for a previous book, and how great it made him feel (which makes *me* feel better about getting cards out, as I've got a chicken-scratch which looks like some bizarre crossing of Klingon and Linear B). This also dove-tails with a bit from Robert B. Cialdini's Influence[8] where a car salesman created a huge business by sending out *thousands* of cards a month to his contact list. I'm additionally reminded of a story from my youth, when my Mom's friend, Bishop Montgomery (who I was amazed to Google is still alive, albeit in his mid-90's) was *always* so prompt with thank-you cards that my Mom jokingly accused him of mailing them on the way *to* the dinner/event they were about.

Anyway, I found The Art of People[9] useful, if not as focused as its subtitle would suggest (it really *is* "11 broad categories" in which the 53 could-be-called *skills* are collected), and it has a good deal to do with the author's life experiences. There was stuff that "raised my hackles", stuff I found exciting, and a lot of stuff that I just didn't connect with at all (hey, according to the book's companion site[10], I'm a "People Rookie" who "*may just not like other people very much*", so there's that!).

At this writing, the book's been officially out for under two weeks, so is likely to be all over the brick-and-mortar stores handing this sort of thing … and, of course, the on-line behemoths have it, with discounts of a bit more than a third off of cover price. I'm sort of on the fence on this one, there's elements I liked, parts I didn't, but generally found it something I'm glad to have read. Given that a lot of my resistance to this is likely based in me being a curmudgeonly misanthrope of a *non*-"people person", I suspect that others … who find the dominant fauna on our planet more engaging that I do … will find this more agreeable as well!

Notes:

1. http://btripp-books.livejournal.com/182048.html
2. http://btripp-books.livejournal.com/151272.html
3. http://btripp-books.livejournal.com/156574.html
4. http://amzn.to/1Zkk7X3
5. http://btripp-books.livejournal.com/180438.html
6. https://en.wikipedia.org/wiki/Fourth_Way_enneagram
7. http://amzn.to/1Zkk7X3
8. http://btripp-books.livejournal.com/181759.html
9. http://amzn.to/1Zkk7X3
10. http://www.artofpeoplebook.com/

Saturday, April 9, 2016[1]

Turning threats into opportunities ...

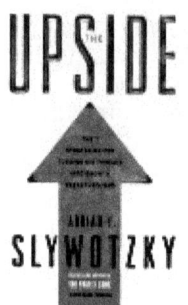

I'm not exactly sure how Adrian J. Slywotzky's The Upside: The 7 Strategies for Turning Big Threats into Growth Breakthroughs[2] got into my to-be-read piles, however, it has been hanging around for *years*, and I suspect that it was one of the titles I got in a big splurge a long time ago on a BN.com clearance sale. I'm also not quite sure *why* this suggested itself to get into my active reading list, except, perhaps, that it *had* been sitting around for so long, and I wasn't particularly inspired by anything else more recent.

This is, as one might guess from the title/sub-title, another of those "business philosophy" books, which I seem to have gotten an inexplicable taste for (after a lifetime of never reading any business books ... I believe my first came a decade ago). While I found this an interesting read, and quite engaging, I only ended up with two bookmarks in it, and those within the last 10% of the book ... which means that I'm going to be doing some "tap dancing" here walking through the book to find specifics to address.

I rather liked how the author launches into the theme of the book by going into military history for an example somewhat analogous to the type of "big threat" situation that would be later expressed in a business setting. Here, the story is of Union Civil War Colonel Joshua Lawrence Chamberlain, in command of the 20th Maine Regiment, that was holding the hill Little Round Top against focused attacks by a much larger Confederate force during the battle of Gettysburg. His troops, reduced by about 1/3rd down to a mere 200, were out of ammunition, and were unlikely to survive another charge by the enemy. Chamberlain positioned a unit of sharpshooters (who, apparently, still had ammo), along a stone wall on the flank, and had his men prepare a bayonet attack. The sharpshooters surprised the Rebel troops with fire from an unexpected direction, and the 20th Maine's charge down the hill resulted in the Confederates retreating in panic. The Union troops ended up taking more prisoners than they had remaining men, and the exchange (and holding the hill), was credited as a key element to the Union winning at Gettysburg.

How is this a lesson? Well, another commander might have just *defended the hill*, but Chamberlain opted to make a desperate "out of the box" (if you will) counter-attack, resulting in what had to have been a surprising success. Much of the *business* stories in the book look at situations of companies taking actions against major threats in dynamically similar veins.

The author frames these threats to one's business as "strategic risks", which differs from the following:

> Traditional risk management focuses on three categories of risk that are widely understood: hazard

risks (fire, flood, earthquake), *financial risks* (bad loans, currency and interest rate swings), and *operating risks* (the computer system goes down, the supply chain gets interrupted, an employee steals). Most companies have risk managers who specialize in handling these kinds of risk.

However, *strategic risks* target "one or more of the crucial elements in the design of your business model". The author lists "seven major kinds of strategic risk your business can prepare for":

1. Your big initiative fails.
2. Your customers leave you.
3. Your industry reaches a fork in the road.
4. A seemingly unbeatable competitor arrives.
5. Your brand loses power.
6. Your industry becomes a no-profit zone.
7. Your company stops growing.

These provide a framework for the stories detailed in most of the book. There are numerous *interesting* charts in here, but they don't seem to be a specific *approach*, but just a display template for the info ... there is also an odd stylistic approach to "handicapping" the odds of a project's success as these cases are being considered – where there is, in the body of the text, small boxes with a bolded percentage number, reflecting what the chances of the thing is question working out were at various points (if I'm recalling correctly, in the examples given these only went *up*, if in small increments – say, 15% to 18%). Obviously, these are subjective numbers, and have the benefit of retrospect, given that most (if not all) of the discussed products were great successes.

One thing I found somewhat distracting is that the author tends to jump around ... leaving one story to get into another, then switching back to the earlier one. This is likely to be that way to allow dealing with the same sorts of risks in different points in different products/companies, but it led to a bit linearity to the telling than had he stayed with one case study all the way through. Speaking of these, the first two are the Toyota Prius, and the Apple iPod. There are numerous steps in the development which are identified (such as the strategy of "creating excess options" by Toyota, which started with *twenty* engine designs ... and this step boosted the odds from 17% to 20% ... or Apple's licensing the player technology from another company that boosted their odds of success by a similar 3%). Slywotzky tracks the Prius up to 90% odds of success, and then flips over to discuss the Mars Pathfinder, and its fast/cheap model.

The book shifts from development to customer relations, and takes a look at Coach handbags, and a Japanese chain of music/video/book stores (that have since expanded into "lifestyle" product lines) called Tsutaya. In both of these cases the focus of growth was on amassing proprietary customer information, with their approaches conducting 10x the "conventional model" of customer interviews and marketing experiments. As both those companies are in the B2C zone, the author also adds in a B2B company, Johnson

Controls, which went from making frames for car seats, to the entire automotive interiors, introducing the video entertainment system, etc., based on what the data showed the customers wanted.

The "fork in the road" risk brings up "synthetic histories" and "double betting" ... and interesting example of the former is a description of what might well have happened to Microsoft had Bill Gates reacted differently to the report of some managers who had gone on a recruiting trip to Cornell in 1994 ... which involved some of the first on-line systems – that the students were enthusiastically using. Gates, in the midst of launching W95, could have (as in the story here) brushed this aside, and Mosaic/Netscape could have ruled the world in a couple of years, but instead he recognized the risk to his product implicit in the Internet, and instituted a crash-development program resulting in Internet Explorer. A similar story is told of IBM ... which in the first half of the last century was the main source of (mechanical) calculators and related machines. The son of the CEO, Tom Watson, Jr., saw the emerging computers (from Sperry-Univac) as a serious threat, and convinced upper management to invest in computer development as well ... this was the "double-betting", as both the calculator and computer lines were being worked on, and by the mid-60's IBM was dominating the latter business just as they had the former in previous decades. A number of other "horse races" are detailed in this, Blockbuster vs. Netflix, Motorola vs. Nokia, Lotus vs. Borland and WordPerfect, etc. The author identifies blocks to "double betting", which are *failure to face reality*, *misplaced strategic logic* (to avoid "cannibalizing" one's flagship products, it frequently ends up that everybody *but* the "threatened firm" will invest in a new technology), and *fear of spending* (although one must "double bet" carefully).

The risk of a "unique competitor" is first framed in the basketball battles between Bill Russell and Wilt Chamberlain, which involves some fascinating analysis of the game, and Russell's quote: *"Wilt played vertical, I played horizontal. I got to his favorite spot first ... so that he'd have to shoot from an angle he didn't like."* This then spins into the Wal-Mart vs. Target story, focusing on Bob Ulrich, who went from a merchandising trainee at Target to CEO of its (then) parent company (Dayton Hudson, since sucked up by Macy's, like so many others). His strategy (among several) was to find "name" designers who were in a slump, such as Isaac Mizrahi, Mossimo Giannulli, and numerous others, and sign them for exclusive product designs ... that had to follow a "3H" – Head/Handbag/Heart – philosophy ... helping to also drive the "non-overlap" dictate that means that only 30-40% of products in a Target could be found (cheaper) at the local Wal-Mart.

There are some chastening data points in the chapter on "brand erosion" (especially for those of us who have been around a lot of decades), with once-dominant companies that are either gone or shadows of their former selves. Two companies which are specifically looked are Sony and Ford, which lost significant brand value in the period from 2000-2006 (27% and 69% respectively), and a table with the declining results of a bunch of other "household names". This is countered with a look at Samsung, which, in that same period, more than *tripled* its brand value ... here another detailed look with those percentage boxes interspersed. There is an interesting table here on "brand risk", with 10 "types of failure", a definition of each, and an example of a company that stumbled due to that particular issue.

The "no-profit zone" largely deals with competition and collaboration … with examples like Steve Jobs convincing the music industry, which was in full battle mode against Napster, etc., to embrace the iPod's proprietary format, and the iTunes marketplace, and the various European manufacturers who came together to create Airbus and compete with the major American aircraft manufacturers. Slywotzky also offers up a "synthetic history" of what might have happened had the assorted players in the auto industry come together ala the players in Airbus, in the mid-90's. In this fantasy, costs have plummeted, fuel consumption has dipped, and emerging economies are producing vehicles that are able to be sold for just a few thousand dollars.

In the "company stops growing" risk, there's another interesting chart here, tracking growth moves, and companies that made these work, as well as stories of a number (oddly, mainly European) companies that responded to stagnating growth with an array of approaches. There's also a piece about Proctor & Gamble's sudden decline in 1999 (their stock lost 50% of its value in *one quarter*), and how they fought their way back by 2004. Part of this was a new direction that asked *"Are there things that professionals do for consumers that consumers could do for themselves?"*, which not only resulted in products such as Crest Whitestrips, but also a focus on "consumer anthropology", a research approach that P&G was dedicating as much as $200 million in 2006.

At the end of each chapter there are questions for companies to ask themselves to assess their level of risk in the various areas, and in the last chapter it looks at "reversing risk" and providing a number of tools to help one get there. These fall in these six main categories:

> 1. *Identify and assess your risks.*
> 2. *Quantify your risks.*
> 3. *Develop risk mitigation action plans.*
> 4. *Identify the potential upside.*
> 5. *Map and prioritize your risks.*
> 6. *Adjust your capital decisions.*

These include things like a "Risk Exposure Map", a "Risk Profile Worksheet", the "Strategic Risk Spectrum", etc. There's a lot of "coaching" here as well, like looking at how companies are often structured to ignore risks, from "killing the messenger" who brings up bad news (like in the Microsoft "synthetic history"), overvaluing confidentiality, and "siloing" information. Slywotzky defines *"three disciplines that can help management teams get consistently better at managing their portfolio risks:"* 1. knowing the true odds, 2. seeing the earliest warning signals, and 3. constantly comparing risk profiles. He provides quite a lot of material about each of these, with numerous example tables, and a worksheet for #3 to compare one's company with a key competitor. One thing that I suspect would be very useful for a lot of companies would be the last part of the book, which outlines, over several pages, a half-day workshop to use the various tools in the book to determine one's "strategic risk and upside profile".

Needless to say, The Upside[3] is not a "general reader" or "all and sundry" book, although it's an interesting enough read, with a lot of fascinating info. It's also getting a *bit* "vintage" at this point, having come out in 2007, so there are sections which seem like real *old news* from today's standpoint. However, it is still in print in the hardcover (so it certainly must have its audience!), and the on-line big boys are offering it at 49% off of cover. It *is* available from the new/used guys too, with "very good" copies that can be had for the ever-popular price of 1¢ (plus shipping). If this sounds like something you'd find of interest, you should certainly have no excuse to not pick up a copy.

Notes:

1. http://btripp-books.livejournal.com/182458.html

2-3. http://amzn.to/1XczIX5

Sunday, April 10, 2016[1]

A writing class with Mr. King ...

As I nearly exclusively read non-fiction books, I rarely have that experience (which appears to be fairly common among novel readers) of hitting a book that "I couldn't put down", but this one has been about as close to that in at least my most recent several years of reading, with my having blown through it in only a day or so. This is also "an outlier" in that I have *no* idea how it got into my hands. I have no recall or ordering it, or buying it in any store ... it was just *there* one day, and I was asking my daughters if it was something they'd be assigned (one could *hope*) from school. No clue.

So, I approached Steven King's On Writing: A Memoir of the Craft[2] with a touch of trepidation (moderated by looking it up on Amazon and seeing massive numbers of 5-star ratings for it). While I'm certainly *familiar* with Stephen King, I don't believe I've actually *read* anything by him (given the whole "no fiction" thing, plus my only being minimally tolerant of horror/suspense), while having seen parts (I don't do movies much either) of a few films based on his books.

This book *is* a bit of an "odd duck", the first third of it is pretty much an autobiographical essay in 38 parts, from his birth in 1947, up till 1981, which is pretty coldly honest about how much his life had "gone off the tracks" into substance abuse. Being a recovering alcoholic myself, I found the following having a certain resonance:

> The idea that creative endeavor and mind-altering substances are entwined is one of the great pop-intellectual myths of our time. The four twentieth-century writers whose work is most responsible for it are probably Hemingway, Fitzgerald, Sherwood Anderson, and the poet Dylan Thomas. They are the writers who largely formed our vision of an existential English-speaking wasteland where people have been cut off from one another and live in an atmosphere of emotional strangulation and despair. These concepts are very familiar to most alcoholics; the common reaction to them is amusement. ... Hemingway and Fitzgerald didn't drink because they were creative, alienated, or morally weak. They drank because it's what alkies are wired up to do. Creative people probably <u>do</u> run a greater risk of alcoholism and addiction than those in some other jobs, but so what? We all look pretty much the same when we're puking in the gutter.

King notes that he never stopped writing, but regrets not being able to recall the creative process of books like *Cujo*, about which he says: *"I wish I could remember enjoying the good parts as I put them down on the page."*

The middle half of the book is the "meat" of it (at least in terms of it being a book about *writing*), broken into three sections: a very brief piece called "What Writing Is", a somewhat larger section called "Toolbox", and then the "On Writing" part. In the first of these, he argues that writing is *telepathy*, and he suggests that the reader has an ideal "receiving place", as he has his preferred "transmitting place", and notes that neither time nor distance are problems, as we can still read the thoughts of Dickens, Shakespeare, and even Herodotus when we pick up their books. King suggests a scenario with a red table cloth on which is a cage, in which is a rabbit, on which, in blue ink, is marked the numeral 8 (which I immediately was wondering if it were actually an infinity symbol – but King doesn't address that). He notes that everybody will see this in their mind slightly differently, the nature of the table, the color and material of the cloth, the type of cage, etc. He adds:

> This is what we're looking at, and we all see it. I didn't tell you, you didn't ask me. I never opened my mouth and you never opened yours. We're not even in the same <u>year</u> together, let alone the same room ... except we <u>are</u> together. We're close. We're having a meeting of the minds.
> ... We've engaged in an act of telepathy.

So, there you know, that's what writing *is* (at least to Mr. Stephen King).

The "toolbox" section starts off with just that, a *toolbox* that had belonged to his carpenter grandfather, and had been hand-made by him. The story involves the author helping his uncle do some repairs, involving said toolbox. He spins this into an analogy:

> I want to suggest that to write to your best abilities, it behooves you to construct your own toolbox and then build up enough muscle to carry it with you. Then, instead of looking at a hard job and getting discouraged, you will perhaps seize the correct tool and get immediately to work.
> ... You'll find you have most of the tools you need already, but I advise you to look at each one again as you load it into your box. Try to see each one new, remind yourself of its function, and if some are rusty (as they may be if you haven't done this seriously in awhile), clean them off.

He lists various things that should go into the different parts of the toolbox (he's envisioning a multi-level box with lots of drawers, etc.). He puts vocabulary and grammar on the top shelf (and even suggests a resource for the latter, *Warriner's English Grammar and Composition* - something I've added to my Amazon wishlist), before getting into details. He talks about active and passive verbs (try to minimize the latter), and warns against adverbs. He says *"I'm convinced that fear is at the root of most bad writing."* and that without the fear you *"can safely energize your prose with active verbs"* and using basic "he/she said" attributes for dialog.

The next layer down in the toolbox is all that stuff in Strunk & White's *Elements of Style* (you *do* already have a copy of that sitting on the shelf somewhere, right?), plus an awareness of sentence and paragraph usage. King suggests: *"In expository prose, paragraphs can (and should) be neat and utilitarian. ... In fiction, the paragraph is less structured – it's the beat instead of the actual melody."* and *"{The paragraph} is a marvelous and flexible instrument ... You must learn to use it well if you are to write well. What this means is lots of practice; you have to learn the beat."*. This brings me to one slight quibble about the book ... it really *is* about writing fiction. Of course, this is the author's niche, it's what he's done all his life ... but there were points where I sort of glazed over as I really don't have that much interest in fiction, and he delves deep down a bunch of rabbit holes in pursuit of what seemed to me to be minutia about that side of things.

This brings us to the actual "On Writing" section. In one paragraph the author pretty much lays out what his intents for the project are:

> *I am approaching the heart of this book with two theses, both simple. The first is that good writing consists of mastering the fundamentals (vocabulary, grammar, the elements of style) and then filling the third level of your toolbox with the right instruments. The second is that while it is impossible to make a competent writer out of a bad writer, and while it is equally impossible to make a great writer out of a good one, it is possible, with lots of hard work, dedication, and timely help, to make a good writer out of a merely competent one.*

King starts the first part of this with another declaration:

> *If you want to be a writer, you must do two things above all others: read a lot and write a lot. There's no way around these two things that I'm aware of, no shortcut.*

One of the "technical" questions he addresses is what is "a lot" for writing ... he visits a story about James Joyce sometimes only managing seven words in a day, and notes others who spewed out reams of copy. As most of my *reviews* these days are clocking in at this level, I was very pleased to read that King's own output is pretty manageable: *"I like to get ten pages a day, which amounts to 2,000 words. That's 180,000 words over a three-month span, a goodish length for a book ..."*, now, I have no idea how he's measuring *pages* but 2,000 words in *my* wordprocessor runs to just 4 pages (the review I wrote just before this one was about 2,200 words), so I'm guessing he's doing editorial mark-up friendly (and magazine submission compliant) multi-line spacing, and there's no accounting for margins (as any highschool student who's submitted a paper with 1.5-2" margins will attest). Anyway, King writes in the morning, up to, and sometimes through, lunch. He has some definite ideas about writing environment as well ... *"most of us do our best in a place of our own. ... it really needs only one thing: a door which you are willing to shut."* ... he goes on quite a bit about "closed door" and public spaces for writing.

He launches into a lot of pages with examples of writing from his catalog, from other famous writers, and some less-famous, and gives opinions, suggestions, and dictates based on these, from writing whatever you want "as long as you tell the truth" to dissuading you from *plotting* (which brought to mind a counter-example of the stories of Frank Herbert's environment in which he penned the *Dune* books, which had everything graphically laid out exactly as he was going to write them). King equates books to fossils: *"Stories are relics, part of an undiscovered pre-existing world. The writer's job is to use the tools in his or her toolbox to get as much of each one out of the ground intact as possible."* and says, in relation to characters, that his job is *"to watch what happens and then write it down"*. Sort of re-visiting the "telepathy" idea, he adds: *"Description begins in the writer's imagination, but should finish in the reader's."*, and suggests a self-hypnosis like approach to putting oneself into an environment (his example is the Palm Too restaurant in NYC), and experiencing that in all one's senses – impressions that can then be translated to the page.

He spends a good chunk of the section talking about dialog, again in both his and others' works … which is probably where I tuned out a bit … but then ends up discussing symbolism. He notes: *"It's that ability to summarize and encapsulate that makes symbolism so interesting, useful, and – when used well – arresting."*, but suggests that it's not something one should go *into* the writing with, but an element that can be polished in subsequent work-overs. He also sort of dismissed "theme", saying that the writer spends all his time with the trees, and it's frequently left to others to go on about the *forest*, although he notes that it's another element that can productively influence one's second draft.

Speaking of which, he says that his books typically have "two drafts and a polish", with the polish in the wordprocessor era coming to be closer to a third draft. He does point out that this is just *his* method, and compares that to Kurt Vonnegut's who *"rewrote each page of his novels until he got them exactly the way he wanted them"*, and when he was done with the book, it was ready for print. He also suggests when that first "door closed" draft is done, one should "let your book rest", which he thinks should be a minimum of six weeks. Once that period of time is over, you can pick it up with fresh eyes, making the editorial re-working much easier. Once that set of edits is over, you can move to the "open door" part, where you're sharing the manuscript with significant others, trusted friends, and associates whose opinions of your writing you trust. Getting this sort of feedback can be a godsend, as frequently these others have whole libraries of more in-depth information on topics that you were writing about, and whose feedback can save you from deeply embarrassing factual gaffes (examples of which from his writing are of an appealingly voyeuristic interest).

He also offers up some "industry" stuff, like *"Formula: 2nd Draft = 1st Draft – 10%"* … a note he'd been given on a rejection slip when he was in highschool, that he still uses as a guide today. He goes into research, how to effectively craft and inject "backstory", and some war stories about the business, with publishers, agents, and the coming and going of magazines.

The book follows with a second autobiographical piece, which follows his near-fatal accident in 1999, which happened to be right in the midst of his writing the first version of this book. He was off on his daily walk up in the backwoods of Maine, when, on the section of his usual route that took him along an actual road, he got hit by a van, and was very badly injured (one of his lower legs was "broken in at least nine places" and the report of the accident indicated that he was *very* lucky to have survived – a bit to the left or right and he'd probably not made it). This section is only peripherally about writing, except in how it helped his recovery:

> I didn't <u>want</u> to get back to work. ... Yet at the same time I felt I'd reached one of those crossroads moments when you're all out of choices. And I had been in terrible situations before which the writing had helped me get over – had helped me forget myself for at least a little while.

This section is followed by a couple of "Furthermore" parts, the first being quite interesting from a writer's perspective, as it's "showing us his work", where he reproduces the first draft of a part of a story (4+ pages worth), and then displays his editorial mark-up on a double-spaced copy of the same text (he evidently works from paper with pen for making these changes), and then walks the reader through the "why" of all the edits ... fascinating. The next two sections are lists of books that he's found appealing and/or useful, one that was in the original On Writing[3] in 2000, and an additional (covering stuff he'd read between the two versions) list put together for the "Tenth Anniversary Editon", featuring nearly two hundred titles between them (of which I've read only about half a dozen, and those mainly due to having been an English major back in the day).

My snarking about this being fiction-centric aside, it *is* quite an excellent book, and should certainly be "in the toolbox" of any writer. It's approachable both as a biographical work, a historical work (as far as the trade of fiction author goes, at least), and a workshop on writing with one of the most successful writers of our time. This is still very much in print (in hardcover, trade paperback, mass-market paperback, audio book, e-book, heck, it might be in *braille* for all I know), so should be reasonably easy to find it in the surviving brick-and-mortar book stores, but you *can* score a "very good" copy of the mass-market paperback for as little as a penny (plus shipping) through the new/used guys, so it's definitely something you should go get if you have any interest in the craft of writing.

Notes:

1. http://btripp-books.livejournal.com/182645.html

2-3. http://amzn.to/1ZMEufT

Monday, April 11, 2016[1]

A blast from the past ...

I know that *somebody* highly recommended this book to me, but I have no clue who that might have been. I suspect it may have been somebody at one of the Transamerica meetings (where I've had other "business philosophy" titles enthusiastically suggested that I should read). In any case, I took the advice and picked up a copy of Robert J. Kriegel's If it Ain't Broke...Break It!: And Other Unconventional Wisdom for a Changing Business World[2] from the Amazon new/used guys (hey, hard to argue with copies for 1¢).

I hate to say it, but the *most notable* thing about this is that it's quite *old* (from 1991 – heck, I was still a PR exec back then), and yet, except for the particulars (O.J. Simpson as a sport celebrity, Arthur Anderson as an innovating company, etc.) this doesn't *feel* overly dated ... which no doubt speaks to the tone/approach of the book. As opposed to many marketing (or certainly *technology/internet*) books, this isn't full of "groaners", but it does have a bit of a sense of coming from a different world ... one, for example, without the web (Mosaic, the earliest WWW browser, wasn't released until 1993!), and where moving functions onto a *computer* is a highlighted achievement.

In the Introduction, Kriegel says:

> The one thing we can count on as we approach the twenty-first century is the certainty that rip-roaring change will challenge our understanding and shake up the basic foundations of the world around us, in every area. Whatever we do, and wherever we do it, everything – workstyles, economic conditions, technology, corporate structures, global communications, lifestyles, environmental responsibilities – everything is changing at a dizzying rate.

... which was certainly borne out by the past quarter century, albeit in ways that he probably had no inkling of at the date this was written.

However, the sense of on-coming change sets up the context for the (on the surface) somewhat counter-intuitive title, in the realization that trying to "keep things as they are" is almost certainly going to result in being passed by ... so looking for ways to "break" things (as they've always been done) looks to be a promising strategy.

There are a couple of odd usages in here, one of which I'd like to address ... "firehosing" ... when *I* use the term "firehose", it's typically in the sense of a massive amount of information coming fast and hard, like water out of a firehose ... here the author uses it in different sense: *"In an attempt to cling to the familiar and stay on safe ground* {the would-be innovator}'s *boss responded like a fireman hosing down a fire. He effectively "firehosed" her, dousing her ideas, enthusiasm, and spirit."* This usage comes up all through the book, and is related to the idea of having passion, or "a fire in the heart". He goes on to frame this as:

> *Firehosing is a common way we undermine or dismiss the daring strategy, the new idea, and even the simplest suggestion for improvement. What's worse, though, is how often we firehose <u>our own</u> dreams and creative ideas without knowing it.*

The basic feel of the book (and probably why it's aged as well as it has) is very "coachy", which makes sense as the author is a former athlete and coach for Olympic competitors, and is more about one's motivations than the specifics of the implementations. This is not, however, much of a *workbook* (which I take it the author *does* have for the various courses and corporate events he mentions doing), although there *are* the occasional fill-in-the-blank sections, and lists of questions and attributes.

Speaking of lists, this covers a lot of thematic ground over its 21 chapters, making a discussion of the whole somewhat challenging, so I think this is one of those instances where indulging in a list of chapter headings might well impart a sense of the "arc" better than my trying for some sort of summation:

1. *Surf's Up! ... Embrace the Unexpected*
2. *Put Fire in Your Heart*
3. *Stoke It ... Don't Soak It*
4. *Dreams Are Goals with Wings*
5. *Try Easy*
6. *Always Mess with Success*
7. *Playing It Safe ... Is Dangerous!*
8. *Don't Compete ... Change the Game*
9. *Sacred Cows Make the Best Burgers*
10. *Think Like a Beginner*
11. *Strange Bedfellows Make Great Partners*
12. *Take Risks ... Not Chances*
13. *Fear Tells Lies ... Break the Cycle*
14. *Mistakes Are a Good Investment*
15. *Failure Is a Good Place to Start*
16. *Plan on Changing Your Plans*
17. *Play Your Own Best Game*
18. *Don't Look Where You Don't Want to Go*
19. *Like It? Log It!*
20. *Joy Pays Off*
21. *Breaking Out*

Needless to say, you can pretty much tell "where he's going" with the various chapters. Again, this works best when it's in the "general" rather than in the particular (aside from now-gone corporations he lauds here, there are quite a few "highly innovative" products, companies, and systems which I've never *heard* of, so the odds are pretty good they were something shiny that caught his eye at the time, but never actually made it). Of course, *far* older books have had on-going popularity (Napoleon Hill's "Think And Grow Rich" comes to mind), largely on being about *process* rather than specific situations, so it's in good company there.

One of the workshop exercises he outlines is that for determining one's own "sacred cows", and he reports that (from over 10,000 participants), more than 90% reported spending more time doing things they disliked than those they *liked*, with the latter being predictably more *productive* activities:

> In almost every instance, doing the things you like – the challenging tasks, the creative work, the people work – is much more directly related to the bottom line of the organization than the paperwork.

... which he expands on, noting that this (paperwork) typically: *"has more to do with mistrust, control, and monitoring than with motivating, innovating, and producing"*.

One of the most useful/applicable bits here is the part about "The Fear Cycle", which has five "links":

> Link I: Imagined Consequences
> Link II: Fear Distorts Perception
> Link III: The Physical Response
> Link IV: Freeze or Frenzy
> Link V: Worse Expectations Fulfilled

The most typical example of this would be in public speaking or doing an important presentation, although the same cycle can be traced out in almost any stress-inducing situation. Kriegel suggests that the cycle can be broken at any of these links, and charts out methods to address the fear at each (such as making a "worry list" and thinking through actions to take if any of the worse-case scenarios *do* manifest).

There were some interesting quotables in the "Mistakes" chapter, including quoting from an early Apple exec that *"success does not breed success. It is failure which breeds success."*, which the author expands on with:

> Mistakes help you to rethink, reconceptualize, and restrategize. The result of "going back to the drawing board" is usually substantially better than the original idea.

Another figure he throws out is good to recall ... *"the average millionaire entrepreneur has gone bankrupt 3.75 times."* (which brings to mind the mindless criticism of Trump's assorted failed ventures, as if only an – impossible – 100% success record is legitimizing!). There's also a number of stories here that talk of world-class winners who hardly started that way ... including a trio of multiple Super Bowl champion head coaches who also managed to have worst-ever first-season records in NFL history.

As anybody who knows me in real life will attest, I have always had a lot of distrust of "plans" (even before I read about the Gurdjieff/Ouspensky "shock points"), and so I had a certain affinity for his "changing plans" section here. Kriegel notes (and I suspect he might be *underestimating* the effect):

> As unpredictable and uncontrollable as things are today, there are three things you can in fact count on. I call these the "triple double." You can assume that anything new will invariably take twice as long, cost twice as much and involve twice as much work as you thought!
>
> ...
>
> Because of the triple double, one of the most difficult phases of any new project or venture is in the middle. This is where the unexpected has wreaked havoc on carefully developed plans. ...
>
> ...
>
> Nowadays, uncertainty and surprise are normal. You can assume that is reality. You can also assume that the unexpected can't be controlled. What you can control, however, is your attitude towards the unexpected. ...

In the "Play Your Own Best Game" he has both one of the most useful parts of the book, and one of the things that most aggravated me. I'm a "confirmed generalist", and the author foreshadows the irritating "ninja/rockstar/one-trick-pony" employment world by *decades* in insisting one needs to "be great at *one thing*", which is just swell if you're a tennis prodigy who's been doing endless hours on the court since you still had your baby teeth, but it's an intellectual death for anybody with any breadth. Just sayin'. The beneficial thing here is a pretty handy "strength assessment", which leads into a bit on "designing your own game". Here's another point where the age of the book is telling ... he's writing from a time when companies couldn't fill the slots they were wanting to hire for (leaving *lots* of employment options), as opposed to today when long stretches of involuntary unemployment are increasingly the norm. I suppose he also semi-predicts the "work for yourself (because nobody is hiring)" reality by sketching out this:

> It is more critical than ever to work in an area in which you are utilizing your strengths and natural skills. You'll not only be more productive and creative, but you will also enjoy what you are doing more, which will further increase your effectiveness.

Again, I suspect the "joy" section here is long past us in the current economy, where it is frequently *impossible* to get work with things one is skilled in, let alone something one *likes* ... but he talks of a study of 1,500 people, where 83 percent were in jobs they chose for making money, and 17 percent were in jobs they loved. At the end of 20 years, 101 of the 1,500 had become millionaires, and all but *one* had come out of the much-smaller-sample "love the work" group. Interesting, but depressing at the same time (although I'm sure he's accuse me of being a "firehoser" for saying that)!

Anyway, I found If it Ain't Broke...Break It![3] a decent read, if not the "essential" book it had been pitched to me as. It covers a lot of ground, is light in tone, and full of enough interesting tidbits to keep the reader engaged, and is remarkably "evergreen" considering its vintage. I think it would have been *better* with more "workbook" aspects, but I guess that's what the author's ultimately *selling*, so he's not wanting to give it away. It appears like this might still be in print, but (as noted up top) you can get a "very good" used copy for as little as a penny (plus shipping) were you interested in taking this particular time-tunnel journey.

Notes:

1. http://btripp-books.livejournal.com/182817.html
2-3. http://amzn.to/1W1N2zj

Tuesday, April 12, 2016[1]

Banking on your unconscious mind ...

About ten years ago I took a hypnosis training course via the Hypnosis Motivation Institute (https://hypnosis.edu), which was very interesting, and in which I did very well (I guess my voice is pretty great for "inductions"), but I never got any traction with figuring out what to do with it (if I was any good at "selling myself", I'd have a freak'n *job*), so it's another of those zillion things that I've studied but never got to apply. Back then I was picking up various materials that they had available, and one of these was Success is Not an Accident: The Mental Bank Concept[2] by HMI founder John G. Kappas, Ph.D., along with its companion wire-bound "ledger". As these were not part of the coursework, they sat on the "other desk" in my office, and sat there, and sat there ... until I picked up the book a week or so back.

Frankly, I had never even seriously *looked* at this when I got it, and only had the vaguest idea of what it was about. What it *is* is a system that Dr. Kappas developed for his clients to allow them to work on themselves, programming the subconscious as "a goal machine", which *"represents the culmination of 47 years' experience in the field of subconscious and behavioral re-programming"*. I also hate to admit it, but by the time I was finished *reading* the book, I was still at a loss about what I was supposed to *do* to put it into action. Fortunately, in the ten years since I picked this up, materials that at one point were purchase/subscription only are now available (posted by the organization) on YouTube. I would *highly* recommend watching this video[3] to get the *instructions* laid out for using the Mental Bank (the video is 2 hours long, and the how-to stuff only comes in half-way through). While I really hate to depend on "ancillary materials" outside of the book I'm reviewing to *make sense* of the book, in this case I'm really recommending that. Heck, if one watched the video first and *then* read the book, it might make more sense all the way around!

Before I get into the book's content, I can't help (wearing my editor/publisher hat) but to bring up a *bizarre* "feature" of the book (at least in the printing that I have). In standard book lay-out there are names for the two facing pages, *recto* and *verso* (which mean "front" and "back"), with recto being on the right and verso on the left, and, nearly universally, the *odd* page numbers are on the recto. While the Foreword and Introduction have standard numbering, Chapters 1-7 have the odd numbers on the verso, only to return to standard numbering from Chapter 8 through the end of the book. As a "book guy" this drove me *nuts*, with the feeling I was in some mirror-reality reading experience. There's a great lyric by Peter Murphy about dealing with esoteric stuff: *"Look for what seems out of place."*, and this is close enough to those realms that I kept wondering what the *message* was of having the book set up like this ... not believing (in my editor hat) that this, if *not* intentional, hadn't been noticed (and thereby *corrected*) before ink hit paper. At this point I'm guessing that it's simply an "inexplicable error", but it was a page-by-page distraction to me for 150+ pages of this 250-ish page book!

The Mental Bank Concept (or System in the video) is a way to "reprogram" your subconscious to change your "life script". Now, if one is looking into a book like this, it is very likely due to being *unhappy* with some aspect of one's life, be that financial, relationships, health, whatever. However, one of the keystones of this approach is the extremely counter-intuitive insistence that each and every one of us *is a success*:

> No matter how down-and-out you may feel, you have succeeded in carrying out your current life script. You were programmed by your past, and success in any endeavor means carrying out your subconscious plans. You have done this well. The only problem is that your subconscious script is not the pattern you want for your present and future. Thus, it is time to change that script so you will have the accomplishments you desire.

Admittedly, this is a fairly substantial leap of faith to take, but it *is* based on a half-century of hypnosis therapy, and it seems to work for a lot of people. This is also *very* regimented, and one is constantly encouraged to follow the steps *exactly* as presented. Now, I am one of the *worst* people as far as "doing things *my* way" (because, hey, I'm "the smartest kid in the room" and all that), but having read through this, I'm seeing how the "doing it as written" thing is probably a real good idea. Also, this requires a whole lot of discipline, as, for it to *work*, you have to do the process (which is generally said to take 5 minutes) *every* night at bedtime.

Back in my "drinking days", *that* would have been a problem, but it's set up that way to get the information into your head just in time for the early phases of sleep. As woo-woo as a lot of this may seem, it does appear that there is some quite solid "brain science" involved in how this is structured. There is also a gauge as to what "type of suggestibility" is primarily active in the individual. Dr. Kappas defines two types, "emotionally suggestible" (responding to inferred suggestions) and "physically suggestible" (responding to literal suggestions), with the two types subconsciously accepting quite different modes of suggestion – so it's obviously very useful to know what your "type" is when coming up with the affirmations that are part of the process. There is a questionnaire and chart to determine which is your dominant mode. The following example is almost ridiculous (I'm assuming it arises from dealing with people in hypnotic states, not in general conversation), but it points to the differences:

> If you ask an extreme literal person and an extreme inferred person the following question: "Would you tell me your name?", the extreme literal person will say "Yes" while the person accepting inferences will give you his or her name.

To come back to the "life script" concept, the book has a number of examples of how various of Dr. Kappas' clients had gotten into patterns that were limiting. One example is a guy whose father earned what was, in the 60's, a very solid income (say $25,000) and that *number* got stuck in his head as "what success was". However, decades later, that dollar amount wasn't an income that he could survive at, yet his subconscious programming somehow kept sabotaging any of his *conscious* efforts to get better pay. This can also work in reverse, with programming to "not be anything like" one's parents ... in any case, most of the information in the subconscious "filter" is set from about ages 8-13 ... dooming most people to lives dictated by their childhood experiences.

I suppose that a lot of people whose problems are *not* financial (wanting to find a life partner, wanting to lose weight, etc.), may have issues with the way the Mental Bank is set up, but, through a lot of trial-and-error, it was determined to use symbolic language to influence the subconscious, in this case the symbol $ and numbers. The way the program works is to fill out an old-style bookkeeping-like *ledger* with dollar values, and keep a running balance. I got *totally confused* with this (I'm *horrible* with financial stuff), until I watched the above-noted video. What you do is come up with your real-life income (or an equivalent if you're not currently pulling a salary), multiply by one factor for your Mental Bank income, come up with an hourly rate, and an over-all target (I've not started using this ... was waiting to get through this review first ... so these are still a bit hazy to me). Once you have your hourly rate, you make a list of tasks for which you are going to "pay yourself" (for instance, writing reviews would be something I'd have on my list), and at the end of the day, total up everything you'd done that was on the list, and come up with your daily "pay". Oddly, any *real-world* income that had come your way is *deducted* from that total before it gets rolled into the daily balance.

One of the things that I have had most "resistance" to here is the insistence that *all the writing* involved in these daily ledgers (and the "contract" you write when you get started) needs to be in cursive longhand. Since I learned to type (back in 10th grade or so), I have maybe filled up *two pages* of cursive writing in the intervening decades ... so the argument that this is a "direct route" into one's subconscious seems to be somewhat iffy to me, as I'm going to have to *re-learn* how to write in script to work this!

I suppose the key part of how the Mental Bank program functions is that the subconscious doesn't make a distinction between *real* income, and *symbolic* income, so that it just sees that it's getting rewarded for doing the tasks you have set up as things you're getting "paid" for. This is very much along the lines of research done for NLP and similar approaches, where the mind doesn't differentiate between things *visualized* and things actually *rehearsed*. Plus, putting this into play just before going to sleep, sets it up for the most suggestible times for the brain ... which is augmented by daily affirmations – again, written out long-hand on the ledger *every night* – which is why that test for suggestibility style is important.

Although there are stories in the book about the Mental Bank producing some remarkable turn-arounds for numerous clients, in the video George Kappas (John's son, who now runs the HMI), describes the process as "dropping pebbles in a bucket of water", where each pebble makes no noticeable difference, but over time there's no water left in the bucket. This is paralleled by one all-caps paragraph in the book which says: *"Remember: changing your mental script after having it serve as a guide all your life is a big change!"*.

As those who have read a lot of my reviews will no doubt recall, I am *quite* hesitant to actually *do* the stuff in most of the books I read – my being more interested in the *concept* or information than taking the time and effort to delve into something that I'm not particularly convinced will be of use. However, this is one that I'm planning to actually implement. While the "broad strokes" of the Mental Bank Concept sound pretty goofy in the "newage sewage" mode, looking at it in the details, and reflecting on similar mind research I've read, makes me think this has solid possibilities and could well be worth the 5-minutes per night (and re-learning how to write in cursive) it involves.

If you want to get a copy of Success is Not an Accident[4] you should probably head over to the HMI site[5], which has the book available, new, at full cover price. Oddly, the on-line guys don't have it as a regular purchase, and the new/used guys have it for *huge* mark-ups, twenty bucks or more above what HMI is charging! Again, this is a bit odd, but I'm going to be "working the program", so I guess that's a solid recommendation for the book ... but if you're interested, I'd say you should probably check out the video[6] first.

Notes:

1. http://btripp-books.livejournal.com/183133.html
2. http://amzn.to/22JKEiC
3. https://youtu.be/JCsX6CeRJNY
4. http://amzn.to/22JKEiC
5. https://hypnosis.edu/
6. https://youtu.be/JCsX6CeRJNY

Saturday, April 23, 2016[1]

Going up against the "Democrat-Media Complex" ...

I have let a number of books linger in the to-be-read piles due to being *certain* that reading them, in the current political climate, would only get me very, very angry. However, after letting it sit there for a couple of years (after having found the hardcover at the dollar store), I finally got into Andrew Brietbart's Righteous Indignation: Excuse Me While I Save the World![2] ... and I was right, it got me pissed off. First of all, I'm pissed off that he's no longer around, and I'm pissed off that I can't help but think his death (just hours[3] before he was supposed to release a damning video about the current POTUS during the 2012 election cycle) was *not* from "natural causes".

One of the most frustrating parts of reading this is that I would have *loved* to have worked for the man, and having that no longer be an option is depressing. This book came out just a year before Breitbart's death, so it really is something of a summation of his life. However, he was, obviously, *not* coming to this in that sense, but in an attempt to re-define the right-left battlefield:

> *The left does not win its battles in debate. It doesn't have to. In the twenty-first century, media is everything. The left wins because it controls the narrative. The narrative is controlled by the media. The left is the media. Narrative is everything.*
>
> *I call it the Democrat-Media Complex – and I am at war to gain back control of the American narrative.*

The autobiographical parts *are* interesting ... he grew up in Los Angeles, surrounded by limousine liberals, and never really questioning that world view (although not being of the "limousine" crowd). He went to college at Tulane, down in New Orleans, selected because it was a notorious party school that still had a reputation for being a quality college, in a town that did debauchery like no other. There he essentially majored in "drugs, drinking, & gambling", barely making it through ... only managing to get his diploma by throwing himself on the mercy of a professor (in a class that he was clearly going to fail) who saw fit to give him a C-, allowing him to graduate with a paltry 2.0 GPA. He returned to L.A. and started out with a job as a waiter (serving college pals who were now in med or law school), eventually moving into a "gopher" job in the movie biz (which, inexplicably led to an offer to be a producer in some B-grade film project).

He had, however, started to have some glimmerings of a conservative awakening ... the Clarence Thomas hearings had been so blatantly unfairly stacked against the judge, that he started questioning the whole Leftist narrative. This, added to his job running around L.A. in a car (where he began to listen to AM talk radio), started to shift the needle to the right. His future father-in-law (TV's Orson Bean) also helped in this, suggesting that he give Rush Limbaugh a listen ...

> I was convinced to the core of my being that Rush Limbaugh was a Nazi, anti-black, anti-Jewish, and anti-all things decent. ...
> ...
> I turned on KFI 640 AM to listen to evil personified from 9 a.m. to noon. ... One hour turned into three. One listening session into a week's worth. And, next thing I knew, I was starting to doubt my pre-programmed self. ...
> ...
> Most important, though, Limbaugh ... created a vivid mental picture of the architecture of a world that I resided in but couldn't see completely: the Democrat-Media Complex. Embedded in Limbaugh's analysis of politics was always a tandem discussion on the media. Each segment relentlessly pointed to the collusion between the media and the Democratic Party.

Breitbart decided that he just couldn't keep working in the movie biz, and was desperately searching for something else ... an old high-school friend told him (in the remarkably early year of 1992) *"I've seen your future and it's the Internet."* - the eight words that Breitbart credits with changing his life. It took him until 1994 to really get himself established on line (I beat him to it by about a decade, but, hey), at which point he says he was "reborn" ...

> The Internet in those days was a free-for-all libertarian haven. I saw, even at the very beginning, that this was a new medium born of unwieldy individualism, of people who so desperately wanted to communicate with the world outside of the Democrat-Media Complex (whether they were aware of that construct or not), that they sought each other out in this technological wilderness. I recognized that for the Internet to exist, and for people to have such a massive desire to get on it, there had to be a driving force – and that driving force was the suffocating ubiquity of the Complex. Here was a place where freedom of speech truly existed, where you could say anything, think anything, be anything. It was no wonder that the first adopters of the Internet were the outcasts of the Complex, libertarians and conservatives.

One of the voices he discovered out on the 'net was Matt Drudge, who he found to be *"fascinating, unique, and worldly, while also being oddly uncynical"*, with that latter feature being what got to him:

> With the Drudge Report and the Internet, I thought, <u>Here, at least, is something that takes itself seriously.</u> I was gaining nourishment from something outside of humor and cynicism; I'd found that reading about big issues and listening to other people's

> *thinking about conservative ideas and morality and societal standards was actually fulfilling.*

It was Drudge who introduced Breitbart to Arianna Huffington, who was looking to create "media-driven websites", and hired him as her "Director of Research" … giving him access to LexisNexis (Ann Coulter's favorite tool). This brings the tale up to the point of the hearings regarding Paula Jones' lawsuit against Bill Clinton … the author was still somewhat willing to believe in the media at that point:

> {reflecting on the Clarence Thomas hearings} *I knew that if they were going to hold Thomas to that standard, they had to hold Clinton to that standard as well.*
>
> *The Clinton hearings became, to me, the living embodiment of the Democrat-Media Complex – and the inherent biases of the media were multiplied when cable news came of age during this era. With an enormous dedication of resources, the Complex went to work spinning Bill Clinton out of peril.*
>
> *Watching {Clinton} get away with sexual harassment … was the emblematic example of the media double standard, where a liberal could get away with anything as long as he toed the politically correct line. … He could get away with it because he was a liberal, and because liberals wanted him to get away with it. I wanted Clinton to pay, and I wanted his enablers to pay – I wanted to see them held to the standard that they had created to destroy their enemies.*

Needless to say, nothing has changed with "the Complex" in the intervening years, as they've been all "see no evil" with the execrable Obama regime, and are totally in the bag for Hillary. It's one of the saddest things about this book – as we no longer have the author around to expose the vileness of the media and their leftist masters.

At this point, the book goes a tour of breaking stories, through the Clinton regime, into the Bush years, and on to the first term of the current administration. Breitbart is one of the few people I've ever seen who wrote about "W" in terms that I've held for a long time … the biggest problem with the Bush years was that he bent over backwards to work with the Democrats, and, like in the story of <u>The Scorpion & The Frog</u>[4], that's a no-win proposition. It's amazing how one can't publicly say any bad about the current administration, given what Bush was besieged with for eight years. Leftist hypocrisy has no limit.

One of Breitbart's biggest "coups" was the creation of the Huffington Post in 2005 …

> *… The greatest victory for the right with regard to the site is that for years, conservatives argued that*

> the <u>New York Times</u>, the most important journalistic entity in the United States, was radically left of center. And for years, the left denied it. But the Huffington Post was different – it was openly and loudly and radically leftist. When you read the Huffington Post, you knew there was a collective mindset, a group-think. And the great irony was that if you looked at the front page of the Huffington Post on any given day and matched it with the front page of the <u>New York Times</u>, they were virtually identical. If you tested the philosophical DNA of the Huffington Post and the philosophical DNA of the <u>New York Times</u>, it was obvious to anyone that they were identical twins. They were fighting the same battles, and the bylines at both places were of people who went to the same schools, married the same kind of people, and voted the same way.
>
> They were all part of the same incestuous, elitist orgy. They were all part of the power structure of Hollywood, Washington, and New York. They were all from the same group of people who made tons of money, vacationed in the nicest places, flew first class – or private, and then dictated to the rest of America how to live "sustainable" lives. ...

What follows is both fascinating and horrific ... as the author takes a look at what enabled "the Complex" to get as massive and influential as it has become. He looks past the present-day funding by George Soros and back into the doctrinal underpinnings, back to Marx, "the Frankfurt School", and others whose *"mission was to dismantle American society by using diversity and 'multiculturalism' as crowbars with which to pry the structure apart, piece by piece"*, and how these people managed to infiltrate the universities, the government, and especially the media. Here too is Obama's philosophical godfather Saul Alinsky ... whose approaches Breitbart looks at closely. Frankly, Breitbart *admires* Alinsky on a strategic/tactical level, and goes into a good deal of detail on the "how" ... noting that *"Every successful ... {leftist} movement in the United States since the 1960s has used Frankfurt School ideology and Alinsky rules."*. What is amazing is that he's able to take this and spin out a "pragmatic primer" for libertarian/conservative action, with a 13-point plan for countering "the Complex" with their own tactics. Brilliant ... and such a shame that we don't have this man still fighting in the trenches for "the righteous cause".

Obviously, I'm a libertarian, and so Breitbart is "preaching to the choir" when it comes to me ... there is nearly nothing in <u>Righteous Indignation</u>[5] that I'm not in full agreement with or at least in visceral resonance with. Of course, if you're a devotee of "the Complex", your reactions to this will no doubt be quite different. This is one of those books that I wish that *everybody* would read, but I know those of a Leftist bent will reject it out of hand ... which is too bad, as they most of all need to hear this side of things.

While I found the hardcover of this at the dollar store a couple of years ago, it *is* still in print, in a paperback edition, which you should be able to connect with at your local brick-and-mortar book vendor. The on-line new/used guys, however, have new copies of the hardcover for under a buck, and "very good" used copies of the paperback for as little as a penny (plus shipping). If what I've presented above sounds at all interesting to you ... *go get a copy*!

Notes:

1. http://btripp-books.livejournal.com/183436.html
2. http://amzn.to/1RZDC4t
3. http://www.infowars.com/breitbart-wait-til-they-see-what-happens-march-1st/
4. https://en.wikipedia.org/wiki/The_Scorpion_and_the_Frog
5. http://amzn.to/1RZDC4t

Sunday, April 24, 2016[1]

Glad THAT'S over with ...

I bought this book used a very long time ago, perhaps a decade, perhaps longer, and it's sat there on various to-be-read shelves, in to-be-read boxes, and amid to-be-read stacks of books, somehow untouchable. Why? It's freak'n *750 pages long*, like 3 normal books. Plus, it's *math*, and as much as I like *physics*, I'm always hesitant to delve into too much math because my mental processing does not lend itself to the necessary discipline (or even bondage ... *waka, waka, waka*). However, this was a "big deal" among circles I was at least in contact with (although it didn't come out until I was past college). Much as I held Lombard for years as an example of a suburban wasteland (eventually finding myself having to spend 2.5 hours each way on public transit commutes to a writing job out there for a period of time), this was something of a *bête noire* in terms of a "mountain too high to climb" reading project – a commitment that would no doubt totally screw up my reading patterns.

And it was.

I started reading Douglas R. Hofstadter's Gödel, Escher, Bach: An Eternal Golden Braid[2] at the beginning of January, and by mid-April, I wasn't quite half-way done. However, earlier this week I went on a journey that, over a 35-hour period, had me on a bus for 18 hours and hanging out *waiting* for a bus for another 8 hours, time that I largely devoted to trying to knock this beast down. I did not succeed in *finishing* it on my trip, but got close enough that I was able triage out enough "in between" times this week to get it read.

I wish I could say it was worth it, but I found this quite frustrating, on a number of levels. First of all, and this is (obviously) "on me", I have never "gotten" music aside from as a listener, no matter how many attempts I've made, the whole "music theory" stuff just flies by me ... and, as one would guess from the title, music (aka the "Bach" parts here) is about a third of the basis of the book. I am also (and, no doubt, relatedly) not particularly good with "pure logic", something that the mathematician Hofstadter seems to think is a delightful game that all of his readers would love to play with ... and invites said readers to "work out" various extremely vague (to me) structures and puzzles in bizarre (again, to me) codings (see pic below for an example). What's *worse* is that the author tends to define his system of symbols *once* and then apparently assumes that "you've got it" and will go back to using it *hundreds of pages later* without any "catching us up" on it, even as little as "name checking" abbreviations like TNT when they crop up a book length past when they're initially defined (that's Typographic Number Theory, if you were wondering).

$$\exists b: \exists c: (((SSSSSSSSSSO \cdot SSSSSSSSSO) \cdot SSSSSSSSSO) + ((SSSSSSSSO \cdot SSSSSSSSO) \cdot SSSSSSSSO)) = (((b \cdot b) \cdot b) + ((c \cdot c) \cdot c))$$

and

$$\exists b: \exists c: (((SSSSSSSSSSSSO \cdot SSSSSSSSSSSSO) \cdot SSSSSSSSSSSSO) + ((SO \cdot SO) \cdot SO)) = (((b \cdot b) \cdot b) + ((c \cdot c) \cdot c))$$

The book rotates between three different types of presentation. The most identifying one of these, and no doubt what got the book its fame, is what is referenced in a sub-sub-title added by its publisher: *A Metaphorical Fugue on Minds and Machines in the Spirit of Lewis Carroll* ... discussions between various characters, beginning with Achilles and a Tortoise, with added others such as a Crab, a Sloth, and ultimately up to Hofstadter himself. As anybody who reads my reviews regularly will realize, I "have issues" with "teaching stories", and these aren't even *necessary* (although being about a third of the book) features, having more the character of trying to present the material in a "cute" way that allowed the author to mess about with framing the logical questions being discussed in the other sections in a "Lewis Carroll" inspired format. Across the course of the book I tended to find these parts irritating rather than illuminating, but I am willing to cede the point that "your mileage may vary" on this, and that it could well be a "it's me" rather than "it's the book" here.

The other two "types" are where the author is going through the various symbolic systems (he has several, most of which are "cutesy" in that they're structured to reflect, as initials, to other elements in the material), which generally made *no* sense to me at all (and, again, this is likely due to my disconnect with that sort of symbolic thinking). And, finally, the parts where he's actually EXPLAINING what the book's about ... like a regular book on a subject. Frankly, were the book *just* this latter material, I would have probably quite *liked* the book ... which might have been only 350 pages or so of lucid prose. But, noooooo.

That "core conceptual arc" would have been fascinating, as it addresses a lot of intriguing issues on logic, consciousness, and artificial intelligence, but it's so munged up with the other stuff that it's rather difficult to follow. I'll try to pull out some of the more cogent bits here to give a sense of where this goes.

First of all, there's this Gödel guy ... Kurt Gödel was a German mathematician whose *"discovery involves the translation of an ancient paradox in philosophy into mathematical terms. That paradox is the so-called* Epimenides paradox*"* which is at its base the statement *"This statement is false."*. This is, perhaps, the *least* convoluted part of it. Hofstadter goes on to say:

> The Epimenides paradox is a one-step Strange Loop ... but how {sic} does it have to do with mathematics? That is what Gödel discovered. His idea was to use mathematical reasoning in exploring mathematical reasoning itself. The notion of making mathematics "introspective" proved to be enormously powerful, and perhaps its richest implication was the one Gödel found: Gödel's Incompleteness Theorem. What the Theorem states and how it is proved are two different things. We shall discuss both in quite some detail in this book. ...
>
> ...
>
> Gödel's Theorem appears as Proposition VI in his 1931 paper "On Formally Undecidable Propositions in Principia Mathematica and Related Systems I."

> ...
> *here is a paraphrase ...*
> *All consistent axiomatic formulations of number theory include undecidable propositions.*

The author refers to that last line as "the pearl" and goes on for several hundred pages exploring it, in the various approaches detailed above.

Of course, none of this is particularly straight-forward ... the concepts, based on Gödel's mathematics, get dragged through the complex recursive musical structures of Bach's multi-voiced fugues, etc. (sometimes in excruciating detail), as well as being cast in reflections of Escher's convoluted graphics (which the characters in the dialog parts spend a good deal of time popping in and out of – acting out aspects of the *mathematics* in doing so), and getting the "Lewis Carroll" treatment at every hand, which seemed to more muddy the waters than anything. There are some truly fascinating bits here, like the discussion on *translation*, looking at approaches taken to convert Dostoevsky to English, or *Jabberwocky* into French and German ... or how viruses use DNA to attack cells ... but these tend to stand out because they're self-contained and *not* bounced around between conceptual frames!

One of the topics examined across the book is consciousness in humans and the possibilities of Artificial Intelligence. Obviously a book that came out in 1979 has a whole different perspective on computers than a reader approaching the information in 2016. At the time of its writing, the first models of the Apple, Atari, Commodore, TRS-80, etc. were out, but most of what is discussed here is far more primitive. On one hand, this is probably a *good thing*, as it keeps the discussion largely in the theoretical/mathematical side, but it's somewhat painful to read, when you realize that the capabilities of machines back then were so minimal that it's hard to even frame a comparison to current tech.

Needless to say, there's so much stuff going on in here, that it's a challenge to even try to summarize in a couple of thousand words. I was somewhat surprised that this eventually rolled around to something of an existential essay by the end of the book. There was a particularly cogent section called "Strange Loops as the Crux of Consciousness" that I think is worth taking a look at here:

> My belief is that the explanations of "emergent" phenomena in our brains – for instance, ideas, hopes, images, analogies, and finally consciousness and free will – are based on a kind of Strange Loop, an interaction between levels in which the top level reaches back down towards the bottom level and influences it, while at the same time being itself determined by the bottom level. In other words, a self-reinforcing "resonance" between different levels ... The self comes into being at the moment it has the power to reflect itself.
>
> ...
> In order to deal with the full richness of the brain/mind system we will have to be able to slip between levels comfortably. Moreover, we will have

> to admit various types of "causality": ways in which an event at one level of description can "cause" events at other levels to happen. Sometimes event A will be said to "cause" event B simply for the reason that the one is a translation, on another level of description, of the other. Sometimes "cause" will have its usual meaning: physical causality. Both types of causality – and perhaps some more – will have to be admitted in any examination of mind, for we will have to admit causes that propagate both upwards <u>and</u> downwards in the Tangled Hierarchy of mentality, just as in the Central Dogmap.

Oh, that last thing there … it's typical of a lot of stuff happening in the book, Hofstadter takes Crick's "Central Dogma of Molecular Biology", spins out his own "version" of it as a "Central Dogma of Mathematical Logic", and "maps" them against each other as the "Central Dogmap" … and, trust me, that's not the "worst" of the groaners that are in here – he weaves puns through the core structures of a lot of the key concepts here that, honestly, don't add anything to the coherence of the presentation (perhaps, as a college professor, the author had gotten into the habit of putting this sort of stuff into class materials to keep his students involved).

Again, I would have both enjoyed and gotten more out Gödel, Escher, Bach[3] had it been cut down to the expository parts, with maybe some subsections dealing with the math/logic behind the assorted theoretical concepts involved. However, it's a "classic" in its own way (Amazon has it listed as the #1 best-seller in the "Artificial Intelligence and Semantics" category, for whatever *that's* worth), and I'm glad to have gotten it moved from the to-be-read limbo into the proverbial rear-view mirror. If you feel like you want to take up the challenge that this book represents, it can be had in various formats … used copies of the 1979 and 1989 editions are available, and the 1999 edition is still in print. Oddly, the used copies of the older editions (this may be a "text book" thing happening) aren't particularly cheap, and you'd only be saving a bit (with shipping) vs. the nearly half-off pricing of the new book.

Notes:

1. http://btripp-books.livejournal.com/183787.html
2-3. http://amzn.to/1POOGRs

Thursday, May 26, 2016[1]

One of the greats ...

This was another Dollar Store find ... I was down in Urbana (home of the University of Illinois) to pick up my engineering student daughter at the end of her semester, and we swung by to grab a couple of things "for the road". I, of course, had to check out the book section and found *five* books of interest (oddly, mostly on a "culinary" theme). I don't know how these all showed up there, and, in particular, the subject of this review – Auguste Escoffier's Memories of My Life[2] – seemed strangely out of place. Not only is this a large-format hardcover, but it's also a 1996 first edition ... which means that it had been kicking around for *twenty years*. Now, I'm used to getting "vintage" books at things like the Newberry Library book fair, or box sales at Open Books[3], but those are typically there via estate liquidations (i.e. "dead people's books"), and this seems to have been in various retail channels for a *long* time (including stickers three deep over the dust jacket's original UPC).

As I no doubt have mentioned, I grew up in the orbit of the food biz, and the name Escoffier was familiar in its own right, but was bandied about a good deal at home, as my Mother had been a long-time member of Les Dames d'Escoffier[4], and a recipient of their "Dames of Distinction" award. Needless to say, seeing Escoffier's autobiography sitting there *for a buck* was NOT something I was going to take a pass on!

As with most dollar store finds, this *was* a bit of a "pig in a poke", with my not having any particular expectations going in, but I sort of anticipated a bit of a dry "book of its time". While Escoffier *had* been putting together a memoir intended for the cooking profession, this was assembled from a lot of additional materials that his family had collected following his death (at age 88) in 1935. The book as it stands, however, is based on a far more recent translation of these materials by a great-granddaughter, Laurence Escoffier, and I'm thinking that she imbued the English version with more than a *soupçon* of modern tone, making this a far easier read than it might have been.

Escoffier was born in 1846 on the Mediterranean coast of France, between Cannes and Nice, and at 13 he was instructed that he was to be a cook at his uncle's restaurant in the latter. He took to this as a discipline, and from his earliest years (barely six months into his training, he came up with a design for serving platters that would eventually be produced by Christofle as "Escoffier Plates") he was dedicated to the craft. He writes of his focus:

> My natural curiosity also encouraged me to look for anything that could develop and embellish the art of our national cuisine. My aim was twofold: to increase awareness abroad of French products and of ways to use them.

By the age of 19, he had found his way (through various recommendations) to Paris, and worked at *Le Petit Moulin Rouge*, where he stayed for five years prior to his being called up for the Franco-Prussian war, and some subsequent military cooking. There are *fascinating* stories of his work at this time, as French military officers were typically nobility, and had their own staffs, including chefs. At one time his part of the army is captured and spent some time as prisoners of war in Germany (this comes back as an uncomfortable point when he later hosts the Kaiser). Upon his return to Paris, he becomes the head chef at *Le Petit Moulin Rouge*, then at a series of other postings, eventually ending up at the *Grand Hôtel* in Monte Carlo, where he meets hotelier César Ritz, and becomes his go-to Chef for major projects such as the Savoy Hotel and later the Carlton Hotel in London, where he creates some of his most famous dishes.

A lot of the book focuses on specific events and dinners produced for "big names" over the years, including menus, and the occasional recipe. There are photo pages that include reproductions of some of these (very ornate) menus, and pictures of a few of the "notables" and venues discussed. Two things that are basic in today's restaurant world were introduced back then: one, the prix fixe menu, and the other being service *"à la russe"*. In discussing his book for chefs, the *Guide Culinaire*, which he dedicates to his friend Urbain Dubois, he notes:

> One of Dubois' greatest contributions was the important role he played in the growing use of the so-called service *à la russe*, that is to say the presentation of dishes one after the other, rather than the service *à la française* that was then popular, with all dishes being presented together at the beginning of the meal.

One of the most shocking (from the modern perspective) aspects of these menus is how *extensive* they are ... there is a section here where Escoffier *looks back* to a time when things were even *more* extravagant ... no doubt reflecting the excesses of the nobility:

> Current fashion and habits are such that one can only spend one hour, or an hour and a half, at any single meal.
> For the last thirty years, even the most substantial menus have generally been made up of only one or two soups, an hors d'oeuvre (hot or cold), a fish, two entrées, a roast, a cold meat, a salad, one or two accompanying vegetables, two hot or cold sweets, and various desserts.
> In the old days, depending on the importance of the host and the number of his invited guests, the expected menu consisted of an incredible number of dishes that we can hardly imagine today ... between thirty and sixty dishes, not to mention the desserts, which were often just as numerous.

Needless to say, I find it amusing that what *his* menus encompass are things that "we can hardly imagine today", let alone those of "the old days"! Another subject I found interesting was the extensive use of truffles (the fungus, not the chocolate). Now, I like truffles as well as (or more than) any other *gourmand*, so I was drawn to this side note (by the translator?) on these:

> Truffles reached their apogee in France in the nineteenth century when nearly every grand meal featured at least one dish that was bejeweled with the prized black diamond. Such liberal use of truffles today is impractical, not only because of their price but also because of diminished supplies. In 1892 two thousand tons of truffles were harvested in France; today only 25 to 150 tons are gathered annually.

As a fan of the truffle, it's a sad thing to think that we only have a tiny fraction of them available compared to Escoffier's heyday (and there certainly has been a lot of effort and money dedicated to finding ways to cultivate truffles, beyond planting spore-inoculated saplings and waiting a decade to see if any fungus forms on their roots).

Oh, and while there *are* recipes here, they are definitely targeted to a professional kitchen's staff, and not to the home cook. There are *some* that one might successfully produce at home (such as the famous *La Pêche Melba*, probably minus the carved ice swan it's supposed to be served in, commemorating the opera singer's appearance in Wagner's *Lohengrin* that enchanted Escoffier), but most involve multiple pre-prepped sauces, etc., and are frequently addressing quantities like *"add about 50 frog legs that have previously been washed, drained on a towel, and rolled in flour"* that might not be practical for the home cook.

The book continues through Escoffier's extensive career, in France, London, on a number of ocean liners, and at the Ritz-Carlton in New York. His recounting of events of the First World War as "seen from London" is also interesting, and that chapter starts out with another side note which tells of a fascinating, if peripheral, historical confluence:

> On the night Germany invaded Belgium in August 1914, Lloyd George and Winston Churchill were dining at the Carlton. Ho Chi Minh, the future communist leader of North Vietnam, was working in Escoffier's kitchen preparing vegetables.

The narrative goes up to 1930, five years before his death, and I guess his family decided to just let it go at that. There is an interesting timeline in the back, which tracks the highlights of his life against world and (generally unrelated to anything in the book) American events, plus a very useful glossary, and some other bits and pieces (photos of letters, brief biographies of people important in his life, etc.) as well.

Escoffier's Memories of My Life[5] appears to be *long* out of print (again, I'm amazed to have found this where I did), but "very good" copies are available for under ten bucks on the new/used channels of the on-line big boys. If you have an interest in fine dining, the restaurant biz, or might be wanting to learn about a notable man who rose from nothing to be lionized by his nation and the world, this is something you might well want to track down.

Notes:

1. http://btripp-books.livejournal.com/183845.html
2. http://amzn.to/1WC2bJ2
3. http://www.open-books.org/
4. https://goo.gl/9i9C1S
5. http://amzn.to/1WC2bJ2

Friday, May 27, 2016[1]

"All day on channel nine"?

This one's been lingering in my to-be-read piles for quite a while, and I really am not sure when it was that I picked it up. I'm pretty sure it was a dollar store acquisition of the "oh that looks like it might be interesting" sort, and with only a buck invested in it, having no particular urgency to get into it. However, I was in a point in my reading where something along the lines of this seemed an appealing thing to throw into the mix, so I got into it.

As is frequently the case with dollar store books, I didn't have much of an expectation of what this was going to be like, and it wasn't exactly how I was imagining it. Listen To This[2] was written by Alex Ross, who has been the music critic for The New Yorker for the past 20 years, and had come to them from a similar position with the New York Times, which are pretty impressive credentials (albeit ones that hadn't gotten him on my radar previous to reading the book). This is primarily a collection of pieces written for The New Yorker from 1997 through 2008 (the book came out in 2010), but his notes indicate that most of the 19 chapters are "based" on those articles, but are expanded and edited here, so it's not just a "best of" collection of his magazine work.

Aside from being a look at various musical subjects, there doesn't seem to much of a "theme" here, Ross doesn't seem to have a particular axe to grind, nor does he press any specific style. Instead, this reads like a collection of individual explorations into a wide range of topics. Of course, this makes it a bit of a challenge to whip up a review that gives attention to *everything* in here ... but I'll try to give you a good sense of it.

The first chapter starts out with a look at the author's relationship with music. It's a bit of a shocker to hear from somebody born as recently as 1968 that: *"I am a white American male who listened to nothing but classical music until the age of twenty."* (especially as *I* started my own rock record collection at age 6). He continues his self-confession with: *"By high school a terrible truth had dawned: I was the only person my age who liked this stuff."*, and adds a cringe-worthy note that following having been dragged off to see Pink Floyd's The Wall movie, his one take-away seemed to be *"that one passage sounded Mahlerian"*. His baptism into rock came in college when he would hang out at the school's radio station, with a bunch of "cerebral punk rockers", who introduced him to Pere Ubu and Sonic Youth. He uses this personal story line as a basis of taking a historical look at what was popular in music in different times, and uses that to reflect on the place of classical music in today's culture.

From there he moves into a piece called "Chacona, Lamento, Walking Blues: Bass Lines of Music History" which starts in 16th century Spain with *"the chacona, a sexily swirling dance that hypnotized all who heard it"*, moves back to the middle ages, and the evolution of musical expressions of melancholy and "laments". This is the first place where the author starts to lose me, as I'm technically fairly musically illiterate, and he picks apart the music in terms and contexts that I just don't have any way to follow. He does, however track these elements into the blues, and ultimately into modern popular music, from the *Mary Poppins* soundtrack to the Beatles, Bob Dylan, and many others on the way to Led Zeppelin's *Dazed and Confused* ... yes, *really*.

He next has a look at music recording, which he argues *changed* music from its earliest use. The famed John Philip Sousa is quoted as testifying before Congress in 1906 that *"These talking machines are going to ruin the artistic development of music in this country"* (in that nobody will *make* their own music if they can just play a recording), and the author traces out the changes in how orchestras perform, with various national styles on particular instruments falling away to the one most amenable to the recording technology of the day.

This is followed by an interesting look at Mozart, both personally, and his musical development. The next chapter (somewhat jarringly) moves into a piece about the band Radiohead, and the book then subsequently shifts to a discussion of the Finnish composer and conductor Esa-Pekka Salonen, and his work with the Los Angeles Philharmonic, and other institutions. From here it shifts back to another classic name, this time Schubert, and then again to a modern act in Björk. At this point the author shifts to a wider stage, and considers classical music in China, particularly as seen around the time of the Beijing Olympics, which he appears to have been covering. He stays on the road in the next chapter, and visits Alaska and idiosyncratic composer John Luther Adams who tries to live "outside culture" in that huge state's sparsely-populated interior. Next it's back to a familiar name, with the life, music, and the performance/recording history of Giuseppe Verdi, including reminiscences of where Ross had heard performances of his music (from New York's Central park to Genoa, Italy). Although the book is not broken into one of its sections here, the next piece, about the St. Lawrence Quartet, seems to close out this part of the book, as the next chapters seem to have a bit different tone.

The shift happens (for me, at least) when he gets to the "Edges of Pop", where he covers a disparate group of acts, from drag-themed Kiki and Herb, to jazz figure Cecil Taylor being compared with Sonic Youth, a brief nod to Frank Sinatra, and then into a look at Kurt Cobain ... quite a mix for one chapter. This then shifts to a chapter on the sorry state of musical education in the U.S., and those who are trying to fix what can be fixed given the low priority the Arts have in that sphere in recent decades. Speaking of musical education, I don't believe I'd ever *heard* of the next subject, described as "The Voice of the Century", Marian Anderson, whose defining moment seems to have been a 1939 performance on the steps of the Lincoln Memorial – a venue arranged by Eleanor Roosevelt after the DAR wouldn't let a black woman perform at Constitution Hall (this episode also plays a significant role in part of another book that I'm currently reading). This is followed by what seemed to be a rather odd look at a summer gathering in Vermont called Marlboro Music (held at the tiny college of the same name – which comes from the local town, not the cigarette brand), and its director Mitsuko Uchida ... this is a retreat that is much sought after, with a tiny fraction of those applying getting accepted to attend.

I'm not clear on why the book's three sections are set up the way they are, but the last three chapters are in the third part of the book. The first of these is the author following Bob Dylan to various performances, from big downtown arenas to rural agricultural fairs, and considering the strange journey that Dylan's been on. Next is a brief chapter on the opera singer Lorraine Hunt Lieberson, which, while interesting in its details sort of missed me in terms of having a point. Finally, the book goes back to a classical composer, in this case Brahms ... not exactly a "big finish" for the book.

One useful (and still active) aspect to Listen To This[3] is the companion site with pictures, videos, audio files and other add-ons that I wish I'd have encountered when actually reading through this (I was frequently looking things referenced in the text up via YouTube on my phone), the URL is here[4] if you want to check that out. This is one of the best companion sites I've encountered, and I highly recommend using it in conjunction with the book as you go through it (although it's pretty informative in and of itself – kudos to whoever developed that, if not the author!).

While the hardcover of this appears to be out of print (new copies can be had for under $5 via the new/used guys), the paperback is still available, so should be something you could get from your local brick & mortar book vendor. While it's not exactly "my thing", the subjects of Ross' pieces were varied enough that it kept being interesting, and there's plenty there to recommend it just on a "learning stuff I didn't know" basis.

Notes:

1. http://btripp-books.livejournal.com/184306.html

2-3. http://amzn.to/1r2dHQE

4. http://www.therestisnoise.com/listentothisaudio/

Saturday, May 28, 2016[1]

From one tormented moment ... to the next

One of the effects of being out of work for *seven years* (and the rejection implicit in having applied to 2,000-3,000 jobs in that time with only a mere handful of serious interviews resulting from that herculean effort), is that I struggle with depression ... a lot. Of course, *another* effect of not being in a job is not having a paycheck, so my options for finding *help* with said depression are somewhat limited. Over the past year or so I've been going to DBSA[2] meetings, which are sort of like group therapy sessions, but (generally speaking) without a *therapist* (yeah, it's a bit like "the inmates running the asylum"). The subject of this review is a book that was *enthusiastically* recommended by the folks who referee one of the groups I attended: An Unquiet Mind: A Memoir of Moods and Madness[3] by Kay Redfield Jamison.

Now, Ms. Jamison is a clinical psychologist, a Professor of Psychiatry at the John Hopkins School of Medicine, and co-author of the "standard medical text" *Manic-Depressive Illness*, so I figured that An Unquiet Mind[3] would be a book *discussing* depression, etc. But, no. This is an *autobiography* focusing on the author's OWN struggles with what is currently labeled as "bipolar disorder". I don't know *why*, specifically, this confused me ... but I guess I was anticipating that somebody might have mentioned (amid all the praise for the book) that it was "one woman's struggle" with the disease, even if from a standpoint of being on the leading expert *on* the disease, rather than presenting it as some definitive text on the subject.

This review may end up being a good deal less "in depth" that I would like it, largely due to it being an intensely personal tale of Jamison's life, with narrative arcs and illustrative details that are, if not "TMI", hard to *generalize* from, as they're intrinsically interwoven with her individual experiences. Early on here she gives the broad strokes:

> For as long as I can remember I was frighteningly, although often wonderfully, beholden to moods. Intensely emotional as a child, mercurial as a young girl, first severely depressed as an adolescent, and then unrelentingly caught up in the cycles of manic-depressive illness by the time I began my professional life, I became, both by necessity and intellectual inclination, a student of moods. It has been the only way I know to understand, indeed to accept, the illness I have; it also has been the only way I know to try to make a difference in the lives of others who also suffer from mood disorders. The disease that has, on several occasions, nearly killed me does kill tens of thousands of people every year
> ...

Although she had, as detailed in the above, been "of the type" for most of her life, it wasn't until her late 20's (*"Within a month of signing my appointment papers to become an assistant professor of psychiatry at the University of California, Los Angeles"*) that the disease hit her full force.

Again, this is a very personal book, and while the particulars are certainly of interest in context, extracting them here seems awfully random. The author was a "military brat", her father being a meteorologist with the Air Force, and her childhood was spent in that rather idiosyncratic environment, reinforced by her D.A.R. mother's appreciations of the social aspects involved. One of the factoids that is repeatedly raised here is that manic-depression/bi-polar disorder is frequently, if not predictably, found within families, and (although it was rarely *diagnosed* in previous generations) her father pretty clearly (from the difficulties of later years) had the disease.

When she was headed to high school, her father left the military, and took a position with the Rand Corporation out in California. This threw Jamison out of the familiar settings of the peripatetic military lifestyle, and into the less structured environment of Los Angeles. She survived high school, and reluctantly (she'd always planned on going to University of Chicago) enrolled in UCLA.

I have no reason to doubt the overall veracity of this book (unlike many others I've reviewed), but I found myself waxing incredulous at several points in the parts discussing her academic career, both as a student, and as she climbed the professorial ladder. If things were as *bad* as she paints them here, how could she have completed her college work? I assume that she is selecting material to discuss based on how it illustrates her disease, and avoiding the less "remarkable" parts, but reading through this made it hard to believe that she managed to get through college, get advanced degrees, do competent work, get tenure, etc. Sure, there were *manic* phases when she could move mountains, but the over-all tone of her academic life (and, OK, what do I know about the realities of those "ivory towers"?) sounded like something that would have resulted in a *business* person having long ugly chats with HR.

One of the pivotal issues in the book is that, for a very long time, Jamison was refusing to medicate. I realize that many of the "popular drugs" for depression, etc. can be quite debilitating (I had a few prescribed for me a decade or so back, and each was worse than the last, and I finally decided that I'd rather be *miserable* than various degrees of *zombified*), but she was a *professional* in the field, and should have known that she should have been on meds.

> I reaped a bitter harvest from my own refusal to take lithium on a consistent basis. A floridly psychotic mania was followed, inevitably, by a long and lacerating, black, suicidal depression; it lasted more than a year and a half. From the time I woke up in the morning until the time I went to bed at night, I was unbearably miserable and seemingly incapable of any kind of joy or enthusiasm. Everything – every thought, word, movement – was an effort. Everything that once was sparkling now was flat. I seemed to myself to be dull, boring, inadequate, thick brained, unlit, unresponsive, chill skinned, bloodless, and sparrow drab. I doubted, completely, my ability to do anything well. It seemed as though my mind had slowed down and burned out to the point of being virtually useless. The wretched, convoluted, and pathetically confused mass of gray worked only well enough to torment me with a dreary lit-any of my inadequacies and shortcomings in character, and to taunt me with the total, the desperate, hopelessness of it all.

Thankfully, I only suffer from "situational" depression (a form of PTSD, I'm told), but that sounds *awfully* familiar to me – waking up to that sort of state several times a week. One thing that I found interesting here (and which I've also gotten a sense of from various people at DBSA meetings), is how *bad* the flip side of depression (*"floridly psychotic mania"* in the above) can be. For somebody whose college nickname was "manic", I never had a *clue* that for some folks "being manic" wasn't just about being up for days at a time cranking out awesome projects ... and Jamison details some of these behaviors (which frequently involve massive spending sprees on things that no *rational* person would think was a good idea) which certainly parallel the horror stories I've heard in group.

Despite the difficulties generated by the manic phases (luckily for the author, her brother was able to "fix" her financial issues from these episodes) and the nightmares of the depressive times (in which she regularly contemplated, and on occasion attempted, suicide), Jamison ends up having a rather sterling academic career, including co-"writing the book" on her disorder. However, her private life was not so lucky, as her initial (seemingly wonderful) marriage was destroyed by her disease, and she ended up having a series of other relationships which she goes into here ... including one really tragic connection which was cut short by the sudden heart-attack death of her (young, athletic) intended (however, at that point she was religiously taking her lithium, and did not have a total crash in the wake of it).

While An Unquiet Mind[5] was not the book that I thought I was getting into, it certainly was an interesting (if somewhat voyeuristic) read, and broadly illuminating on the subject of manic-depression / bi-polar disorder. It is, however, not a particularly *comfortable* read, and I don't think that's just from the perspective of somebody dealing with depression ... but that could also be due to my having expected something more "clinical" here than the personal outpouring that this is.

This has been out for 20 years at this point, and is still in print (in the paperback edition), being a "classic" in its niche, so you should be able to get a copy from your local brick-and-mortar book vendor, although the on-line big boys have it at a substantial (40% off at this writing) discount. You can also find "very good" copies in the used channel for as little as 1¢ (four bucks with shipping), if you want to go for maximum affordability. I found a good deal of what the author presents in here of use, but (as noted) it wasn't the sort of book I was expecting, so my enthusiasm isn't quite up to that of the folks who had suggested my getting it. I guess if you know going in it's an autobiographical look at one (top professional in the field) woman's struggle with this disease, you won't be trying to extract the sort of info I was hoping for here ... and probably get more out of it.

Notes:

1. http://btripp-books.livejournal.com/184328.html
2. http://www.dbsa-gc.org/
3-5. http://amzn.to/1sbUey1

Sunday, May 29, 2016[1]

From "funnel" to "radar" ...

I'm really embarrassed about this one ... I attended an event that was functioning as a local book launch, hosted by a friend from the Social Media Club, featuring this book (which I got free, signed by the author) about *two and a half years ago*. Now, this, in and of itself, isn't the embarrassing part, but the fact that I told the author that evening that there was a *chance* that I'd be getting to his book (for reading & review) "in a week or so", and it took me all this time for that to happen. *Oops*. Frankly, I think it was the "sale" in the title that kept letting other books slide up the to-be-read queue ... despite nearly 40 years in marketing communications, I've always been hostile to anything "sales" oriented – hating to be sold to, and *really* hating to have to "sell to" others. So this sat there and sat there and sat there, until one day (due to the other stuff I'd been reading) it sounded like a good change of pace.

I was chastened to find that Tom Martin's The Invisible Sale: How to Build a Digitally Powered Marketing and Sales System to Better Prospect, Qualify and Close Leads[2] is a really great book ... informative, entertaining (even *funny* in places), and full of useful information ... I swear, if this had "market" instead of "sale" in the title, I'd have been read/reviewed it by the end of 2013. *Bad* Brendan!

Now, don't get me wrong, this book is very much about *selling*, with lots of stuff that's way out of my "sweet spot" like taking about sales teams and sales calls and sales emails and sales "closes", and similar stuff that "makes me throw up a little bit in my mouth", but it also has a lot of "philosophical" material (which reminded me a bit of some of Gary Vaynerchuck's work), and about 1/3rd of the book which is in-depth on content creation. Structurally, the book is in four sections (well, three sections and a bit of a coda), "Selling the Premise", "Capturing the Invisible Sale", "Creating Your Content", and about a dozen pages on "Closing the Deal" ... across these are distributed seventeen chapters, each of which has a half-dozen or so specific subject headers.

So, what *is* this "Invisible Sale" thing (no, it's not like my poetry collections, which have *nonexistent* sales – which is, sadly, quite different), anyway? I'm sure Martin has a handy definition in there *somewhere*, but I wasn't able to dig up a nice compact statement about it to drop in here, instead, here's something from one of his promo web sites that I think comes pretty close:

> Today's digital savvy buyers are sophisticated and silent. They're doing recon work on your brand, product or company -- searching for product reviews and tapping into social networks for recommendations and first-hand experiences. These invisible buyers are slipping past your sales team, stepping out of the shadows only after they've decided that your company is in the running for their dollars.

He notes that, in a whole lot of settings, the traditional "sales funnel" of pro-spects => contacted => qualified => proposed => sold is no longer a working model, being replaced by what he calls the "sales radar"[3] which has six segments, each referencing a different approach, with "sales contact" being at the center – the contact being pretty much at the point of sale, rather than four levels previous.

One of the things I rather liked in the book was the "Power Points" sections that show up at the end of most of the chapters ... these are more editorial than simply recapping the info from the chapter, putting it in a bit different frame. You can actually download these as Powerpoint slides (which he notes are "minimally formatted" so you can add your own organization's look-and-feel – clever!). This leads me to a somewhat early mention of the companion web site[4], which has a bit of stuff related to the content of the book, but really is more of a "sales page" for the author's speaking and training ventures. There are Amazon links to assorted "tools" mentioned (microphones, etc.), and links to videos he references, but those parts seem, unfortunately, like an afterthought, plus the "community" site one has to join to download the Power Points seems to have been abandoned but for those download links, as it has four segments for content, all of which (nearly 3 years down the road) say "coming soon" with links that head off to blank pages ... disappointing. However, a lot of the material *is* available via his corporate site[5] in the form of blog posts ... too bad these two elements didn't get linked up.

Good thing that the book is otherwise chock-full of useful stuff. I probably have a dozen of my little bookmarks[6] stuck in here, however, digging into them for this, I'm finding that most are for key points of info that I could use in projects, and not "choice quotes" ... although, in context of this particular book, those nuggets might be as useful as anything. Now, again, I'm not a "sales guy" and am a marketing *writer* and not some MBA, so it's possible, or even likely, that stuff that I find somewhat revelatory might be "old hat" for another reader. So, with that caveat, I guess I'll walk us through some of these.

The first of the bookmarks is on a page in the long look at what camera store Adorama does in their digital marketing, with a goo.gl link to a video/post on "How To Embed Website Links in YouTube Videos"[7], and, while I've done a decent bit of video in various contexts over the years, this is not something I've even *thought* to do (well, outside the context of a project I worked on with the WireWax platform). The next deals with a "Behavioral Email Logic Diagram"[8], which, given that I've done precious little email marketing, is not surprisingly "new to me" ... Martin says:

> Planning the BEL is the most important and most difficult step of these programs. To create a BEL, you first need to define the core message content of each email you plan to send. You don't have to develop finished creative executions – you just need to know the core content each email will include. Then you hypothesize what a prospect's behavioral pattern is telling you, based on how the person moves through the BEL.

He describes a client program where they had 1,600 email prospects, and managed to filter that down into 249 "warm prospects", and 12 *"whose behaviors indicated they were ready to buy"*. Speaking of email campaigns, the next bookmark I had is at the place where he talks about "proper URL naming" and Google Tags ... which he shows how to set up and how to get detailed "click reports" from using these.

Of course, the part of the book that I had the most resonance with was the content creation part ... and this was where I had the most bits of paper marking pages. He starts out here with the idea of "Right Sized Content":

> *The RSC concept is based on matching the quality of your content, in terms of production quality and cost, to the content need you are filling. Simply put, a Facebook video doesn't need to be shot or produced at the same quality level as a television commercial. The digital world has trained the buyer to accept – or, in some instances, desire – lower-quality content. In fact, overproduced content often can be just as ineffective as underproduced content.*

Part of this is further framed into what he calls "Cornerstone Content" and "Cobblestones", the former being *"big pieces ... such as white papers, major presentations, and eBooks"*, with the latter being "easily distributable" bits of these. The chapters here deal with Video, Photography, Audio, Text, and live/recorded Webinars & Tutorials.

In the Video discussion he goes into details on "Desktop Video Editing" ... I have, regrettably, never moved beyond Windows Movie Maker (not horrible, but not what I'd hope to be working with), so I found his suggestions here of particular interest (even though he's an Apple "true believer", and I'm *not*). He also lays out various levels of set-ups for doing podcasts and webinars, which may be very useful if I ever get around to creating programs using these. One interesting thing he talks about is using Dragon on his phone to *write*, with his getting in about 1,000 words on his 15-minute commute. I've actually passed along that suggestion to a couple of people who have a hard time sitting down to craft blog posts!

He goes down a bit of a rabbit hole in the photography section, with something called the "Gestalt Principle" which starts with a <u>duck/rabbit</u>[9] graphic as an illustration of how people can see completely different things in a single image ... and you will always default to seeing the image as you first saw it ...

> *The Gestalt Principle tells us that the deconstruction of a visual message occurs at the point of reception. The decoding of an image's meaning happens during the buyer's decoding process versus your encoding process – where you decide that the image you're using is a duck versus a rabbit.*

Obviously, the duck/rabbit dichotomy is not a particularly applicable case, but he then details how he did research on images of "escape" and how images got sorted to match that concept were *vastly* different between what one might think were fairly close coteries: married adults with or without children. What you select as images might totally miss one (or both) groups!

I guess I can't do a review of this book without touching on the concept of *propinquity* that the author is quite enamored of.

> marketing propinquity results from increased interactions between a prospective customer and a brand or company ... Two types of marketing propinquity exist: physical and psychological. The first, physical, also has two dimensions: time and place. The latter is strictly a subjective measure to the prospective customer. It's harder to formally define, but I think it's more powerful.

In this he contrasts classic "Top-Of-Mind Awareness" (TOMA) with what he posits to be TOMP – top-of-mind *preference*. There's a whole system he builds on this with a "propinquity map" that defines a "home base" and various external points.

Obviously, there is a *lot* of material in The Invisible Sale[10], which is interesting, and assortedly applicable, depending on how close you are to the sales function. I really wish I had gotten around to reading this when I first received it, as it's a very useful book ... but there was that "sale" thing that spooked me. This, being a relatively recent release, is still in print, and so could well be sitting at an actual bookstore that carries business books, but the online guys have it at about 20% off of its (fairly steep) cover price. Oddly, copies don't seem to have filtered down into the "used" channels in any great quantity, and there are (as of this writing) no significant deals to be found there. Again, this is one of those "your mileage may vary" recommendations ... the book is a fairly fun read, and a bit of a "firehose" of information, with some fascinating new-ish concepts being bandied about ... but it is targeted to sales, and depending on how that works for you pretty much equates to what you'll get out of it.

Notes:

1. http://btripp-books.livejournal.com/184596.html
2. http://amzn.to/1SnDQ3u
3. https://goo.gl/SaHD4i
4. http://conversedigital.com/theinvisiblesale/
5. http://www.conversedigital.com/
6. https://goo.gl/3MwGxh
7. http://goo.gl/TQsoj
8. https://goo.gl/99PnkC
9. https://goo.gl/9vYDCX
10. http://amzn.to/1SnDQ3u

Friday, June 10, 2016[1]

War is Hell ...

This is one of those books that has been sitting around for years ... I got it in one of those post- post-holiday sales on BN.com, possibly as long as a decade ago, and it sat in a pile of books from that order since then. However, in a book I recently (well, in the past year, and I'm not sure which one it was) read, Lt. Col. Dave Grossman's On Killing: The Psychological Cost of Learning to Kill in War and Society[2] was highly recommended, and I had a "oh, wait – I *have* that" light bulb moment, and shifted this from the stack of unread books in an obscure corner and onto one of the "recent acquisition" stacks that are more-or-less at eye-level on my way in or out of my office.

Now, as I've noted before, stuff that I get from those sales are pretty much "pig in a poke" deals, as I scan through book listings looking for "interesting sounding" titles, but without my having much background info on any of them. I was unclear on the nature of this, but recently noted that it's got about a 4.5 star rating on Amazon, and is in the libraries of nearly a thousand users over on LibraryThing.com (which is pretty high – making me suspect that this is being used as a college text). Structurally, it's in eight sections, with two to eight chapters each ... giving it an orderly progression through the factors involved in the main points of the book. The thrust is military, psychological, and societal, with some brain science, and zoology thrown in for good measure (like the factoid that when piranha fight among themselves, they primarily use tail-slaps rather than biting).

The piranha info (among others) sets up early on that most in-species conflicts across nature *tend* to have non-lethal results, which leads up to one of the most startling bits here – up through the Vietnam war, very few regular soldiers ever actually *killed* anyone (with most casualties coming from artillery fire, etc.). The first options in a conflict situation are between *posturing* and flight. Posturing can be anything from ridiculously large head gear, making the soldiers look bigger, to intense *yelling* that could make a smaller force *sound* like a more formidable foe. With amazing frequency, one side or the other in an exchange of posturing will opt to *flee*, and avoid the conflict. If both sides stayed engaged, the choices shift to fight, submit, or, again, flee. Bizarrely, firearms in most conflicts have mainly served to be loud sources of *posturing* ... here's a bit about Civil War era battles:

> Muzzle-loading muskets could fire from one to five shots per minute, depending on the skill of the operator and the state of the weapon. With a potential hit rate of well over 50 percent at the average combat ranges of this era, the killing rate should have been hundreds per minute, instead of one or two. The weak link between the killing potential and the killing capability of these units was the soldier. The simple fact is that when faced with a living, breathing opponent instead of a target, a

> *significant majority of the soldiers revert to a posturing mode in which they fire over their enemy's heads.*

I was *shocked* to see that small kill rate, but the author reports studies that have looked at other conflicts which reported 252 rounds fired per hit, 119 rounds fired per hit, and on up to Vietnam, where there were firefights *"when more than fifty thousand bullets were fired for every enemy soldier killed"*. The author goes into quite a lot of detail on the *ways* that soldiers avoided actually killing the enemy … from muskets found with multiple loads crammed down the barrel (where the soldier was going through the process of prepping his weapon, but simply never *firing* it), to a look at how subtly aiming can be shifted to shoot over the heads of the enemy without looking like one was "trying to miss". The point here is that this can't be laid at the feet of the arms themselves (even in the smooth-bore musket era, 75% hit rates should have been possible at the average distance of engagement), or marksmanship (a chimpanzee messing with an AK47 is going to do better than 1 kill for 50k rounds!), but it has to be put squarely on the soldier's unwillingness to *kill*.

While the kill rate didn't "improve" in Vietnam, the *firing* rate did … in earlier conflicts the firing rate had been as low as 15 percent, was around 55 percent in Korea, and (through "classical or operant conditioning", the details of which appear to still be classified) got up to 90-95% in Vietnam. This leads the author off to Freud, and discussing Eros and Thanatos, the "life instinct" and "death instinct" and the psychological factors … and a note that the chances of becoming a "psychological casualty" *"were greater than the chances of being killed by enemy fire"*. He presents a fascinating chart that tracks "combat effectiveness" against days in combat, rising through the first 10 days, maximized over the next 20 days, being high but declining over the next 15 days, and rapidly crashing over the next 15, to being "vegetative" by 60 days in combat. Some really horrific examples of the mental breakdowns of battle are described, and ways that modern armies try to avoid these. One approach is to rotate out troops exhibiting psychological damage to situations with *proximity* (as close to the actual battlefield as possible), and *expectancy* (that they will be returned to their units as soon as possible), this helps to both avoid the worst of the psychological wounds, *and* "evacuation syndrome", where "acting crazy" would seem to offer a way out. Grossman notes:

> *War is an environment that will psychologically debilitate 98 percent of all who participate in it for any length of time. And the 2 percent who are not driven insane by war appear to have already been insane – aggressive psychopaths – before coming to the battlefield.*

The author dedicates chapters to Fear, Exhaustion, Guilt & Horror, and Hate, before moving into "Fortitude". This is used rather than "courage", as it encompasses a wider range of reactions. Here are some quotes: *"heroism … is endurance for one moment more"*, *"it is willpower that can be spent – and when it is used up – men are finished"*, and that 98% figure keeps cropping up, as in *"In sustained combat this process of emotional* bankruptcy *is seen in 98 percent of soldiers who survive physically."*.

The third section of the book looks at "Killing and Physical Distance", with a chart which maps "resistance to killing" against "physical distance from target", going from one end at the oddly-named "Sexual Range" to "Max Range", representing bombers or artillery (or, I suppose, ICBMs). As one might expect, the closer the enemy, the more "difficult" the act of killing. On the far end of the spectrum the author uses the July 1943 fire-bombing of Hamburg, where 70,000 died, but *"from twenty thousand feet the killer could feel fascinated and satisfied with his work"*, contrasted with the Assyrian destruction of Babylon in 689 BCE, where *"someone had to personally hold down tens of thousands of men, women, and children, while someone else stabbed and hacked at these horrified {victims}"*, and the hideous stories from the Nazi death camps. The *personal* nature of the up-close kill seems to be emotionally scarring, while the distance kill is emotionally detached. Interestingly, the *survivors* of bombing attacks are less traumatized as well, with their considering themselves as *"incidental victims of an act of war"*, and able to put it behind them, when the survivors of the concentration camps were haunted by the idea of *"members of my own species actively seeking my end"* – even if the machine guns and gas chambers were not *as* horrific as the face-to-face butchery in Babylon. Grossman walks the reader through chapters looking at killing at various ranges, from the maximum-range forms: *" Artillery crews, bomber crews, naval gunners, and missile crews – at sea and on the ground – are all protected by the same powerful combination of group absolution, mechanical distance, and ... physical distance."* ... and on to that "sexual range" where *"much of the attraction to the killing process, and much of the resistance to close-in killing, revolves around the vicious side of ourselves ..."*.

The fourth section is a deep psychological dive into human behavior, with looks at "demands of authority", the just mentioned "group absolution", the physical and emotional (including cultural and similar factors) "distance from victim", the "target attractiveness of the victim", and the predisposition of the killer, across several chapters. Not surprisingly, this starts with the work of Stanley Milgram (and Freud to the extent that he perceptively warned: *"never underestimate the power of the need to obey"*), and his iconic Yale experiment[3]. One thing I found fascinating here (that had obviously not gotten on my radar previously) was that in proposing the experiment, Milgram's colleagues estimated that only a fraction of 1% of the subjects would keep going until the maximum (supposedly *lethal*) voltage was applied. As it turned out, with no more established authority than a clip board and a lab coat, the orders of the assistants running the experiment were complied with by a shocking *sixty five percent* of the test subjects. As the author comments, if 65% of test subjects could be convinced (what they thought was) to *kill* an innocent victim with just some "window dressing" of authority, how much more coercive is the authority of a military chain-of-command? Another interesting discussion in this section is that of the various strategies (either "institutional" by way of propaganda, or internal justification) of "dehumanizing" the enemy, making them emotionally less relevant. Another chapter deals with "disposition", this can be achieved via training (the Rhodesian security force in the 70's had an over-all kill ratio of 8-1 against rebel guerrillas, with their elite units achieving as high as a 50-1 ratio), or by personal experiences: *"the recent loss of friends and beloved leaders in com-*

bat can also enable violence on the battlefield", on to the "natural soldier". This is the previously-mentioned 2% … the author is careful to note that:

> *It would be absolutely incorrect to conclude that 2 percent of all veterans are psychopathic killers. Numerous studies indicated that combat veterans are no more inclined to violence than nonvets. A more accurate conclusion would be that there is 2 percent of the male population that, if pushed or if given a legitimate reason, will kill without regret or remorse.*

He goes on to point out that those very low (non-artillery) kill rates from the Napoleonic wars through WW2 could indicate that *most* of the kills came from these, uh, *motivated* soldiers. I couldn't help but think both of lyrics[4] by Arlo Guthrie, and a famed H.L. Mencken quote[5]. This leads into a related subject in the fifth section, that of "atrocities", but I'll spare you the details on that.

Section six is on "killing response stages" and relates to a fairly complex chart that seems to show that "all roads lead to PTSD[6]", with even more unpleasant results along the way. Again, this I'll skip here. The next section takes a specific psychological look at the Vietnam war, and how *"between 400,000 and 1.5 million Vietnam vets suffer from PTSD"*. Once the previously mentioned low rates of firing in earlier wars (as low as 20% in WW2!) were discovered, the military set out to fix the problem. This started in Korea, where a 55% firing rate was achieved, and moved towards a *"boot-cam deification of killing"* which, coupled with (operant) *"conditioning techniques to develop a reflexive 'quick shoot' ability"* got up to a 95% rate in Vietnam (although, not particularly *efficient* shooting, as detailed above). The author also notes that Vietnam involved very young soldiers:

> *They were teenagers leading teenagers in a war of endless, small-unit operations, trapped together in a real-world reenactment of* The Lord of the Flies *with guns, and destined to internalize the horrors of combat during one of the most vulnerable and susceptible stages of life.*

This coupled with increasingly high-tech equipment, pharmacological interventions to keep the troops engaged, and the disgraceful way that the media handled the war, created stress levels almost unique to that conflict. And, one of the primary coping factors was missing … instead of returning to a welcoming and thankful nation, the Left had created an atmosphere where soldiers coming home were cursed, spit upon, and exiled … driving an additional aspect to the PTSD equation.

Now, up through here, the book hasn't suffered from its age (written in 1995), but when he gets to the "What Are We Doing to Our Children?" section, it begins to sound very dated. Grossman latches onto some "pop psychology" of the time about movie violence, and "video arcades". A couple of decades later, the level of violence in entertainment vehicles hasn't gone *down*, but things haven't gone out of control in the *"pathological spiral"* he forecasts. Most unsettling, he ends up taking serious anti-Constitutional stances directed (especially) to the 1st and 2nd amendments, which makes my Libertarian blood boil. Given that the rest of the book is *fascinating*, this last bit could well be lopped off to make its reading (in a whole new technological world) much improved!

Again, On Killing[7] is likely being used as a textbook, as not only is it in a lot of hands on LT, but it's still in print at this point, with no substantial cheap used presence 20 years on. In fact, the on-line big boys have the 2009 paperback edition at a very reasonable price (admittedly, something not typical for a textbook!) that's not much more than the cheapest used copy plus shipping – so if you thought this was something that you'd want to check out, might as well order new.

This is a deeply engaging look at human nature, within the context of killing in war. I suppose, having been a reader of military history, it possibly had more of an interest for *me* than it would for somebody who was less familiar with the niche, but the level of psychological insight and "looking under the hood" into these mental-emotional factors should make it attractive to a wide range of serious readers.

Notes:
1. http://btripp-books.livejournal.com/184946.html
2. http://amzn.to/1rcTHuT
3. https://en.wikipedia.org/wiki/Milgram_experiment
4. https://goo.gl/Gu3oCE
5. https://goo.gl/7ZzWSH
6. https://en.wikipedia.org/wiki/Posttraumatic_stress_disorder
7. http://amzn.to/1rcTHuT

Monday, June 13, 2016

Preaching to the choir ...

Nearly a decade back, I was "in a mood" and decided that I needed to get up to speed with all the current anti-theist thought out there, and ordered in a bunch of books ... while I'd gotten to quite a few of them at the time, I eventually hit a "meh" point, and these started to drift down the "to be read" piles. This is one that I got back then (new in hardcover at retail, even), but only got around to reading a month or so ago. I'm sort of embarrassed to admit that part of the reason this went so long without my getting to it was that, when I was in the thick of my job hunt, part of me "didn't want to get on Santa's naughty list" just in case there *was* some bronze-age sheepherder's vision of a vindictive Sky Father up there who'd get mad at me for reading stuff saying he didn't exist. Sort of a Pascal's Wager deal there, but after cranking out nearly 3,000 resumes over a 7 year period, I figured "how much *worse* could the job search get?" ... if there IS a God, were he to "smite" me, it would be a blessed release at this point and provide life insurance funds to my family while I'm still covered!

Anyway, I finally got around to reading the late Christopher Hitchens' <u>God Is Not Great: How Religion Poisons Everything</u>, and figured that today was as good as any for getting into the review. One thing I found frustrating here was that Hitchens would get into really engaging territory, and look like he was about to produce some pithy *bon mot* that I'd be able to quote for you here, but pretty much every time roll into a long digression riffing on the point that I was wanting to highlight. While this didn't mar the flow of the *reading*, it was frustrating when I was eager to drop in a "gotta use this" bookmark.

While there is no indication that this was a compilation of previously existing pieces, the chapters are sufficiently self-contained that the book *does* read more like a collection of pamphlets on assorted rants against religion than one coherent narrative arc. So, I'm afraid that I'm going to seem to be "cherry-picking" here through the chapters, in an attempt to find quotes illustrative of where the author's taking his arguments. Oh, and sometimes his prose gets a bit *florid*, as is somewhat exemplified by the end of this quote from early in the book, which otherwise fairly concisely (following a rambling bit about the certainty of death and the implausibility of any afterlife) frames the book's main thesis:

> We believe with certainty that an ethical life can be lived without religion. And we know for a fact that the corollary holds true – that religion has caused innumerable people not just to conduct themselves no better than others, but to award themselves permission to behave in ways that would make a brothel-keeper or an ethnic cleanser raise an eyebrow.

Speaking of Pascal, Hitchens compares him with C.S. Lewis, and notes *"... the appalling load of strain they have to bear. How much effort it takes to affirm the incredible!"* ... which he follows (after a brief side trip to the Aztecs' daily human sacrifices), with the rather arch *"How much vanity must be concealed – not too effectively at that – in order to pretend that one is the personal object of a divine plan?"*.

I mention the Aztec reference above to suggest how much of the narrative in these chapters is not overly *linear*, with the author pulling in items seemingly off the top of his head ... which, while perhaps engaging in a chat over a pint, makes it tough to extract bits here. This results in one of the most telling chapters, "Religion Kills", not having any of my little bookmarks in it ... despite being gripping, informative (Hitchens had been all over the world as a correspondent, and had a lot of eye-witness material to a wide array of horror stories where he *"could sense that religion was beginning to reassert its challenge to civil society"*), and truly shocking.

Interestingly, "Religion Kills" is followed with a brief chapter about pork (subtitled "Why Heaven Hates Ham"), and, I suppose, religious dietary restrictions in general. While this visits a range of items, some quaint, some brutal, the most illuminating (for me, at least) tidbit of info here is that the delightful culinary tradition of the *charcuterie* platter arose from the Spanish Inquisition (no, I didn't *expect* that either) as a way to ferret out the less-sincere among forced Jewish and Muslim converts, by presenting them with a splendid array of *pork products*, and gauging their reactions. Or, as he puts it: *"In the hands of eager Christian fanatics, even the toothsome jamón Ibérico could be pressed into service as a form of torture."*.

The next chapter deals with issues of health, and how religion rather predictably messes up even the most positive attempts at improving people's lives. He notes a UNICEF program that was trying to eradicate polio. This was moving along quite well in India until a group of Mullahs decided that the drops (the treatment was a couple of drops of liquid on the tongue – but had to be administered twice) were a "conspiracy by the United States to sterilize true believers". This rumor (and eventual *fatwa*) spread to Africa (particularly Nigeria) and then all across the Muslim world. Oh, those crazy Muslims, you say? Well, this comes in close parallel with the Vatican's "President of the Pontifical Council for the Family" who put out warnings that *"all condoms are secretly made with many microscopic holes, through which the AIDS virus can pass"*, creating massive surges in AIDS infections in countries like Brazil, Nicaragua, Kenya, and Uganda ... with some Catholic Cardinals asserting that women who die of AIDS rather than use condoms are "martyrs"! Needless to say, a good deal of the "health" restrictions pushed by religion deal with sex ... and Hitchens lists off a litany of quite disturbing examples. He starts a section here with:

> Violent, irrational, intolerant, allied to racism and tribalism and bigotry, invested in ignorance and hostile to free inquiry, contemptuous of women and coercive towards children: organized religion ought to have a great deal on its conscience.

... yet he suggests that in the heart-of-hearts of the religious the *opposite* is true, noting that the "church father" Tertullian promises that *"one of the most intense pleasures of the afterlife would be the endless contemplation of the tortures of the damned."*.

Next comes the rather directly titled "The Metaphysical Claims of Religion are False", which features at its start a list of assorted quotes, including Ignatius Loyola's *"We sacrifice the intellect to God."* and Martin Luther's *"Reason is the Devil's harlot."* ... and Hitchens does not seem to be in a mood to "play nice" with a whole roster of historical religious notables whose writings bear the marks of the basest credulity on one hand, and vile manipulation on the other. He contrasts these with notable scientific thinkers, and the likes of Jefferson and Franklin, who, despite being *deists*, *"managed to seize a moment of crisis and use it to enshrine Enlightenment values in the founding documents"* of the USA. There are several superb runs in this, but aren't quite of the quotable variety (although the line "the pathetic vestiges of this can still be seen in modern societies", when referring to times and places where "the clergy has the power to dictate its own terms", is too rich to not pass along here!). One thing he does use to highlight the differences between the religious and scientific sides is: *"today the least educated of my children knows much more about the natural order than any of the founders of religion"*.

He spends a good chunk of the book in a chapter dealing with evolution vs. "design", which is, perhaps, more *combative* than others as the idiots pushing religious delusions are still very much on the forefront of assorted "culture wars", thus providing extremely tempting targets for Hitchens' attacks ... and he shreds many of the designists by name here.

Next comes the subject of the Bible, divided, naturally, into two chapters: "The Nightmare of the Old Testament" and "The Evil of the New Testament". This starts off with a dissection of the Ten Commandments (*"the monarchical growling about respect and fear, accompanied by a stern reminder of omnipotence and limitless revenge"*), and delves into the horrors of that tribal document (although, not to the extent where it is eviscerated elsewhere). Similarly, he does a fairly broad-stroke review of what H.L. Mencken described as *"a helter-skelter accumulation of more or less discordant documents"*, pointing out the more egregious idiocies believed by so many in the New Testament. Pointedly, Hitchens frames this review:

> *The contradictions and illiteracies of the New Testament have filled up many books by eminent scholars, and have never been explained by any Christian authority except in the feeblest terms of "metaphor" and "a Christ of faith." This feebleness derives from the fact that until recently, Christians could simply burn or silence anybody who asked any inconvenient questions.*

While Christian fundamentalists have been largely stripped of their more lethal reactions (institutionally, at least), the Muslim world is still quite enthusiastic about torturing, murdering, and enslaving those who offend its evidently rather delicate sensibilities. These would, no doubt, be much abused by the chapter "The Koran Is Borrowed from Both Jewish and Christian Myths", which gives you a good sense of the subject matter. Of course, having *just* detailed what a hot mess *those* mythic traditions are, you can imagine what the Muhammadan mash-up looks like in Hitchens' view. Of course, one of the main problems here is the murderous nature of the faith:

> *Not only did Islam begin by condemning all doubters to eternal fire, but it still claims the right to do so in almost all its dominion, and still preaches that these same dominions can and must be extended by war. There has never been an attempt in any age to challenge or even investigate the claims of Islam that has not been met with extremely harsh and swift repression.*

Hard to live long enough to become the "Muslim Martin Luther", I suppose. One of the aspects that Hitchens focuses on here is the inconvenient bit about how nearly all the early figures in Islam were *illiterate*, and yet cobbled together a *book* which is supposedly "the final revelation". The hadiths are even more muddled, with illiterate hearsay reporting illiterate hearsay, going back through various repetitions. The author notes there were some actual scholars involved, such as Bukhari, a compiler living nearly *a quarter of a millennium* after Muhammad, who sorted through 300,000 "attestations" and determined that 200,000 of those were *"entirely valueless and unsupported"*, eventually whittling the remaining 100k down to a collection of 10,000 ... but, still:

> *You are free to believe, I you so choose, that out of this formless mass of illiterate and half remembered witness the pious Bukhari, more than two centuries later, manage to select only the pure and undefiled ones that would bear examination.*

... with the result including *"great chunks of more or less straight biblical quotations"*.

Hitchens then takes a side trip into considering the concept of Hell, and how it's manifested in various religious traditions, how it was developed, and how *useful* it has historically proven for those running religions, along with how "tawdry" most miracles are when actually examined. This is followed with a chapter on the *beginnings* of religions, starting off with a quote from Sigmund Freud: *"Where questions of religion are concerned, people are guilty of every possible sort of dishonesty and intellectual misdemeanor."* In this the author looks at "Cargo Cults", the Mormons (which he notes has similarities to Islam in their "miraculously delivered" documents), and the one-time child evangelical star Marjoe Gortner, who famously developed a film in the early 70's exposing the vileness of the "religious revival" scam. This is followed by a brief "coda" chapter on "How Religions End", primarily looking at a handful of assorted the-world-is-ending cults from various points in history.

The next chapter asks "Does Religion Make People Behave Better", with a long listing of examples of religion being either the justification or vehicle for the most appalling behavior. From Thomas Jefferson having to negotiate with ambassadors of the Barbary (pirate) states ... before sending the Marines to Tripoli ... to issues with the British leaving India, and Hitchens' own experience in Bosnia, there are some fascinating historical bits here. Most telling, though, is an exchange between a noted humanist and a prominent Bishop ... the former claimed that "he saw no evidence at all for the existence of any god", to which the latter animatedly responded with the rather telling *"Then I cannot see why you do not lead a life of unbridled immorality!"* – clearly implying that the churchman would, if not for his "imaginary friend" constantly looking over his shoulder, be some licentious reprobate! {Penn Jillette has a great take[3] on this as well}

At this point the book turns East, and has a go at "Eastern Religions", which don't fare much better than the Major Monotheisms. The following chapters look at how almost *any* religion is going to be fundamentally flawed, ask "Is Religion Child Abuse?", and religion's "last ditch" arguments against secularism. This has these choice bits:

> *If I cannot definitively prove that the usefulness of religion is in the past, and that its foundational books are transparent fables, and that is a man-made imposition, and that it has been an enemy of science and inquiry, and that it has subsided largely on lies and fears, and been the accomplice of ignorance and guilt as well as of slavery, genocide, racism, and tyranny, I can most certainly claim that religion is now fully aware of these criticisms. It is also fully aware of the ever-mounting evidence, concerning the origins of the cosmos and the origins of species, which consign it to marginality if not to irrelevance.*
>
> ...
>
> *... it is interesting to find that people of faith now defensively to say that they are no worse than fascists or Nazis or Stalinists. One might hope that religion had retained more sense of its dignity than that.*
>
> ...
>
> *For most of human history, the idea of the total or absolute state was intimately bound up with religion. ... The slightest infringement – of a holy day, or a holy object, or an ordinance about sex or food or caste – could bring calamity.*

This latter chapter goes on through quite a lot of material, showing how, in nearly every case, most "secular totalitarian states" were working hand-in-hand with the religious institutions of the day. Fascinating, but ugly, stuff here.

The book concludes with two chapters somewhat looking forward, "The Resistance of the Rational", and "The Need for a New Enlightenment". The former takes a look at philosophy (*"Philosophy begins where religion ends, just as by analogy chemistry begins where alchemy runs out, and astronomy takes the place of astrology"*), starting with Socrates and others of the ancient Greeks, and meanders through various traditions up through the centuries. The latter takes a look at the world around us (or at least that of a decade ago), and cries out for more sanity. One key quote here is *"Religion* has run out of justification.", and closes with the warning: *"it has become necessary to know the enemy, and to prepare to fight it."*.

Needless to say, despite my caveats regarding the difficulties of extracting elements to illustrate this for the review, I was quite engaged with God Is Not Great[4], and would recommend it to all and sundry (although the more preachy types might want to have antacids on hand). It appears that the hardcover edition I have is no longer in print, but the 2009 paperback is out there, with the on-line big boys having it a discount bringing it under ten bucks (oddly, there aren't many quality used copies of the hardcover out there, but "good" copies can be had for around a buck plus shipping).

Notes:

1. http://btripp-books.livejournal.com/185178.html
2. http://amzn.to/1SLecFc
3. https://goo.gl/fawp8N
4. http://amzn.to/1SLecFc

Tuesday, June 14, 2016[1]

Stuff you probably didn't know ...

This was another book that the "Almighty Algorithm" matched to my book collection over on LibraryThing.com for their Early Reviewers program. As is frequently the case, "early" doesn't necessarily mean "pre-release", although the copy in hand *is* an ARC (review copy), as this hit the shelves the first week of April. I guess that's "my bad" as this was a February LTER[2] selection that showed up here mid-March.

Anyway, Juan Williams' We the People: The Modern-Day Figures Who Have Reshaped and Affirmed the Founding Fathers' Vision of America[3] is an odd concept, as one might gather from the cover graphic, this is sort of setting up "new founders" for the *changed* America that some love and some loathe.

I'm always somewhat surprised by Williams, as I identify him with Fox News, and so expect a level of conservatism that he only exhibits on occasion. However, it turns out that he had a long career at leftist bastions *The Washington Post* and *National Public Radio*, that I'd not been previously aware of, so that explains a *lot* about how much this book grated my sensibilities.

While this is not *blatantly* some "progressive" screed, it certain reflects the author's preference for stances, movements, legislation, and cultural shifts that I think are wrong, bad, or just plain *evil*, so I was grinding my teeth a lot while reading it. However, Williams anticipates this, and starts the book with the (quoted) question *"What happened to my America?"*, and points out that, during the 2012 election

> One poll found 53 percent of white Americans saying the changes in culture, economics, demographics, and politics were coming too quickly and damaging America's "character and values."

Interestingly, in the same poll, 51 percent of *African Americans* also felt these changes were too much ... so it's not just me as a middle-aged white male! There is a big divide here, though ... with the author clearly admiring people, movements, and organizations that I *loathe* ... so take that as a caveat to my impressions of the book.

This is structured in chapters that address one societal issue and the figures Williams identifies as being related to the changes in that. As I have just three or four of my little bookmarks in this (pointing out places that I felt had information good to present here), I'm going to resort to, basically, walking you through the TOC initially to give you the "30,000 ft view" on this. The following are the sub-headers of the chapters, which present the characters and the contexts for each:

> JFK, Ted Kennedy, and the Immigration Reform That Changed America
> Earl Warren, Thurgood Marshall, Martin Luther King Jr. and the Fight for Civil Rights

                              Bill Bratton and Modern Policing
        General William Westmoreland and the Rebirth of the U.S. Military
     Milton Friedman's New Math of Free Markets, Big Business, and Small Taxes
            Eleanor Roosevelt and the Fight for Global Human Rights
              Robert Moses, William Levitt, and the American City
        George Meany, the Labor Unions, and the Rise of the Middle Class
              Billy Graham and the Power of the Christian Right
                    Betty Friedan and American Feminism
             Henry Kissinger, Richard Nixon, and the Opening of China
                   Pat Moynihan and the War on Poverty
                Harry Hay, Barry Goldwater, and Gay Rights
        Ronald Regan, Ed Meese, and the Remaking of the Judicial System
                 Social Security, Medicare, and Robert Ball
              Rachel Carson and the Environmental Movement
      Martin Luther King Jr., Jesse Jackson, and the Fight for Racial Equality
                      Charlton Heston and the NRA

Now, even in a 400+ page book, that's quite a list of stuff to cover, so nothing is covered particularly *in depth*, although at an average of 20 pages each, these are not trivial looks at the subjects. Obviously, the majority of the individuals discussed are "household names", but with a sprinkling of folks I'd never heard of. The time periods covered also shift around quite a bit, from Robert Moses, active in the first decades of the last century, to Bill Bratton, whose influence first manifested in the 1990s.

The book gets off on the wrong foot, as the figure of Ted Kennedy (whom Williams obviously greatly admires) is, to me, more the elite power-abusing monster that bought his way out of the Chappaquiddick incident and regularly championed causes I disliked. The author argues that the Kennedy brothers had a deep connection to immigration via their Irish background … but I wonder how real that is, being raised in power and privilege by their bootlegger Nazi-supporting family patriarch. It appears that the 1964 Civil Rights Act only got passed because Lyndon Johnson and Ted Kennedy used the trauma of JFK's assassination to "guilt" it through congress.

The chapter dealing with Earl Warren, Thurgood Marshall, and Martin Luther King Jr. is the first place where Williams tries to envision the thoughts of the original founders about demographic realities of recent decades, and spins off from the founders supposedly not being able to imagine or accept how the Constitution has been construed by modern Courts, and into territory which in danger of "throwing the baby out with the bathwater" in attempts to push "progressive" (Leftist) goals. Johnson is a key player in this chapter as well, but I guess didn't make the cut for the sub-header.

The next chapter is entitled "Broken Windows, Urban Crime, and Hard Data", and focuses on the figure of Bill Bratton, the police figure (former Chief of Police in Boston, New York, and Los Angeles, and current NYC Police Commissioner) who developed the "data driven" approach to policing, which drove down crime rates by responsively assigning resources where they were needed ... but more controversially following the "broken windows" theory of reacting to small crimes before they create perceived permission for more serious crimes. This, with advanced surveillance has raised a lot of civil liberties questions, and Williams indicates that Bratton was instrumental in hooking in local law enforcement with Homeland Security under the Patriot Act.

The chapter on General William Westmoreland is fascinating in its look at the history of America's military, from the early days when many were unwilling to *have* an army, on up through Vietnam. Of course, Westmoreland had been the commander of the efforts in Vietnam until 1968, and got to see up close how debilitating that conflict, and the systems involved in it, were for our forces. It was he, and his successors, who pioneered the present highly-trained all-volunteer force.

Next comes a look at economic theory, featuring the famed economist Milton Friedman (whose *Free To Choose* video series and accompanying book in 1980 were huge successes). One gets the sense that Williams doesn't much like Friedman's stances on things (repeatedly contrasting him with Paul Krugman), but he's presented here due to his *influence*, both in economic theory and the ideas of freedom.

The concepts of American-style "liberty and justice" applying world-wide is the key point in the chapter on Eleanor Roosevelt, who had become the head of the United Nations Commission on Human Rights in 1946. Williams says:

> Mrs. Roosevelt offered the Founding Fathers' claim of natural rights as the new baseline for judging how any government, in any place, treats the poor, political dissidents, racial and ethnic minorities, women, and children.

Aside her work in these areas, this chapter has quite a lot of interesting information regarding her life, which was extraordinary by any measure.

The chapter on the rise of cities probably has the least-known names here, Robert Moses and William Levitt, both operating in New York City, although in different eras. Moses was born in 1888 and became a very controversial figure, on one hand, fighting corruption and ingrained political factions, on the other, "bullying" his way toward tearing down whole swaths of housing to build highways, and other personal pet projects. While Moses operated in the governmental sphere, Levitt was to be instrumental in developing the suburbs: *"It was Levitt who was the first to build middle-class residential communities off the exits of the parkways and highways."*, his family company initially having contacts to build housing for defense workers in Norfolk, VA, they devised new building techniques for "assembly-line" housing construction that was able to pump out hundreds of times the units of traditional builders.

I suppose the name George Meany is familiar to older readers, as I suspect he's not much on the radar of anybody under 40 at this point. He ran the AFL (American Federation of Labor) which later merged with the CIO

(Congress of Industrial Organizations), to form the familiar AFL-CIO union structure. This piece is fascinating to read as a union outsider, as it represents a time when the unions were massive, powerful, yet stridently anti-communist ... a world away from Leftist monstrosities like the SEIU or government employee unions these days!

Williams does a great job at backgrounding the chapter on the Christian Right, both in tracing Billy Graham's history but also outlining assorted laws, etc., such as the 1948 Supreme Court case that prevented the teaching of religious doctrine in public schools. Much of this is focused on the 60's and 70's, however, with the rise of evangelical broadcasting, and the all-too-familiar names involved in that (he quotes Jerry Falwell saying that people were fascinated to be able to see him on TV in the morning and then get to see him live at an event that night). Frankly, Graham isn't the "main player" in here, but he seems to be the one who got the ball rolling, and much of the later figures are, essentially, his protégés.

Another name that might have faded with the years is that of Betty Friedan, whose 1963 book *The Feminine Mystique* (based on research initially begun in 1957), was a ground-breaking look at women in the post-war world, and the *"nameless, aching dissatisfaction"* they felt. She ended up publishing the book, because she was unable to interest any magazine in taking the article she had originally planned to write ... of course, when the book sold *over 3 million copies*, the magazines, talk shows, and other media were all too happy to cover it ... and it has been described as *"a good example of a book that permanently shifted the society in which it was published"*. She was President of the National Organization for Women (and was instrumental in developing that group's "Bill of Rights for Women"), a founder of the National Women's Political Caucus, and a key player in numerous other organizations.

One of the most fascinating (for me) chapters here is the one on the Opening of China, which is largely centered on the still-imposing figure of Henry Kissinger. That noted anti-communist Richard Nixon was the President to begin normalizing relations with Mao's China was a shock at the time, and is still a pretty amazing episode in American history. Kissinger's background is remarkable (and I'd not previously seen anything on this), including hunting down Gestapo agents in post-war Germany. He was largely responsible for much of the Cold War strategy of fighting "little wars" (like Korea and Vietnam) and avoiding full-on conflict with the USSR. The tales of back-channel negotiations (and even cloak-and-dagger operations such as his going on a trip to Pakistan that was a ruse to fly to China to work out Nixon's eventual visit) should be the stuff of movies.

Pat Moynihan is another of those names that I *remember*, but generally just as a whiny liberal Senator that always seemed to be on the wrong side of issues. It appears that his upbringing in and out of the lower end of the middle class, set him up for being very sensitive to poverty, and became an Assistant Secretary of Labor in the Kennedy administration, and continued into the Johnson administration where he wrote *The Negro Family: The Case For National Action* (more commonly known as the Moynihan Report) in 1965. This report was seminal to Johnson's "war on poverty", and argued that *"the problems of poverty and unemployment were rooted in common problems of broken families, poor education and training"*. He worked in the

Nixon administration (and became an ambassador) before winning a Senate seat in 1976 (to which he was reelected three times, retiring in 2000), and even co-sponsored bills with the Reagan administration. There is quite a lot of detail about his career, and the legislation involved, here ... plus some interesting personal details about the author's life.

While I have always been a big fan of Barry Goldwater, I did not recognize the name Harry Hay. It turns out that he was an English immigrant who came to the U.S. in 1917 and was very active with political organization to support the rights of gays. His long career (he died at age 90 in 2002) spanned a lot of cultural territory, which was further complicated by his being a member of the Communist Party. It turns out that Goldwater was one of the strongest supporters of gay rights in the mainstream political world *"arguing that conservative reverence of the Constitution and its guarantees of persona liberty include the right to make personal choice about sexual preferences"* ... a stance that's more associated with the Libertarians these days.

As one might expect, a writer who had been with the *Post* and *NPR* probably never had Ronald Reagan or Ed Meese on his Christmas card list, and the "Remaking of the Judicial System" chapter, while remarkably detailed in its look at the courts, has that sort of feel of adversarial attitude about it. Of course, he's pretty even-handed here, saying regarding Meese: *"The height of his effort to get back to the Founder's original intent was to select judges on the basis of their fidelity to strictly interpreting the law on the basis of the Constitution."* ... which I think is a shame that that is *notable* rather than *required*.

One name that I doubt any but hard-core policy wonks will know (I certainly didn't) is that of Robert Ball. The first third of this chapter walks the reader through the history of social programs in the U.S., up through the Truman administration, during which a Senate panel was formed to look at Social Security, the head of this panel was Ball, a former Social Security official noted for his expertise and abilities to do high-level presentations on the intricacies of the system. He was, essentially, the go-to guy for the program on up through the Reagan administration (serving on panels and commissions even after his official retirement in 1973).

Rachel Carson is probably still a recognizable name as her *Silent Spring* is an environmental classic. After WW2 she had gotten a position with the U.S. Department of Fisheries as an aquatic biologist and began writing materials for the government in the 50's. She published an award-winning book, *The Sea Around Us* in 1951, and continued publishing through the decade. Her research into the deleterious effects of the insecticide DDT led her to writing *Silent Spring* in 1962, which is credited (although she died two years later) with being the foundation for the Environmental Protection Agency.

Everybody knows the names of Martin Luther King Jr. and Jesse Jackson, and the chapter on "the Fight for Racial Equality" largely looks at how their messages, in very different styles, interacted. This takes detailed look back at social and legal history leading up to King, and how Jackson, essentially, tried to push himself into the leadership of the movement after King's assassination (including wearing his blood-soaked shirt constantly at meetings and rallies for days after). As much as Jackson wanted to be *seen* as the natural inheritor of King's mantle, he was not much liked by others in those circles, and even MLK at one point told him (in public): *"If you want to carve out your own niche in society, go ahead, but for God's sake, don't bother me"*! Williams details Jackson's political ambitions, and frustrations with never getting the power he was seeking (leading, no doubt, to the bitterness he's frequently shown regarding Obama).

Finally, there's Charlton Heston, and the NRA. This is another case where I think Juan Williams had to "stretch" a bit, as Heston, while universally known, and active (at one point President) in the NRA, was hardly a central figure. In fact, his initial involvement was being *hired* for some commercials. This chapter is very interesting, however, in looking at the NRA, its history (at one point it was a quasi-governmental organization to train kids to be better shots), and the whole "gun issue". Needless to say, this is a topic very much "of the moment".

Anyway, that's pretty much what's in We the People[4] … each of these is fleshed out with enough detail to make it worth reading, but not so much as to make it unbearable (I'm pretty sure I'd take a pass at reading an entire book on some of these). While I don't agree with the author's "spin" on a lot of these (and think the whole *premise* is somewhat off), he's certainly presented something that shines new light on a lot of areas of American life. This just came out in April, so should be generally available, but the on-line big boys have it for nearly half off at the moment (making it nearly a wash with what the new/used guys have it for, with shipping).

To be honest, this is *not* a book that I think I would have picked up "free range" to read, but I don't think I wasted my time reading it. I suspect that someone of a more Leftist bent might have been more enthusiastic about it than I was … so there's that to consider.

Notes:

1 http://btripp-books.livejournal.com/185419.html

2. https://www.librarything.com/wiki/index.php/HelpThing:Er_list

3-4. http://amzn.to/253oFUP

Saturday, June 18, 2016

Another play ...

So, here's another of those always-useful Dover Thrift Editions ... ideal to pad book orders up to free shipping levels, or to plug holes in one's education. I suspect I ordered this (before getting Amazon Prime and not having to worry about shipping), for both reasons. I'm actually on the fence here regarding if I've seen this play or not, as it seemed awfully familiar when I read it, and may have been one of the things I saw ages ago when in London.

Anyway, George Bernard Shaw's Arms & The Man has been a popular play for a long time. Having been both an English and Religion major in school, I kept bumping into Shaw from both sides, on the latter especially for the arch "Shavian Satan" (oddly, that term might have been idiosyncratic to my university, as almost all searches for "Shavian" just turn up the phonetic alphabet Shaw had had developed, which appeared posthumously, but attributed to him), who, in *Man and Superman* is quoted (in reference to Milton's writing) as saying: *"The Englishman described me as being expelled from Heaven by cannons and gunpowder; and to this day every Briton believes that the whole of his silly story is in the Bible."* ... as a perfect example of how most people have a vaguely formatted, culturally filtered, view of their own religions!

Shaw is a fascinating figure in his own right (I must find a good bio of him to read at some point), being almost larger than life in the extremities (political, religious, cultural, etc.) he embraced over his long life (he died at 94 in 1950). He was born in Ireland, but moved to London at age 20, seeking to establish himself as a writer – which he did, initially as a theater critic, and "pamphleteer" for a Socialist society. During this time he was also writing plays, and these eventually found an audience.

One of the odd, yet attractive, features of this Dover edition is the inclusion of the rather extensive (it's 8 pages here of fairly small type) Preface to a collection of plays he published in 1898. This is snarky, gossipy, cynical, yet self-disparaging, as in this bit: *"I half suspect that those managers who have had most to do with me, if asked to name the main obstacle to the performance of my plays, would unhesitatingly and unanimously reply 'The Author'."*. Frankly, this section is well worth the very small cost of admission (the cover price on the book is all of $2.50), but I'm avoiding the temptation to quote several pieces of it here, as it is, after all, not the point of the book.

I do feel like I need to apologize that I managed to get through this without putting in *any* of my little bookmarks indicating where I found good things for the review ... as this means that I'll be "winging it" here more than I'd like. The play premiered in 1894, and deals with a scenario towards end of the (don't feel bad, I'd never heard of it either) Serbo-Bulgarian War of 1885 – so it was a relatively current topic for audiences of the day – which appears (after some Googling) to have been as complicated as anything Balkan tends to be. The location of the action is sufficiently near the front lines so that a Swiss mercenary, fighting for the Serbians, is able to seek refuge from his pursuers in the home of a moderately well-to-do Bulgarian family.

The action in the play certainly owes a good deal to the typical Shakespearean comedy, with people and items being shuffled around, just out of the view of those whose attention would be disastrous, and shifts happening in romantic affiliations as the story unwinds.

OK ... now here's my warning as a non-fiction reader (who is particularly tone-deaf as to what might or might not be seen as a "spoiler") ... anything from here on in deals with the specifics of the plot, so if you want to be *surprised* at either reading the book or seeing a production of the play, you should probably stop here.

One thing to note, this is a very *brief* read ... the whole play is slightly more than 50 pages (I have no idea how long it takes to stage) ... and it is divided into three Acts, which are (of course) fairly compact. The main character here is Captain Bluntschli, a Swiss professional soldier who is fighting in the Serbian army. Upon his side losing one of the latter battles of the conflict, he takes flight, and attempts to hide in an upper room of a house. The room, however, is occupied by Raina, daughter of Major Petkoff and his wife, Catherine. She is quite impressed with her family and its (somewhat questionable) achievements – such as having *a library* (in the description of the stage set for Act III, Shaw describes it as: *"It is not much of a library. Its literary equipment consists of a single fixed shelf stocked with old paper covered novels, broken back, coffee stained, torn and thumbed; and a couple of little hanging shelves with a few gift books on them ..."*), or the favorite of her father, an "electric bell" – and really thinks that they are the cultural elite (after all, they do *"go to Bucharest every year for the opera season"*), at least for their small border town. Bluntschli is threatening enough to convince her to not raise an alarm, even with him hidden behind a drape, first when her mother and the insolent servant girl Louka enter, and then when the Russian/Bulgarian troops arrive. Aside from protecting him, she also lets him have the remnants of a box of chocolates, which earns him the nickname "chocolate-cream soldier". The ruse is discovered by Catherine, who assists by providing one of the Major's coats for him to escape in ... although the first Act ends with him falling asleep in Raina's bed.

It turns out that Raina is engaged to Sergius Saranoff, a Bulgarian officer who led a successful, albeit poorly-thought-out charge that ended up scattering Bluntschli's force – a charge which would have been massacred had the Serbian guns not malfunctioned. It appears that between the first and second Acts, a peace treaty has been signed, allowing Bluntschli to show up at Petkoff's house, unannounced, to return the coat given to him for his escape. It also appears that Sergius has encountered Bluntschli in the time since the cease-fire, and has even heard the broad strokes (although not the *details*) of his escape. Catherine is *horrified* to see Bluntschli, as she's claimed the coat had gone missing. The head servant, Nicola, unaware of all this, not only brings out Bluntschli's luggage, but later brings the coat to Major Petkoff. Petkoff, introduced to Bluntschli by Sergius, insists he stay for lunch and (recognizing his expertise in the military) asks his help with a problem of troop movements in decommissioning the forces. Later, when Raina appears, she is shocked to see Bluntschli, and lets slip "the chocolate-cream soldier" ... and then has to come up with a whole back story about a decoration she'd made for a dessert, that had gotten ruined by Nicola (who gets a lot of things blamed on him).

The third Act begins in the Library after lunch, where Bluntschli is working up orders for troop movements, and Sergius is reduced to just signing them, while Petkoff keeps trying to be "useful", he eventually asks about his old coat ... which is now hanging back in a closet where he'd looked for it previously, and is brought to him by Nicola. Later, Raina and Bluntschli are having a discussion and she asks what he thought of her giving him her portrait – with a note to the "chocolate-cream soldier", which she had put in the pocket of the coat – and Bluntschli hadn't discovered. In the meanwhile, Louka has rejected Nicola (to whom she had supposedly been engaged), and has been sought after by Sergius (who is less dedicated to Raina than she declares to be to him), who claims to want to marry her. Much confusion ensues, and eventually the truth of the situation of Raina's room being where Bluntschli had hidden comes out. More confusion ensues and Raina finds that Sergius has been pursuing Louka ... and the couples come together (Raina with Bluntschli – who has been revealed as being the heir to a substantial hotel chain – and Sergius with Louka). The play rather oddly ends with Bluntschli heading off to take care of other matters, and promising to come back in two weeks.

I'm sure this is quite charming on the stage, and I hope to see it performed at some point. While hardly a "deep" work, it's well written, and reasonably well developed for its fairly brief length. It is an enjoyable read, and something that pretty much anybody could appreciate. As noted above, the Dover Thrift Edition of Arms & The Man[3] is quite inexpensive, with a $2.50 cover price, however, at this writing Amazon has it at *only a buck*, which is pretty remarkable.

Notes:

1. http://btripp-books.livejournal.com/185778.html

2-3. http://amzn.to/1THscB5

Sunday, June 19, 2016[1]

The tyranny of good intentions?

A few months back, I did a review of Jeremy Rifkin's The Zero Marginal Cost Society[2], which referred frequently to his previous book (or, perhaps the central concept thereof), The Third Industrial Revolution: How Lateral Power Is Transforming Energy, the Economy, and the World[3] ... and I was interested enough to order a copy. Now, I probably mentioned that I didn't have a particularly positive initial image of Rifkin, although I rather liked his newer book, probably due to his being connected in my mind with the felonious Clinton regime. Well, this book, while quite interesting and thought-provoking, clarified what I was disliking about him – he's an out-right "anti-Libertarian" (which says to me that he's a wipe-your-butt-with-the-Constitution type, like the current POTUS), and a *HUGE* fan of Big Government, in fact (judging from this book), pretty much "the bigger, the better", with shifting as much control as possible from individuals to smarmy bureaucrats and cold, faceless, governmental departments. Do. Not. Like.

In the course of this book, he advocates for tyrannical control over pretty much ANYTHING you can think of under governmental organizations, and preferably *global* government – based on the model of the E.U., not the U.S.A. It's telling that the (relatively few for 124 copies) 4 reviews of this over on LibraryThing.com are all in languages other than English (3 French, 1 Spanish) ... which seems to make sense as most of his actual work has been with foreign governments and institutions.

He also evidently "got deeper into it" as the book went on, as I have a half-dozen bookmarks in the first half of the book, and none in the second half. The book is in three Parts, "The Third Industrial Revolution", "Lateral Power", and "The Collaborative Age" all nice catch-phrases with nasty underlying dynamics, from a rejection of the sorts of economics which are the core of American values, to a really frightening re-visioning of education into lowest-common-denominator *"webs of shared relationships"* where excelling would be seen as degrading for the average, and would (*à la* Diana Moon Glampers[4]) be driven down to the level of a bland, uninspired, and easily-controlled sheep-like mass.

That being said ... let me turn to the parts of this that I *didn't* hate.

First of all, there's the title concept, that of the "Third Industrial Revolution", which he shortens to TIR (certainly not to be confused with Týr[5]) though most of the book. I'll admit that there's something to be said for his idea of pairing power sources and communications technologies to define the nature of various "industrial revolutions". Here's basically how he breaks these out:

        1st Industrial Revolution:
        19th Century
        Steam Power
        (Coal)
        Letterpress Printing

> 2nd Industrial Revolution:
> 20th Century
> Combustion Engine
> (Oil)
> Electronic Communications
>
> 3rd Industrial Revolution
> 21st Century
> Renewable Energies
> ("Green")
> The Internet

He also defines "5 pillars" (*religious imagery* much?) of the Third Industrial Revolution – these are:

> 1. shifting to renewable energy;
>
> 2. transforming the building stock of every continent into green micro–power plants to collect renewable energies on-site;
>
> 3. deploying hydrogen and other storage technologies in every building and throughout the infrastructure to store intermittent energies;
>
> 4. using Internet technology to transform the power grid of every continent into an energy internet that acts just like the Internet (when millions of buildings are generating a small amount of renewable energy locally, on-site, they can sell surplus green electricity back to the grid and share it with their continental neighbors); and
>
> 5. transitioning the transport fleet to electric plug-in and fuel cell vehicles that can buy and sell green electricity on a smart, continental, interactive power grid.

Sounds swell, until you realize that this will require the replacement of nearly every building, and having government control over ALL construction EVERYWHERE. Plus, Rifkin isn't particularly visionary on the energy side of the equation ... he's convinced various European cities to slap up low-efficiency solar panels over nearly every surface, but he doesn't even *mention* GenIV nuclear reactors (being actively pursued by both India and China) that can be powered by consuming spent fuel from old-style reactors, and solve two problems at once ... but I guess the idea of having a "neighborhood" reactor is too "individualistic" for Rifkin, whose entire focus appears to be on government control of all aspects of society.

In the early chapters, Rifkin describes himself starting out as *"a young activist weaned on the anti-Vietnam War and civil rights movement of the 1960s"* and describes his growing up in the same parts of Chicago that were the home turf of the vile Saul Alinsky[6] (beloved of both Obama *and* Hillary Clinton[7]). While he claims to have affinity for Jefferson, Franklin, Paine, and Washington (my favorites among the founding fathers as well), as opposed to his youthful associates' heroes of Mao Tse-tung, Ho Chi Minh and the butcher Che Guevara, you'd never guess it in his end-game here. Frankly, much of this book sounds like an echo of the current administration's "you didn't build that" lie.

Now, this book came out in 2011, and it's never really fair to judge projections on "20/20 hindsight", but he pushes a lot of agendas here which, as far as I know, have completely "fallen off the table" (what happened to the promise by the chairman of auto company Daimler to *"mass produce hydrogen powered fuel cell cars, trucks, and buses in 2015"* ... I must have missed the articles on those). So much of this book deals with meetings of panels, task forces, and mid-level governmental functionaries (OK, plus some heads of state), all churning through a lot of verbiage. But what's getting *done*? It's like throwing the future of the race on the mercies of the DMV ... take a number and they'll get to you when they feel like it. While I've not delved into these topics in any particular depth, it seems to me that *businesses* are far more efficient in delivering these new technologies.

However, Rifkin doesn't see it that way, he describes entrepreneurs as *"predatory and unsavory, consumed with self-interest and unconcerned with the public welfare"* ... but I'd sure trust an Elon Musk, Peter Diamandis, or Jeff Bezos over the [Dolores Umbridge][8]-style bureaucrats that seem to populate his vision of the future.

I am probably being too hard on [The Third Industrial Revolution][9], but for every "inspiring" bit in here there are 2-3 "aggravating" things that totally triggered me (and I'm not the only reviewer having issues with it, [this][10] is a very telling over-view from a German source). The world that Rifkin seems to *want* sounds like it's to be run with some global version of the IRS, wielding total control on where you live, how you live, what you can do, what you can *think*, and how you can relate to others. That sounds like a classic dystopia to me ... but you might be more aligned to his views and be more "gee wiz" on the programs that he *has* put in place in various locations around the globe.

This is still in print, in both hardcover and paperback, but the on-line new/used guys have "very good" copies of the hardcover for a penny (plus shipping), and I'd hope you wouldn't pay more than that for it. Again, there's a lot of interesting stuff in here, but what there is lies buried in a matrix of tyrannical big government wet dreams, with a decided Leftist bent, so it's sort of hard to take from where I'm sitting ... but, as usual, *"your mileage may vary"*.

Notes:
1. http://btripp-books.livejournal.com/186076.html
2. http://btripp-books.livejournal.com/171323.html
3. http://amzn.to/1TU4IAx
4. https://goo.gl/IsrwX5
5. https://goo.gl/PBXSju
6. https://goo.gl/fphniZ
7. https://goo.gl/BWGqwA
8. https://goo.gl/eWQNMb
9. http://amzn.to/1TU4IAx
10. https://goo.gl/QTMXL0

Tuesday, June 21, 2016[1]

Looking for Emmanuel Goldstein?

This wasn't something that I sought out, although I certainly knew the author from his late-night show *Red Eye* from back when I was up all night, every night, but was only sort of vaguely aware that he'd published books (he has four out in his current role as a punk/conservative gadfly, plus one from a previous manifestation). However, when I saw Greg Gutfeld's mug staring out at me from the dollar store shelf a couple of months back, I was pretty quick to toss The Joy of Hate: How to Triumph over Whiners in the Age of Phony Outrage[2] into the shopping cart.

Frankly, if I were involved in the editorial/marketing process on this, I'd have fought for a different title ... sure, "The Joy of Hate" is semi-cute, playing on iconic books such as *The Joy of Cooking* and *The Joy of Sex*, but it's not *that* cute, and really doesn't reflect the main thrust of the book (unless one takes this – quite possible if one is of the right mindset – as an invitation for an Orwellian "hate"[3] directed at the objects of the author's derision). A better (or, more descriptive) title could actually be spun out of the *subtitle*, "How to Triumph over Whiners in the Age of Phony Outrage", as that's pretty much what the book is *about*, although, admittedly, rolling it around in my head, I wasn't coming up with anything particularly catchy to suggest as an alternative.

Gutfeld is a bit of an acquired taste, as his *shtick* is sarcastic, smarmy at times, and laced with a lot of fairly bizarre bits of self-deprecating humor. He also tends to spew out somewhat rambling rants here, making it challenging to pull out pithy quotes (although, as you can see from the picture over there ==>, I did manage to plant a veritable *forest* of my little bookmarks in it). As noted, the book deals with the "whiners" (liberal/left types) and the ever-present "Phony Outrage" they (and the MSM) are so fond of promulgating. Gutfeld distributes his 225 pages across 27 areas where different varieties of this "outrage" get expressed – generally orbiting around a concept that he describes as "repressive tolerance", the Left's eagerness to embrace anything that is destructive to how America has been much of the past century or two, and unwilling to allow for anything that disagrees.

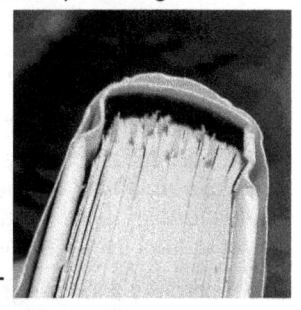

To be honest, this was a *very uncomfortable* read for me, as the stuff that Gutfeld shines his snarky light on are exactly the type of things that keep me from watching the MSM ... or, have me *screaming at the TV* if I make the mistake of actually exposing myself to the so-called "news" shows ... and so walking through this particular mine field was an adventure in spiking blood pressure and intense teeth grinding. It would probably have been "more fun" if there *was* an organized "hate" for each of these ... not only pointing out how monstrously hypocritical the Left is in their intolerant "tolerance", but also having a good stress-releasing go at them! Of course, that's *me*, and I'm, if anything, *angrier* than Gutfeld at those sorts of morons, so consider your placement on the left-right scale before you opt to go venturing into The Joy of Hate[4], because if you're "on the other side" you may well find some of your most cherished group-think beliefs made fun of, if not gored like the proverbial sacred cow.

It probably wouldn't be overly useful for me to list the topics, and certainly not the chapter headings (which are delightful, but more evocative than descriptive, from "Working at the Death Star" which is about his career at Fox News, on to truly delightful ones like "I'm OK, You Should Die"), but suffice it to say, he covers a *lot* of territory, pretty much hitting all the possible hot spots of Lefty intolerance for anything that doesn't agree with their world view. So, I guess I'm going to take a little walk through all those bookmarks, and cherry-pick bits and pieces to give you a sense of what's in here.

Let's start with a sample from the Introduction:

> *The media, for the most part, tends to dismiss the "outrage" perpetrated by the left, often dismissing the slurs and smears as the product of "edgy comedy", only because they rabidly agree with whatever's being said. ... This liberal pass, however, is not afforded to those on the right. If Maher calls somebody a slut, the outcry lasts a few days. When Rush says it, the outrage lasts as long as a case of herpes. It flares up and never really goes away ...*

He goes on to note:

> *... because of tolerance, there are no repercussions for bad behavior. And bad behavior won't just continue, but will accelerate, because the tolerati ... provide the grease for the wheels.*

In the nicely alliterative "The Bigot Spigot" chapter, Gutfeld describes the health care bill's being *"rammed through Congress like a torn-up dollar bill in a Coke machine"* as making *"Caligula's method of government seem positively modest"* ... which does beg for various lines of comparison being drawn to the current administration and its co-conspirators!

The next bit is a longer grab since I couldn't ellipsis it enough to make it pithy and short, but it has a good message (in the chapter dealing with various ways the Left has attempted to "spin" repeated Islamist attacks into categories that better fit their on-going narrative):

> *Now, somehow I just don't think viewing these threats as potential examples of workplace violence is going to be our most effective method of attack. What are we going to see on the walls next to the "no smoking" signs? Posters that exclaim, "No massacres in the name of Allah"?*
>
> *Fact is, we are living under a government that's head over heels in love with euphemisms. Whether it's "man-caused disasters" or "workplace violence",*

> our leaders can't stop creating new lies out of old words. Taxing the rich is now "paying our fair share". Class warfare is now called "a war on inequity". As I've said before, calling the Fort Hood massacre workplace violence is like calling Pearl Harbor an air show.

... and you get the idea that had that attack happened under the current POTUS, his vile administration *would* call it a freaking "air show"!

The above-mentioned "Death Star" chapter has lots and lots of good bits, but you don't want to have me type out *pages* of quotes, do you? Here, however, *are* a couple of choice ones:

> Freedom of expression and tolerating points of view are {whiny liberals'} expressed desires ... unless you, um, disagree with them on something. Then it's sooo over, you Nazi!

and

> All entertainment options came saddled with {liberals'} approved assumptions: Movies, theater, the art world, magazine publishing, newspapers, comedians ... – you name it – they all uniformly turn left as if they're performing in an ideological NASCAR event.

... which is one of the best lines in here! He goes on to discuss having Leftists on *Red Eye*, etc.:

> Because I'm confident in my mission, presenting liberal perspectives should *only* make whatever else that much stronger. Seriously, put a leftist on any show and you see how much more sensible the right is. You have me sitting there sounding reasonable and anyone to my left morphs into one of those LSD experiments from the fifties ...

Fun. One of the useful rules of thumb he comes up with there is this gem: "Whenever you see the word <u>dialogue</u> in a political context, you are in the presence of pure, unadulterated bullshit of the liberal variety.", which he then points out in any subsequent bit that involves the d-word.

In the "I'm OK, You Should Die" chapter he goes on about the gross double-standard of "wishing ill" on one's ideological opponents. He cites numerous examples where those on the conservative side slipped into this zone and got roundly chastised by their fellows, which leads into:

> If you're going to be intolerant of that kind of thing when it's said about people you like, you gotta do the same for those you don't. ... The left isn't so consistent. You can wish death or ill will on anyone from George Bush to Sarah Palin, and you'll proba-

> bly get a grin from every liberal blogger, comic, and talking head. But say anything like that about a precious liberal icon and you will be run out of town.

In the also delightfully-titled chapter "Stalin Grads", which largely deals with the cretinous Occupy Wall Street "movement", there is the one point in the book where the author drops the "ironic" filter and goes direct:

> But historians know: What begins as a utopian vision always – <u>always</u> – ends in bloodshed. Because you have to force utopia on a free people. Free people want to pursue their own happiness, but a one-size-fits-all approach requires herding the free, against their will, into the state's idea of what's right. Then it's not utopia. It's Uganda. It's 100 million dead. ... And it's not like the folks behind the {Occupy} movement have hidden their intentions. ...

Finally, here's one bit about how the left gets to be as violent, racist, and misogynistic as they want ...

> What's truly amazing is how the left seems baffled by the revulsion it causes. ... To them it's daring comedy. Why is that? It's because liberals are surrounded by liberals all day, and so they develop a massive blind spot concerning what's acceptable to everyone else ... you essentially spend all your time around people who share your assumptions, which makes it exceedingly easy for you to say what's on your mind.

I'd mentioned that there's a lot of self-deprecating humor in this, and a number of the ellipses inserted in the quoted bits above were to present the concepts without the sidebars, but I guess I'd be remiss if I didn't put in at least one example. This is how the "Harmed Forces" chapter starts:

> I love a man in uniform. And I'm not talking about my house-boys (sarongs hardly qualify as a uniform). But for the left, tolerance is rarely afforded to the military.

Most of these involve his stature, bad habits, and assorted sexual elements ... which I figured I could spare you. Again, The Joy of Hate[5] is not a read without challenges, as Gutfeld is strategically "in the face" of the reader, making it somewhat uncomfortable for all (well, I'm sure whackjobs like Pelosi or Feinstein would *really* get their panties in a wad over this, while fundies like Huckabee somewhat less). One of the more interesting personal stories here is how the author was a Punk, and has numerous notables from the music biz name-checked ... so on one level I guess he's channeling Johnny Rotten's attitude here.

The paperback of this is still on the on-line big boys' sites at very nearly full retail, so I guess I lucked out hitting the hardcover at the dollar store (which gets stuff being rotated off of Walmart's shelves) when I did. The latter has, as is frequently the case, found its way to the new/used vendors' listings, with many "very good" copies to be had for a penny plus shipping ... were this sounding like something you'd like to check out.

Notes:

1. http://btripp-books.livejournal.com/186326.html
2. http://amzn.to/1UkKw6T
3. https://en.wikipedia.org/wiki/Two_Minutes_Hate
4-5. http://amzn.to/1UkKw6T

Wednesday, June 22, 2016[1]

Memories ... tasty, tasty memories ...

This was another dollar store buy ... it seems like a few months ago a *lot* of food industry related titles started showing up, and (at a buck) I figured "why not?". As I've noted in previous reviews, I "grew up in the food industry", or at least in the consumer food products end of things (and the PR/marketing end of that) ... heck, there's a picture out there of me at 6 months old, reaching for product up on the shelf of the Swift test kitchens ... so the food biz is very much in my blood, and I have a lot of background in it, making books like Gail Simmons' Talking with My Mouth Full: My Life as a Professional Eater[2] more interesting to me than one might assume from the past couple of decades of my career.

Oddly, I don't know if I've ever seen Ms. Simmons' show, *Top Chef: Just Desserts* ... in fact, I've not been able to come up with a mental image of the Top Chef show at all, which is strange, as the cooking shows are one of those "fall back" options when nothing else is on, and I've watched a lot of Iron Chef and Chopped, etc. over the years. Maybe we don't get Bravo, or it's off in one of those backwaters not an easy up/down channel from the other stuff I watch (I just discovered that we *did* still get Fox News a few weeks ago, after assuming our TV provider dropped it a couple of years ago from the cheap/free package we have – yes, I *do* find the on-screen menu thing totally unworkable, thank you). Anyway, this led me to come to Talking with My Mouth Full[3] with a reasonably blank slate as I didn't know either the author or her show (although I was quite familiar with *Food & Wine* magazine, but the names I would have known there probably preceded her by a decade or so).

When I picked this up, I wasn't expecting that it was going to be so much of an actual *autobiography*, and sort of thought it was going to be more generally about the industry, but this is tightly connected to Simmons' life/career, so while there are bits that are *generalized* out of those experiences, the book closely follows the specifics of where she was and what she was doing. I suspect that it was this that led to there being almost *none* of my little bookmarks in here for interesting stuff to stick in this review ... meaning that you're going to be getting more "broad strokes" in this than I probably would have preferred.

The book starts, as one might expect in an autobiography, with her family and childhood. One of the on-going threads here is her Jewish heritage, with her father being a South African immigrant to Canada, and her mother hailing from Montreal, and how they met in Toronto. Aside from the Jewish milieu she grew up in, the whole Canadian thing is a major part of the story, especially when it came to visas, etc. necessary to stay/work in the U.S.

Her exit from college sounded very familiar to me:

> Was I the only person without a clue about the next step? It sure felt that way. My parents and my

> friends' parents expected great things from their children, and great things usually involved post-graduate degrees. Graduate school is great if you know what you want to do. But I didn't have the foggiest idea. None of the things my friends were doing interested me. ... I felt at the time like the only one in my crowd – full of so many bright, strong young women – who really didn't know what she wanted to be. So where did that leave me?

Fortunately for her, a friend of the family came by while she was sulking in her parent's basement following graduation, and told her to *"Make a list of what you like to do. Not jobs. Just anything that comes into your mind."* ... what she ended up with was the rather non-specific: *"Eat. Write. Travel. Cook."* (my list from the same stage in my life might have read quite similarly, likely with "drink" replacing "cook"). Needless to say, those four words eventually came to embody her career path.

She attended McGill University and began to write restaurant reviews for the school paper, which eventually led to an internship with *Toronto Life*, then to the *National Post*, where she was a bit at loose ends, and was told *"If you want to write about food, you need to speak the language. ... Go learn how to cook and how to eat."*, which led her to New York, and Peter Kump's cooking school (I'd had some contact with Mr. Kump, who died in '95, via the Beard Foundation back in the day – nice guy).

Now, the chronological arc in the preceding leaves out a *lot* of material ... a good deal of the book involves places she ate, places she traveled to, what she ate when she was there, the culinary interests of her family (there's a recipe for her father's pickles), etc., but it's all so enmeshed in the matrix of the telling, that it seems pointless to try to extract any of the individual elements here.

She details her experience in cooking school, which she anticipated would lead to working at a top-tier test kitchen, but she was told by the career services head at Kump: *"... you still don't know how to cook ... the only way to truly solidify your skills is to work in a restaurant and cook on the line"* they were able to place her in some amazing restaurants, however:

> I would go on to work in two kitchens: Le Cirque for only six weeks and Vong for a few months. In that whole time, I was the only woman in both."

The stories she tells of life in the kitchen are quite interesting, especially as I've not read a lot (such as Anthony Bourdain's notorious *Kitchen Confidential*) in that area. What is more amazing is the tale of her time working as fabled *Vogue* food critic Jeffrey Steingarten's assistant. The author had read his *The Man Who Ate Everything*, and was fascinated by his descriptions of his assistant – the things that she was doing was exactly what Simmons wanted to do – and went back to the culinary school to see if they knew of any jobs *like* that ... remarkably, the placement guy had just seen Steingarten the week before and he'd said he was looking for a new assistant, and, somewhat implausibly, she got the gig (she notes her timing ended up being perfect, as Steingarten was at the point of getting desperate to have a new person in place). If you're not familiar with some of the "bigger than life" characters in the food industry, you may find the stories of her working with him hard to believe, but they're something to see (read) ... for example, while working on a story about espresso machines, they had *eighteen* ordered in, and, after testing these for weeks *"Jeffrey decided that it was basically impossible to make a good espresso unless you had a $10,000 professional upright Italian espresso maker with a brass eagle on top"*.

After two years of working for Steingarten, she felt she had to move on. She'd contacted restauranteur Daniel Boulud for advice (Steingarten dined at his place frequently so she'd become a friend) on a new position, and his marketing gal expressed interest, but couldn't afford the hire at the time. Simmons then went on a vacation, where she contracted Epstein-Barr, and had to return to Canada (and back in her parents' basement) to recover ... leaving her boyfriend in New York. Towards the end of her convalescence, she heard from him that she'd had a call from the marketing gal, who was asking if she was available ... so she returned to New York for that job. Again "the stars were aligned" for her, because their restaurant group had numerous foreign-born staff members, and kept an immigration lawyer on retainer, so her needing a visa (which had been a problem at other job options) was easily taken care of.

The stories of the years she worked at *Daniels* are also informative, as she breaks down a lot of the "technical workings" of the restaurant biz ... including an amazing 2-page diagram of all the positions, and how they fit into the organizational chart. At the restaurant she did most of the special event work, and some other marketing functions, but there was only one marketing director (the gal who had hired her), and she wasn't going anywhere, so Simmons had to consider her next move. This came along via another serendipitous connection, a marketing guy from *Food & Wine* had become a friend, and when he was getting ready to leave his gig there, he outright asked her "do you want my job?"! She also had good timing because not long after she was on staff, the organizer of the *Food & Wine* Classic in Aspen went on maternity leave, and she got to step in. One of the features of the Classic was a head-to-head competition between two chefs, which set her up for the eventual TV gig at *Top Chef*.

The rest of Talking with My Mouth Full[4] is stories from the TV show, talking about her wedding, and the development of the *Just Desserts* spin-off ... lots of name dropping here, lots of insider insight into the TV cooking biz, and a lot of food and travel mentioned (like serendipitously getting to go to the tuna auction in Tokyo's Tsukiji Fish Market when on her honeymoon). The last dozen pages are an interesting concept ... her taking a look at a day's food, in recipes that track bits of the book – from eggs she learned to make during a summer in Israel to the Welsh Rarebit that was a feature of her proposal "picnic" – and, as noted above, the recipe for her dad's pickles.

This is one of those dollar store finds that's still evidently in print, and selling well enough that the on-line big boys have it at just a normal discount (so should be available in the surviving brick & mortar book vendors). It is, however (as is often the case when they've hit the dollar store), available for cheap via the new/used guys ... with "like new" copies of the hardcover going for as little as 1¢ (plus $3.99 shipping, natch).

If you're interested in these areas of the food biz, but aren't already in it, this would be a very interesting read, given that Ms. Simmons' career takes her through so much of it. It's also very rich with food memories (again, I barely touched on that aspect here), making it one of those literally mouth-watering reads. This isn't a ground-breaking "must read", but it's well worth the effort if you have a hankering for this stuff.

Notes:

1. http://btripp-books.livejournal.com/186370.html
2-4. http://amzn.to/1UGRz5C

Thursday, June 30, 2016[1]

Unless It Comes with a Comfy Chair …

This is another of those LibraryThing.com "Early Reviewer" program books. As I've noted previously, these typically have a only a paragraph or two on the site describing them, so users have to put in their "requests" for the offered books based on fairly sketchy information … so while a book may sound like it would be "interesting", it's rare that one really knows what one's getting into until it actually shows up. I was sort of expecting that *"a world-famous theoretical physicist with hundreds of scientific articles and several books of popular science to his credit"* would have been producing a more "sciency" book, but Marcelo Gleiser's The Simple Beauty of the Unexpected: A Natural Philosopher's Quest for Trout and the Meaning of Everything[2] is a somewhat muddled combination of science discussions, autobiographical sketch, travelogue, and an enthusiast's paean to fly fishing.

The author hails from Rio de Janeiro in Brazil, where he first got hooked on fishing as a boy, hitting the famed Copacabana beach several times a week. As he grew up, he left fishing behind, eventually becoming a physicist (from a country that has only a handful of jobs for physicists), doing his graduate work in the U.K., and eventually moving to the U.S., ending up as a Professor of Physics and Astronomy at Dartmouth College.

Gleiser and his (second) wife were out walking on the Dartmouth campus one day, and encountered a class of novices being introduced to fly fishing. He was evidently smitten by the activity, and his wife decided to get him that class for their anniversary. He took the class, bought all the requisite gear, and made a go of it a few times, but was unable to balance the time required with the frustration involved … he notes: *"you have to embrace it full-heartedly in order for it to work"*. After a few years had passed, his wife prodded him to try again … and he began to get up before dawn, and head down to a local river to fish. This is the first point where the "metaphysical" aspects of the book come to play, as he's constantly having "encounters" with his young self who encourages him in his efforts.

The book is set up in four sections, each anchored to a particular event (usually an international conference somewhere around which he is able to schedule time with a fishing tour guide), and generally themed with a "scientific philosophy" issue. These are:

- Cumbria, Lake District, UK
- São José dos Ausentes, Rio Grande do Sul, Brazil
- Sansepolcro, Tuscany, Italy
- Laxá River, Mývatnssveit, Iceland

To be honest, I really did not connect much at all with the fishing parts of this … although some sound to be in amazing locations, and are quite beautifully written about … but that material reads like any enthusiast's enthusing about their particular "thing" (it could be model railroading, cosplay, or wine collecting), no doubt interesting to the extent of exposing one to information not previously encountered, but not having the pull to make the reader really *care* if they're not already into the particular activity.

Oh, and I think I have an actual *spoiler* to pass along here (unusual in non-fiction reading) … so if you don't want to see it, quickly skip to the next paragraph. OK. Here it comes … ready? You sure? Last warning … One of the sub-themes here is his epiphany of how his vegetarian diet is poorly reflected in his fishing. Generally speaking, I felt like the tone "devolved" somewhat over the course of the book, and while I wouldn't necessarily call the direction as being into the "shrill" zone, it certainly gets to feeling "preachy" and "holier-than-thou" at points. While one can congratulate the author for trying to resolve the implicit cognitive dissonance of his vegetarianism and the "violence" being done to the fish, the "journey" to that point (in parallel with flag-waving for some popular leftist "scientific" stances) turns what is, for the first two-thirds or so, a reasonably pleasant read into something that feels like it's subtly brow-beating the reader … leaving *this* reader, at least, feeling somewhat abused by the time the pontificating (and book) ends.

The U.K trip is anchored by a "workshop on classical field theory", and that section starts off quite promisingly with Gleiser sort of free-form "riffing" about fields. While this is entertaining to read (going from pre-Socratic philosophers to current research), it's also a bit hard to cherry-pick coherent quotes from. He goes from familiar field concepts and then veers off into discussing "matter fields" and even "communication fields" (he at one point writes: *"for physicists like me who deal with the inner structure of matter and the cosmos, everything is a field of some sort"*), which then flips over to a discussion of quanta, and waves. This leads into a story of a Scottish engineer in 1834 who encountered a "solitary wave" ("soliton" - *"a bundle of particles interacting with each other so as to behave as a single non-changing entity"*), which leads to musing on "solitary activities", such as fly-fishing, as well as intros the topic of his presentation, that of "oscillons"[3] (too complicated to try to define here – click on the link if you want to read up on this).

It turns out that his fishing guide has a PhD in theoretical chemistry, from the same school (King's College in London) that the author attended, and this leads off into more philosophical pondering on the nature of reality, with much name-checking of leading lights of science, from Galileo to Planck, and the question of *belief* within the scientific community, including the big cosmic divide in theoretical physics between the supersymmetry and multiverse camps – with mention of research currently being done at the Large Hadron Collider which is targeted to shed some light on which of these hypotheses is more likely.

The bulk of the book (about 40%) is in this first section, and the author goes into a lot more side discussions than in the later, shorter, ones. One of these is a story from his teenage years (further illustrating the "faith" angle), when his father fired a cook who (only discovered *during* a dinner for a very important guest) had been drinking all the whiskeys, etc., in the liquor cabinet and replacing the liquid with *tea*. Unfortunately, said cook *"was a high priestess of the Macumba, a syncretic religious practices widespread in Brazil"*, who openly put a curse on the house in response. The author was the witness of what seemed to be the fulfilling of this as he was mysteriously drawn to the dining room, just in time to see the glass shelves of the liquor cabinet and serving cart simultaneously collapse, destroying all the crystal, etc., with no evident (non-occult) cause. This leads to a sub-section on "Reason, Faith and the Incompleteness of Knowledge", which includes looking at the concepts of our "cosmic horizon" (*"the bubble of information defined by the distance that light has traveled since the Big Bang"*), "worm holes", and assorted philosophical backwaters such as the "Ionian Fallacy" (the belief that all genuine questions have one true answer) ... which also provides the first point for the book to start slipping into politics. There is a lot of navel-gazing going on here, including another return to the author's youth, and the loss of his mother, which drove him to desperately try to "see" her ghostly form, but whenever he managed to evoke the vision *"she would vanish in thin air, like a rainbow made of hope"*. The fishing story is almost an afterthought here, wedged in between his mother's ghost and his father's insistence that he be an engineer (saying *"who is going to pay you to count stars?"*).

The section on Brazil continues with the "belief" theme. He's back in his home country for a promotional tour for a novel he'd published, and was lured to a book fair in the far-southern city of Porto Alegre with the promise of actual Brazilian fly-fishing. His talk centered around "changing views", scientific, religious, and, at their intersection, cosmological. He spins off of this into a discussion of atheism (which he practices), and how that concept has developed through history. One bit that I marked to illustrate this is:

> *I find it quite ironic to see {a religious fundamentalist} happily using a GPS, talking on a cell phone, or, when illness comes, taking antibiotics or going for radiation therapy. How is it that the technological offspring of quantum and relativistic physics may be conveniently used as needed but not the revolutionary worldview they brought forth? The same science used to build these gadgets is used to date fossils, Earth's age, and life's evolutionary trajectory from bacteria to people. It's mind-boggling. And yet, this eyes-tightly-shut perspective is the only option for an alarmingly large number of people, not just religious extremists.*

And, it's not just the assorted flavors of "fundies" that get his derision, he also notes that *"some in the New Age movement ... ground their beliefs in a science pulled completely out of context ... using concepts like 'energy', 'quantum', or 'field', in ways that have very little to do with their physics counterparts"*. The bits on fishing are somewhat more expansive here, veering off into a contemplation of our urge to take the biggest/strongest fish (or any hunted species), which ultimately weakens the gene pool. He also muses on returning to places ... he avoids his old neighborhood *"to hold on to the little of my past that my memory can preserve"* ... and our "place" in the world.

The Italy section is centered on a conference of the International Astrobiology Society, taking place in Florence. On this trip, he starts with the fishing, then returns to Florence for the conference. Here his guide introduces him to fishing in the dark ... which led to dreams of his younger self and his mother. Most of this section (the shortest of the four) is taken up with discussions of general cosmological theories, from the gas composition of the primordial universe, to the life-cycles of stars, leading up to the formation of our solar system, and the origin of Earth. Gleiser goes on to trace the development of terrestrial life, and what that might imply for life elsewhere. He has an interesting view on what makes humanity stand out:

> *Humans have an urge to explore the unknown, what lies beyond their immediate reach. This may be our species' most distinguishable trait. Animals want to be safe, living within familiar boundaries that don't expose them to any extra risk. They keep to their tried, well-adapted behavioral patterns, a recipe that allows them to thrive. … Humans, on the other hand, have a need to lunge into the unknown, to expose themselves to what is uncomfortable, even threatening. We take risks as individuals and as a species, continually pushing ourselves beyond established limits. We like our boundaries elastic, safe but expandable.*

He finishes this section with a look at the "is anybody out there?" question, and isn't particularly optimistic of there being any, despite the large numbers of likely habitable planets that both *should* be out there statistically, and are almost daily being identified by our space-based telescopes.

The Iceland section comes from an opportunity made available to him by a Dartmouth alumni group, which invited him to lead a series of lectures on a cruise around the island. However, he brought his very pregnant wife (and their 5-year-old son), and, while her doctors back in the states had OK'd her for the trip, the ship's officials felt it was too hazardous to have her on board due to some of the very isolated areas they'd be in. They had to disembark, and change the schedule from several lectures across the whole of the cruise, to one substantial "seminar" at the end, which caused them to have to improvise their own tour of Iceland. One of the fascinating things about that part of the world is that: *"The belief in* Huldufólk {in the book it's written *hundúfolk*, but I was unable to find any references to that on-line} *(hidden people) is so pervasive that construction projects often have to deviate from sites and stones where elves are believed to dwell.".* There's a lot about the volcanic nature of Iceland, and some of the issues with recent and historical volcanism, and a discussion of creation myths. Interesting, both the Icelandic narrative, and one from China (around 300ce), describe the creation of the world from the corpse of a slain giant, whose skull becomes the sky, blood becomes rivers and oceans, bones forming rocks and mountains, hair turning into trees, etc., and in both cases, humanity arising from the maggots eating his flesh!

The author spins from this to a look at current views of cosmic origins, from the Big Bang onward, and eventually comes to a point where he points out that *"all that exists has a common origin"*. This is where the "soapbox" comes out and we're into the vegetarian lecture … which, while raising assorted very valid ethical points, is quite aggressive. But, he's not done with beating the reader up at the end of *that* … as this leads right into a whole "global warming" (at least he's not using the "climate change" euphemism) tirade, which, admittedly was what he was scheduled to be talking to the Dartmouth alumnae about during the cruise. Lecture completed, he sends his wife and son back to the States, and heads off for his Icelandic fishing adventure. However, while in the midst of this: *"Something had changed inside, a feeling of complicity with the fish, of humility as a fellow living creature sharing the same planet. ... We can be close to Nature without maiming its creations."*. I guess he's presenting this as his big "enlightened human" moment, but in the arc of the book, it's a real downer for the ending.

The Simple Beauty of the Unexpected[4] is a mixed bag (one might be tempted to say "neither fish nor fowl"), but is interesting on various levels throughout (even in the "soapbox" parts). At this writing, the book has just been out a few weeks, so it's likely to be available via your local still-extant brick-and-mortar book vendors ... however, the on-line big boys are offering it at about 1/3rd off of cover price, which is likely your best bet if this sounds like something you'd like to check out.

Notes:

1. http://btripp-books.livejournal.com/186705.html
2. http://amzn.to/1XZPxF2
3. https://en.wikipedia.org/wiki/Oscillon
4. http://amzn.to/1XZPxF2

Wednesday, July 6, 2016[1]

An excellent introduction ...

This was another LibraryThing.com "Early Reviewers" selection that the "Almighty Algorithm" matched up with my collection over there. At first I was sharing some of the other reviewers' consternation that this book originated out of a *children's* program at a Hawaiian Zen temple, *"based on* {the author's} *experience as a Zen priest and an elementary school teacher"*, a data point not suggested *at all* in its descriptive paragraph in the LTER listings. However, if one takes a step back from that genesis, one is faced with a really very good "introductory" book about Buddhism (albeit primarily from a Zen perspective).

Richard Gentei Diedrichs' Living in Blue Sky Mind: Basic Buddhist Teachings for a Happy Life[2] covers a lot of ground, with over 80 chapters (each illustrating one particular point from the Buddhist perspective) in its brief 162 pages. Each chapter is 1-2 pages of text, followed by a "Reflecting" section featuring 1-5 questions for the reader to contemplate regarding the material in that chapter (ranging from the very basic like *"How does being good help us and everyone around us?"*, to the technical as in *"What is a mental formation"*, to the more obscure such as *"What did Chogyam Trungpa mean when he called Sangha 'clean friendship'?"*).

Obviously, nothing here is considered *in depth*, but I was very pleased to find what it lacked there, it made up in *breadth*, as the book is a quite attractive (and certainly *accessible*) over-view on Buddhism (although, with its Zen grounding, a Theravada practitioner might not be as enthusiastic about it). I have been *reading* Buddhist books for decades (part of me wishes I had been *practicing* all that while, but *no*), and this is, I think, one of the best introductory pieces that I've seen.

If I had one gripe here, personally, it would be that I would have liked to have seen more *structure*, even to the point of pedagogical presentation of the material. The sections of this are, however, fairly evidently crafted to appeal to an audience of children, so the text is light-handed in doling out the information, such as this paragraph at the start of the chapter ("How to Solve the Problem") which introduces the concept of "the Middle Way":

> *If we know that craving causes us so much trouble and sadness, as Buddha indicated, we might also know that we are happy when we stop craving. If we understand how life works, we also are happy.*

There are also, notably, eleven indexes and a glossary. I would have liked to have had more of this material interspersed in the book itself, but the component elements of these *are* the main subjects of most of the "chapters", so I guess it would have created a situation of the author "getting ahead of himself" repeatedly through the book ... but these are as short as *six words* (and that's including the heading). I suppose listing these out here will give you a good sense of what's in the book (although it doesn't march through these in order): "Eightfold Path", "The Four Noble Truths", "The Six Virtues/Perfections/Paramitas", "The Four Wisdoms / Methods of Guidance", "The Three Refuges / Three Treasures / Three Jewels / Triple Gem" (quite a heading for a 3-word appendix!), "The Four Sublime Attitudes/Immeasurables or Brahma Viharas", "The Seven Factors of Enlightenment", "The Three Poisons", "The Five Strengths", "The Four Bodhisattva Vows", and "The Three Marks of Excellence". The Glossary, while only covering three dozen terms, included a handful that I wasn't familiar with (such as *"**Piti:** joy, rapture, happiness"* – go ahead, say it like Mr. T[3]), which either indicates the author was delving into a particularly technical level of Zen in his word choice, or that I had somehow managed to not have encountered (or, possibly, remembered) these from previous reading.

Diedrichs uses his background and childhood for a lot of the illustrative bits here, be it when he stole something, lied about something, failed at something, etc. Here's a paragraph from the chapter discussing the "Right Speech" aspect of The Eightfold Path:

> Besides never lying or trying to never lie, we also do not talk trash. We try to talk kindly to people. I watched a video of my brother and me playing baseball when we were kids. I was probably twelve, and he was nine. I hit the ball and ran towards the base where he was standing. The sun shone in his face, and he laughed. I saw my mouth move as I ran up, and I said something to him. Suddenly, his face darkened, and his expression turned to a mean scowl. He said something angry back at me. My heart broke when I watched that. I was so nasty to him. These hurtful actions sill bring me suffering as Buddha said they would.

I think this illuminates the dual level of the book ... while this is certainly *targeted* to being something that children can relate to, it also has a payload of reflective material for the adults reading it. That's what makes this as useful as it is – not only does it cover nearly all the "main points" of Buddhist teaching, making it informative to nearly everybody (and, as I mentioned, it includes stuff that I'd not recalled seeing in *dozens* of Buddhist books), but presenting it in a form that anybody can connect with.

In the chapter introducing the "Three Poisons" (greed, anger, and ignorance, although the particular chapter here is mainly about greed), one of the "Reflecting" questions is *"Where does your happiness come from?"*, which points the reader back to this bit:

> We understand the truth about life, and we realize that our happiness, sense of well-being and worth, and our joy come from inside our own hearts and minds. No one can give them to us. No one can take them away from us. Our own hearts and minds are the most joyful and happy when we are loving, kind, caring, peaceful, and giving.

Again, the message is applicable to anybody, but how great would it be if more kids got those messages *when they were kids*? Similarly, introducing children to these concepts (in the chapter discussing "impermanence", or *annica*, the "Buddha's First Mark of Existence") early on would be awesome:

> I said that you should not believe anything I or anybody else says until you have explored it for yourself. You must make every truth you own. Take a look at the truth of impermanence. See if anybody or anything in your life stays around forever, without ever changing. Buddhists call this fact the true nature of reality.

A few chapters later he adds:

> Buddha observed that our thoughts, a Fourth Mark of Existence, become words. Our words become actions. Our actions become habits. Our habits harden into character. ...

He then leads into a consideration of attachment to mental formations with:

> A thought appears in a flash. It disappears just as quickly and completely. A thought cleanly completes its cycle unless we attach to it. ... Once we grab a thought and hold on, like clutching the mane of a bucking stallion, confusion, contortion, and regret ensue. Caught in a stream of consciousness, we manufacture more thoughts. We form our captured thoughts into ideas, beliefs, opinions, and personal philosophies. We believe these fabricated formations of thought. They become our identity, which we take as our past and our life story. ...

Admittedly, this is pretty "deep stuff" for the kids ... which serves as an additional example of how the book speaks to both children and adults. As mentioned above, Living in Blue Sky Mind[4] is only 162 pages (and "really" is considerably shorter than that, as there's a *lot* of white space involved in those 80 chapter breaks), so it's a quick read ... and possibly reasonably appealing to older kids. However, I don't think this is something you'd just hand to a 10-year-old to read, but could well be used to have "weekly Zen sessions" when you read one chapter *with* your kid and then discuss the "Reflecting" questions. Alternately, this *is* something that could be a quick, easy, and uniquely informative "first contact" for those unexposed to Buddhist thought ... I would certainly contemplate suggesting this to anybody in that state.

As one would expect from an LTER selection, this has just been released (it came out this April), so it is likely to be available via your local bookstore, but the on-line big boys have it at about a third off of cover price, putting it, very affordably, under ten bucks. This, while coming from a "kids book" place, is hardly a book that should be limited to that audience, and I'd have to say this comes in as one of my "all and sundry" recommendations, as I think anybody would benefit from the very direct approach to a wide range of Buddhist thought that's presented here.

Notes:

1. http://btripp-books.livejournal.com/187062.html
2. http://amzn.to/290ipFy
3. https://youtu.be/-sQELbOflO4
4. http://amzn.to/290ipFy

Thursday, July 7, 2016[1]

Managing emotions within negotiations ...

I've had this one sitting around for quite a while. I'd attended parts of the Ayn Rand Institute's conference down at the Hyatt Regency a few years back (it could have been as long ago as 2010, can't remember or dig up an identifiable reference for it), and at one of the receptions I was chatting with a guy who was *highly* recommending this book. I jotted down a note on it, and ended up ordering a used copy, which sat in my to-be-read piles for years. As is frequently the case in my selections of what I'm going to read next, this sort of suggested itself as being sufficiently different from what I'd been reading (and the other options in those piles) that it got picked.

This goes to point out that I didn't have any particular expectation or agenda going into Roger Fisher and Daniel Shapiro's Beyond Reason: Using Emotions as You Negotiate[2], which was probably a good thing, as when I took a look at the Amazon reviews (yeah, I know, *"bad form!"*), a lot of people in the actual target audience for this were sort of dismissing it as too basic, or not presenting anything new. As I *wasn't* in the audience for this (which I take to be people who are frequently in situations where they're having to do high-stakes negotiations), and so didn't have much background information with which to contrast it, I found it fairly interesting. At the end of the first chapter there's a section which pretty much sets up the book:

> This book offers negotiators – and that means everyone – a powerful framework for dealing with emotions. Whether or not you acknowledge emotions, they will have an impact on your negotiation. As the following chapters suggest, you can avoid reacting to scores of constantly changing emotions and turn your attention to five core concerns that are responsible for many, if not most, emotions in a negotiation. These core concerns lie at the heart of many emotional challenges when you negotiate. Rather than feeling powerless in the face of emotions, you will be able to stimulate positive emotions and overcome negative ones.

Do you think they mentioned negotiation enough times in that paragraph? Yeah, me too ... which is sort of the downside here, rather that presenting what would have been a somewhat more interesting (OK, *to me* at least) over-all survey of the "Five Core Concerns" structure (which is the really valuable part of this), they're constantly re-focusing this as a "serious business book" ... which, I suppose, is a minor quibble for what is, obviously, intending to *be* a *serious business book*, but, still ... it's like they're verging on the *"doth protest too much"* territory with that.

Anyway, let's cut to the chase ... the Five Core Concerns (they don't typically capitalize the phrase, but as it's the pith of the book, I'm going with that).

Discussion of these in sequence takes up about half the length of the book (which is in five sections, with various chapters or other elements in them, these coming in the second section bearing the somewhat *"huh?"* title "Take The Initiative"). The Five Core Concerns are:

- Appreciation
- Affiliation
- Autonomy
- Status
- Role

These are defined at the outset:

> <u>Core concerns</u> are human wants that are important to almost everyone in virtually every negotiation. They are often unspoken but are no less real than our tangible interests. ... Core concerns offer you a powerful framework to deal with emotions without getting overwhelmed by them.

I'm going to *try* to convey the essence of each of these concerns here, but extracting this might be a bit uneven, as the structure of the chapters on each tend to be a bit rambling. The authors are, evidently, experienced negotiators, and dip into their histories quite a bit here ... perhaps to the detriment of clarity. Rather than, say, discussing a "negotiation" that one of them had with a wood carver for a souvenir when he *"was in Tbilisi, working with South Ossetians and the government of Georgia (a former Soviet republic)"*, they could have presented a scenario less rife with cultural baggage that would be more direct in transmitting the dynamics involved (which in the story presented, makes the teller sound awfully smarmy). Frankly, the "situational name-checking" involved in many of the "personal examples" outlined here have that "humble brag" vibe to them ... yes, they're *personal experiences*, but it sounds like they're in there more to highlight the authors expertise than to present the clearest possible framing of the specific negotiation issue ... or I may just be cranky.

The first of these is "Appreciation", which is presented as having three elements: *"to <u>understand</u> each other's point of view", "to <u>find merit</u> in what each of us thinks, feels, or does",* and *"to <u>communicate</u> our understanding through words and actions"*. Illustrative scenarios here include making arguments in front of the Supreme Court (no doubt useful for the next time *you* find yourself having to do that), and doing negotiation workshops in Macedonia during the Kosovo conflict ... along with other scenarios illustrating various points related to the central concept. Maybe it's my "allergy" to parables or teaching stories, but I kept wanting them to get to the key ideas, and a lot of that is buried in these reminiscences ... although, they do eventually set up specific suggestions and guidelines for applying the concepts within one's own negotiation situations.

Next comes "Affiliation", which is pretty basic on the broad strokes – developing connections which will make working together easier. The stories here are all over the place, from working with Serbian Parliament members to negotiations between the South African government and the ANC, to attempts (unsuccessful) to get corporate and union representatives to sit interspersed at a large round table rather than on opposing sides of a long rectangle. The affiliation dynamics break down into two basic categories, "Structural Connections" – links one has *"with someone else based on your common membership in a group"* (age, rank, family, background, religion, hobbies, etc.), and "Personal Connections" – *"personal ties that bond you with another"* (they present a table of "Affiliation-enhancing Subjects That Reduce Emotional Distance" vs. "Safe Conversation Subjects That Maintain Emotional Distance", such as "personal opinions about politics" vs. "favorite TV programs" … although this one is pretty touchy in *my* experience, and as likely to cause a total communication break-down as to minimize emotional distance!).

"Autonomy" follows this (and I sort of wished they'd quoted the Buzzcock's song[3] by that title, whose lyric *"I, I want you, autonomy"* would have fit in quite well here!), and has two primary elements, "expanding your own autonomy" and "avoid impinging upon the other person's autonomy". This has an interesting story where one of the authors had been contacted by the Carter White House to be a back-channel negotiator with the head of the Iranian Islamic Republican Party during the Tehran embassy crisis in 1979, which included him finding a basis to argue for cessations of sanctions, a key point on the Iranian's side. One of the factors in this is what they call "Joint Brainstorming" for which they have a five-point plan of action that could be implemented in various situations. They also present what is called the "I-C-N Bucket System" for determining the "right" amount of autonomy in a given setting. These are: I for *Inform*, where one feels it is appropriate to decide on something and simply inform other parties of the decision, then C for *Consult, then decide*, where it's important to get other parties' feedback before making a decision, and finally, N for *Negotiate joint agreement*, where the eventual decision needs to have all involved parties on board.

The next Core Concern is "acknowledging Status", which has a wide range of particular applications, including "be aware of social status", "be courteous to everyone", "look for each person's areas of particular status", "give weight to opinions where deserved", and "beware of status spillover". An example given here was of a patient in a hospital almost dying because the doctor wasn't interested in hearing what a nurse had to report – he was unwilling to realize that the nurse had more case information on the patient that he did, and acted on his assumptions, not on the reality she was trying to convey to him. The "spillover" concept is familiar from commercials – an actor who plays a role on TV is often tapped to appear as an expert on the subject to pitch products.

Lastly there is the topic of "Role" … a fulfilling Role has three key qualities: it has a clear purpose, it is personally meaningful, and it is not a pretense. They have a table of "conventional roles" which is primarily job descriptions ("travel agent") and relationships ("grandparent"). They also offer a four-point approach to "shape your conventional role", which involve naming the role, analyzing the activities involved in that role, adding activities to make it more fulfilling, and deleting the more unfulfilling activities. There are also "temporary roles" which one "chooses to play" – such as "problem solver", "competitor", or even "joker".

The section following the Core Concerns looks at ways to deal with "strong negative emotions", including a framework for gauging your and others' "emotional temperature", and having plans to deal with highly-charged emotional situations. There are some very uncomfortable example scenarios sketched out here, plus a four-part plan for moving to more calmer discussions. Next comes a chapter on preparation, including a table on "using seven elements to prepare". There is also the suggestion of reviewing every negotiation and classifying things as "WW" – "worked well", or "DD" – "do differently" … and a recommendation to chart out how things unfolded regarding Core Concerns, with a list of specific questions to consider for each.

The book (almost) ends with an odd, but interesting piece written by the former President of Ecuador, Jamil Mahuad, dealing with his negotiations with Peruvian president Alberto Fujimori over a border dispute that had been simmering (and occasionally flaring into open conflict) for over 50 years. Mahuad had taken negotiation courses with the authors and used the approaches outlined in the book to help work out a mutually acceptable solution. Following this there is a 2-page "section" of a Conclusion, followed by *another* section called "End Matter", which includes a re-stating of the "Seven Elements of Negotiation", a brief "Glossary" (more re-framing of the key elements), and a very interesting "Works Consulted" piece, which, rather than just listing a bibliography, is a walk through various concepts involved in the book, and other resources that relate to them … including this bit (in discussing The Handbook of Cognition and Emotion and the work of Paul Ekman):

> … in Beyond Reason, we have chosen to focus on five core concerns. One need not analyze which of the various emotions the other person is feeling, nor their causes, in order to use the core concerns to enlist positive emotions. Rather than focusing on dozens of emotions, a negotiator can take action with five core concerns.

Beyond Reason[4] is still in print in the paperback edition, and so should be obtainable from your local brick-and-mortar book vendor, but the on-line big boys predictably have it at a fairly substantial discount, and "very good" copies of the hardcover (which is what I have) can be had for a penny (plus $3.99 shipping), if you want to go that way.

While a lot of the material here is quite interesting, from a psychological perspective, I would have much preferred the book had that been its thrust … having this more set in the boardroom made it consistently "less relevant" to me … and I'm guessing that would be the case for *most* readers. It's certainly worth the read … but it involves a lot of mental gymnastics to try to filter out the parts that one could use in one's own life from the high-level international or organizational examples which serve as illustrations of these concepts here.

Notes:
1. http://btripp-books.livejournal.com/187177.html
2. http://amzn.to/28J9Y2k
3. https://youtu.be/NK9YtcSA1Rs
4. http://amzn.to/28J9Y2k

Tuesday, July 12, 2016[1]

"Souls of Poets dead and gone ..."

As regular readers of this space will no doubt recall from my previous blitherings, I've been a big fan of the Dover Thrift Editions for a long time. For many years (before I finally broke down and got Amazon Prime and its free shipping), I relied on these as a way to nudge an order up over the free-shipping threshold, which then also gave me an excuse to "fill holes" in my otherwise excellent liberal arts education.

The latter, however, wasn't a specific concern bringing me to this edition of John Keats' Lyric Poems[2], as I'd been conversant with his poems from back in high school (when I wrote a bit of doggerel which started out *"Shelley, Byron and Keats / do not the oiseau to eat / ..."*), so I probably picked this up for its inexpense (cover price $3, currently going for a buck) as for anything else. The collection "contains 30 of his finest poems" which appear to have been excerpted from a number of publications, both released during his life and posthumously.

Keats died in Rome in 1821 at the age of 26 from tuberculosis. His writing career barely spanned five years, so his fame and influence (as one of the "Romantic Poets" - albeit not a group with whom he had much actual contact) is remarkable, especially as "He published only fifty-four poems, in three slim volumes and a few magazines."[3]. So, excepting his longer pieces (not included here), the poems collected for this book are a fairly substantial chunk of what he wrote.

Speaking of "slim" ... this is going to be a fairly brief review, as I'm not going to try to dig into an analysis of Keat's poetry ... where I rather liked this back in my school days, my tolerance for rhyming poetry has not improved with age, and I found myself being frequently cranky when reading this in regards to the frequency of (what sounds to *me* as) tortured convolutions to get a rhyming word (or some abused variation on a word) where it needs to be in one of these odes or sonnets (there was a time in my teens when I was hell-bent on writing "sonnet cycles" much like these here, but could not stand to indulge in the necessary word-wringing to get concepts to fit within the rhyme schemes).

So, I'm just going to do some re-typing of bits that stood out to me to give you a bit of the flavor here (although sparing you some of the noted "groaners") ...

> From *Isabella; or, The Pot of Basil – A story from Boccacio*
>
> XXII
> And many a jealous conference had they,
>   And many times they bit their lips alone,
> Before they fix'd upon a surest way
>   To make the youngster for his crime atone;

> And at the last, these men of cruel clay
>   Cut Mercy with a sharp knife to the bone;
> For they resolved in some forest dim
> To kill Lorenzo, and there bury him.

Obviously, there's nothing to fault with they/way/clay, alone/atone/bone, and dim/him in this one … and it does give some sense of the somewhat cinematographical feel of Keats' depictions of his subjects.

From <u>The Eve of St. Agnes</u>:

> XIV
> 'St. Agnes! Ah! It is St. Agnes' Eve –
> 'Yet men will murder upon holy days:
> 'Thou must hold water in a witch's sieve,
> 'And be liege-lord of all the Elves and Fays,
> 'To venture so: it fills me with amaze
> 'To see thee, Porphyro! - St. Anges' Eve!
> 'God's help! My lady fair the conjuror plays
> 'This the very night: good angels her deceive!
> 'But let me laugh awhile, I've mickle time to grieve.'

This certainly points towards the classical/literary influences brought out in Keats' writing … themes that are most famously on display on the piece that eventually launched a thousand "drachma jokes" :

From <u>Ode on a Grecian Urn</u>:

> IV
> Who are these coming to the sacrifice?
>   To what green altar, O mysterious priest,
> Lead'st thou that heifer lowing at the skies,
>   And all her silken flanks with garlands drest?
> What little town by river or sea shore,
>   Or mountain-built with peaceful citadel,
>   Is emptied of this folk, this pious morn?
> And, little town, thy streets for evermore
>   Will silent be; and not a soul to tell
>   Why thou art desolate, can e'er return.

OK, that one comes close to having painful word pairings (there are much worse examples than *priest/drest*, trust me), but who am I to complain about something that nearly every English major (or well-rounded high school student) has had to deal with in class?

Anyway, <u>Lyric Poems</u>[4] is a great way to get familiar with Keats (even if it doesn't have some of the *"most highly regarded works of his maturity"*, in the longer <u>Endymion</u>, <u>Lamia</u>, and <u>Hyperion</u> – all of which can be found <u>online</u>[5], if you want to go with free), for a very low price, and, frankly, a minimal time investment.

Notes:
1. http://btripp-books.livejournal.com/187637.html
2. http://amzn.to/294t9bn
3. https://goo.gl/IHmSKt
4. http://amzn.to/294t9bn
5. http://www.john-keats.com/

Wednesday, July 13, 2016[1]

When the going gets weird ...

This is one of those books that has been lurking in my to-be-read piles for quite a while. I got it as a throw-in on another order about five years ago (it apparently was on some sort of special, as the packing slip, still stuck in the back of the book, lists a price that should be in the "used" category – less than 1/5th of cover price – but as part of a regular order ... go figure! ... perhaps I ordered it just *because* it was so cheap) but only got around to reading it now.

I'm pleased to report that William McKeen's Outlaw Journalist: The Life and Times of Hunter S. Thompson[2] is a pretty amazing book ... and I'm sort of kicking myself that I didn't get into it previously. To be perfectly honest, I think I *enjoyed* reading this more than 90% of the books that get processed through my eyeballs in my general run of non-fiction consumption. It is informative, entertaining, poignant at times, and gives the sense of a comprehensive look at its fascinating subject.

Now, I'm assuming that anybody reading this is at least somewhat familiar with the figure of Hunter S. Thompson – a "journalist" who cut a fairly wide swath through the consciousness of the 70's, 80's and 90's. First coming to national attention with his 1966 book *Hell's Angels*, which detailed his time hanging out with (and occasionally getting beaten up by) that notorious motorcycle gang, which was a book-length expansion of a magazine article he'd done in 1965. He is probably best known for *Fear and Loathing in Las Vegas*, and subsequent "fear and loathing" titles (most focusing on political campaigns).

As familiar as I thought I was with Thompson, it turns out that I'd not actually *read* much of his stuff (except as published in *Rolling Stone* back in the day – when he was a key player in that magazine's image). Looking into my LibraryThing.com collection[3], I only appear to have two of his titles, *Generation of Swine*, and *Songs of the Doomed*, and not any of his "famous" books (an oversight that I suppose I'll have to correct eventually).

One of the main take-aways from this look at his life is how *serious* he was about the *craft* of writing, no matter how insane the details of what he was writing about. That being said, it's also pretty clear that he had issues with deadlines (OK, probably "with authority" in general), and was constantly months, if not *years* late with various projects promised to various publishers.

Outlaw Journalist[4] starts with Thompson's early years (a fairly rough childhood, leading to one of those classic "military or prison" choices being presented to him), which fortuitously ended up with his landing a writing gig at a large Air Force base. It quickly became apparent, however, that he was not cut out for the discipline of military service, and was soon separated (in 1957) from same. While Thompson seemed to want to have a career of writing *novels*, none of his projects got much traction until the later years of his career (when publishers figured that they could make money putting out *anything* with his name on it). The book goes into quite a bit of detail on the assorted jobs (most fairly briefly held) he had in the late 50's and into the early 60's. He saw an opportunity in 1962 to head to South America, and managed to talk his way into a contract with a new publication by the *Wall Street Journal* for him to file reports from his journeys.

McKeen points to this time as the start of "Gonzo"[5], which he puts in a very particular context:

> In these letters to Ridley, {HST's editor at the short-lived *National Observer*} Hunter's Gonzo style began it rear its head. One of the characteristics of the style Hunter developed was his preoccupation with getting the story. In fact, getting the story became the story. His writing could be classified as metajournalism, journalism about the process of journalism.

Oddly, this made me reflect on my own writing (especially these reviews), with that "meta" element certainly coming into play.

Thompson parted ways with the *Observer* in 1965, and one of the subsequent projects he landed was an article for *The Nation* about the Hell's Angels. As noted above, this led to his break-out book, which opened up other opportunities with a wide array of significant publications. One of these was *Sports Illustrated* which assigned him to produce a 250-word caption for photos of a motorcycle race in Las Vegas in 1971. Thompson ended up submitting a 2,500-word essay, which was rejected, but later picked up by *Rolling Stone*, giving him the encouragement to expand it into the notorious *Fear and Loathing in Las Vegas*, which featured his alter-ego Raoul Duke (initially listed as the author).

Raoul Duke was a repeating character that Thompson employed to be able to, essentially, write about himself ... and the character ended up with enough "substance" that he was included for years on the Rolling Stone masthead, being listed as the "sports desk" (having been supposedly a crazed sports writer, going back to "notes" in Thompson's pieces for *his* sports-writing gig with the Air Force). An interesting side-bar here is that for most of his life, Thompson *hated* the "Uncle Duke"[6] character in the *Doonesbury* comic strip. When the character (very plainly based on Thompson's appearance, and Raoul Duke's proclivities) appeared in 1974, it created a type of fame that Thompson was not prepared for ... as it mixed up *his* personality, and that of Raoul Duke, and suddenly everywhere he went, people were expecting him to *be* that character. While the author notes that Thompson eventually became OK with the whole "Uncle Duke" phenomena, the inability of him to move "invisibly" in the background of events to actually work on *stories* seems to been one of the key elements to his retreat to near-isolation in Woody Creek, CO.

Another part of the book that I found surprising is that Thompson was pretty much working hand-to-mouth for most of his career. Even after becoming famous, he was still not particularly financially secure. This was an on-going stressor in his personal life. By the early 60's he was married with a young son, but until he got on the speaking circuit (which was still touch-and-go, as he was frequently at odds with the agendas of the schools, etc. which were hiring him to speak), he was constantly in search of just survival money.

His personal relationships are discussed at length here, both with the women in his life (not only the romantic relationships, but also the "support" people that rotated through his world), as well as the wide network of people in the publishing business. Again, this is fascinating reading, but not put in the sort of form that would be useful to quote in this context.

Late in his career, he was having a lot of professional success (with awards and recognitions that seemed to greatly please him), but not producing notable work. Another on-going theme was that when he encountered cocaine, it allowed him to be up and writing, but not of the quality of his earlier material … *and* he'd have long periods of not being able to write at all. Most of his later books (like the ones I've read) were collections and re-processing of older stuff. The book notes that there were massive amounts of material that he left behind, so there's likely to be more Hunter S. Thompson titles appearing. Of course, the novels and similar pieces that he'd written in the past (and hadn't been able to get published), such as *The Rum Diary* (made into a Johnny Depp film in 2011) eventually were widely released.

Thompson's physical decline is also given a particular consideration, probably to put his eventual suicide in context. As the years went by, he was less able to get around, and he was well past his "expected" death in his late 20's … one day in 2005 (at age 67) he stuck a gun in his mouth and killed himself.

Again, I was very impressed with the depth of research that William McKeen put into Outlaw Journalist[7], and the whole thing is quite exceptional. He had previously done another project on Thompson, and reproduces a letter sent to him saying *"I warned you about writing the vicious trash about me."*, a sure sign of affection from the Gonzo man himself. This is one of the best biographies I've read, and I really would recommend it to anybody with an interest in any of the wide-ranging topics on which it touches.

Obviously, I'm not the *only* one who thinks so, as the hardcover (which has been out since 2008) is still in print, as well as a paperback, e-book, and audio edition. The prices are all over the board (I'm still confused as to why the hardcover I got back in 2011 was as cheap as it was), with "very good" used copies of the hardcover being the least expensive option (you can get those for as little as 40¢, plus shipping), with the on-line big boys having this now only a bit off of cover price. You could certainly *order* this through your local brick-and-mortar, but I'm not sure, this many years past publication, that it will be on the shelf there. In any case, this is a great look at an amazing figure, and I can't imagine anybody not finding this a fascinating read!

Notes:
1. http://btripp-books.livejournal.com/187776.html
2. http://amzn.to/28T7Bck
3. http://btripp-books.com/
4. http://amzn.to/28T7Bck
5. https://en.wikipedia.org/wiki/Gonzo_journalism
6. https://goo.gl/GMGguE
7. http://amzn.to/28T7Bck

Saturday, July 23, 2016[1]

You really should read this one ...

I don't think that Wayne Allyn Root is the type of guy who gets embarrassed much, but I suspect he's somewhat so when it comes to this book. Root made his name in sports prognostication, and then turned to being a political commentator. Back in 2008, he was a hopeful for the Libertarian Party's Presidential candidacy, and was in third place with as much as 26.7% of the vote through five rounds of balloting at their national convention. The top two contenders, former GOP Congressman Bob Barr, and LP "true believer" Mary Ruwart, were locked in a virtual tie on each of these, and following the fifth ballot, Root reached out to Barr to offer his support, in exchange for a spot on the ticket. This was enough to give Barr the nomination, and landed Root in the VP slot. That was, of course, when everybody was expecting Hillary to roll to the White House, and the LP was seeing this as a great opportunity to get some exposure with a wider swath of the voting public. Of course, instead of the "abysmal" Hillary winning, it was the "horrific" current POTUS, which changed the game ... the threat of the abuses of the current administration (which has been every bit as monstrous as anticipated, with even more anti-Americanism than anybody could have thought possible) made "standing on principle" a sucker bet.

Root wrote The Conscience of a Libertarian: Empowering the Citizen Revolution with God, Guns, Gold and Tax Cuts[2] in 2009, when he was gearing up for a LP Presidential run in 2012. He was elected to the Libertarian National Committee in 2010 (and re-elected in 2012), and this book was very much the vehicle that he was using as a cornerstone of his campaign. However, as the first term of the current POTUS marched on in its disgusting Alinsky debasing of the country, it became obvious to Root that it was more important to try to get a new administration in place than to make a quixotic (if noble) run as a 3rd party candidate, and resigned from the LP in order to help with the Mitt Romney campaign.

Root was roundly *savaged* by the Libertarian "true believers" (sort of like food fetishists, but neurotically doctrinaire on *political* stances) for this ... they felt he was a "carpet bagger" anyway from his previous run (and deal with "Libertarian of convenience" Barr), and having him jump back to the GOP was seen as a betrayal, at best.

Frankly, I feel that Root has gotten a bad rap in this ... as his beliefs (certainly as set out in this book) are solidly Libertarian in the Goldwater sense of the term. Indeed, Conscience of a Libertarian[3] is inspired by Barry Goldwater's 1960 Conscience of a Conservative[4] (although three times as long as the earlier book), and he spends much of the first part of it dipping into the far-sighted wisdom of Mr. Goldwater.

I also have a somewhat unusual problem with this review – I have over *two dozen* bookmarks stuck in here for "good parts" that I wanted to share. Root and I have a very similar view of government – that it is *the enemy* most of the time, so there's a "preaching to the choir" aspect here. Things like:

> ... government entitlement and welfare programs have never been about helping the poor. They've always been about giving more power and control to politicians and government.

are such a relief to see expressed by somebody other than myself (when swearing at my computer monitor).

Again, Root was out-front with this being his call to action for a substantial 3rd party run as a potential LP Presidential candidate, and it's set up very much in that context. The book is in four parts, "A Revolution Is Brewing" which sets out the case that both major parties are leading the country down the drain with bigger and less responsible government, framed with material by Goldwater and the Founders; "Let's Talk Money and Politics" which looks, in horrifying detail, at just how bad things had gotten by 2009 (needless to say, they've gotten worse since); "Solutions for the Mess We Are In" which presents a fairly coherent plan for how to reverse much of the madness of not only the past couple of decades, but on back to the post-WW2 lurch into big government; and "Protecting and Preserving our Inalienable Civil Liberties", which details all the areas where our Liberties are being ground out of existence by *both* major parties. It's really a shame that a GOP candidate hadn't won in '08 (aside from the obvious blessing it would have been to have avoided the disastrous Leftist rampage of the current execrable administration!), as it would have been a lot of fun to see Root running at the head of the LP ticket in 2012, trying to make the stuff in Conscience of a Libertarian[5] come to be.

One of the key values of this book – and why I would recommend it to *everybody* – is that it gets into gory details on HOW BAD THINGS ARE ... stuff that you'll never hear a peep about from the progressive-conspirator MSM. Living in Illinois, we're especially at the mercy of a kleptocratic state government that has for generations solidified its power with sweetheart deals for the unions – and especially the government employees unions – deals that are now totally bankrupting the state. Cynical politicians like Mike Madigan have been promising insanely high pension packages to the unions and leaving the taxpayers of the state on the hook for these billions of dollars. Root has a chapter in here, "Government Employee Unions Gone Wild" which outlines exactly how this scheme has played out, and he very kindly gave me permission to do a .pdf version of that chapter, which you can download HERE[6]. If you're in Illinois, I *urge* you to download that, email it to friends, print it out (I formatted it so it will print front-and-back on four sheets of paper), and get the word out on this particularly vile situation.

As is often the case when I find myself with a "forest" of bookmarks in a book I'm reviewing, I can find myself being unsure exactly what it was on those pages that I was wanting to use (although enough of them were in the above-noted chapter that I decided to contact the author to simply bring that whole thing to you). One bit that I found illuminating, however, is in the "God and Government" chapter where Root (who grew up Jewish but converted to some evangelical Christian sect in order to marry his fundy wife, as I noted in my review[7] of his *Relentless* book) discusses religious matters, he writes:

> *... my religious views should not allow me to use government as a hammer to smash those views down your throat. I want to explain to Christians who support all my fiscal views of smaller government, less government spending, lower entitlements, lower taxes, and more freedom, that asking for government to enforce our religious and moral values is in fact <u>big government</u>. And it's also a <u>big</u> mistake.*

Given that I first came to the Libertarian Party because its "religion neutral" positioning (in the face of having Armageddon-desiring fundy Dan Quayle being "a heartbeat away from the Presidency" in Bush I's administration), I find Root's stance on belief reassuring.

One of Root's most dramatic propositions here comes in the "Eliminating Federal Taxes and the IRS" chapter ... which, in the briefest setting is:

> *We propose eliminating the income tax and all other sources of federal tax revenues, including payroll taxes (FICA), excise taxes, and import duties, and replacing it with only one tax: a tax on each state in proportion to its population, with each state deciding for itself how to raise its share of the money. ... With no other source of revenue to the U.S. government, the balance of power would be forever dramatically reversed back to the states (just as our Founding Fathers envisioned).*

He goes on to quote Jefferson in support of a number of points, including the remarkable:

> *"The true theory of our constitution is that states are independent as to everything within themselves ..." and even went so far as to recognize the right of states to nullify federal laws within their own borders, describing federal intrusion into state matters as "interference by a foreign government".*

In the chapter "Eradicating Capital Gains", Root, the serial entrepreneur, gets on his soapbox (yeah, I'm cheering him on), about risk and reward, and how *"Capital gains are the only ticket out of poverty. Capital gains are the only ticket to success and upward mobility."* He goes on to show what the Left is leading us to:

> *What do you get when you turn off that {investment} faucet? Cuba. Before Fidel Castro, Cuba was a prosperous country. A huge class of professionals and business owners lived a wonderful life. Then Castro decided that capitalism was bad and socialism was good for the people. Now the country is frozen in time. Homes, cars, roads, government buildings – they are all dilapidated and bro-*

> ken down, frozen in time because without motivation, no one has invested in anything since 1959 (the year of Castro's revolution). ... Cuba is the country that time forgot. Liberals whine all day about "fairness". Life is completely fair in communist and socialist countries. In liberal utopias like that, taxes are so high that <u>everybody</u> lives in poverty and misery.

Since we're on the subject of liberals … here's another great bit (which dovetails back to the damned union deals):

> Why do liberals want to spend ever-higher amounts of your money? So they can buy the votes of people too ignorant to understand that the very policies that they are voting for are keeping them poor, helpless, hopeless, aimless, and clueless.

It's almost like Root was forecasting the whole BLM thuggery that the current administration has encouraged over the past year or two!

Root also has some very interesting suggestions about reforming Congress. It turns out that his home state, Nevada, has a "part time" legislature, which manages to run the state just fine. In the chapter "The Magnificent Seven (Times Two)" he features two 7-item lists. I was hoping to find a source to point you to on these (rather than listing them all out), but one of the highlights of this is to *significantly* expand the number of representatives by having each Congressperson represent only 100,000 citizens (versus the average of nearly 700,000 each now), making it not only a far more *responsive* office, but also making campaigns much less expensive. He also suggests, instead of unlimited 2-year terms, making each term for six years, and only allowing two terms. Another feature of this much larger Congress:

> Today a lobbyist needs to buy a majority of the 435-member House in order to get the appropriation they desire, or the special favor they are seeking. That's downright <u>cheap</u>. It becomes almost 10 times as expensive for any corporation or lobbyist to accomplish this with a 3,000-member House.

Among the other items Root puts forward here is:

> No proposed bill should be enacted into law unless it has been read out loud in its amended form in the presence of a quorum in Congress, and then posted to the Internet at least one week prior to a scheduled vote.

This will not only discourage massive bills with layer upon layer of "hidden" pork, but it would ensure that never again will some cretinous psychopath like Nancy Pelosi be able to pontificate that the public *can't see the bill* (that's tens of thousands of pages long) until it's passed.

Additionally, there are suggestions for "Presidential line-item veto", the elimination of "earmarks", a system to put into effect the First Amendment's "right to petition the government for a redress of grievances", and a rock-solid constitutional test of any bill … *"if a spending bill is not authorized (or enumerated) by our Constitution, the money should not be spent"*.

Another section that should get anybody's blood boiling is the "Nanny State" chapter where Root lists case after case of callous elitist politicians destroying "the little people" because they *can*. He has a great rant in the middle of this that I'm 100% behind:

> *Never trust government. Never trust politicians or government bureaucrats. Never trust moral crusaders. Never let others define morality for you. Because the people doing the crusading and defining and prosecuting often have an agenda, and out-of-control ego, and an outsized sense of entitlement. They certainly do not have your best interests in mind.*

Gotta love that. He follows later with a campaign-like call to action:

> *It's time to put candidates in office whose goal is to give the power back to the people. Whose goal is limit the size, power, and scope of government. Our wise Founding Fathers wrote about power of the people, by the people, for the people. They did not write about putting power in the hands of morally corrupt, power-hungry, ego-driven, hypocritical politicians and government bureaucrats.*

Speaking of the Founding Fathers, he opens one chapter with an *awesome* quote from George Washington, which should be always remembered: *"Government is not reason. It is not eloquence. It is force."* … after all, every "give away" from the government is based on money being forcibly taken (or at least under the *threat* of force – if you're not Al Sharpton and don't pay your taxes, somebody's eventually going to show up at your door with guns to take you to jail) from somebody else.

Root hits a lot of hot buttons here … "third rail" topics like Education, "affirmative action", and global ~~cooling~~ ~~warming~~ *climate change* … and he's right pretty much across the board (although I have issues with his particular favorite cause of on-line poker). He certainly strikes the right chord late in the book with this call for economic sanity:

> *We cannot possibly continue to spend at the same levels as when things were going good, now that things are going bad. There just isn't enough tax revenue coming in to keep spending at the same baseline. We can't keep spending far more than we take in, while at the same time the national debt from decades past keeps piling up unpaid. We are so broke, we can't pay last year's bills, let alone the new bills from this year.*

Frankly, I think that Conscience of a Libertarian[8] is a very important book (which *everybody* should read), and it's unfortunate that the situations around this (Root returning to the GOP to help in the fight against the continued usurpation of the Executive Branch by enemies of America) have scuttled its primary context. As noted above, I would have *loved* to see a Root run for the Presidency ... it would be "popcorn ready" from start to finish!

I was pleased to see that this appears to still be in print, in both the hardcover and paperback editions, so you could likely get this at your local brick-and-mortar book vendor ... and, as much as I'd like to throw some coin Wayne's way, you can get "very good" used copies of the hardcover for as little as a penny (plus the $3.99 shipping) from the new/used guys, so you *really* don't have much of an excuse for not getting a copy (if nothing else, do remember to grab the .pdf[9] of Ch.13)!

Notes:

1. http://btripp-books.livejournal.com/187995.html
2-3. http://amzn.to/29iEAeE
4. http://amzn.to/2a5dtAC
5. http://amzn.to/29iEAeE
6. https://goo.gl/92huFh
7. http://btripp-books.livejournal.com/172545.html
8. http://amzn.to/29iEAeE
9. https://goo.gl/92huFh

Sunday, July 24, 2016[1]

Why religion?

As I noted in a review[2] a few weeks back, I recently decided to get caught up on several "atheist" books that I'd gotten in a number of years ago, and so Daniel C. Dennett's Breaking the Spell: Religion as a Natural Phenomenon[3] got out of the "to be read" limbo and into my active reading mix. This is one that I pretty much ordered "by reputation", without having a lot of particular info (and, hence, expectations) about it. I guess Dennett was quoted enough in other books that I figured that I should get around to reading this one as well.

Dennett writes with a bit of a wry attitude – and brings (what in context of Dawkins, Harris, and Hitchens is) a fairly gentle counterpoint to religions here. I suspect that this comes from his being, by profession, a *philosopher* (holding a Chair at Tufts University, and being a director of the Center for Cognitive Studies there), and, while the *sciences* are more specifically his area of study, religion (as in the sub-title here, "as a natural phenomenon") seems to be a professional interest, rather than the *bête noire* that it is for most of his "teammates" on the Atheist side of things. However, I take it that he's a big wheel in The Brights[4] movement, so there's certainly no hesitancy to make fun of the religious.

Now, I just finished reading this, so it's not been sitting around draining out of my head ... but I still don't have a good summary about what the book's "about" ... while not being "academic" (although chock full of citations), it sort of rolls through what it rolls through and didn't leave a solid impression on me. This may be "my bad", or it might be something about the book ... I certainly *enjoyed* reading it, but it's a good thing that I bookmarked a bunch of stuff, because if I was going to do this review from unaided recall, neither of us would be happy with the results.

Structurally, it's in 3 "parts" with various thematic chapters, which are broken up into numerous topical sections. The "parts" are: Opening Pandora's Box, The Evolution of Religion, and Religion Today (followed by four Appendixes), which gives you the broad-strokes of what's in here.

Tellingly, this starts out looking at parasites that cause "suicidal" behavior in various animals, from a microscopic fluke that infects ants' brains and causes them to climb high on grass, just so the fluke can get into the digestive tract of a sheep or cow – which is necessary for the fluke's reproduction, to the parasites that get into mice or rats and make them fearless around cats, because the parasite needs to get into the *cat's* digestive tract to reproduce. One of the recurring questions here is *Cui bono?*, the Latin phrase that means "to whose profit?" ... which certainly gives a starting place for explaining bizarre behaviors in the host creatures for these various parasites – which could well include the entire concept of religion among humans.

Dennett puts forward a rather convincing call *for* the study of religion:

> *We have particularly compelling reasons for investigating the biological bases of religion now. Some-*

> times – rarely – religions go bad, veering into something like group insanity or hysteria, and causing great harm. Now that we have created the technologies to cause global catastrophe, our jeopardy is multiplied to the maximum; a toxic religious mania could end human civilization overnight. We need to understand what makes religions work, so we can protect ourselves in an informed manner from the circumstances in which religions go haywire. What is religion composed of? How do the parts fit together? How do they mesh? Which effects depend on which causes? Which features, if any, invariably occur together? Which exclude each other? What constitutes the health and pathology of religious phenomena?

He does suggest caution, however, referring to the knee-jerk move to low-fat dietary guidelines (driven by politics, of course), where *"the demands of the public for simple advice – run up against the confusing ambiguity of real science"*. He goes on to say:

> Good intentions are not enough. This is the sort of misguided campaign that we want to avoid when we try to correct what we take to be the toxic excesses of religion.

Again, much of the book is involved in delving into specific *philosophical* questions dealing with belief, with historical indications of how modern cultures arose, with brain function, with cultural insularity, etc., etc. etc. This is presented in a very accessible format, with humor and reference to a wide array of cognitive frames. Unfortunately, none of that makes for quick-and-handy quotes or summaries. Here, however, is one section that did sort of stand out:

> Belief in belief in God makes people reluctant to acknowledge the obvious: that much of the traditional lore about God is no more worthy of <u>belief</u> than the lore about Santa Claus or Wonder Woman. … {he references Dawkins' famous line: "… modern theists might acknowledge that … We are all atheists about most of the gods that humanity has ever believed in. Some of us just go one god further."} *The trouble is that, since this advice won't be heeded, discussions of the existence of God tend to take place in a pious fog of indeterminate boundaries. If theists would be so kind as to make a short list of all the concepts of God they renounce as balderdash before proceeding further, we atheists would know just which topics were on the table, but, out of a mixture of caution, loyalty, and unwillingness to offend anyone "on their side", theists typically decline to do this. … This double standard is enabled if not actually licensed by a logical con-*

> *fusion that continues to defy resolution by philosophers who have worked on it: the problem of <u>intentional objects</u> ... the <u>things somebody can think about</u>.*

The start of that, "belief in belief in God" is featured through this quite a bit, which eventually gets contrasted with various scientific theorems ...

> *Do you believe that <u>$E=mc^2$</u>? I do. We all know that this is Einstein's great equation, and the heart, somehow, of his theory of relativity, and many of us know what the <u>E</u> and <u>m</u> and <u>c</u> stand for, and could even work out the basic algebraic relationships and detect obvious errors in interpreting it. But only a tiny fraction of those who know <u>"$E=mc^2$"</u> is a fundamental truth of physics actually understand it in any substantive way.*

He goes on to quote from Richard Feynman's <u>QED: The Strange Theory of Light and Matter</u>[5], where in a lecture that great mind said:

> *It is my task to convince you <u>not</u> to turn away because you don't understand it. You see, my physics students don't understand it either. That is because <u>I</u> don't understand it. Nobody does ... It's a problem that physicists have learned to deal with ...*

Lots of other threads are woven through here: anthropological studies of obscure cultures, "teaching stories" from various traditions, atrocities committed in the name of various religions (Kosovo, the destruction of Buddhist statues in Afghanistan, etc.) – with the comment *"This is the great danger of symbols – they can become <u>too</u> sacred"*, with a look at how religion has been historically studied in the West.

In the "Morality and Religion" section there is an interesting discussion of a key element that appears to be preventing Islam from evolving into something less medieval:

> *It is equally unknown how many Muslims truly believe that all infidels and especially kafirs (apostates from Islam) deserve death , which is what the Koran (4:89) undeniably says. ... of the Abrahamic faiths, Islam stands alone in its inability to renounce this barbaric doctrine convincingly. The Koran does not explicitly commend killing apostates, but the hadith literature (the narrations of the life of the Prophet) certainly does. Most Muslims, I would <u>guess</u>, are sincere in their insistence that the hadith injunction that apostates are to be killed is to be disregarded, but it's disconcerting, to say the least, that fear of being regarded as an apostate is apparently a major motivation in the Islamic world. ... Even Muslims "on the inside" really don't know*

> *what Muslims think about apostasy – they mostly aren't prepared to bet their lives on it ...*

Reflecting back to the science example, Dennett talks about "division of labor", where there are "experts" in various areas, and he suggests that this is frequently what drives most bodies into the pews, and despite quoting H.L. Mencken's *"For every complex problem, there is a simple answer – and it is wrong."* he notes:

> *... if you decide, after conscientious consideration, that your moral decision is to delegate further moral decision in your life to a trusted expert, then you have made your own moral decision. Your have decided to take advantage of the division of labor that civilization makes possible and get the help of expert specialists.*

Of course, this hinges on the "conscientious consideration" part ... people *thinking it through* (which I suspect is a sucker bet every time) ... with the problem coming with those who *"have an unquestioning faith in the correctness of the moral teachings of their religion are a problem"*. Dennett defines these (probably the majority of believers) as *"taking a personally immoral stand"*, which he suspects is the *"most shocking implication"* of his studies in this area.

The book closes out with a chapter "Now What Do We Do?", where he summarizes much of the material, while still introducing some new elements. I liked this piece in the early parts of this chapter, where's he sort of setting up his "closing arguments":

> *Religion provides some people with a motivated organization for doing great things – working for social justice, education, political action, economic reform, and so forth. For others the memes of religion are more toxic, exploiting less savory aspects of their psychology, playing on guilt, loneliness, the longing for self-esteem and importance. Only when we can frame a comprehensive view of the many aspects of religion can we formulate defensible policies for how to respond to religions in the future.*

Dennett does eventually get around to "politics", and he gets into some territory sure to irritate the Left (which, needless to say, got my attention), including a discussion comparing dangerous religious believers to dangerous political believers, and here's a bit of that:

> *There were Marxists working very hard to bring about the revolution, and it was comforting for them to believe that their success was guaranteed in the long run. {according to the doctrine that "the revolution of the proletariat was inevitable"} And some of them, the only ones that were really dangerous,*

> believed so firmly in the rightness of their cause that they believed it was permissible to lie and deceive in order to further it. They even taught this to their children from infancy. These are the "red-diaper babies," children of hardline members of the Communist Party of America, and some of them can still be found infecting the atmosphere of political action in left-wing circles ...

Heck, one of them regrettably managed to "infect" the White House!

Again, Breaking the Spell[6] is both rather wide-ranging and in-depth in its philosophical consideration of its numerous subjects. Dennett's prose is fortunately "light" in the sense of a college professor adding humor into the lectures, making this less of a slog than it might be. However, my take-away is that this would make a *wonderful* series of symposia, each taking up discussions on the 50 or so specific sections here ... and that it's more of a *starting place* for consideration of "Religion as a Natural Phenomenon", than a definitive *statement* on the topic.

This is still in print (in various formats), with the paperback being quite reasonably priced once the on-line big boys have knocked nearly 40% off of cover ... nice for a book that could easily be in that stratospheric "textbook" pricing zone. Being as it's been kicking around out there for nearly a decade at this point, used copies are available, with "very good" hardcovers being offered for under a dime (plus shipping). This, of course, will not be for *everybody*, as it requires a good deal of *thinking*, which goes against the proclivities of *the faithful*, and those seeking the "simple answers/advice" mentioned a couple of places above ... but it's really a quite enjoyable read for those who like to get their synapses stretched, and I'd recommend it heartily to that demographic.

Notes:

1. http://btripp-books.livejournal.com/188328.html
2. http://btripp-books.livejournal.com/185178.html
3. http://amzn.to/29e0vE5
4. http://www.the-brights.net/
5. http://btripp-books.livejournal.com/78009.html
6. http://amzn.to/29e0vE5

Tuesday, August 2, 2016[1]

Training camp for the emotional side ...

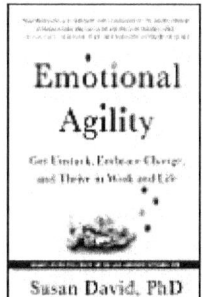

As regular readers of this space no doubt know, I get a book to review from the LibraryThing.com "Early Reviewer" program pretty much every month. However, as opposed to what's implied in the program's name, it's a fairly rare occurrence that the books are actually *early*, as in pre-publication ... I guess the LTER program is seen by most publishers as a way to get a bit of a bump in visibility well after the book is out there (even if they're sending out ARCs – advance review copies). This one, however, is not due out for another month yet.

Of course, one of the *downsides* of reviewing an ARC is that it's frequently "unfinished", with assorted bits and pieces noted as "TK" ("to come"). Also, one of the standard notes to the reviewer is to *not* quote from these as the copy may change between the ARC and the final release version ... which also goes for notes on the graphics (I almost bitched about an ARC of one of Gary Vaynerchuk's books[2] for crappy looking images when reviewing it, but the publisher fortunately sent along a copy of the beautifully-illustrated publication version before I got that posted). I bring this up because there is a lot of what I'm hoping are "place holding" rough graphic pages here that are probably going to be much nicer looking in the actual hardcover when it appears next month.

Anyway, I seem to be on a roll of getting semi "self-help" books from the LTER "Almighty Algorithm" (nice to know it *cares*), and so I wasn't overly surprised to find that I was going to be receiving Emotional Agility: Get Unstuck, Embrace Change, and Thrive in Work and Life[3] by Susan David, PhD. This is set up in something of a flowchart (with an arrow-line that runs through the book between chapters) for a "system" of moving from a starting point of being "Hooked" to an ending state of "Thriving". While I can't exactly duplicate how this lays out in the book, here's the general idea:

>   Hooked ==>
>   Showing Up ==>
>   Stepping Out ==>
>   Walking Your Why ==>
>   Moving On ==>
>   Thriving

... each step of which involves assorted other elements. The term "hooked" here relates to the idea of a "hook" in a movie ... a narrative in our head that serves to explain, rightly or wrongly, our experiences ... once we get into one of these "hooks", we start bending all other aspects of reality to fit with that narrative. The author provides several very interesting examples of automatic responses, such as filling in the missing word in *"Mary had a little _____"* ... pretty much every English speaker is going to stick "lamb" (and not, say, "velociraptor") in that blank, but we have automatic responses to situations in our life which are as predictable as that – if unhelpful, and ultimately not "reality based" – but are things which got plugged in at some point and have become our default response. She also presents some *fascinating* research on some brain science, like the relation of words to shapes, with sounds and outlines being perceived across cultural and linguistic boundaries with as many as 98% of people studied associating the same sounds (words?) with the same (sharp or bulbous) images ... and then relating this to the ability to process metaphors ("sharp" cheese, "loud" shirt, etc.), which appears to take place in the *angular gyrus* of the brain (damage to which will render people unable to make sense of metaphors, and which is 8x larger in humans than other primates).

There are four most common hooks: "Thought Blaming", "Monkey Mindedness", "Old, Outgrown Ideas", and "Wrongheaded Righteousness" ... which are pretty much what they suggest. There is the sense (although I don't think that the author outright *says* this) that these are nearly as hard-wired as the sound/shape patterns noted above. She moves from defining these to looking at how we attempt to "unhook", and offers up a 3-question quiz (with 3 options each) which shows how one typically tries to unhook ... one set of responses indicate that you're a "bottler", which means you *"try to unhook by pushing emotions to the side and getting on with things"*, and another indicates a "brooder", who is likely to *"stew in their misery, endlessly stirring the pot around, and around, and around"*. Not surprisingly, there is a definite gender disparity between these, with the "bottlers" typically being male, and the "brooders" typically being female.

One of the things she brings in at this point – which certainly got my curmudgeonly attention – is the benefit of negative moods ... *"The paradox of happiness is that deliberately striving for it is fundamentally incompatible with the nature of happiness itself."* (which reminds me of a phase an associate of mine was going through where he was constantly trying to [force][4] happiness, which was really irritating to everybody else around him) ... which is followed up with sections on "Good News About Bad Moods", and "The Upside of Anger".

There was a third option in that brief survey, and those who selected that other option were "being present", which is the topic of the first step of the process here ... "Showing Up". This step is broken into three elements: "Practice Self-Compassion", "Choose Willingness", and "Learn from Thoughts and Emotions". In the first of these the author goes into quite a lot of detail contrasting *guilt* from *shame* ... *"Guilt is the feeling of burden and regret that comes from knowing you've failed or done wrong."*, while *"Shame casts one not as a human being who did a bad thing, but as a human being who is bad."*, with the difference being "self-compassion". Interestingly, she notes that criminal recidivism rates are higher for those who exhibit shame over those whose equivalent emotion is a sense of guilt. The "willingness" is largely framed here in terms of cravings – that if you are willing to accept the *fact* of a craving, you are more likely to avoid it, rather than struggling with the whole concept (sort of like the A.A. idea of "not drinking today"). In the "learning" part, she introduces a question: *"What the func?"*, a shorthand for *"What is the function of this emotion?"*, the analysis of which can reveal a lot of deeper realities hidden beneath the external levels of things like anger.

The next step is, well, "Stepping Out", which includes sub-elements of "Notice with Curiosity and Courage", "Create the Space in Between", and

"Let Go". One piece of this that I (predictably) found of interest was the research of James Pennebaker where:

> *In each study ... the people who wrote about emotionally charged episodes experienced a marked increase in their physical and mental well-being. They were happier, less depressed, and less anxious. ..."*

... which reminded me of the "morning pages" discipline (see here[5] or here[6]). She relates this to a project with a group of 100 senior engineers who got down-sized late in their careers, a third did a writing discipline like this, a third did a more neutral writing assignment, and a third didn't write ... *"the degree of change between them was astonishing ... the men who had delved into how they truly felt were three times more likely to have been reemployed than those in the control groups"*! Referring to a wider study of similar situations she notes: *"by dissolving the entanglement that had built up between their impulses and their action so they could see their experience in context, and from a broader perspective, they flourished despite it all.".* She also offers up some techniques for "becoming more mindful", and shows an interesting "perception" quirk, where context determines meaning ... how (written out differently than here) A B C and 12 13 14 can have exactly the same lines being seen as "B" in one and "13" in the other.

The next step, "Walking Your Why", just has one part: "Choice Points: Make Towards Moves" ... both of which are sort of "huh?" to my ear ... the former is defined as *"the art of living by your own personal set of values – the beliefs and behaviors that you hold dear and that give you meaning and satisfaction.",* while the latter comes to bear in the face of a matrix of influences that enables the environment (culture) to make decision *for* us, ranging from "social proof" situations (buying stuff because those around us are buying) to "dangerous groupthink" ... *"The more you choose moves that are toward your values, the more vital, effective, and meaningful your life is likely to become."*

The last of these steps is "Moving On", which has two chapters, each with one multi-element part to it, first: "The Tiny Tweaks Principle" which includes "Tweak Mindsets", "Tweak Motivations", and "Tweak Habits". I was interested to see in the "mindsets" section some research I'd read in other contexts (I don't recall where, or I'd toss in a link here), which involved planting the idea among a group of hotel maids that their daily activities *"were, in fact, exercise"* which met the surgeon general's daily recommendations ... with no other changes, just having that one piece in their "mindset", the test group had lost weight, lowered blood pressure, and improved body-fat ratios compared to the control group who had not been told that what they were doing (although having the same activities) was meeting those exercise levels. Similar examples with children being exposed to information of how the brain can grow and improve with study, and elderly subjects who had varying views on the aging process, showed that just a few cognitive factors could result in significant positive changes. In the "motivations" topic, the thrust is largely regarding activities that one "had to do" versus "wanted to do" ... with the complication that *"our baser instincts have a head start ... according to brain imaging, when we're faced with a typical choice, basic attributes like taste are processed on average about*

195 milliseconds <u>earlier</u> than health attributes", meaning that the brain is likely to have made the decision that it wants that cupcake *"well before willpower even enters the picture"*. There's also some interesting research outlined in the "habits" section, where different signs (encouraging the same behavior) had different levels of effectiveness depending on their location in relation to the activity (i.e., taking the stairs), the author uses elements of this to present a number of suggestions on how to best develop the behaviors that one wants in various situations.

The second "Moving On" chapter features "The Teeter-Totter Principle", which has the elements "Live at the Edge of Your Ability", "Choose Courage over Comfort", and "Opt for What Is Workable". These hew pretty close to what you'd expect reading those sub-headings, and are presented with a fire-hose of references to well known sources as Bruce Springsteen, Jim Collins, Pierre de Fermat, Malcolm Gladwell, and many others ... way too much stuff to try to summarize here ... however the "teeter-totter" image is meant *"to illustrate the idea of balance, the sweet spot in which challenge and mastery are in a state of creative tension"* ... with the further note that *"emotional agility ... involves moving towards clear, challenging, yet achievable goals that you pursue ... because you want to, because they're important to you."*

Oddly, when the line reaches "Thriving", it starts with an extensive look at "Emotional Agility at Work", as in at one's business. This seemed to be a somewhat odd progression, but I could hardly argue that there's some seriously twisted thinking involved in current contexts:

> *The prevailing wisdom of today's business culture is that uncomfortable thoughts and feelings have no place at the office, and that employees, particularly leaders, should be either stoic or eternally optimistic. They must project confidence and damp down any powerful emotions bubbling up inside them, especially the negative ones. But as we've seen, this goes against basic biology. ...*

Dr. David has evidently done a lot of work with clients in the corporate sphere, and goes into a number of "case studies" here, looking at "hooks" that effect both individuals and groups. In a sub-section called "The Why of Work" there was another assertion which is very close to my own concerns:

> *... work provides far more than a meal ticket. It can give us a sense of identity and purpose, as well as a framework around which we organize our other activities and interests. Work can also bring substantial mental health benefits.*

This is followed by a chapter on "Raising Emotionally Agile Children" which includes a few stories of the author's own parenting efforts, and walks through suggestions for various aspects of childhood development (how to think, caring, ways to coach your kids, etc.). The book ends with a visit to the classic *The Velveteen Rabbit*, and the concept of "becoming real" ... I have always found that a serious tear-jerker, which made the close a bit of a gut-punch to me.

Anyway, Emotional Agility[7] will be hitting the store shelves on September 6, but the on-line big boys have it for pre-order at a generous 36% off of cover. This is one of those books that *could* be "for all and sundry", but that depends on how you feel about the self-help/personal-development niche. I'm glad to have read it (and have picked up a number of things to talk about with my therapist – to whom I suspect I'll be lending my copy), and think it's one of those that may end up being a long-time go-to book in the popular psychology category.

Notes:

1. http://btripp-books.livejournal.com/188662.html
2. http://btripp-books.livejournal.com/151726.html
3. http://amzn.to/29S5Qyy
4. https://youtu.be/y6Sxv-sUYtM
5. http://morningpages.net/
6. http://750words.com/
7. http://amzn.to/29S5Qyy

Wednesday, August 3, 2016[1]

Once upon a time, there was a ...

It's a fairly defining feature of shopping trips to the dollar store that one is never sure what you're going to be coming out of it with ... as stuff that's been there each of the past half-dozen times predictably *isn't* when you're up there looking for that specific item. And this is even moreso when it comes to the supply of books. I had a nice haul a couple of weeks back, coming out with four hardcover books (with a combined cover price of over a hundred bucks), and this is one of those. Of course, one of the *other* factors at the dollar store is that I'm rarely specifically *looking* for any particular book, so most of my purchase decisions are made on fairly shallow investigations into what I'm buying ... after all, they're *just a buck* if I end up with a clunker.

Well ... this one is sort of in that *"hey, what do you want for $1?"* zone ... not that it's *bad* but I had NO idea (until I'd logged it in my "reading" list and had started in on it) that this was not a discussion/analysis/system book, but was one of those "business parable" fictional narratives. As I have pointed out numerous times in the past, I do *not* relate well to this style. Give me structure, give me bullet points, give me charts and end notes and references ... don't just tell me a dopey story!

Now, Dennis Bakke's The Decision Maker: Unlock the Potential of Everyone in Your Organization, One Decision at a Time[2] is not *as* "dopey" as a lot of these sort of things are ... but it's still "neither fish nor fowl", as it were, not a straight-forward dissertation on the program of corporate re-organization that the author is pitching, nor is it particularly gripping *literature* (although, I have to admit, I was engaged enough by the telling that I didn't find this as irritating as I usually do with these "teaching story" things).

Of course, that's me ... others, I'm sure, quite like having their information cross-platformed into a parable (sort of like the jibe at the Waldorf schools where one might have a student doing their chemistry final in the form of interpretive dance or a P.E. exam satisfied with a toothpick sculpture) ... but I kept wishing Bakke would get to the point – and, unlike some other books of this sort, he did not upgrade the story with direct presentations of the material in sidebars, etc. (although there *is* a "slide deck" in the Afterword, and available on SlideShare which summarizes it fairly well).

As I was not interfacing particularly deeply with this, I also didn't end up with a lot of bookmarks in it for the "key points" (indeed, it appears that there were only *two* here, one marking a bit which reminded me of a famed Lorne Michaels quote[3], which really didn't have anything to do with the material being presented, and one marking the part with the graphics of the "slide deck" that can also be found on the book's companion site[4]), so you're going to get a lot of vague paraphrasing in this review. Sorry about that.

So ... there are these two guys who had worked in a very buttoned-down and obsessively hierarchical corporation, and they had wanted to get out there and forge their own path. They ended up buying (with the substantial assistance of an outside investor), a medical supply/device company, that, as it turns out, *also* was very regimented. The story picks up fairly early on in their tenure at the company, and with a significant catastrophe ... one of the main machines on the production line had exploded, and was a total loss. The fellow running the machine survived, because he was off trying to find the right supervisor to get the required approvals to *shut down* the machine, which he could clearly see was about to have a problem. This "institutional inability" of this worker to shut down the machine in an emergency situation is the start of the whole re-structuring of how the company does business.

There are several "stress points" here ... one of the new owners is the "idea guy" and the other is the "money guy" and they are both beholden to the lady investor who has substantial say in the company (although she's not involved on a day-to-day basis). The "idea guy" starts with setting up situations where individual workers on the production floor can stop the machines mid-run, and then expands that to a more generalized system of "decisions" ... and ultimately into "The Decision Maker Process", which (from the slide deck) is:

> *In a decision-maker organization, the leader leads by choosing a decision-maker.*
> *The decision-maker must ask for advice.*
> *The advice process brings multiple perspectives together to guide a successful outcome.*
> *But the decision-maker makes the final call – and takes responsibility for it.*

Needless to say, there is a lot of institutional inertia that the "idea guy" has to fight against to get these things implemented, aside from the resistance from his partner and their main investor. Assorted parts of the company are involved in the story at points – from the R&D teams whose specs aren't always "doable" when it gets down to prototyping, and there isn't enough communication between them and the techs (or the manufacturing) ... at one juncture somebody orders in a full product run's worth of an alternative material because, on paper, it's much cheaper and nominally to spec – but it (*spoiler alert!*) is too brittle and easily breaks – leading to the company having to absorb those costs. In another situation (*another spoiler alert!*) a long-time employee in charge of the shop floor figures he knows the manufacturing better than anybody, and doesn't need anyone else's opinions, and not only won't go through the "advice process" but he's also in the habit of simply filling in the government regulatory forms from the R&D spec sheets, rather than actually *testing* the products. One of the operators (of course, the same guy who was trying to shut down the machine) *had* tested the product and noted discrepancies – problems that had the potential of destroying the company were the government apply maximum fines. Ultimately, the owners made the manager the "decision-maker" on whether he'd be fired or not!

I guess this brings us to another good place to dip into that slide deck. Here's a list of considerations for choosing the decision-maker:

> **Proximity.** *Who's close to the issue? Are they well acquainted with the context, the day-to-day*

details, and the big picture?
Perspective. *Proximity matters, but so does perspective. Sometimes an outside perspective can be just as valuable.*
Experience. *Has this person had experience making similar decisions? What were the consequences of those decisions?*
Wisdom. *What kinds of decisions has this person made in other areas? Where they good ones? Do you have confidence in this person?*

As you might have guessed from the scant outlines above, the guy on the floor who wanted to shut off the machine takes over the job the guy who was fudging data had (who stayed on as a consultant), and there are lots of other "blossomings" of people from being given the ability to make essential decisions. Along the way a lot of people are worried about losing their jobs, but eventually find new roles, plus there's another character who had been at the same company the two owners had come from, and when *he* tries to implement this system, it's a disaster, but that's blamed on the other fellow being a total "bottom line" guy, more interested in the dollars than the work environment. This, of course, presents something of a caveat: these ideas might not be universally applicable – at least without totally over-hauling the "personality" of one's company.

As the story plays out, everything falls into place as one might expect it to (frankly, I was thinking that they should make this into a Bollywood musical, culminating in a big dance number involving the penultimate scene of the big happy company barbecue), with everybody (well, except for the "bottom line" guy at the other company) living happily ever after. La-di-da ... but I guess if you're a "parable person" this will be a *lot* more appealing to you than it was for me.

That being said, I liked The Decision Maker[5] a lot more than I typically do for things in this format, the core concepts were interesting, and the potential of this being a "business model" is quite enticing (I'd like to work there ... but, after 7 years mired in a job search, that's not a particularly high bar). This is fairly new (it came out in 2013), and the on-line big boys still have it at pretty much full price ... suggesting that this was only on the dollar store shelf due to the rotation of books in and out of Walmart (where a lot of the dollar store stock originates). However, having found its way to that channel, it also is available via the new/used guys, with "like new" copies going for as little as a penny (plus shipping).

While not what I was expecting (nor being in a format I much care for), I felt this was a worthwhile read, and can recommend it to anybody with an interest in running businesses. And, again, if you're a fan of fiction, you'll no doubt be more enthusiastic about this than I was.

Notes:
1. http://btripp-books.livejournal.com/188887.html
2. http://amzn.to/2a1cj8q
3. https://goo.gl/qcrfJe
4. http://decisionmakerbook.com/
5. http://amzn.to/2a1cj8q

Sunday, August 7, 2016[1]

Observing culinary history ...

This was another delightful, if surprising, dollar store find. Surprising in that this is relatively new (it's only been out for three years at this point), and the on-line big boys have it at *full cover* ... which means that I was *very* lucky to have run into it for a buck as it must have just have made that strange journey off of the Walmart shelves.

As my previous life had been in food publicity, I knew *of* the author (although I don't recall if I'd ever met him), and he's certainly only a one-degree-of-separation connection, having name-checked an old family friend in passing here (as somebody he'd assumed was getting the *New York Times* job instead of him). But, I'm getting ahead of myself. The book in question is Steal the Menu: A Memoir of Forty Years in Food[2] by Raymond Sokolov, who I *think* I know best from his magazine work.

To start off, I want to say this was a *delightful* and engaging read, but with the caveat that, having spent much of my early career in the PR outlands of the food biz, this could well be more appealing *to me* as a "trip down memory lane" than it might be for a random reader picking up the book.

As one would gather from the subtitle, this is a *memoir*, and not some high-concept treatise on the food/restaurant/media world. It's about where Sokolov was, what he was doing, and how it effected him. The book's set up in five sections, which largely walk through his life and experiences. To be deeply presumptive when commenting on a book by somebody with the sort of C.V. he has, I really think this would have been significantly improved if it had been broken up a bit ... as the five chapters tend to carry a *lot* of material each, and having those broken up into 3-5 thematic sections would have made this "tighter", not that it particularly *rambles* or anything, it's just that there are narratives in here which sort of meander from one into the next, where they might have been more definitive were they to stop, summarize, and then move into the next topic. Again, who am I to kibitz on his (or his editors at Knopf's) decisions? But there it is, all the same.

The book starts with a recollection of a lunch that he had with the legendary Craig Clairborne and his managing editor in 1971, in the cafeteria of the *New York Times*, when Sokolov was preparing to transition into Clairborne's role at the newspaper. The book's title comes from the advice that the legend gave his woefully unprepared successor (*"In Craig's world, I was indeed a nobody. I'd never taken a cooking class, published a restaurant review or written a recipe ... in the kitchen, I was a cipher ... I had no business at this table ..."*) during lunch ... because if you *ask* for a copy of the menu, you might well not get it (and, of course, restaurant reviewers are ideally incognito when doing their forkwork, so there's no good reason for the staff to agree to let a random person have a menu).

The initial section, "First Bites", does what one would expect in a memoir, tracing his life from his birth in Detroit a few months before the attack on Pearl Harbor. His family was more interested in food and eating out than the average, and so he ended up getting a varied basis in assorted cuisines. A bit of a child prodigy (at least in spelling), he ended up at Harvard, and then Oxford, and was working towards a doctorate in the Classics (his proposed thesis topic focused on *"rare Homeric vocabulary in Theocritus"*). In the early 60's he was one of multitudinous American youth who took advantage of the post-war exchange rate to bum around Europe, which not only allowed Sokolov the ability to deepen his connection with the classics, but also get a very good grounding in food – if mainly in the lower-end eateries affordable to the traveling college student. He passed his PhD orals at Harvard in 1965, and took a job as a correspondent in the *Newsweek* Paris office, where he frequently found himself with *"almost nothing to do"*, and an expense account ...

> ... I busied myself with entertaining "sources" ... at restaurants of high gastronomic quality. No one in the office minded. In fact, the bureau chief seemed glad to not have me nagging him for work, and it amused my colleagues that I was putting so much energy into establishing contacts in corners of French life they had no time to investigate.

His timing proved to be excellent, as it was in these years that *"the nouvelle cuisine revolution had already begun simmering in the provinces"*, and he had his first food piece published (anonymously) in *Newsweek* in 1967 based on an assignment he'd been given to check out the awarding of a third Michelin star to an Alsace restaurant, *L'Auberge de l'Ill*, which was a replacement for an initial pitch for a story about an up-and-coming chef by the name of Paul Bocuse.

Soon after, he was offered a spot back at the New York offices of *Newsweek*, and he (with his young family) landed back in the US on his 26th birthday, in August of 1967. His main responsibility in his new position was doing book reviews, which included a number of cookbooks. He had tried to angle some freelance work with magazines such as *New York*, but that hadn't gone anywhere. However, in 1971, an associate had suggested that he apply for the *New York Times* food job, who additionally mentioned the idea to *another* associate, who ended up speaking with Claibourne's editor, resulting in a lunch appointment. On the way back from that lunch, he was told that because he didn't have much of a food track record, they'd want to get "some tryout pieces" from him, which they'd pay for, and cover his expenses. They liked these and he was hired.

The next section "The Ungatronomical Me" starts out with a note (much like his impression on Craig Clairborne) about his wife's belief that he *"was radically, hopelessly unqualified for the job"* and his reflection that:

> If you had told me then that I would spend the rest of my life writing and reporting on food in major publications and in many books, I would have laughed at you.

He goes into a long-ish side track here to describe his youthful spelling bee fame (at 10 he was the youngest contestant ever in the National Spelling Bee). While this *does* seem a bit self-indulgent, it serves as a key turning point – amid all the press attention he experienced, he got *"fatally interested in journalism"*. which led him to working (doing movie reviews) on the *Harvard Crimson*, which in turn opened the door for his getting that *Newsweek* position, without which he suspects that he'd have ended up *"a disappointed retired professor of Greek at some provincial university"*.

This leads into the meat of the story, the "Food News" section, which starts with a humorous reminiscence of his first week at the *Times*, and his introductory interview with the HR department – which had evidently not been clued in that he was the new *food editor* – when asked what he had been hired for, he said he would be "handling food", and they ended up putting through the paperwork for him being an *assistant salad handler* in the cafeteria ... the error being first discovered by the rather substantial discrepancy on his first paycheck between what he was expecting and what showed up!

There is a vast lot of material in this section, and quite varied – making it somewhat difficult to cull out specifics for highlighting here. He starts with a bit of reflection of just how Clairborne had changed the "food editor" gig in his 13 years at the *Times* (including discarding *"the old food-page model of recipes handed out by food-product companies"*, a trend which would eventually doom my family's PR firm a couple of decades later), how their operation functioned (including minutia such as who answered phones in what order – he was the fourth option if everybody else was already on a call), and a look at the early growth of Chinese regional cuisine in the New York market (originating with one of those "tryout pieces" that he rushed into print when Clairborne opted to not do his last week's projects). From there he wanders off into politics (sort of – it starts with a rambling recall of a story based on presidential offspring Tricia Nixon's wedding cake, but circles back to his spelling bee days and then fast-forwards to the opening of the LBJ library, all of which anchored in the author's animosity towards Richard Nixon). He gets back to the *Times* job, and mentions that he *"was not happy with the mediocre gastronomic outback I found myself in"* (New York???) and describes how he took a rather "activist" stance in knocking down some restaurants and building up others that *"reminded me of my time in ... Paris"*, including taking credit for launching *Lutèce* into its run *"for the next thirty years as the top restaurant in the United States"*. He follows this with a return to France, and this time succeeding in connecting with Paul Bocuse. Then he's back talking about Chinese food, which leads (in a vague way) to his dismissal from the *Times*.

However, before he got canned, he was still *connected* with the paper, in the form of an (embarrassingly to all involved) at-that-point still upcoming cookbook. This is the lead story in the "Upstairs In Front" section (named for what he'd put down for "where he worked" on forms – being a description of where his desk was in their house), which covers his freelancing years. He wrote for *Time*, the Sunday magazine at the time of the *Chicago Sun-Times* called *Midwest*, he still did book reviews for the Sunday *New York Times*, and magazines like *Travel & Leisure*. Also, notably, he began writing for *Natural History* magazine, a monthly from the American Museum of Natural History (which I used to subscribe to, and so best know Sokolov's writing from), where he wrote a food column for 20 years.

One of the more significant projects of this period was his work on the book *The Saucier's Apprentice*[3], a definitive text on the art and array of classic

French sauces, that Julia Child's co-author Simon Beck noted: *"no one, not even in France, had written anything like it"*. Given that Sokolov had arranged to do the book when he still had a test-kitchen staff, it's especially a remarkable work, as his experience was at the table, and not at the stove. He says:

> *My idea was to match up the assembly-line efficiency of the old sauce system with the preservation magic of the deep freeze. ... giving directions for twenty-five brown sauces, following recipes for their most unremittingly orthodox versions in* La-rousse gastronomique. *These "small or compound" brown sauces fitted neatly into a family tree, ranging from* africaine *to* poivrade, *plus two game sauces descended from* sauce poivrade, *which constituted a third generation, demi-glace's grandchildren.*

His description of what he had to go through to get this done in his home kitchen is rather off-putting, yet the thrust of the book is to make these heretofore arcane culinary gems accessible to the home cook, to be poured out into ice cube trays, frozen, and doled out as needed. I need to get a copy of that!

In another veer (one of the points that I think would have been better served with a break into a sub-section), he goes from the efforts for making these old-school French sauces approachable to everyone, to a look at the spread of *nouvelle cuisine* into the U.S. (and global) markets. Here he name-checks chefs, restaurants, cook books, and gets into quite a lot of technical detail on how the "new cooking" was conceived and composed. Oddly (again, a sub-section split would have been useful here), this leads to his tenure at *Natural History*, where his column was framed as needing to *"reflect the various fields in which the {Museum} intersected with what people ate"* ... which he discovered was pretty wide-open as *"anthropologists had by and large ignored what the people they studied ate"*. Needless to say, with two decades of stories to draw from, this part of the book is a bit of a fire-hose of Sokolov trying to put out a wide array of the sorts of things that he covered, from cannibalism myths, the history of Navajo fry bread, Cornish vs. Finnish pasties, to the botany of the Key Lime. This leads to a discussion of the Oxford Symposium on Food and Cookery, which then leads off into more info on industry organizations and individuals, and eventually gets around to his work at the *Wall Street Journal*, initially with the short-lived *Book Digest* where he would identify books to buy excerpt rights for, and subsequently at the WSJ proper, managing a daily "arts" page.

The last section "With Reservations" starts off on September 11, 2001, with Sokolov taking his dog for a walk in southern Manhattan (*"the Journal's offices had look directly at the Twin Towers from across West Street"*). He mentions that he'd been hired to do a story on the innovative food-service network that Joe Baum had designed for the World Trade Center, back before it was constructed in the early 70's ... so he had a long history with the location ... including him having been scheduled to have lunch there in 1993 when the first terrorist attack (with a van full of explosives in the basement garage) happened. The chaos and subsequent difficulties following 9/11 caused a major shift in the WSJ, and he ended up losing the job there in 2002. This led him to starting a new book project, and picked up work at Harvard on his *"long-abandoned PhD"*. He goes into a discussion of the details of going back to academia after such a long period (unsurprisingly, his extremely obscure thesis topic had *not* been scooped up by some later Classics student). His subsequent brief foray into academia ends up with a return to the WSJ to write restaurant reviews … which then morphs into his doing "pop-food odysseys" which he compares to some of the "American folk food tradition" stories he did for *Natural History*. This rambled through searches for "the best hot dog" and different BBQ traditions around the country, the growth of Las Vegas as a culinary hot-spot (especially for insanely expensive experiences that could hardly be sustained elsewhere), the explosion of high-quality cuisine across the country (notably even in small backwaters, of which he details several), and the evolution of cutting-edge work in "molecular gastronomy" and other "modernist" experiments. His later work with the *Journal* expresses itself in notes on dozens of up-and-coming (in 2013) restaurants and chefs … which is pretty much where the book stops.

Again, because I love the subject matter (and how I ache to have some of those meals he reproduces menus of!), Steal the Menu[4] was a gripping read for me. If you are a fan of fine dining (and perhaps publishing) this should be attractive to you as well. It is certainly still in print, so you could find it at your local brick-and-mortar, especially as the online big boys aren't presently discounting it. However, as it's found its way to the dollar stores, the new/used guys are also offering it, with "very good" copies going for as little as a penny (plus shipping), so it's not going to set you back much to pick this up. I quite enjoyed this (despite my occasional bitchiness in the above), and am pretty sure you'll like it if "it's your thing".

Notes:

1. http://btripp-books.livejournal.com/189110.html
2. http://amzn.to/2a5CL18
3. http://amzn.to/2aYgzKt
4. http://amzn.to/2a5CL18

Monday, August 8, 2016[1]

My choice is "nope!" ...

This was another book obtained at the dollar store. Sometimes I get great stuff[2] there, some times "not so much". I wonder had I taken the time to look at this more closely if I'd have bothered to put it in the cart. At the time I must have figured that if it had Richard Branson and Jack Canfield involved, how bad could it be? Well ...

Choice Point: Align Your Purpose[3] by Harry Massey and David R. Hamilton, Ph.D., is based on a film (that I'd obviously never heard of) by the same name, which evidently was primarily set up by stringing together interview clips with a lot of people in fields related to the interests of the authors. More on this in a bit. It also came out in 2012, and was evidently part of the "Mayan Calendar Ending" the-sky-is-falling mania from back then (interesting, the book has no copyright date, although the Foreword, Preface, and Introduction are dated – all to late 2011 – with Amazon listing the publication date as February 1, 2012). It purports to be a "personal blueprint of transformation", but is pretty much New Age twaddle serving as a loose matrix to hold quotes from "names" interviewed for the movie.

The guy behind this, Massey, is a co-founder of NES Health Ltd., which peddles *"a 21st-century system of natural holistic health care based on integrating physics and biology"* ... this is one of those books that actual physicists *hate*, and every time the text floated a physics term, the Inigo Montoya (from *The Princess Bride* movie) quote *"You keep using that word, I do not think it means what you think it means"* came to mind ... over and over again. Almost every scientific term in here is twisted around to some cringe-worthy "unicorn fart" interpretation.

And, of course (it wouldn't be New Age without it!), they're selling a course ... which seems to follow the general outline of the book, with out-takes and transcripts from the movie (which they're also selling DVDs of).

As regular readers of these reviews know, I typically have several little slips of paper to guide me back to the "good parts" ... I had *one* in here, in the Preface (notably, not written by either of the nominal authors), which seemed pretty promising:

> The knowledge of how a cycle begins and ends is the key to using choice points. Whether the cycle lasts for one day or thousands of years, the principle of when it starts, when it ends, and what happens in between is the same. Each cycle begins with a seed event – something that sets a pattern of energy in to motion. Before the pattern repeats itself as the next cycle, however, it ends with a window of time where the pattern is absent. This place of no patterns is the choice point of the cycle. The choice point is the greatest window of opportunity for each cycle because it holds the greatest oppor-

> *tunity to change patterns of the past before they repeat. In this way, cycles of time and our power of choice are closely related.*

This reminded me a lot of the Gurdjieffian enneagram concept with the "shock points" (deleted in the since-popularized corporate "enneagram" crap) and motion ... which made me hope that the whole "Choice Point" thing would be a system along those lines. Nuh-uh.

The book *is*, however, structured to be a system of sorts. It has ten chapters across three "phase" Parts, with 3-6 topics per chapter. The "parts" are "Understanding Your World", "Align Your Purpose", and "Be The Change" ... which would be fine, I suppose, with less "fluffy" filler. What's frustrating here is that it's hard to *totally* reject the project, as there are some pretty substantial quotes from the 20 "visionaries" (some of whom *hardly* qualify for that label, being simply "newage" activists of various stripes that fit the authors' paradigm). Frankly, this whole thing reminds me (embarrassingly) of some of my college papers, which strung together more-or-less applicable blocks from multiple sources with narrative copy steering everything toward the point I was trying to establish. I wonder just how "involved" the bigger (or less woo-woo) names included here actually are/were with the project, as in a lot of cases it feels like they were interviewed once, and had various "sound bites" extracted, first for the movie, then for the book, and eventually for the course!

There *was* one thing that I actually liked here ... but it's more "structural" than anything ... at the end of each chapter there's a list of "Things To Remember", which gives one the outline of the material without being burdened with the saccharine blah-blah-blah of the actual text. Here's an example, from Chapter 7, "How To Be The Change":

> *1. Changing ourselves ensures that a change is a lasting one.*
>
> *2. We need to be a match for what we want.*
>
> *3. There is an interplay between destiny and free will.*
>
> *4. We can choose how we act within natural cycles and choose to align with specific patterns.*
>
> *5. The outer world reflects the inner world.*
>
> *6. If we look within, we can discover our inner world.*
>
> *7. If we want to see peace in the world, we need to be peaceful.*
>
> *8. If we look inside and deal with any emotional wounds, we can discover our true selves.*

Sounds great, yeah?

Now, I have to admit that I'm a cynical, curmudgeonly, cranky font of darkness, so all that "peace & love" stuff makes me snarl ... and I suspect that somebody more on the "flower power" side of the gauge would likely have *no* problem getting behind this. However, it's one of those reads that had me channeling Michael Ironside's "Ham Tyler" from the original "V" TV series[4], with his contempt for Marc Singer's "Mike Donovan" character, with the book's authors standing in as the nauseatingly light "gooder".

Needless to say, it's a good thing that Choice Point[5] only cost me a buck. This had the potential of being a valuable book, but it would have to have been taken out of the hands of its authors and put into the control of some less hearts-and-flowers types. If you're into that stuff, hey, you might like this. Bizarrely, this appears to still be in print (the on-line big boys have it at full cover price), and even stranger, the new/used guys are actually charging a few bucks for it.

Again, if they hadn't played fast-and-loose with the science, went with fewer "gooder" types stuck in as "visionaries", and wrote out the 2012 "Chicken Little" vibe, this could have been a worthwhile read … but that would be a different book, wouldn't it?

Notes:

1. http://btripp-books.livejournal.com/189425.html
2. http://btripp-books.livejournal.com/189110.html
3. http://amzn.to/2a9LDCc
4. http://v.wikia.com/wiki/V_Wiki
5. http://amzn.to/2a9LDCc

Sunday, August 21, 2016[1]

How does that work, again?

I'm always pleased to find a book like this at the Dollar Store ... which I've come to understand is often (as I'm sure is the case here) "pure luck" of my swinging by to look at the shelves when some particularly choice titles have been rolled out of Walmart and into the aftermarket. Certainly, it beats the old system of having the covers stripped off and returned to the publisher with the actual books going into the trash! I used to be confused about this, as a recent release (this one's only 4 years old) that's still at full price through the on-line big boys seems to be an unlikely find for a buck ... but now I'm just happy to get 'em!

Needless to say, that's how John Long's Darwin's Devices: What Evolving Robots Can Teach Us About the History of Life and the Future of Technology[2] got into my hands. This can be seen as a rather odd book, as Long is a *biologist* (he's Chair of the Department of Biology at Vassar), although he's also a professor of "cognitive science", which I suppose does get one into at least the neighborhood of robots. He was a PhD candidate who got enticed into studying the backbones of marlins – a fish that is incapable of surviving in captivity, so can't simply be brought into the lab. In Hawaii, he was able to obtain the backbones of recently processed marlins, and was able to study in detail the fine structure and various motions achievable via that bit of organic architecture, but this wasn't something that could be functionally *tested* as the backbone was missing the marlin.

One of the most *interesting* factors of Darwin's Devices[3] is it's very much a "science book", no so much a "popular presentation" of the subject matter, but a tracking through the *process* of "doing science", including discovering one's big errors, bad assumptions, experimental challenges, and limits caused by both funding and available technology. Early on here, the author frames what's coming with:

> At this point the best model of a marlin backbone is not a marlin backbone. Because we couldn't study it any further in the living fish, we were left with three choices. One: quit and do another project. As depressing as that sounds, sometimes it is the only practical alternative. In the hopes of finding a species that works really well for answering a ton of different questions (which would make it a "model organism"), switching species is a common response. Two: try to build a new instrument or experimental procedure to answer the question. For the stubborn and electromechanically minded, this is often a way to work out your frustrations and keep busy while you come to grips with the fact that you really, truly are stuck. Three: build a model

> of your fish. For those of us who need to keep writing papers so that we can earn tenure and win research grants, this is the way to go – we model.

While modeling offers a lot of flexibility as far as how/what you're looking into he notes *"... we always have to make, even in the most accurate models, many simplifying assumptions. The trick is to make the right ones."*. His initial "capstone" to his doctoral research involved a computer model of the dynamics of the marlin backbone in action. One can model in either the computer or in a physical device, but, as he's reminded *"every computer model is doomed to succeed"*, and *his* had the unfortunate factor of violating the laws of physics (in this case, the 2nd Law of Thermodynamics), something that did not faze the computational environment at all ... he subsequently outlines why it's often more useful to go with a physical model: *"If an engineer's design violates the laws of physics, the machine won't go on forever: instead, it just won't go."*

At this point Long goes into a discussion of the surprisingly wide array of backbones and related structures (notochords, etc.), various of which appear to have evolved independently in a number of different phylogenetic lines. This sets up the choices made for the first physical model, the Tadro (shortened form of "tadpole robots"), which *"are based on the tadpole-shaped larvae of sea squirt chordates"*, each having *"for its axial skeleton a notochord of differing stiffness"*, the stiffness controlling the swimming performance of the model, and which is genetically coded, allowing that variable to evolve from one generation to the next.

Here the author goes into a bunch of technical detail about natural selection, and how traits will change in a population across generations ... even getting into some delightfully obscure (to me) mathematical short-hand such as "delta x-bar equals delta p", which indicates how genes relate to phenotype, and logical formations such as *ceteris paribus*, a Latin phrase meaning "all else being equal", which is the method by which *"we isolate one variable and understand how it influences the whole system"*.

The Tadro model went through various stages until they had Tadro3, which was a simplified system (basically a small computer in a bowl) which, like its tadpole-ish larva predecessors, responded to light, and whose tail stiffness could be varied (the stiffness standing in for vertebrae). The "success", evolutionarily speaking, was the Tadros navigating to a light source, which was its "food". Through a number of equations, the ability to do so defined the "fitness", and so determined what particulars the next "generation" would exhibit.

Here the book wanders into a look at robotics and "intelligence", noting that the evolution of these robots involved "embodied intelligence", each generation got more efficient via optimizing chordate stiffness, not getting any "smarter" except in a body sense (the entire program that ran these is reproduced here, and it's only about 50 lines of code). There's a reasonably detailed look at the competing intelligence theories of Alan Turning and John Searle, and how these different stances can create dramatically divergent ways of considering what's happening with the robots. This then leads into a thread about the work of a number of neuroscientists, whose research points to yet another whole "world" in which the Tadros operate (and the author does admit – even celebrates – the confusion inherent in these different cognitive contexts).

There is a LOT of material being backgrounded in these sections – with discussions of if a "brain" (what one MIT professor calls a "cognition box") is really necessary, when a palette of "reflexes" might be as functional, or even more so. Various versions of these frames are charted out as both organic and electronic diagrams, and reduced into some more Greek-abbreviated mathematical formulas. It's all fascinating (and not oppressive) in context of the read, but a bit complex to summarize in this review.

While not *evolving* per se, the Tadro3 gets supplanted by the Tadro4, which is equipped to model predator avoidance. It ends up with two light sensors (to better determine direction), and "an infrared proximity detector" which is designed to some extent mimic the "lateral line" of sensing cells on fish. One of the other interesting "sciency" things here is that one of the factors that they'd set up to determine "fitness" in the Tadro3 turned out to be messing up the data. They had decided that "body wobble" was a negative, but discovered that penalizing for wobble ended up degrading the feeding efficiency ... as it was *"functionally dependent of swimming speed"*, and the faster moving units were exhibiting more wobble, but could maneuver better. There are various tables and charts looking at how they processed this info, but it stands out as big "oops", and a cautionary tale of how one's initial assumptions when setting up models need to be *very* carefully considered!

Another significant change in the Tadro4 was the addition of "vertebrae". They took the gel-based notochord of the Tadro3, made it a consistent stiffness and length, and added bead-like vertebrae ... as the other elements are constant, the flexibility of the "backbone" was only determined by the width of the "intervertebral joints", which was variable in relation to the number of vertebrae placed on it (more vertebrae, less joint space, stiffer spine). They also made two versions of the Tadro4, an evolving "prey" unit, and a non-evolving "predator". The Tadro4 was modeled on a different type of critter, an early (400 million years old) jawless vertebrate fish, *Drepanaspis*[4]. Having multiple sensors allowed the team to test for the relation of sensory systems and vertebrae, with the hypothesis that having the sensory system (to determine the presence of predators) would spur the development of (propulsion-enhancing) vertebrae.

It pains me to do so, but at this juncture I'm going to throw my hands up and say "too much stuff – can't summarize it!" ... the author bounces around between some very technical evolutionary theorizing, overviews of the experiments his team did, and charting out "adaptive landscapes" (which, short of scanning and including those graphics in here, are kind of hard to describe). He also shifts from the development of the tail-mobile Tadros, and into an "ET" (Evolutionary Trekker) called Madeleine, which has four flippers ... and is named for its vague similarity in shape to that small French pastry. This takes side trips off into considering Plesiosaurs, and aquatic vs. terrestrial tetrapods (where there are 1,679,616 possible different mobility options ... needless to say, only a tiny fraction of those being tested with models).

It's at this point that a lot of the action shifts from the college lab to the R&D centers of various robotics companies ... and ultimately off into the acronym

-laden world of DARPA and military applications of robotics. However, it's hardly just *our* folks looking at this ... he quotes an expert in the field as saying that at least *fifty-six* countries are developing robotic weapons. He quotes an associate as saying that military robots should be *"unmanned, expendable, and cause maximum damage"*, and gives an example of something called the MicroHunter which is a palm-sized torpedo-like vehicle, with just one moving part – the propeller. These were tested against a SEAL diver, and the SEAL was only able to stop these from hitting the target 50% of the time (they have otherwise been getting 100% marks) – and that was with just *four* in play. The book ends up with a "philosophical" look at how to manage this sort of technology, but with a "SkyNet" dystopian vibe hanging over it all.

As noted, [Darwin's Devices](#)[5] is still in print, and the on-line big boys seem to have it a full cover price. However, having gotten into the Dollar Stores, "good" copies are available from the new/used guys for a penny plus shipping, and "new" copies can be had for under a buck (plus shipping). Again, this isn't exactly one of those "popular science" books, as it's more focused on the experimental/research/theory aspects than most of those would be ... which is one of the reasons I'm looking to pass this along to my robotics-obsessed (she's currently off developing an aerial mapping drone on a summer internship!) engineering student daughter ... but it might be a bit overwhelming for some (I'll admit that I got a bit lost at a few points here). It is, however, a fascinating look at a line of research, with all the complexities involved in that, with an over-all arc which charts out the (somewhat disturbing) development of this sort of robotic system. A definite recommendation for all science/engineering geeks out there (others' "mileage may vary" on how you'd like this).

Notes:

1. http://btripp-books.livejournal.com/189661.html
2-3. http://amzn.to/2aEsyOK
4. https://en.wikipedia.org/wiki/Drepanaspis
5. http://amzn.to/2aEsyOK

Monday, August 22, 2016[1]

The Odd Couple ...

This was another Dollar Store find ... with the standard "didn't go looking for it" aspects involved in seeing something that looked plausible staring out from the shelf for a buck. I don't think that I'd have acquired this if it *hadn't* been in that channel, as I really didn't *care* that much about the authors (and their legendary mis-matched relationship), but it was "interesting enough" to get into my cart a few months back.

I'm glad that these various factors conspired to get me into Mary Matalin and James Carville's Love & War: Twenty Years, Three Presidents, Two Daughters and One Louisiana Home[2], as it was a thoroughly enjoyable read. I'd been hesitant, because I'd hated the Clintons so much, and Carville was their personal media pitbull ... and I wasn't sure that I wanted to put myself through some glorification of that sorry period in our nation's history. Similarly, I wasn't sure that I really wanted to follow behind Matalin's track through two Bush administrations ... with the emotional scars still left from those years.

However, while the political stuff is certainly in here, it's much more a dual memoir of two completely different political players (if you're not familiar, Matalin is a conservative Republican, who is remarkably fond of her former boss Dick Cheney, and Carville is a co-conspirator with the Clinton Crime Family – and otherwise a supporter of the worst of leftist politics), and how their lives have played out. The dichotomy here is perfectly clear, as the book is set in two typefaces – one for the "Mary" parts, and one for the "James" parts – so you always know who's talking.

If there was one pivotal element here, it would be when the couple (well, *family* at that point) up and left D.C. for New Orleans. Carville, of course, was from down there, and still had a huge extended family around, but Matalin was from *Chicago*, and as hot and humid as our summers can be, it was certainly a change for her (although, oddly, she favors open windows, while he wants heavy-duty AC). Of course, their having their daughters (and the various stories of the kids growing up) is another thread here, but the "good stuff" is really the fly-on-the-wall look into the world of Washington, politically, socially, and its accompanying media.

Flipping through this, I'm seeing that most of my little bookmarks are highlighting places with "gotcha" reminiscences (needless to say, mainly from Matalin), which throw a particular light on stuff that usually goes unseen. The book sort of (it jumps around quite a bit) starts with the biggest conflict between the two, the re-election loss of Bush Sr., for whom Matalin was deputy campaign manager, to Clinton, whose campaign was being run by Carville. Following the election, Matalin couldn't find any work in her field, and ended up being hired by CNBC to co-host a "girl-gab show" with Jane Wallace, called *Equal Time*, that had been described as "*Wayne's World* on estrogen" (something with which it initially shared a lot of production values). This started out as pretty much just a time-filler, but ended up building up a devoted cult following, which eventually got noticed. She says:

> It turns out, when your ratings are lousy and nobody's watching, you are left alone to die a quiet TV death. It's when you have a hit that the problems start. Once we were "discovered" by the TV critics, the CNBC suits appeared like Death Eaters and tried to suck the blood and soul from _Equal Time_ ...

The "last straw" for her was that she did _not_ want to do anything about the O.J. Simpson trial:

> The rest of television was doing the O.J. Trial _non-stop_. What intelligent or edifying thing could I possibly add to that? What intelligent or edifying thing could _anyone_ say about that? The O.J. Trail clearly marked the early stages of cable crapdom: the dumber the story, the greater the coverage.

This then moves into the couple's work on _Crossfire_ and their long friendship with the late Tim Russert, with various stories from each of them regarding how that show impacted both sides of the political spectrum.

Again, this is very much a _personal_ memoir for the two authors, and it here shifts into discussing Mary's multitudinous pets, and James' dislike of them all ... followed by a chapter on raising their kids ... followed by a very brief chapter on, well, "bedroom stuff" (largely summarized by its last line: _"none of your damn business"_) ... followed by a look at how they had grown up, and how James is a classic case of ADHD (and how different they are in their personality types – she's big on spontaneity, and he's a stickler for a locked-in schedule).

This takes us to a chapter called "The Dark Ages" which is about the "hanging chads" end to the 2000 Presidential election. Just about the only thing (well, aside from the kids) that seemed to save their marriage is that Carville thought Gore was an ass, so didn't have quite as much blind devotion to him as he did to Clinton ... but it wasn't something that he was prepared for when Matalin got tapped to work for V.P. Dick Cheney. She had _insisted_ that it was only going to be for six months, although this wasn't going to be the case. One part here that drew my attention was in her discussion of how hectic these transitions can be ...

> Meanwhile, it turns out that there _is_ something worse than a transition hell that's smooshed into a few short weeks. And that is transitioning from an administration with a civility and maturity level lower than Animal House's, a comparison that is actually a compliment to the outgoing Clinton administration.
>
> You think I'm being a partisan exaggerator? Well, would you call this mature and civil? Once into the White House, we found all the W's had been stripped from our computer keyboards and our desks were full of molding garbage, uneaten fast food and/or porno – and those were only the

> *cute stunts. The vice president's office were the worst because, as it turns out, Al Gore is not what you'd call graceful in defeat. Instead he lived up to his reputation as a real loser.*

Because of the destruction of the White House facilities by the outgoing regime, the VP transition was happening from Cheney's *home*, with a single phone line for communications. Matalin ended up with a pretty impressive dual title, Counselor to the Vice President, and Assistant to the President, giving her remarkable access across the Bush Jr. administration. By August 2001, she had the office of the VP, *"a (mostly) well-oiled machine"*, and she and James took a cruise together without the kids, and things began to look like she was ready to start her own transition out of the White House.

And then it was September 11, 2001. That morning Carville was speaking at a conference and said, regarding Bush *"I hope he doesn't succeed, but I am a partisan Democrat."* ... minutes later cell phones started buzzing around the room, with the news of planes flying into buildings. Matalin had arrived at work "spiffed up" in designer duds (and spike heels) to make an impression at a labor meeting scheduled for later that day ... a bad choice as things turned out.

Perhaps the most fascinating part of Love & War[3] is the play-by-play from within the White House (and subsequently those "undisclosed locations" that the V.P. was being shuttled off to) on 9/11 and the time following. As you may recall, Bush was out of town (reading to school kids in Florida) when the attack came, and the Secret Service whisked (here described as being physically picked up and carried) Cheney off to a safe room in the sub-levels of the White House, while most everybody else was told to get away from the building, as it was expected that a plane (perhaps the one that was taken down by its passengers) was headed for there. Matalin was a few blocks away (in her stiletto heels) when she got a call from the Secret Service – Cheney wanted her there, and they managed to find her and get her back and down to the WW2-era PEOC (Presidential Emergency Operations Center) ... evidently the first time this space was used for its intended purpose, and what had been *"state-of-the-art in FDR's day"* was poorly equipped for current tech. Plus, with as many people who ended up being in that space, they found the ventilation was less than needed. One poignant bit here was in her discussing trying to get in contact with key administration members ... *"Secretary of Defense Donald Rumsfeld was literally incommunicado ... We discovered later that he was pulling his injured and dead colleagues out from the smoke and debris of the Pentagon carnage."*

I don't believe I've read any specifically "post-9/11" books (although I've seen quite a bit online), so I don't have other examples to compare this to ... but being able to look over Matalin's shoulder, as it were, as she discusses what was happening in the upper reaches of government over those days, weeks, and months of doubt, rage, and chaos is remarkable here. The details are revealing, and they confirm my counter-to-the-MSM-story gut reaction about the *nobility* of the Bush administration, especially when compared with its venal predecessor. Needless to say, being part of Cheney's team, her family life was deeply disrupted, as Matalin was off at whatever "undisclosed location" that they were keeping the V.P. (one story she tells was of a Christmas trip out to Wyoming when they were able to have their families join them ... she had shipped out – on *Air Force Two* – all of their holiday ornaments, and requested the advance team find a tree for their living quarters, which she describes: *"{it} wasn't a tree so much as a spindly shrub with a few errant branches, a very small version of a freaking Charlie Brown tree"*, which caused a major break-down ... James came through, however, and notes: *"the tree was kind of puny, in a comical way"*). Needless to say, as time rolled on, the Iraq war became an issue in their household, and in 2003 she finally disengaged from the White House job. In the course of this both authors do a lot of musing on the reality of the D.C. scene ... I found this bit by Carville worth noting:

> Most times people do something because they actually think it's going to work out. Most times, they are not evil people trying to undermine America. Most times, there's not some underlying conspiracy or motive. ... There's a great tendency to overestimate conspiracies and underestimate stupidity.

Of course, this is a guy who worked hand-in-hand with the Clintons, so you'd expect him to try to sweep as much "evil people trying to undermine America" under the rug as possible. But, I digress.

As one would expect in a memoir, there's a lot of "personal" stuff in here, a lot of family issues with the Carvilles (including its matriarch, his mother, dying during this time), the lingering death of their much-depended-on housekeeper/nanny, and even their getting re-married. It turns out that their original nuptials were not up to snuff in the view of the Catholic church (Mary had been previously married), and, as she was starting to get into that brand of imaginary friend stuff, this both became an issue and an excuse to throw a big party down in Louisiana. Lots of stuff about new friends, new experiences, and other revelations of their shift to New Orleans, including their girls growing up and heading off to college.

Amid this there's also a section when they "get partisan" again, with reflections on some of the campaigns and opposing sides of issues they'd been on. Matalin has a *great* "rant" in here about dealing with the MSM (in parts worthy of Limbaugh or Gutfeld), which of course spoke to me. Here's some of the key bits:

> Eighty-nine percent of journalists self-identified as liberal. ... Who were the 11 percent who confessed to not being liberal? ... As annoying as it is to the public, I much prefer today's open partisanship of the media. Nothing produced more hair pulling, breast thumping and chain-smoking in GOP camps than reporters professing no bias while reporting like Democratic operatives. ... Do you ever see even a scintilla of fair and balanced reporting from MSNBC ...?

To his credit, Carville takes a less aggressive tone in this part (despite his clear loathing of many of the players in both Bush administrations), and has a lengthy entry taking a look, on various levels, at "what's wrong with Washington", and this bit certainly rung a bell:

> *I sincerely believe that part of the problem is that so many of the people in positions of power in Washington truly, utterly, do not understand the struggles of average people. They literally can't wrap their minds around the battles ordinary people have to fight every single day ...*

The book, which came out in 2013, sort of peters out (being something of a "snapshot" from their lives, things don't get all tied up with a ribbon), taking a look back at the Katrina disaster, and how it is still effecting things down there, and has a final "punctuating" event of the BP *Deepwater Horizon* explosion (and subsequent major oil spill), which happened in 2010 (a scant few months past the Saints winning the Super Bowl – an event that the authors had been heavily involved in – which was a huge thing for the New Orleans community). This part isn't long, but it sort of puts a pin in the timeline as a place to leave off the chronological narrative, and allowing them to finish with some "looking to the future" stuff.

I really enjoyed reading Love & War[4] ... the back-and-forth between Matalin and Carville (although not *in response* to the other's writing – they appeared to have written this separately, but in tandem, taking up a topic and letting the editors piece the bits together) is an appealing format. It does, though, go without saying that this would be *far* more engaging for "political junkies" than it would be for those whose obsessions lie in other realms. That being said, however, the "behind the scenes" looks at those challenging times following 9/11 are well worth the price (and I'm talking retail, not Dollar Store here).

It appears that the hardcover is now out of print, but there's a more recent paperback version out there, so is a pretty good bet to be available at your local brick-and-mortar book vendor As I noted up top, the hardcover has gotten out to the aftermarket and the on-line new/used guys have "like new" copies of it for 1¢ (plus shipping), so if you can't find a Dollar Store copy, that would be your best bet. Again, it's an engaging read, with some really fascinating material in amid the "Mary & James' life together" stuff.

Notes:

1. http://btripp-books.livejournal.com/189931.html
2-4. http://amzn.to/2bc4O44

Saturday, September 3, 2016[1]

An amazing look at an icon ...

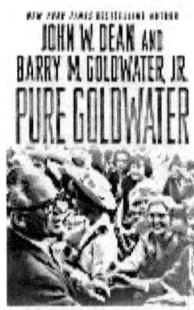

This has been sitting in my "to be read" piles for a few years ... I picked it up at the Dollar Store down in the Back of the Yards neighborhood when I was working with "the worm guys" ... which was a strange place to find a book on Barry Goldwater. That's the old stomping grounds of the nefarious Saul Alinsky[2] (philosophical godfather to both the execrable current POTUS, and the equally vile Democratic presidential candidate), but maybe the hard-left skew of the area is the reason this was still sitting on the shelf for a misplaced Libertarian to find it.

This might have sat around longer, waiting for me to randomly develop a hankering for some "political history", if not for my recent read of Wayne Allyn Root's *The Conscience of a Libertarian*[3], which was primarily inspired by Goldwater's *The Conscience of a Conservative* (which Root claims to carry with him everywhere) ... and my curiosity was piqued enough to delve into Pure Goldwater[4].

I'm am very glad I decided to finally get around to reading this, as it is a *fascinating* book. It is put together by Goldwater's son, Barry Jr., and John Dean (yes, Nixon's White House lawyer), who have been friends since their early teens – both, obviously, having close connections to the subject of the book. However, this is not *written* by them, but *assembled* from the vast stores of archival material held by the Goldwater family and the Arizona Historical Foundation. There is so much material because Goldwater was a dedicated recorder of his activities, both carrying around a portable typewriter and camera (he was an award-winning photographer), and later making taped notes for others to type up. In the Preface the "authors" write:

> In fact, this is a book by Senator Goldwater about himself, although he did not write it for publication. Throughout his adult life he paused from time to time – albeit on an irregular basis, yet with sufficient frequency to create a meaningful collection – to gather and share his thoughts and put them down in written form.

The current book is nearly 400 pages, and they note that it was seriously trimmed down to reach *that* length, as the amount of available material is quite voluminous (not even counting official government/legal transcripts – some of which *are* excerpted here), and they eventually had to bring in outside editorial help to tighten things up and bring down the page count.

The primary source material for Pure Goldwater[5] is the journals that he intended as a record of his life to provide to his children ... so this is quite personal (and occasionally somewhat pedagogical in a "Dad says" mode), and, by extension, revealing of the man far beyond what an intentional autobiography would provide. In fact, the authors point out that there were several significant items in there that *they* had never known, including that Nixon had at one point promised Goldwater the ambassadorship to Mexico (which they say he would have *loved*), and that Ford had asked him to be his Vice President ... which, if it was news to his family, it's probably the first time this info has gotten out to the public.

Again, this is collected of various materials in various forms, and from various dates ... and while Goldwater had put down a number of "recollections", much of what is in the earlier parts are pieces he composed some 50 years after the fact, so they are, understandably, not as immediate as his later journals. One amazing item (which is where the book starts) is a letter he wrote to Thomas Edison when he was 14 years old, letting the famous inventor know that he was operating a radio station and was very interested in electricity – this having surfaced in Rutgers' Edison archives in 1989, and sent to the Senator. One of the first recollections here was of how early his interest in flight appeared ... he pegs it to 1917 (he would have been 8) ... and he got his pilot's license in his late teens (and flew for the military – eventually reaching the rank of Major General – as well as personally for decades, with many of the notes here recorded while in flight).

Goldwater's family owned a mid-size department store in Phoenix, AZ, and when his father died at the end of his freshman year at University of Arizona, he opted to join the family business rather than continuing with college. Instead of being a "silver spoon" kid coming in to run the show, he wanted to learn the business: *"I started literally at the bottom in the piece goods section ... after that I worked in every department in the store except for corsets and shoes ... I gradually worked my way up until I was merchandise manager of ladies ready-to-wear ..."*. He helped the business navigate the depression (*"the business didn't make any money but it didn't lose any either"* and they *"were able to maintain our employees and our salary scale"*), and he was elected as president of the board in 1937, running the company until he left for military service in 1941.

As a Libertarian (a movement strongly influenced by Goldwater, although he was a life-long Republican), I was amazed at how much what he wrote fifty (or more) years ago could just as easily be put out there today as criticisms of the government. In a 1937 piece directed at FDR he says *"Instead of the businessman having confidence in you today, he distrusts you and fears your every utterance."*, and *"Are you going further into the morass that you have led us into or are you going to go back to the good old American way of doing things ...? I would like to know because I like the old-fashioned way of being an American a lot better than the way we are headed for now."* – how 2016 of him!

Goldwater started out slowly in politics, getting involved in local Phoenix and Arizona politics as an outgrowth of his activities as a local business leader with the Phoenix Chamber of Commerce ... eventually being elected to the Phoenix City Council, and becoming the campaign manager for a Republican candidate for Governor. Here's a bit from a speech he gave in that campaign:

> *Our founders pledged their lives, their fortunes but most important of all they pledged their sacred honor. Today, because of the almost total ignoring of*

> those basic concepts, we find our nation treading on the threshold of socialism. Our government's being run by people who think one way and act another. Whose fault is this? It is yours and mine – the people of this state and nation. Plato once said, "The penalty that people pay for not being interested in politics is to be governed by people worse than themselves." Now, hasn't that come true?

The briefest glance at D.C. would confirm that! He, obviously, *did* have an interest in politics, and mounted his first Senate campaign in 1952, creating quite a splash by defeating the sitting Senate Majority Leader. There are numerous pieces here that Goldwater wrote as he was acclimating to the way that things get done in Washington ... the last bit of this particularly stood out:

> While I am trying to learn to be patient, I find it exasperating. It is difficult to get used to the time that is wasted here, for it is a fact that much time is wasted. Nonetheless, this may be just fine. For I subscribe to what I heard someone say the other day: It isn't the laws that are passed here that help the country; it's the legislation that doesn't pass that really does the country more good.

This clear distrust of the ever-growing power of the government is also reflected here (my edits to focus on the main point):

> I have learned some things in this year. I have learned that our fears in the West about people in this country wanting to circumvent the Constitution are certainly true. And I am just as fearful as I was a year ago when I was heading to Washington that this could and might happen to this country. People here don't recognize rights of the states. Rather they laugh at them. The concept of government here is one of federal domination. It's one of the federal operations doing everything. ... Members of Congress ... have lost sight of this basic fundamental concept of government that the power of the federal government stems from the states and the people, and not in the other direction.

And this was decades before a dictatorial madman decided that he could completely "circumvent the Constitution" by *pen & phone* fiat! Interestingly, in the (highly recommended) book[6] referenced above, Mr. Root charts out a superb plan for re-organizing government – no doubt originating out of these sorts of concerns initially voiced by Goldwater.

Oddly, there is very little from Goldwater's 1964 presidential campaign, as it appears that he had largely put aside his journal writing during that time. There is material here indicating that he and JFK were friendly (there's a pic of Kennedy included with a note he'd written on it encouraging Goldwater to follow his "talent" and become a pro photographer rather than a politician!), and they had discussed the upcoming campaign, even to the extent that *"we talked about the possibility of staging an old-fashioned cross-country Lincoln-Douglas type debate on the issues of the day"*. However following the assassination, Goldwater was certain that he didn't have a chance, with the Democrats using JFK's death to push through massive legislation that would have been hard to pass otherwise, and Johnson into the White House.

Another thing I found strange is that about 1/3rd of the book is looking at Richard Nixon. Sure, the Nixon years were those when Goldwater was strongest in the Senate, but it seemed "off tone" for the rest of the book (perhaps this is due to John Dean being as familiar with that administration as he is). I didn't flag a lot to bring up in here from that part of the book, but there is one bit that I hope is top-of-mind for the aforementioned Mr. Root in his current political ventures ... this in a meeting with other Congressional leaders and Nixon, where each was able to raise key concerns:

> *I minced no words in saying the administration reminded me of when Eisenhower came into power and failed to remove some thirteen thousand Truman appointees, and went on to subject himself to eight years of abuse from people in government who actually hated the Republican Party and who would never follow the policies laid down by the leadership. I reminded the president that only a few weeks after his inauguration I had advised him that if he did not get control of his government by May he would never get it, and I said, frankly, Mr. President, you don't have control now and I don't see how you are going to get it unless something drastic is done.*

Needless to say, the past 50 years have been a long ugly slide away from greatness in this country, and Goldwater saw this all too clearly. At several points here he is questioning remaining in the Senate because of how bad things were even then, and this is part of his thinking on that:

> *We are following the same paths that were followed by the ancient government of Rome and by the government of Austria when it brought on the depression of the late 1920s and 1930s. We are becoming a military power of second rate stature at a time when the world only understands strength and needs more of it, not less of it. ... I am deeply concerned at this point in our history and my life, as to whether or not this country is going to remain a free Republic or whether we have gone so far down the road to socialism, particularly now that we have controls over the economy here in Washington, that we will find it impossible to return. No country in the history of the world has ever made an exploration into government control and then*

> *found it possible to completely extricate themselves from that situation. ... It is a terrible time in our history, a very particular one, but not unusual in the sense that we might think no other country or people have ever faced it; in fact they all have. The sad and terrible thought is that none of them has had he guts to come back after facing the failure of the loss of freedom.*

Oh, one thing to note on the Nixon material ... I don't know if this has surfaced in other sources, but it appears that Nixon kept his VP, Spiro Agnew, totally "out of the loop" on nearly everything, to the extent that it became a recurring point of contention in Goldwater's journals. Another factor that I had not been aware of was how much a "player" General Al Haig had been in the Nixon White House – as Chief of Staff ... as my view of him was almost exclusively from his tenure as Reagan's Secretary of State.

The last parts of Pure Goldwater[7] look at his stands of a wide range of issues, many of which might surprise you (there's a *lot* of reasons he's an icon to Libertarians), plus a very detailed chronology of his life. By the time I was done with this, I felt I'd been able to follow a great man around and be privy to his thoughts over his whole life. Needless to say, this makes the book stand out as something special. It's not an outsider telling a life story, nor is it a "for publication" somewhat sanitized autobiography, but something else, with the protagonist telling his story, but in a manner intended for his kids, and not for the whole world.

It sadly appears that this is out-of-print, except for an e-book edition, even though it's a reasonably recent publication (2008). There are numerous copies in the new/used vendors channel, however, with "like new" copies offered for as little as a penny plus shipping ... so it's available. Obviously, 400 pages of a politician's reminiscences isn't something that's "for *everybody*", but if you're libertarian-inclined, or have an interest in politics in general, I *urge* you to pick up a copy, as it brings a near-mythic figure to life in a way that I certainly didn't expect when I got mine!

Notes:

1. http://btripp-books.livejournal.com/190034.html
2. http://www.conservapedia.com/Saul_Alinsky
3. http://btripp-books.livejournal.com/187995.html
4-5. http://amzn.to/2aZ068O
6. http://btripp-books.livejournal.com/187995.html
7. http://amzn.to/2aZ068O

Sunday, September 4, 2016[1]

Originally nothing. Where is dust?

This may be a bit into the "TMI" zone ... as I came to be reading this book through a "very personal" route, one that many might not choose to volunteer in public. I quit drinking 31 years ago ... but have just recently begun to attend A.A. Meetings because, while I evidently "got" the *first* step way back in 1985, I've been feeling that I "missed something" regarding the full *program*. As regular readers know, I'm at *least* "deeply agnostic", if not enthusiastically "antitheistic", so the second (and third) steps[2] in A.A. were a wall that I could not figure a way around. A couple of weeks back, I had a discussion with a fellow following a meeting who suggested the Korean Zen concept of "don't know" might provide me with a way to have a "higher power" that did not seem to be a lie (which would, in my view, taint all the subsequent steps as being built on a falsehood).

This struck a chord with me, as I had long quoted a bit of this (as I recalled it) from a talk I'd attended at the 1993 Parliament of the World's Religions here in Chicago, where a Korean Zen master (possibly Samu Sunim, but I wasn't able to find definitive identification) did a talk, and said something to the effect of *if you say "yes", I hit you with stick, if you say "no", I hit you with stick – what you gonna do?*, with the intent of getting into that pure "don't know" consciousness. Inspired by this, I went off to Amazon and found Don't-Know Mind: The Spirit of Korean Zen[3] by Richard Shrobe and dug into it. While I didn't have a "lightbulb moment" with this (the "don't-know mind" is still pretty abstract, but perhaps less so than *gravity*, which was what I was otherwise coming up with as a "higher power" that I had *faith* existed), it certainly fleshed out the concept to the point where I suspect I might be able "to work with it".

Anyway, embarrassing "breaking of anonymity" out of the way ... this is quite an interesting read. First of all, there is an approachability of this being issued under the author's "birth name", rather than his "Zen name", Wu Kwang ... this alone is enough to indicate this isn't some newage twaddle, as it's the opposite of what frequently happens in those cases where somebody without much in the way of credentials starts "spewing in public" based largely on some "sacred name" they've come up with! Shrobe is the main teacher at the Chogye International Zen Center in New York City, and this book is primarily a collection of talks that he's given there.

The book operates on several levels. There is a goodly amount of the *history* of Zen presented here, with discussions of the various "schools", and the key figures involved in these. There is the presentation of teaching materials, and explanations of how these work, and there is the underlying offering of what one might hope is possibly enlightening. The book is divided into three sections, "Origins", "The Classical Period", and "The Modern Period", each looking at highlighted teachers and approaches. Because this is based on *talks*, this does not hew to a particularly academic voice, with the author "breaking the fourth wall" here and there to add context and commentary for the reader, which is attractive when it happens. Because it's coming from a Korean Zen standpoint, the names of the protagonists are given in their Korean forms, but – very usefully – these are followed by their Japanese and Chinese forms, which are (for me) typically more familiar.

Now, when I was reading this, I was primarily focused on bits I could *use* in wrapping my head around the "step" thing, so most of my little bookmarks are leading me back to things I found illuminating, rather than illustrative quotes. So, bear with me. The first of these deals with a teacher named T'aego, born around 1300ce, when the Mongols ruled the region. T'aego had established a mountain Zen center near what is currently Seoul, and sought to bring together the feuding "Nine Mountain Schools" into a single school that would revitalize Korean Zen. The kong-an (koan) that grabbed my attention was:

> The ten thousand things all return to one.
> To what though does the one return?

The author cites a book[4] that came out some time back on the teachings of this T'aego, and notes that he was inspired by parts of this. This section is exemplary of how the "discussing" vibe comes across here, as there are bits detailing how the various elements work in this, how things (a presentation at the palace for the King) would have been perceived at the time, and the offering explanations such as:

> T'aego is establishing that on the one hand you can look at this thing as being something which is before name, before form, before speech, before words, never moving, never coming, never going, just universally covering everything. But at the same time, you can find this truth revealed in every activity, in every function, because everything is expressing it just as it is. These are two sides of the coin.

For a historical example, there's a look at the transmission between the Fifth and Sixth Patriarchs, where the head monk of the Fifth Patriarch's monastery was assumed to going to be the one to get the nod. However, the Fifth had requested that everybody there write a poem to demonstrate their "understanding and attainment". The head monk wrote his poem on the wall (rather than directly presenting it to the Fifth Patriarch), which was noted as being a "good poem", however, Hui-neng, a newcomer who could neither read nor write, heard the poem and realized that *"it did not go to the heart of Zen Dharma"*, and dictated a new poem to be put up next to the head monk's. The Fifth Patriarch saw that the author of the second poem was the one to pass along the transmission to, but he had to do so in secret, and then send Hui-neng (now the Sixth Patriarch) away from the monastery, as he knew the internal politics would not accept him. For several days the Fifth Patriarch gave no teachings, and the monks began to wonder, and he eventually said "the Dharma has left here" and explained that the lay brother who had been working in the rice shed had become his successor!

Another snippet which resonated for me was from the teachings of Kyong-Ho, a "modern" figure (1849-1912):

> *What does this which is now seeing, hearing, and thinking look like? Examine and observe this matter carefully. ... Let your examination and observation be focused at the one point and do not forget it. Keep it before you by raising doubt and questioning yourself.*

Shrobe notes that "doubt" here is perhaps better rendered as "perplexity", and that "don't-know" is the feeling of trying to frame the "this" in the above. Later there are a few other pithy statements from Kyong Ho, including one that reminds me of one of my favorite Hunter S. Thompson quotes[5]:

> *Don't expect to practice hard and not experience the weird. Hard practice that evades the unknown makes for a weak commitment.*

While this didn't get me where I was hoping it might, I certainly enjoyed reading it, and found the approach taken by its author ideal for presenting the material. Having previously only had that one brush (at the '93 PWR) with Korean Zen, this certainly filled in more details than *"I hit you with stick"* (although that element *is* touched on here). Of course, I came to this specifically looking for details on the title state, and might have benefited more from something more conceptually focused, but that would have no doubt been a lot less enjoyable read that this proved to be.

Don't-Know Mind[6] must certainly have its audience out there, as it's not only still in print (a dozen years later), but the on-line big boys have it at full cover price, and the new/used guys don't have it for cheap (well, it can be had for 1/3rd to ½ of cover). I would certainly recommend this for anybody interested in Zen, and the Korean manifestation thereof ... but it's probably not an "all and sundry" thumbs-up because it's really for those with those sort of interests. It is certainly an engaging read, however, from where I'm sitting.

Notes:

1. http://btripp-books.livejournal.com/190421.html
2. http://www.aa.org/assets/en_US/smf-121_en.pdf
3. http://amzn.to/2b97hdz
4. http://amzn.to/2cqs6mM
5. https://goo.gl/7S8CKv
6. http://amzn.to/2b97hdz

Friday, September 9, 2019[1]

A lucky tale ...

As one might imagine, much of the time when picking up books at the dollar store, they are purchased more on the fact of *being* only a buck, rather than my having a particularly burning desire to read the book in question. This leads to a lot of dollar store "finds" sitting in the to-be-read piles for long stretches of time. The current book went through this, having been bought nearly 4 years ago (when it had just been out 3-ish years), and only in the past few weeks fitting in the mix of what I was feeling like reading.

Anyway, Jere Van Dyk's Captive: My Time as a Prisoner of the Taliban[2] grabbed my attention, and got into the reading queue. I will admit that I took a peek at some of the existing reviews before jumping into it, so I was a bit hesitant, having noted the slams like *"selfish, careless guy cries for your sympathy"* ... and, frankly, that's not *uncalled for* here ... but it hardly encapsulates the story.

Jere Van Dyk is a journalist, writing for the *New York Times*, CBS News, and others. In the 1980's, he was embedded with the Mujahideen during their struggle against the Soviet invasion of Afghanistan. In 2008, he got the idea of doing a similar type of story, and set about getting himself hooked up with connections to the Taliban. What he seems, at least on some level, to assume is that he can set up the trip he's intending like it's a rafting adventure on the Brahmaputra or something ... which is certainly *not* the case. Early on here he's pretty clear on that point (albeit this certainly could be in 20/20 retrospect once he was home and writing the book), saying:

> It is a very murky world here, a place of ancient tribal ties, betrayal, warfare, double-crossing, and where a man's honor and tribal codes count for everything.

Unfortunately, the above is the *only* thing I had bookmarked in the whole tale ... perhaps more indicative that the book is pretty much set up like an on-going journal than featuring major expository bits – so it was sort of hard while reading through this to pick out the "key elements" on the fly. Perhaps I'll drag a few out while writing this, perhaps not ... we'll see.

For somebody who has spent as much time as he has in that part of the world, the author seems awfully *naive*, beginning with the concept that it would be "a good idea" to illegally cross the border into Pakistan. While the author describes himself as living "like a Pashtun", and I guess – unless he opens his mouth – he can "pass" in a crowd. He also notes that he has "sneaked into the tribal zones" in Pakistan several times previously ... I guess giving him the confidence that this project was workable. The problem was that there were so many inter-related forces involved, sometimes working together, sometimes killing each other. There was the Taliban, there was al-Qaeda, there was Afghan Intelligence, there was Pakistani

Military Intelligence, and various tribal structures running back and forth within these. At one point he finds his driver crying, because one of his brothers is being held by the Afghans, and one by the Pakistanis. And, even in the tribal groups, even within individual families, there were deep animosities, so that almost everybody in the tribal areas was armed – especially when relatives came to call. He notes that he was entrusting his life to *"a man who had killed the brother of my oldest friend in Afghanistan"*, just because he seemed to have the necessary connection to get Van Dyk where he was wanting to go.

One thing that I have to agree with the other reviews who found the author somewhat "whiny" on is that he's *constantly* in emotional flux. I don't know if this is some attempt to paint a picture of how changeable the situation was there, or what, but he'd go from really liking one of his captors or fellow prisoners and feeling very hopeful that he'd be released (or, early on, sent of his way to meet Abdullah), to being angry, scared, and hopeless … often through multiple cycles on the same page. It was not particularly clear how he was keeping notes … as it was only halfway or so through his 45 days of captivity that they deigned to give him back his notebooks. One could imagine if he was making 1-2 sentence notes on paper scraps that one would be "hate this guy", the next would be "this guy's great", etc., and those might have be strung together in the book.

Although he *looked* like a Pashtun (including a full grey beard), he didn't have much linguistic skills for somebody who had lived over there (the "ugly American"?), and hadn't even prepared himself with the basics of "passing" as a Muslim – like memorizing the core prayers and rituals that *everybody* there would have as a matter of course. When they are first captured, he is asked where they came from and where they were going:

> When I said "Peshawar" I pronounced it Pesh-hour, as I had always heard it pronounced. That is the English pronunciation. No one had ever corrected me. I learned later that here it is pronounced Peck-a-waar.

It really is a miracle that he didn't get his head cut off within the first 18 hours of the escapade.

So, he (and those with him) get captured … and are driven off, blindfolded, to some tribal village somewhere (again, the details are murky) in the border region. They are put in an enclosure with minimal facilities – cots and a drain, basically. They get water for the ablutions necessary for the Islamic prayers, and he is *very strongly* encouraged to learn these. In fact, the figure who seemed to "have them" was quite enthusiastic to have Van Dyk *convert*.

Later on the presence of the drain becomes a problem, as sufficient water is coming out of their enclosure that it is notable to people in the area. The fellow whose home they seem to be being held at is worried that his relatives will notice and realize that he has "guests" (albeit ones frequently chained to their cots), which could cause rumors to get to other factions. Even the head guy is playing a bit of a game, as he's unwilling to have the author's group transferred to a regional headquarters – although at points his co-captives are brought there (feeding paranoia that they're part of a plot). This was probably good for Van Dyk, as it sounds like the odds of him being executed there were a lot higher than where he was. Again, there are factions and sub-factions, and various interests all playing against each other … and it's unclear who's working for what goal.

It appears that one of the things that keeps Van Dyk alive is that he's perceived as being a high-value captive, and the ransom figure varied from a million bucks to a couple of hundred thousand. I don't think the amount eventually paid (by CBS, evidently) was ever specifically determined, as everything was constantly in confusion in the telling.

Obviously, the main part of the book is the period of time he was in captivity, but this is, as noted, a bit of a jumble of repeated and/or developing scenarios … they're interrogated, they're fed, they pray, they talk, and the author goes through every possible emotion around each of the other characters – as mentioned, frequently paragraph-to-paragraph (this *is* quite irritating, honestly).

The most interesting thing here, and pretty much the #1 take-away from the book, is how massively backwards these various sub-cultures are. Their focus on religion takes precedence over *everything else*, with the stress being on how one's going to be in the *afterlife* rather than anything in *this* life. The fundamentalism is total, and stifling. The only thing acceptable to study is the Koran and the Hadith, and *ignorance* (of anything else) is seen as a positive. While Van Dyk doesn't explicitly frame things this way … it's quite a cautionary tale regarding "the sort of people" we appear to be in global war with at the moment.

Captive[3] must be a reasonably popular book, as the later paperback edition is still available (at full price) from the on-line big boys. The hardcover (which is what I got at the dollar store), however, is offered *new* by the new/used guys for as little as a penny (and, for the first time that I can recall, you can get that with free shipping if you're an Amazon Prime member), so if this sounds interesting, it can be had for cheap!

Again, my take on this is mixed. It's an interesting tale, with a lot of stuff happening around the main story line … but it's also a real yo-yo on the author's emotions, and you (or at least I) really want to "bitch slap" him and yell at him to get his act together. Yes, he's in constant hazard of being executed, yes, it's not a nice situation that he's gotten himself into, but most of this is *his fault*, and the "I like him" / "he's going to help us" / "he scares me" / "I don't trust him" / "I hate him" vacillation (over and over and over) gets old real fast. As mentioned previously, it's remarkable that he made it out alive.

Notes:

1. http://btripp-books.livejournal.com/190687.html
2-3. http://amzn.to/2bEradI

Saturday, September 10, 2016[1]

A snapshot ...

Another thing that was staring out of the dollar store shelves recently ... I'm not proud to say it, but the main reason I picked this up (being that I'm generally *quite* disinterested in "celebrities" unless there's a compelling story arc in the book) was that I was *hoping* it would be providing an insider view into one of the more notorious entries on the "Clinton Body Count"[2] ... JFK Jr., having tragically died in a "mysterious" plane crash (with his wife and sister-in-law) just before making a run for the New York Senate seat that a certain current Presidential candidate had her eye on back in 1999. Unfortunately, there is *nothing* in Matt Berman's JFK Jr., George, & Me: A Memoir[3] on this (I was disappointed), but, frankly, there was nothing *political* in here at all. Of course, I would have worked pretty much all the way through to book to get to the potential Democratic Senatorial primary, so the absence of that did not notably detract from the reading ... although, I suppose, part of me was waiting for it to turn up.

So, I sailed into this hoping for juicy political intrigue ... and got ... well, a breezy look inside the glossy magazine biz. As this is "A Memoir", it's ultimately more about Matt Berman than it is about JFK Jr., but is (obviously) focused on the part of Berman's life when he was helping to develop Kennedy's *George* magazine. The author was *"a shy, self-deprecating, artistic kid"* who grew up in Connecticut (and had a significant trauma in his life a year following the JFK assassination, when two raccoons ripped up his 5-month-old face – permanently scarring him). He was a good enough artist that he attended Carnegie Mellon, and got his degree from the Parsons School of Design ... and managed to talk his way into the Art department of the American *ELLE Magazine* in 1986. The parent company of *ELLE*, Hachette, was launching the JFK Jr. project *George*, and his boss thought he'd be a good match with Kennedy ... after getting the nod from JFK Jr.'s then-girlfriend (later wife) Carolyn Bessette – who'd been asked to come in to check out the logo that Berman was working on – he got the gig as Creative Director of the magazine.

The book is about 1/3rd dishing about the magazine business (and especially characters around the Hachette New York office), about 1/3rd dishing about the various celebrities who were featured in the magazine (with lots of stories about famous cover shoots), and about 1/3rd talking about himself and John:

> We were an unlikely team. John was confident, charismatic, the son of the most beloved president in history. I was self-conscious, self-deprecating, and son of the most beloved restaurant supplier in all of Fairfield County, Connecticut. John loved football in the park on a Saturday; I loved a good Twilight Zone marathon on cable. ... When I was blearily hitting the snooze button at seven in the

> morning, he was plunging into the Hudson River in a kayak. This split-screen idea always made us laugh.
>
> ...
>
> My brothers ... always seemed so cool ... I felt that way about John, a brother who led an impossibly cool life.

There's lots of "fun" stuff in here about the famous and/or beautiful ... including separate sections on "The Shoot" featuring tales of photographing Cindy Crawford, Demi Moore, Barbra Streisand, Drew Barrymore, Kate Moss (who was a last-moment replacement for Pamela Anderson – no, *really*), Elizabeth Hurley, Barbara Walters, and Ben Stiller (who was doing a feature sending up John). I'm sure that those who enjoy celebrity "stuff" will find these quite appealing.

On a more obscure (for most) plane, there's also a lot of talk of fashion industry photographers, make-up artists, stylists, etc. ... plus (on an even *more* rarefied level) talk about "legends" in the magazine (fashion primarily, and European at that) biz. It's interesting to read Berman's take on these folks, but, without a whole other book to fill in the back story on who these people are and what they've done, and why I should care about it ... it seems a bit "niche".

Having "gone a-googling" a bit, it turns out that Berman (following the changes at *George* brought on by JFK Jr.'s death) ended up moving to Paris, and working in the fashion magazine field for more than a decade, before returning to the states to work for a while as an executive with a clothing company (where he was when this book happened), and eventually hanging his own shingle out as an advertising design consultant.

Oh, being the cantankerous old geezer that I am (who well remembers the way things were "back then"), I found another subtle sub-theme here endearing ... how all this happened in a very primitive technological context ... Berman talks about doing manual paste-up, doing photo research by looking at sheets of *slides*, and notes towards the end of the book:

> It's amazing to think that I never received an email from John. We didn't use it yet at George; we used telephones, FedEx, and fax machines. I wonder what John would think about an iPhone or Facebook, and then I realize he didn't even live to see the tsunami in Phuket or the horrors of September 11, only blocks from his home.

It would be easy to say Matt Berman is using the fame of JFK Jr. to "sell" his memoir (and, honestly, *would* it have seen print without that connection?), but this is a sweet and loving recalling of his boss from those years, providing the over-all arc to a look at the many elements which made up *George*, from the stars on the cover, to the quirky folks in the office.

JFK Jr., George, & Me[4] is still in print, in a paperback edition. It is somewhat odd that it found its way to the dollar store, as it's only a couple of years old, and the new/used guys don't have it at a *deep* discount (you can, however, get new copies of the hardcover for about a quarter of what the paperback is going for). While this wasn't the book that I was thinking it might be when I picked it up, it was an engaging read, and an interesting look at a part of the publishing world that I wasn't particularly familiar with. If you're "into" fashion and celebrities, I'm pretty sure you'll enjoy this even more than I did.

Notes:

1. http://btripp-books.livejournal.com/190910.html
2. http://goo.gl/bkygCl
3-4. http://amzn.to/2bsypEQ

Sunday, September 11, 2016[1]

The "Pathfinder of the Seas" ...

There was a time when I "stocked up" at the Newberry Library Book Fair[2], however in recent years (when I've been broke – and since I discovered the dollar stores as a source of books) not so much. I typically go on the last day (Sunday) when everything's half-priced, and see what I can find. This year I ended up with just a couple of books (and a few CDs), one of which was Chester G. Hearn's Tracks in the Sea: Matthew Fontaine Maury and the Mapping of the Oceans[3], which was not only "like new" (frankly, it looked like it had never been opened), but only setting me back $2.50. I'm somewhat surprised that it managed to get right into my reading rotation, as the subject isn't necessarily one that's in my main thematic groups ... but perhaps that's *why* it appealed – as a change of pace.

I had actually anticipated this being a *science* book, looking at the technologies enabling the "Mapping of the Oceans" in the middle of the 19th Century. However, while there is a not insignificant amount of material on that, this is much more a *biography* of Matthew Fontaine Maury, whose vision of amassing, condensing, and processing data about sea conditions enabled a huge leap in the development of reliable nautical charts.

This is also one of those cases where I've not put any little bookmarks in while reading, so I didn't have any particular "ah-hah" moments with key points that I could string together for a review ... and the book is *so* full of details of ships, journeys, captains, countries, companies, and conspiracies (as well as minutia about Maury's life), that it's likewise going to be hard to summarize. So, I'm leaning towards doing some "cherry picking" of bits that (although not marked during the reading) will give you a sense of the book. The following seems a good place to start:

> Navigators shared their knowledge of winds and currents with other seafarers, passing down through generations a combination of wisdom and rumor. But it remained for Matthew Fontaine Maury, a self-educated lieutenant of the nineteenth-century U.S. Navy, to apply any sort of scientific discipline to the collection and analysis of meteorologic and oceanographic data. His research led to publication of wind and current tables for the Atlantic, Pacific, and Indian Oceans and later, in 1855, to the first textbook of oceanography, his Physical Geography of the Sea.

The development of accurate navigation technology was long in coming. East-west traffic was reasonably predictable, with a compass for direction and angles figured to celestial objects providing a rough estimate of north-south position. However:

> *An accurate timepiece for calculating longitudes took six thousand years to develop; even after John Harrison's chronometer was recognized by an act of the British Parliament in 1773, it took another fifty years for the maritime world to adopt the chronometer for common use.*

While, contrary to common myth, navigators in Columbus' era (and long before) were aware that the earth was round, it took a combination of those accurate timepieces and some rather esoteric "spherical trigonometry" to create accurate charts and the ability to plot reasonably precise pathways from point A to point B. While there are historical examples of some fairly sophisticated mapping (such as exhibited in the famed Piri Reis map[4]), it wasn't until the late 18th Century that sea voyages weren't very much a matter of dead reckoning and luck (Hearn illustrates this with the story of the *Peggy*, whose 1765 "40 day voyage" ended up running over three times as long – with the crew descending into cannibalism – yet, when finally rescued the captain discovered *"that he had drifted to within a few hundred miles of the coast of England"*). Among the many ships and sailors "name checked" here, there are many familiar ones, from Cook to Bligh (yes, who was a historical figure), and many more.

Matthew Maury was born in 1806, the seventh of nine children of a less-than-prosperous Virginia farmer, whose family re-located to Tennessee when Maury was still a child. Inspired by an older brother who had joined the Navy in his early teens, Maury aspired to the service and by 1825 he was serving on the brand new (he'd watched her being built) *Brandywine*. Maury had a natural curiosity, and despite the lack-luster training available, managed to wrest as much knowledge of navigation that he could out of the senior staff.

The book goes into a great deal of detail of journeys made by various ships at various times, and elements of the conditions that they encountered … including the round-the-world trip Maury was on (the first for a U.S. Navy ship) aboard the *Vincennes*. By 1831 he was the "sailing master" for the *Falmouth* which gave him opportunity to manage the logbook:

> *When the cruise began, Maury planned to emphatically demonstrate his skill as a navigator. He expected the cruise to be his opportunity to establish a reputation, so he took a keen interest in the winds and currents. Why such information was not available to seafarers baffled him, so began keeping remarkably precise records of his daily observations.*

The year 1834 was a big one for Maury, not only did he marry his long-romanced cousin Ann, but the *American Journal of Science and Arts* published his "On the Navigation of Cape Horn", as well as an instrument design he'd developed. He was promoted to lieutenant in 1836 (the rank he'd carry for most of his life – there were only a handful of ranks at the time). Publishing was one of the key ways that Maury gained notoriety, and in 1837 the Navy put his 1836 book *Navigation* "on every ship in the Navy".

He had been set up to be the "acting astronomer" for a scientific expedition … but this had been delayed numerous times (partially due to other people actively trying to sabotage Maury's efforts for their own purposes), and he had been back in Tennessee in 1839 when he got orders to report for sea duty … on the stagecoach trip to New York, there was an accident, and Maury was seriously injured, and by the time he was able to get to the coast, the ship had sailed without him. During this period of disability, Maury wrote more, notably the pseudonymously-released (as Harry Bluff) "Scraps from the Lucky Bag", which voiced his criticisms of the Navy (both on issues of training *and* pointing out how much more expensive ships for the Navy were vs. their commercial counterparts … padding government invoices appears to be a long tradition) – and offered a plan for correcting the failings. These publications were *very* popular with the rank-and-file Navy, but understandably less so among the established authorities. This came to be an on-going problem for Maury, as at nearly every point in his subsequent career, he had other factions' candidates trying to take positions for which he was seeking.

In 1842, Maury became head of the Navy's Depot of Charts and Instruments … Hearn notes:

> *That Maury could jam all the records and instruments into the lower level of his home and still have room for his family on the second floor indicates how modest the Depot of Charts and Instruments was in 1842.*

One of the "suggestions" made in the "Lucky Bag" material was for the establishment of a facility which would not only serve as the Depot (for *"… a library of charts and nautical books issued to departing vessels and returned at the end of each cruise"*), but as an observatory to ensure the accuracy of astronomical info … fortunately, the Secretary of the Navy at that time was one of the fans of "Harry Bluff", and managed to get an appropriation pushed through Congress, resulting in the construction of the U.S. Naval Observatory. In the meanwhile, Maury was organizing the materials he'd inherited in his new position:

> *… he found little of value for the navigator, only heaps of disorganized data and a thousand dusty logbooks that had been kept since the birth of the United States Navy. His predecessors referred to the logbooks as depot rubbish, but Maury began to slog through them. The more he read, the more excited he became. Although some logs offered little information of value, other logs contained enormous detail. They might be dead storage to the navy, but to Maury they represented a treasury of priceless information, for they contained records of weather and sea conditions for every month of the year in all parts of the world.*
>
> *…*
>
> *… he laid out a simple program for excising data on the force of winds, rain, for, unusual ocean cur-*

> rents, the distance covered during a daily run, all
> natural or unusual phenomena observed, and any
> other detail that might prove significant or insightful
> ...

Amazingly (by today's standards), the mid-19th century Navy had only 37 ships at sea ... so Maury devised a standardized logbook, and got the Navy to approve offering free charts to merchant ships, in exchange for keeping data in the new format. Fortunately, this was approved, and the value of updated charts was enough of a "carrot" that many shipping companies agreed to the deal (more as the ships using the new charts cut time off their voyages). This ended up providing ever-increasing amounts of data for Maury to work with.

As head of the U.S. Naval Observatory Maury was able to amass ever more data (especially as the merchant shipping got on board), and produce more accurate charts for ever expanding parts of the ocean. In 1853 he pioneered the first international marine meteorological conference, in Brussels, which led to his getting a great deal of attention from the participating countries (many offering him gifts that he had to refuse). This eventually created further problems for him at home, as he was accumulating "enemies" elsewhere in the government ... many (with academic credentials) resenting that a "self-taught" figure was getting the advancement that Maury was seeing, and others (such as the head of the Smithsonian) seemingly just engaging in a "turf war".

There's quite a bit on the nature of charts, the issues with various oceans, the voyages of numerous ships whose logs were particularly useful, races between different ships, and how much time, as more captains adopted the charts, was being cut off of long journeys. One of the more fascinating (to me, at least) things here were the reproduced chart figures, such as the grid that represented the ocean, but rather than have coastlines, etc., it has a disk with all the data on winds at different times of the year. The navigator would use these to mark out specific pathways to take advantage of the conditions at the time of their being there.

The issue of his health arose as a part of the political maneuvering against him, and in 1855 he was "plucked" from active duty ... a move he fought until getting re-instated in 1858. This episode (with the unpleasantries that preceded it) not doubt influenced his decision in 1861 to join the Confederacy. The people that took over his position did not have the vision that Maury did regarding his nautical charts, and his knowledge of these provided a great advantage to the tiny CSA Navy, whose raiders seemed to be able to strike and disappear at will (and were able to use the very charts that the whaling fleet used to find their prey, to attack those ships). With the defeat of the rebel states, Maury had a difficult decision, and opted to move to Mexico and work for their military, even becoming naturalized. Maury, with many other Confederate officers, was pardoned in 1868, and returned to the U.S. for a position at the Virginia Military Institute, where he worked until his death in 1873.

Needless to say, Maury's life was a remarkable one, that changed the ways that people got around the planet. Unfortunately, he seems to be all but forgotten, as his revolutionary systems of obtaining and processing log book data into accurate maps and reference books began to fade as sail power gave way at first to steam power, and then to diesel (and nuclear). As noted, I was less interested in the parts covering his personal life, and the political in-fighting that he had to put up with, but for many these would be quite interesting.

Tracks in the Sea[5] appears to be out of print in the hardcover edition that I found, but seems to still be available as a later paperback edition. Both are in the new/used channels, if you want to save a few bucks. Again, there's a lot to be said for this book, Hearn was able to put together a very wide look at Maury's life, so it offers angles of approach for people with varying interests, in the science (that was what got me to pick it up), as a Navy book, as a look at a developmental stage in our country's history, as a cautionary tale about professional jealousies, and as a basic biographical sketch.

Notes:

1. http://btripp-books.livejournal.com/191115.html
2. https://www.newberry.org/newberry-book-fair
3. http://amzn.to/2bFdyLI
4. http://amzn.to/2cPlXOh
5. http://amzn.to/2bFdyLI

Saturday, September 17, 2016[1]

Useful and Transcendent ...

This was yet another Dollar Store find. I noticed that it had an unusually large number of reviews over on LibraryThing.com, and took a look and discovered that it had been an "Early Reviewers" selection back when it came out. I'm not sure if I requested it then, but it's interesting to get an LTER book via the dollar store channel six years later.

Kevin Starr's Golden Gate: The Life and Times of America's Greatest Bridge[2] is an interesting little book. Its author is a history professor at USC, and is a former "state librarian of California", who has a dozen or so books out, mostly about California, and the majority of those in a 7-part series *Americans and the California Dream*. So, he's no "carpetbagger" when it comes to things iconic about California.

The book could be seen as a series of inter-linked essays, as each chapter is focused on one aspect, and could almost be free-standing. These are "Bridge" (introductory material), "Icon", "Site", "Vision", "Politics", "Money", "Design", "Construction", "City", "Suicide" and "Art" ... each (obviously) taking a look at these varied aspects of the Golden Gate Bridge.

As regular readers of my reviews know, I typically will put in little slips of paper to note places where I feel good "example passages" are to give some flavor of the original in these scribblings. While I quite enjoyed the read, and found the material very interesting, I only ended up with three of these bookmarks stuck in here, and all of those in the first 10% of the book ... not sure why at this juncture, but I do find it somewhat surprising. I guess I'm going to be winging it for most of this.

The first of these was right at the start ... and I was wondering if the whole book was going to be as "florid" as this part of the introductory paragraph:

> ... Like the Parthenon, the Golden Gate Bridge seems Platonic in its perfection, as if the harmonies and resolutions of creation as understood by mathematics and abstract thought have been effortlessly materialized through engineering design. Although the result of engineering and art, the Golden Gate Bridge seems to be a natural, even inevitable, entity as well, like the final movement of Beethoven's Ninth. In its American context, taken historically, the Bridge aligns itself with the thoughts of Jonathan Edwards, Ralph Waldo Emerson, and other transcendentalists in presenting an icon of transcendence: a defiance of time pointing to more elusive realities. Were Edwards, Emerson, or the Swedish theologian Emanuel Swedenborg, a mystic thinker of great importance to the formation of American thought, alive today, they would no doubt

> see in the Golden Gate Bridge a fusion of material and trans-material forces, held in delicate equipoise.

Needless to say, the book does *not* continue in this mode (how could it?), but it sets things out in a modality that is hardly the standard "let's take a look at this piece of engineering" or "ain't that a cool landmark?" tones that might be expected in a book about a bridge. However, Starr isn't *quite* done with the "highfalutin" verbiage, as later in the "Bridge" chapter he adds:

> From an iconic perspective, the Golden Gate Bridge offers a West Coast counterpart to the Statue of Liberty, announcing, in terms of American Art Deco, American achievement and the higher purposes of American culture. And it does this with its own element of historical narrative, subtly contained in the Art Deco stylization of its towers played off against repetitive cables descending into a reversed arch against an interplay of city, sea, and sky. ...

Again, the book starts out in a philosophical mode, and in the "Icon" chapter, these issues are tied to historical antecedents (both conceptually and bridge-wise), and assorted poetry (including one that gets the rather "purple" description of being *"elliptical and elusive, modeled on the vatic Ur-Poem of the twentieth century, fully cognizant of the perils and terrors of modern life"*!). He notes here that:

> The American Society of Civil Engineers ranks the Golden Gate Bridge as one of the Seven Wonders of the Modern World, along with such other choices as the Channel Tunnel, the Empire State Building, and the Panama Canal.

Which is followed by an interesting name-check of the authors of the *original* "seven wonders" (in the ancient world), which were *"Greek historian Herodotus and the poet-scholar Callimachus of the Library of Alexandria"* (I don't believe the latter had ever made it onto my radar). The last thing that I flagged was the introductory paragraph for the "Site" chapter ... which, if memory serves, is pretty much when Starr buckled in and started to actually write *about* the bridge, in its various aspects ... but I figured I'd throw it in here for you:

> The Golden Gate Bridge serves as the focal point and organizing principle of a fusion of nature and history that is at once a matter of geography and public art. In the perceptions of those encountering it, the Bridge and its site reflect eons of geological time and a shorter period of human association. As drama, then, the Bridge celebrates that interaction of nature, technology, and social purpose that created Native American, Spanish, Mexican, American, and ultimately global California across centuries of human development.

While the preceding might seem a bit over-blown, it does introduce a number of themes brought up in the "Site" chapter, including the geological development of the San Francisco Bay through the exploration of the region my mariners going back to the 16th century. However, it was not until the mid-18th century that the Bay was discovered. This was due to the narrowness of the Golden Gate itself, which *"acted as a funnel and stabilizer for fog"*, which meant that unless a ship was running right up the coast (a hazardous venture), the passage would be virtually impossible to see. In fact, it wasn't "discovered" until a group of Spanish soldiers in 1769, exploring the coastline to the south, crested a ridge and *"beheld a great inland sea stretching north, south, and east as far as the eye could see"*, and it wasn't until the fall of 1775 that a ship ended up sailing into the Bay, and only in 1776 was the first permanent settlement established. When gold was discovered in the region 70 years later, everything changed, and the urban San Francisco swarmed up and over the hills.

In the "Vision" chapter, Starr traces the ultimate concept of the bridge to *"El Camino Real – the Royal Highway, the King's Highway"* of the Spanish, which *"linked the twenty-one missions founded between 1769 and 1823 at intervals of a day's march"*, which ended up having a bit of a hiccup at the Golden Gate, requiring either a *very* long circumnavigating of the Bay, or ferrying across the strait. He suggests that, after 1937: *"the Golden Gate Bridge completed the vision of Spanish Franciscan missionaries of an Alta California unified by one Royal Highway"*. In the 19th century, there was a lot of interest in getting *something* built there, especially from railroad concerns, who found themselves having to re-route trains through the central valley, or ferrying across the channel. With the popularization of automotive transportation, the ferry business became a huge operation, and a major bottle-neck, with commuters having to wait in lines hours long to get their turn on the ferries. It's also in this chapter that some key players in the bridge's development are introduced, including San Francisco city engineer Michael O'Shaughnessy, and Chicago-based bridge engineer, Joseph Baerman Strauss (another Chicago connection in the story is that of Daniel Burnham, who had developed a "Burnham Plan" for San Francisco, delivered just before the 1906 quake/fire that destroyed much of the existing city … in their haste to rebuild, even less of his plan got built there than was the case in Chicago).

One of the interesting aspects of the bridge is that it was a *local* development, and managed by a local board, the Golden Gate Bridge and Highway District. The "Politics" chapter goes through the extremely convoluted pathway it took to make this happen (it was structured to take advantage of existing legislation *"authorizing multi-county irrigation districts empowered to issue bonds, raise money, construct irrigation projects, and administer ongoing irrigation programs"*). There were numerous interests both supporting and opposing the bridge, and from its initial approval in 1923, there were on-going lawsuits and challenges. These were still going on when the stock market crashed and the Depression started, and even though the project won what should have been a "final" vote (carrying by a 3-1 margin), more lawsuits were launched at it. In the "Money" chapter, the details on the financing are looked at, noting the influence of banker Amadeo Peter Giannini, who founded the Bank of Italy (in the Italian areas of S.F.), later to become Bank of America and the Transamerica Corp.. His backing of the bridge (agreeing to purchase the first offering of bonds) gave it a key boost in the wake of "the fire" and amid the Depression.

There's more dirt being dished in the "Design" chapter, as it appears that Strauss' initial design was quite uninspiring, Most of the "heavy lifting" in terms of the mathematical calculations necessary to build the largest bridge in the world, were coming out from the pencils of Charles Alton Ellis, a professor of structural and bridge engineering at University of Illinois … although he was later all but erased from the project by Strauss (who liked having the credit to his firm) … in cooperation with engineers Leon Moisseiff, Othmar Hermann Amman (who had designed the George Washington Bridge in New York), and Charles Derleth, Jr., along with geology professor Andrew Lawson (who was key in certifying the stability of the bases of the bridge's pylons). Two architects were largely responsible for the Deco "look" of the bridge, John Eberson and Irving Morrow, neither of whom had any background in bridges, the former making his name in theater houses, the latter being a "thought leader" in the architectural community. This chapter also dips its toe into Pythagorean theory, and discussions of some of the extreme technical challenges faced by the design team. One fascinating point discussed here was about the bridge's "International Orange" color … it was not necessarily an *intentional* choice, but was the color of the lead-based primer used to protect the components of the bridge as it was being built. Despite numerous other suggestions being put forward from everybody from the Navy to some of the engineers, the orange-red seemed to have *"compatibility as far as the site and atmospherics were concerned"*, helped make the bridge more visible in foggy conditions, and ended up as the iconic hue it has become.

The "Construction" chapter is fascinating, as there are elements involved that I never suspected … such as the cables needing to be spun from 0.196" wire *on site*, with carriages holding the spinning mechanisms moving 640ft/min. When there were 452 wires spun, they were banded into hexagonal strands, which were the put into groups of 64, and six circular hydraulic jacks compressed these into a single cable. Pretty amazing. One notable thing here is that Strauss established a hard-hat requirement, soon to be an archetypal element of construction sites, and set up a safety net, which saved many workers. In the "City" chapter, more construction factors are covered, including the shocking news that the bridge might have been destroyed (much like the Tacoma Narrows Bridge collapse in 1940) in a violent windstorm with 69mph gusts in December of 1951 … the report noted that had the winds kept up another half-hour, the bridge likely would have failed … this led to an update *"which increased the torsional rigidity of the Bridge by a factor of thirty-five"*, completed in 1954. Similarly grim is the "Suicide" chapter, which notes that the Golden Gate Bridge is the second "most popular" place on the planet (behind a volcano in Japan – go figure) for folks to kill themselves. Starr goes into a lot of statistics here, both on numbers of deaths, and the tech issues (velocity achieved on the way down to the water, etc.) involved, all of which I think I'll spare you (although the paragraph with the *"chum for sharks"* comment was very tempting). This is filled with demographic info (85% of jumpers are locals, for instance), and touching stories about notes, interventions, and even a movie (*The Bridge*) about these suicides. The final chapter, "Art", is (predictably), an over-view of how the iconic structure has manifested in photography, painting, film/video, and popular media.

As noted, Golden Gate[3] was quite an engaging read, and I think most folks would find it of interest. It's still in print in a paperback edition, but the hardcover I found at the dollar store is in the new/used channels with "like new" copies going for as little as a penny (plus shipping), so it can be added to your library quite reasonably if it sounds like something you'd like to have.

Notes:

1. http://btripp-books.livejournal.com/191325.html
2-3. http://amzn.to/2cvVbyx

Monday, September 19, 2016[1]

Fair & Balanced ...

Here's another score from the Dollar Store ... I was on the way back up from dropping my daughter at college, and stopped at an exit on the south end of Kankakee (where they had the trifecta of a Dollar Tree, a Walmart, and a Speedway with gas a buck a gallon cheaper than it would be in Chicago), and found this, and another interesting title, on the shelf down there. As I've noted elsewhere, the way that these get into that channel always makes it worthwhile to check every place, because there's no way of predicting which stores get which books.

Regular readers of this space will appreciate that I'm certainly in the "Ailes camp" as far as anti-Left sentiment is concerned, so I was really hoping that Zev Chafets' Roger Ailes: Off Camera[2] would be a sympathetic look at the phenom who invented Fox News. I had a concern, as right up front in the author's info is the flagship of Leftist misinformation, the New York Times, but fortunately, this book is about as straight-forward without spin as one might hope.

If one were looking for the broadest of the broad strokes for what this book is about, one could do worse than this snippet from the Preface:

> ... Ailes is not another working-class stiff who got ahead through hard work and the power of positive thinking. For fifty years, he has navigated the waters of show business, national politics, and big-time media. He taught Dick Nixon new tricks, stepped in as Reagan's emergency debate coach when the Great Communicator needed help communicating, and held George H.W. Bush's hand all the way to the White House. He more or less invented modern political consulting and made a small fortune along the way. When he left politics, he talked his way into the number one job at CNBC and then convinced Rupert Murdoch to gamble a billion dollars give or take, on an idea and a handshake. The gamble become Fox News, one of the most lucrative and influential news organizations on the planet. ...
>
> ...
>
> Roger Ailes has his admirers, some of them surprising, and his detractors – entire organizations dedicated to discrediting him and all his works. I talked to a great many people on both sides.

While this is a biography (and so starts with a lot of family stories, school stories, etc.), it's also framed a bit with Chafets' search for the story. Key of the factors from Ailes' childhood is his hemophilia, a recurring issue in his youth, but something of a non-factor in the story here. More lingering was the damage done to his legs when hit by a car in second grade, and perhaps more developmentally important, was his father "throwing him out" once he graduated high school ... he ended up going to Ohio University (*"it was cheap, it had a reputation as a party school, and he could get in with less than stellar grades"*), but found himself "homeless" soon after (*"when he came home for Christmas break, he found his house sold and his belongings discarded"* – his mother having run off with a guy she'd met at a convention).

At several points in the book Chafets "gets involved with the story", and when Ailes talks about missing an old friend who'd he'd lost track of decades previously, the author looks him up, finds him living in New York (teaching acting), and connects the two. This ends up providing him with a lot of "good material" from Ailes' early years, and lets him stick in info about Ailes' time in the early 70's when he was producing theater (including winning three Obies for *The Hot l Baltimore*).

The book really picks up at the end of Ailes' college years – he managed to take a run of shows on the campus radio station (he'd majored in TV) and make a pitch to a Cleveland TV station to be a segment producer on a new "daytime variety show" they were developing, featuring soon-to-be the famed Mike Douglas. The main producer (who would later be tapped at Fox) asked Ailes to come in with a hundred show ideas, which he did and he was hired on the spot. That was 1961. In 1967 his producer left to do Dick Cavett's show, and Ailes got the executive producer slot on *The Mike Douglas Show*. I don't know if the author was trying to "humanize" Ailes in the eyes of his more rabid detractors, but he spends a lot of time featuring stories of Ailes bringing Black icons to the airwaves at the time ... Muhammad Ali, MLK Jr., Dick Gregory, Richard Pryor, Bill Cosby, and even Malcolm X ... the latter connection coming in handy many years later in proving to hostile elements in the Congressional Black Caucus that he didn't just have a "sudden interest" in civil rights.

One of the guests on the show was Richard Nixon, who was traveling around the country trying to build support for his 1968 run. He and Ailes (who was only in his 20's at the time), had a chance to talk, and Ailes convinced Nixon that TV had to be a key part in a campaign. He was called into New York to meet with Nixon's media team, which grilled him for four hours ... before offering him the job of producing Nixon's TV presence – which he took, infuriating Mike Douglas. Once Nixon was elected, Ailes was being frozen out by the White House staff, and in 1969 he left D.C. to move to New York and start his own company. This period he spent producing plays, documentaries, TV shows, and even tried to get a conservative news service (funded by Joseph Coors) off the ground.

In 1980 he was approached by Al D'Amato to help him oust Jacob Javitz from his Senate seat ... he succeeded, and became something of a GOP power-broker, working on numerous campaigns, and winning most. One of the interesting things that comes up here is that he really had very little interest in the *substance* of the politics, just getting the candidates elected ... *"it was always a matter of sizing up the opponent, finding his weaknesses, or turning his strengths against him"*. In 1984 he was called in by the Reagan campaign to help with preparation for the second debate with Mondale. Under his coaching Reagan came up with the classic line reversing the "age issue" where he stated *"I am not going to exploit, for political purposes, my opponent's youth and inexperience."*. In 1988 he handled Bush's media, including the classic spots with Dukakis looking silly in a tank ... but by the end of that, he was getting sick of the political work. He did some minor consulting on the 1992 campaign, but was pretty much out of the game at that point.

He was, however, producing a lot more TV, including the Tom Snyder show which was the precursor to the Letterman show on NBC. In 1991, he connected with Rush Limbaugh, and developed a TV version of Rush's phenomenally popular radio program – which ran for four years. Rush was quoted as describing some key coaching he got from Ailes:

> *"Roger told me that he had detected in me a common fault that newcomers to TV make when being interviewed by mainstream journalists. He said, 'Rush, they don't care what you think. Don't try to persuade them of anything. Don't try to change their mind. They are not asking you questions to learn anything. So don't look at this as an opportunity to enlighten them. Whatever they ask, just say whatever you want to say.'"*

(Which is, if I recall correctly from setting up media tours in my PR agency days, pretty good advice for most interview situations!) Limbaugh eventually wanted out (he disliked all the extra stuff needed to get a TV show done), but it had gotten the attention of the management (and ownership – Jack Welch of G.E.) of CNBC, and they reached out to Ailes to run the channel. This was good for all involved, as Ailes doubled the asset value in two years. Many familiar Fox News faces (Neil Cavuto among them) were on board there. There was a management change above CNBC, and Ailes was faced with reporting to somebody he didn't care to work with, so he left. Rupert Murdoch was waiting ... he had an idea for a more conservative cable news voice, and presented the idea to Ailes, asking if it was doable ... Ailes assured him that it was, but could cost a billion dollars to launch. And, so Fox News was born ... and more than eighty CNBC people followed Ailes into the new venture.

There's a middle section here with a lot of details about personnel development at Fox News, with some familiar names, some less so, some building up individuals (Bill O'Reilly, Shep Smith), some getting rid of others (Jim Cramer, Paula Zahn). Lots of names, lots of scenarios ... too much to try to cherry-pick examples here. This is followed by a bit about Ailes' personal life in upstate New York, and the (very liberal) community he lives in there. The narrative then switches back to Fox, and how hated it is by the Left – and regularly smeared by them. One quote I thought was worth bringing in was this bit by Ailes in response to some of the vitriol being hurled at Fox:

> *"The first rule of media bias is selection,"* Ailes says. *"Most of the media bullshit you about who they are. We don't. We're not programming to conservatives, we're just not eliminating their point of view."*

This is prefaced by a story that Ailes tells about meeting a Liberal at a cocktail party who complains about Fox News coverage:

> Ailes asks him if he is satisfied with what he sees on CNN, NBC, ABC, CBS, MSNBC, and PBS. The man says he is very satisfied. "Well," says Ailes, "if they all have the same take and we have a different take, why does that bother you? The last two guys who succeeded in lining up the media on one side were Hitler and Stalin."

In support of these points Chafets brings in a very interesting mix of quotes ... from Chris Matthews admitting to the Liberal stance of Walter Cronkite (who openly mocked Barry Goldwater during his 1964 campaign), to the *New York Times* public editor Arthur Brisbane admitting that there's a "culture of like minds" that "share a kind of political and cultural progressivism" that taints nearly every word hitting their pages. The bias in most of the media creates what amounts to hostile work environments for anybody *not* part of the leftist hive-mind, which the author notes enables Ailes to *"scoop up most of the really good conservative talent"*. Chafets notes that Fox also hires a lot of overt liberals to provide counter-point to these conservatives ... probably having more of these than all the leftist media outlets *together* have non-lefty voices.

An interesting thing that's pulled in here is UCLA Poly-sci professor Tim Groseclose's PQ[3] (political quotient), which measures how political viewpoints range on a scale from 0-100. The data is based on the rankings of Lefty group "Americans for Democratic Action", so the higher the number, the more leftist the stance (the vile Nancy Pelosi is close to 100, the current execrable POTUS is around 88). The "average voter" is right about 50 on the scale. The MSM network shows were all up around 65, while Fox was at 40 ... however, most damningly: *"Professor Groseclose puts the PQ of the average political reporter for a mainstream organization at 95"* ... and that's the "echo chamber" that drives political news – everybody (but Fox) being on the extreme Left end of the spectrum, leading the liberals to think something like an 80 would be "middle of the road" and Fox is way off to the right!

There's a chapter that largely deals with how Ailes manages the day-to-day news cycle at Fox, then a chapter about his hiring, firing, and people management (including some of the odd connections that he has with people *not* in Fox's camp), followed by a chapter looking at race and religion, noting Ailes' efforts to boost Black and Latino involvement in the organization. I found this illustrative, however, of his basic philosophy (especially vs. the pandering on the Left):

> Racial identity politics are not Ailes's "thing." He belongs to a generation that was raised in a time and place where forward-thinking people accepted MLK's famous exhortation to judge people by the content of their character, not the color of their skin, as the gold standard for racial aspiration. In Ailes's America, everyone would share Middle American, middle-class values and blend into a single national

> *culture. He sees the celebration of racial differences as balkanizing. "Every month is something else," he said, "I'm waiting for Lithuanian Midget Month. ..."*

Chafets then takes a look at how Ailes gets along with his famous boss, Rupert Murdoch, and starts this off with a story about how when he called Murdoch's office to try to schedule an interview for the book, he was surprised to get a call back from Murdoch within 15 minutes (Chafets, assuming he'd get a time penciled in some weeks later, had *nothing* prepared, so just had Murdoch chat about Ailes – he's obviously a big fan of his hire). In this chapter he also looks at how Ailes runs the show from a financial basis, noting that he's totally self-taught in business. One quote I found amusing was how Ailes is very leery of getting the "next big thing", especially with technology, and he's quoted as saying:

> Let CNN buy the new stuff and test it out, and when the technology is right I'll come in like a ton of bricks. ... When I see that the [Framistan](#)[4] is working, we'll get one. Hell, we'll get two. But in the meantime, let CNN waste their money.

The last few chapters are largely adding perspective on different fronts, including how the current POTUS has called Ailes "the most powerful man in America", and how his administration tried very hard to keep Fox out of the White House press pool (to their credit, all the other major news organizations stood up for Fox). There's talk of how ultra-Left organization Media Matters considers Ailes one of it's two "Great Satans" (Rush Limbaugh being the other), and how they are constantly trying to cause trouble for Fox. There's a bit about his young son (Ailes started a family *very* late in life), and how he's handling being a dad in his 70's, with other family reminiscences. The book closes with a look at election night 2012, which reinforces some of the previous bits about how Ailes, for all his success as a political consultant and political broadcaster, really *isn't* a "political junkie", caring a whole lot about getting the message out and not so much about the actual "stuff" involved.

[Roger Ailes: Off Camera](#)[5] is a fascinating read, and is something that I think anybody with an interest in politics (especially if you're not a Leftist), or broadcasting, would find quite interesting. I can't tell if this is currently in print or not ... Amazon lists the hardcover at full retail, but notes that it won't ship for a couple of months. The copy I got at the dollar store was the paperback, but the new/used guys have the hardcover available for 1¢ in "like new" condition, so that's probably your best bet if you want to snag a copy.

Notes:
1. http://btripp-books.livejournal.com/191534.html
2. http://amzn.to/2co7xp4
3. http://timgroseclose.com/calculate-your-pq/
4. https://goo.gl/BpflC6
5. http://amzn.to/2co7xp4

Friday, September 30, 2016[1]

Must be crazy ...

This is another book that got suggested to me at a DBSA[2] meeting, much like the Kay Jamison book[3] I reviewed a few months back. I certainly *liked* Ruby Wax's Sane New World: A User's Guide to the Normal-Crazy Mind[4] a lot more ... but that is likely because the tone of this is much less oppressive – reflecting, no doubt Wax's background[5] in acting/comedy (primarily in the UK, although hailing from Evanston, IL), as opposed to the other author's psychology roots. Wax, who had suffered from depression and related conditions for most of her life, responded to the dwindling of her performance career by *going back to school*, and ending up with a Masters from Oxford in "mindfulness-based cognitive therapy", so she has the chops to really get into the subject here.

While the book does spend a lot of (entertaining) verbiage dealing with specifics of Wax's life, it's not specifically autobiographical, and is in five parts, each (confusingly) containing a differently-named chapter from the name of the "part" (so what's on the Contents page isn't what's up top on the individual pages – go figure – must be the "crazy" manifesting), each containing assorted thematic sub-sections ... including her various "my story" bits. Since these are ambiguously titled, I'm just going to give a description: the first part covers the sorts of neuroses that pretty much impact *everybody* to some extent, the second part's chapter is called "Depression – Broken Brains", so deals with the more damaged among us, the next part looks at "neuroscience", which is followed by an overview of mindfulness, and finished with "the manual", which has (as one might expect) suggested exercises, homework assignments, handy forms, and other useful information.

Rather than trying to summarize all this, I'm going to mainly go with the parts I dropped in bookmarks for – some of which are more for their humor or out-of-the-box approach than being specifically "pithy" as to the actual arc of the book. This starts with the following from the sub-section "The Fix of Happiness":

> *... There are some lucky people who feel they experience happiness when they gaze at a cloud or walk on the beach, but the rest of us get that special tingly buzz only when we've bought, won, achieved, hooked, or booked something. Then our own brains give us a bit of dopamine, which makes us feel good. We don't need substances; we are our own drug dealer.*
>
> *The problem is, the hit of happiness usually lasts as long as a cigarette, so we have to continually search for the next fix. It's as though as a species we had no brakes, just breakdowns. ...*

She goes from this to defining her version of Maslow's hierarchy which takes fourteen steps to go from food/water to "Meeting Oprah" (with five steps of increasingly posh air travel in the mix). Did I mention that there's an awful lot of great stuff in here (and much of it's *a hoot*)? Because I feel guilty flipping through to get to my next little paper slip … but we don't want this review being 20,000 words, do we? Some of these are informative (in the Johnny Carson-esque "I did *not* know that." mode), such as:

> If you watch a face it will tell you everything. For instance, you cannot fake a smile. There is a muscle under the eye called the periocular that will not become active if you aren't genuinely smiling. The mouth is easy to upturn but if you don't find something funny, that periocular muscle just doesn't move; your eyes are dead as a trout's.

Again, this is a complex mix of what Wax *knows* from grad school, and what she *knows* from being saddled with psychological issues … here's a very telling one coming from the latter type of expertise (moving from a discussion of sadness/unhappiness pinned to a particular quote from *Hamlet*):

> Depression is a whole other beast; it is not situation appropriate. Here's something you get absolutely free with this illness: a real sense of shame; it comes with the package. And you feel such extreme shame because you think, "I'm not being carpet-bombed, I don't have anything to complain about." Your thoughts become so punishing for your selfishness – like bombs, incoming over Dresden – so loud, so relentless you get not one voice but about a hundred thousand abusive voices; like if the devil had Tourette's. Depression doesn't care if you're famous, if you live in a mud hut, or what culture you come from, it just loves everyone.

(While I really like that bit, it *is* slightly incoherent – but I'm considering that it's coming from something of a "performance art" place rather that "outtakes from my thesis" on the author's part. A tidbit which *does* sound like it's from the latter category is: *"The World Economic Forum estimates that the global cost of mental illness will be about $16 trillion by 2030."*, and that as many as 1 in 4 people suffer from some degree of clinical depression.) In this section she comes up with what I thought was a great suggestion (actually DBSA is quite a bit like this) following a rant about finding a "buddy" who understands that *"you are not making it up and you are not a self-indulgent, self-obsessed narcissist who's looking for pity or an excuse not to show up at work or school"*:

> Alcoholics Anonymous has a system where you call your buddy when you feel you want a drink and they will talk you down. Why can't we have meeting places like in AA, where they all get together for their twelve-step thing and have cigarettes and cookies? How did they organize these get-togethers so well? They have meeting places on every corner of every block; more places than there are Starbucks. How did they figure all this out? Why can't we do that?

Oddly (given my interest in the subject), I didn't drop a single bookmark in the central "neuroscience" chapter. This is *not* due to it being lacking ... in fact, Wax does a remarkable job of presenting a quite detailed look at brain biology, function, and the like in fifty-some-odd pages. It's more that this has such a "fire hose" of information that it would be hard to sufficiently cherry-pick factoids to give you and adequate sense of what's in there. I did note one thing right at the end of the section, which I thought was important:

> ... I just want to bring your attention to how misguided we are in insisting the external world is exactly as we see it. Much of what you see out there is manufactured by your brain, painted in like computer-generated graphics in a movie; only a very small part of the inputs to your occipital lobe comes directly from the external world. The rest comes from internal memory stores and other processes.
> ...

The next part of the book is about "mindfulness", which is where this all is heading. She backgrounds this initially with her own experiences, and then discusses the history of the discipline. This approach started in 1979 with Dr. John Kabat-Zinn, who *created a method to use with patients whose pain was too chronic to remedy, those who were given the diagnosis of "You're going to have to live with this."* Obviously, there's a disconnect between physical and emotion pain, and it was a group of researchers (John Teasdale, Zindel Segal, and the professor Wax studied with, Mark Williams) who took Kabat-Zinn's work and applied it to psychology, developing MBCT (mindfulness-based cognitive therapy). I am currently undergoing a course of therapy related to this, and found it amusing that something we were working on *this very morning* (for managing depression/panic related emotions) is essentially covered in this section as a coping structure with the acronym RAIN – Recognition, Acceptance, Investigation, Nonidentification ... along with some suggested exercises.

When she gets around to addressing stress, there's this which stood out to me:

> ... Thanks to our ever-speedier culture, most of our lives are now lived in a state of hyperarousal, and almost everything out there seems scary. We're in a constant downpour of adrenaline and cortisol, muscle tension, high blood pressure, and lack of oxygen to the brain – all of which can make us very, very ill. <u>Notice</u> when you feel the beginning of stress; closely explore where it is in your body, the size, the edges, the sensations. <u>Notice</u> how your breathing and your posture change. <u>Notice</u> if your mind starts to kick in with suggestions to get coffee, cigarettes, or tranquilizers. You don't have to suppress the thoughts or the feelings of fear, anger, or hurt but recognize that they are the dandruff of a flaky mind.

The "mindfulness" chapter closes with a fairly lengthy section on "Facts About Mindfulness", which, while interesting in terms of all the multitudinous conditions and studies she cites, almost approaches "snake oil" territory with the feeling that it *"cures what ails ya"* no matter what the issue. Or that might just be me being a cynical old coot. The last part of the book is "The Manual" if you're going by the chapter/page headings, or "Alternative Suggestions for Peace of Mind" if you're looking at the Contents, which is more the second of these than what you might expect from the shorter one. A significant portion of this is taken up with looking at Cognitive Behavior Therapy (which she then contrasts with MBCT – claiming the latter is twice as effective), with some other stuff thrown in. I rather liked her framing this part, which I've shortened somewhat:

> If mindfulness isn't for you, I'm going to suggest some alternative practices to help you deal with everything from life's little hiccups to the gale force ten, brain-shattering breakdowns.
>
> The important thing is that you find something to anchor you when the winds of "shit happens" get rough. So many people I know don't have an antidote for life's turbulent weather and suffer because of it. ... Dissatisfaction is part of the deal of living because simple existence is full of contradictions; we want individuality, to stand out from the crowd, yet we want to be part of a tribe. We're driven and busy and yet we want peace. And, worst of all, we want things to stay the same despite the fact that everything changes (that's the ultimate bummer).
> ... Impermanence is the law of the universe – no can do. Even if you rage through the night, before you finish reading this sentence, billions of your cells have died and been reborn. Because we have consciousness, we suffer about the fact we suffer, and this second arrow of suffering is constructed in our brains. But if our brain can create this pain, it can also create happiness.

OK, so I'm not so convinced about that last point, but the rest is pretty much on-target. Sane New World[6] is relatively new (the hardcover came out in 2013, this paperback edition a year later), and (as a "#1 UK Bestseller") is very likely to be available from brick & mortar book vendors who carry self-help and/or psychology titles. The on-line big boys, of course, have it ... and the new/used vendors have "good" copies for as little as a penny, and "like new" for a couple of bucks (plus shipping). I quite enjoyed this, and found it both entertaining *and* informative, and figure it should be a "must read" for most folks (that's 1 in 4, remember) struggling with depression, and a worthwhile thing to get into for everybody else.

Notes:
1. http://btripp-books.livejournal.com/191810.html
2. http://www.dbsa-gc.org/
3. http://btripp-books.livejournal.com/184328.html
4. http://amzn.to/2cSZqjE
5. https://en.wikipedia.org/wiki/Ruby_Wax
6. http://amzn.to/2cSZqjE

Saturday, October 1, 2016

No cure for meaninglessness ...

This book came to me via the LibraryThing.com "Early Reviewer" program. As I've noted previously, it is a somewhat rare occasion that books from LTER are actually *early*, but this is one of those cases – as this is not due to be released until January 2017, four months hence. I must admit that it always makes me feel like "one of the cool kids" (often quite a stretch for a "bookish" person!) to get an ARC (advance review copy) of a yet-to-be-released title, but there are some challenges. First of all, it's "standard procedure" that one should not kvetch too much about internal issues with the book, since things are frequently still in flux and not quite how they're going to be when the book gets released into the wild (I've seen some that were missing all graphics, for instance), but I thought I'd mention one thing here – there are fairly extensive endnotes, but they're not connected to the location in the text as yet ... which created a bit of a disjointed experience (I was reading them *en masse* after finishing each chapter) ... the reader of the finished version is likely to have a *much* richer experience, as they'll be able to catch the background info as they work through the book (yeah, I'm bitching, but it's sort of to compliment the author for the level of citation).

I must admit, I had been very excited about Emily Esfahani Smith's The Power of Meaning: Crafting a Life That Matters when I started into it, as she sets up the book with material on her family's Sufi ties. As long-time readers of this space know, I've read quite a lot of Sufi material over the years (probably over 50 titles by Idries Shah and related authors), so was enthused that this might have been in that tradition. While I'm sure that, to some extent, this is *informed* by the author's roots in that area, it's not *emerging* from it to any significant extent. Smith has a degree in psychology, and "writes about culture, relationships, and psychology" for such notable publications as the *Wall Street Journal*, *The Atlantic*, *Time*, *Newsweek*, and the *New York Times*, and the tone (and to some extent, the focus) here is what you'd expect for something targeting those sorts of audiences.

The book's main chapters are "The Meaning Crisis", "Belonging", "Purpose", "Storytelling", "Transcendence", "Growth", and "Cultures of Meaning", with the middle group of those being "the four pillars" of meaning (plus "Growth" tacked on, I suppose). The author's investigation of Meaning seems to have begun in the realms of psychology (and philosophy), but quickly branches out to look at how these elements operate in the lives of what she describes as remarkable individuals:

> Some of their stories are ordinary. Others are extraordinary. But as I followed these seekers on their journeys, I found that their lives all had some important qualities in common, offering an insight that the research is now confirming: there are sources of meaning all around us, and by tapping into them, we can all lead richer and more satisfying lives – and help others do the same.

Much of the book is anchored by stories of these folks, and, frankly, while *some* are quite iconic for the points being made, most were just sort of "meh", for me. Of course, I'm not much of a "story" aficionado, so I'm always trying to figure out what the point *is* when approached from those angles, and in a lot of cases here I was "getting" less than a "people person" (or fiction fan) might have.

In the areas where she's not talking about people, she's name-checking like crazy, and mashing together philosophy, psychology, and other disciplines to get to some destination. She uses an appearance of comedian Louis C.K. on the Conan O'Brien show to tie together threads of Tolstoy, Camus, and Sartre ... I don't know if she *started* there (it was unclear if the comic cited these writers) but she says he *"described coming into contact with something like Sartre's nausea, Camus's absurd, and Tolstoy's horror"* ... which gives her a pivot to bounce around between the three, only to flip into *The Little Prince*. In the opening chapter, she is often introducing a different "character" (be that a famous writer or *"a twelve-year-old boy with cancer"*) every paragraph or so. Again, I'm a cynical curmudgeon, so I may be an outlier here, but I very quickly got to the "don't care!" zone through this.

In discussing some previous studies of meaning (a philosophers' book in the 30's, and *Life* magazine's research in the 60's) she gets to what frames her thesis:

> ... Yet there were some themes that emerged again and again. When people explain what makes their lives meaningful, they describe connecting to and bonding with other people in positive ways. They discuss finding something worthwhile to do with their time. They mention creating narratives that bring order to life and help them understand themselves and the world. They talk about mystical experiences and self-loss.
>
>   As I conducted my research for this book these four themes came up again and again in my conversations with people living meaningful lives and those still searching for meaning. These categories were also present in the definitions of a meaningful life ... that meaning arises from our relationships to others, having a mission tied to contributing to society, making sense of our experiences and who we are through narrative, and connecting to something bigger than the self. ...

The "Belonging" chapter starts with the story about a small island off the Virginia coast, where the locals have pretty much their own culture – certainly their own accent – and looks at one fellow who left there, but still visits frequently. This then shifts into a look at the changing theories of infant and child care, and how one researcher, René Spitz, shifted things from a non-contact model to one that emphasized a lot of physical interaction (much of the casework being done in orphanages). From here she moves to looking at loneliness, and there's some interesting figures here:

> ... About 20 percent of people consider loneliness a "major source of unhappiness in their lives" and one third of Americans 45 and older say they are lonely. In 1985, when the General Social Survey asked Americans how many people they'd discussed important matters with over the last six months, the most common response was three. When the survey was given again in 2004, the most common response was zero.

It's not a big jump to examining suicide from there, and she quotes numerous studies that indicated *"people are more likely to kill themselves when they were alienated from their communities"*, and the odd factoid that *"wealthy countries have higher suicide rates than poor ones, and that their inhabitants are less likely to consider their lives meaningful"*. This eventually meanders into a longish tale about the Society for Creative Anachronism (think "ren faire" if you're not familiar with the SCA), and various dynamics in it, including dealing with a suicidally depressed member. Of all the stories in the book, the one that struck me the most was that of a guy who buys a newspaper from the same vendor every morning in New York, and they always had a bit of a conversation, which eventually builds into a connection. One day, the guy only had big bills, but the vendor didn't have change – and he said to pay for it the next day – but the guy insisted he should pay, went into a store, bought something just to get change, and paid the vendor. This chilled their relationship, as the guy rejected the kindness, and pulled the exchange down to a simple transaction. This leads into the author discussing other studies of rejection, and how some people devalue others' work (doctors and hospital cleaners).

The second "pillar" is Purpose. This starts out with a story about a zookeeper in Detroit, moves to a story of a drug dealer in New York (who turns his life around in prison, and now runs a fitness company based on his jailhouse workouts), and into the story of an Indian photographer doing a series of major works based on the Hindu deities, which then veers into a look at the movie *Good Will Hunting*, which is part of a riff on Kant:

> Though living with purpose may make us happier and more determined, a purpose-driven person is ultimately concerned not with these personal benefits but with making the world a better place.
> ... That idea was expressed forcefully by the eighteenth-century German thinker Immanuel Kant. ...
> To Kant, the question is not what makes you happy. The question is how to do your duty, how to best contribute ...

This leads into a look at current research at places like the Yale School of Management and Wharton: *"Adam Grant, a Wharton School of Business professor ... points out that those who consistently rate their jobs as meaningful have something in common: they see their jobs as a way to help others."*

Next comes "Storytelling". This starts with a horrific tale of a teenage girl getting hit by a car, and having severe neurological damage ... the payoff on the story is the whole trauma center staff coming in to introduce themselves to the girl ... for *their* benefit because only about 1 in 10 with these sorts of injuries survive, and having the example "keeps them coming back to work". One thing I actually dropped a bookmark on here was part of a story-telling event/site called *The Moth*, and this comment from their Artistic Director is pretty sharp:

> The most moving stories ... are rooted in vulnerability, but they are not too emotionally raw. The stories should come ... "from scars and not wounds." They should have settled into the storyteller's mind so that he or she can reflect back on the experience and pull out its meaning.

Smith goes on to define this "pillar" a bit more coherently than the others with:

> Our storytelling impulse emerges from a deep-seated need all humans share: the need to make sense of the world. We have a primal desire to impose order on disorder – to find the signal in the noise. We see faces in the clouds, hear footsteps in the rustling of leaves, and detect conspiracies in unrelated events. We are constantly taking pieces of information and adding a layer of meaning to them; we couldn't function otherwise. Stories help us make sense of the world and our place in it, and understand why things happen the way they do.

She goes on to talk about a semi-pro football player who breaks his spine, how college fund-raisers who used personal stories raised more money, the life of a Cuban refugee, and ends up discussing the book/movie *Life of Pi* (which should have come with a "spoiler warning").

The final "pillar" is "Transcendence" and, interestingly, she starts this off with a story of a visit to the McDonald Observatory in Texas, which moves into a lot of scientific space info, and then into ancient beliefs about the cosmos. This was pretty good at describing where she was going here:

> You might expect the insignificance we feel in the face of this knowledge to highlight the absurdity and meaninglessness of our lives. But it in fact does the opposite. The abject humility we experience when we realize that we are nothing but tiny flecks in a vast and incomprehensible universe paradoxically fills us with a deep and powerful sense of meaning. A brush with mystery – whether underneath the stars, before a gorgeous work of art, during a religious ritual, or in a hospital delivery room – can transform us.

She goes off into the work of William James (*The Varieties of Religious Experience*) who was a great fan of nitrous oxide to "stimulate the mystical consciousness" (*maaaaan ...*), and offers up his four qualities of this, being *passive, transient, ineffable,* and *noetic* (imparting knowledge or wisdom). She digs up an "expert on transcendence" from the University of Pennsylvania (I assume there *have* to be some out there ... although I doubt he's on the Wharton faculty), and tracks down some researchers doing actual empirical studies into stuff like "awe". This leads into story of some guy who decided that he really wasn't interested in finance, and ran off to a monastery in Burma, where the author details, over several pages, the predictable whining of the Western seeker who is disappointed to find that traditional spiritual training centers don't sport the comforts of a Four Seasons hotel. He nevertheless sticks to it and eventually gets to a point where he claims he's *"seen so clearly what an illusion the self is"*. She bounces off this story into an interesting (but brief) look at some researchers investigating what's happening in the brains of meditators via SPECT (single photon emission compound tomography), which I've seen covered in other books previously.

This next goes into a story of Jeff Ashby, who was inspired at age 6 by one of the early NASA manned flights, and who eventually made it into space at age 45. The thrust here (*heh*) is on how, once his life-long dream had been achieved, he looked for "bigger issues" ... which then flips back into a look at John Muir, who founded the Sierra Club, and how he got into Transcendentalism via the work of Ralph Waldo Emerson. This then leads off to a review of assorted "transcendent" experiences, including those generated by hallucinogens (with mention of some research studies), and a story about a cancer patient using these to smooth the transition out of this life.

The "Growth" chapter isn't one of the "pillars" that Smith lists, but gets about as many pages devoted to it. This starts with a rambling story of some of the people involved in a group called "The Dinner Party", which is set up for young adults who have lost close loved ones. This is all pretty predictable but for the quote from one of them: *"That's what nihilism is for"*, which, of course, appealed to *my* sensibilities. This then rolls into a story of a Vet suffering from PTSD who ended up killing somebody in a drunk-driving episode, and, in dealing with this, forms a group called Dryhooch to provide places where vets can hang out together without booze. This leads to tales of other folks who have survived traumatic experiences and "grown" from them ... including some research on how there's quite a range of how resilient individuals can be, which may have a substantial genetic component.

The penultimate chapter is "Culture of Meaning", which starts with the story of a church in Seattle that does a late-night service involving chanting a 4th-century ritual, which has been a counter-culture fave for decades. The author quotes dozens of attendees' passionate comments about the program, but doesn't offer much concrete about it (no researchers had wires stuck in the audience, evidently). Smith uses this chapter to try to support her "four pillars" model, and runs through a bunch of different groups, organizations, companies, etc. that are "cultures of meaning" and tries to map them onto her framework. Frankly, I thought the connection was pretty weak across the board here, but if you're the type that gets entranced by the sort of stories that make up much of the book, you may be sufficiently enthused at this point that you'll be totally on board with whatever Smith's pitching. Me, not so much.

However, the book somewhat redeems itself in the "Conclusion", which – while brief – takes a fascinating look at death and suicide. It starts with a rather arch quote: *"Death ... poses a grave challenge to the ability lead a meaningful life.",* and the search for *"a meaning that cannot be annulled by death."* The core story here focuses on researcher William Brietbart (with Sloan Kettering) ... who discusses working with the AIDS community, considers the work of Dr. Jack Kevorkian, and the movement for legalization of assisted suicide. He found that:

> *those who desired a hastened death reported feelings of meaninglessness, depression, and hopelessness. They were living in an "existential vacuum".*
> *... Brietbart knew he could treat depression ... but he was stumped when it came to treating meaninglessness.*

Unfortunately, what he ended up developing (a multi-session group therapy approach) was specifically targeted to the terminal cancer patients with whom he worked, and not a generally applicable approach for the rest of us. The book (somewhat predictably) ends with a meander through the story of Viktor Frankl[3], before coming up with the "big reveal":

> *Love, of course, is at the center of the meaningful life. Love cuts through each of the pillars of meaning and comes up again and again in the stories of those I have written about.*

I wonder if the author has an appreciation of how *empty* and *pointless* that sounds to somebody struggling with suicidal depression. Needless to say, that's a throw-the-book-across-the-room mic drop ending (especially following the rest of that chapter).

Obviously, The Power of Meaning[4] was not "my sort of book" ... I don't care for "teaching stories" in general, and all these tales of people in various situations were frequently just *blah-blah-blah* to me. But, that's *me*, and I realize that a lot of people *live* for this stuff. If you like to read about "remarkable individuals" (and not in the 4th Way[5] sense), you'll no doubt like this far more than I did. Again, I had high hopes for this when it started, and if it had concentrated more on the research, psychology, and philosophy (& Sufi thought), and not on these folks that the reader is supposed to have an empathetic reaction to (I always feel like I'm being "played" when authors try to get me to *feel* instead of *think*), I would have likely been raving about it by this point. But no.

As noted up top, this is not coming out until January, so you've got a few months to wait if you're wanting to pick up a copy. You can, of course, pre-order from the on-line big boys (who have it at a bit over a third off of cover price), so you'll have it as soon as it ships. I just wish I could have been more enthusiastic about this.

Notes:
1. http://btripp-books.livejournal.com/192067.html
2. http://amzn.to/2c90akK
3. http://btripp-books.livejournal.com/136125.html
4. http://amzn.to/2c90akK
5. http://amzn.to/2dzp250

Saturday, October 8, 2016[1]

... if I sang out of tune

The publishing biz can be pretty brutal. I got this book at the dollar store ... which is, of course, not in and of itself unusual ... but it's quite a decent read, and is out-of-print (in the hardcover, at least) a mere 3 years after its release. Sure, I'm happy that this means that I got it for a buck, but this is one of those that I would have thought might well have a better run (it *is* still available in a paperback edition, however).

Anyway, I didn't expect that I was going to much like Carlin Flora's Friendfluence: The Surprising Ways Friends Make Us Who We Are[2], but the way the info here is presented won me over. I'm somewhat surprised that I didn't end up with a whole lot of little bookmark slips in this (and the ones that are here are at the beginning and end of the book), so I'm going to be probably doing "broad strokes" over most of this.

As I noted in the above, I found the *structure* of the book one of the most appealing things here ... the author (a former Features Editor for *Psychology Today*) starts out with a section trying to define friendship, then moves into "Finding and Making Friends", and then to a series of chapters looking at friendship dynamics at various ages, from kindergarten on up, before switching to a consideration of "bad company", and the evolving domain of digital friendship. What could have been an overly touchy-feely presentation flows logically through these chapters, and builds on each stage.

Now, looking through this, one of the challenges I have is that there's lots of rapid-fire examples in most of the chapters, which make it a bit difficult to grab some "summary" sense ... however, an on-going theme here is, not surprisingly, how friendship differs from family relationships, which expresses itself on many levels, from the legal (a patient may have only a friend for support, but hospital rules might only allow *relatives* to visit in certain situations), to organizational (taking time off to grieve the loss of a friend is likely to be more difficult to arrange that that of a relative), to dynamic (especially among siblings).

The author includes some autobiographical information here as well, such as how she encountered her BFF – a Peruvian gal, who showed up at her dorm room looking for her roommate, and they totally clicked. This sets up a look at theories of friend connection, starting with the "proximity theory" where those you come into contact with frequently have a better chance of becoming friends. I found this spin on that of interest:

> But also familiarity breeds positivity. Called the "mere-exposure effect," it's a phenomenon that is widely documented: Just seeing someone over and over can make you like him or her more. It's probably because familiarity feels good to brains that would rather process stimuli using worn-in neural pathways than forging new ones."

She injects an interesting factoid from some research here, that *"You'll give off a better first impression ... if your name is easy to pronounce."* – which is likely due to similar "brain preferences". She rattles through a number of other settings which lead to friend formation ... shared activities, major life events (the new mom finding other new moms to hang with), etc., before turning to Dale Carnegie and his (still applicable) tactics, which are then contrasted with people who have diseases which make things, such as reading facial expressions, difficult.

Unsurprisingly, Flora checks in with the well-known work of Robin Dunbar, and extracts a very good brief over-view of his work:

> The British anthropologist Robin Dunbar, Ph.D., discovered that the size of a primate's brain is correlated with the size of the social group within which its species typically lives. The magic number for humans – extrapolated from our average brain size – is 150.
> More specifically, Dunbar conceives of the number 150 as embedded with a number of layers. "In effect we have five intimate friends. Fifteen close friends, 50 good friends, 150 friends," Dunbar says. "The 15 layer has long been know in social psychology as the 'sympathy group' (those whose death tomorrow would seriously upset you). Beyond 150, we have acquaintances, and here they are more often asymmetric (I know who you are, but you don't necessarily know who I am). The 1,500 layer seems to equate to the number of faces we can put names to."

She adds an interesting bit to this:

> Another team more recently found a correlation between the size of the amygdala, a brain region that processes emotional stimuli, and both the size and complexity of a person's social network.

I found this fascinating, as the amygdala is usually described as the part of the brain that creates reactions like jumping back from a rope because it might be (i.e. looks like) a snake.

This takes us to the "childhood friends" chapter ... with has several thematic sub-sections (again making it tough to summarize). I guess what I'll do is drop in some quotes that catch my eye flipping through these parts (where I didn't drop in bookmarks). Here's one:

> Many childhood friendships dissolve, leaving behind just a few fuzzy memories; others ... lend a steady beat of continuity to life. Whether or not you're still in touch with your old pals – or even can recall them clearly – they surely helped shape you, for better or for worse.

She then runs through some examples, and media expressions of childhood friendships, from Charlie Brown to Harry Potter. I also found this bit of interest:

> Friendships sprout much earlier than you might think. A one-year-old who has the chance to interact regularly with other little ones will indeed choose favorite playmates – first friends. Toddler buddies frolic in more complex ways than do non-friends. They might engage in pretend play ... which requires more cognitive skills than tag or other literal pursuits.

It's also notable that gender is a major differentiating element in patterns of friendship – although the author doesn't particularly wander into the minefield of "nature vs. nurture" in that – and it seems that the gender differences are largely permanent (albeit expressing differently at various ages and in divergent contexts), and later parts of the book take a look at ways that individuals might try to improve, and/or enrich, these dynamics. Flora presents a wide array of sample situations here, from kids who were together for ethnic support (i.e. being the only Iranians in their school), to ones who gravitated around common interests (gamers, jocks, fashion fanatics, etc.). A data point that comes in here is *"A Harris Interactive survey of Americans ages eight to twenty-four revealed that 94 percent had a close friend."*, so this does seem to be something fairly hard-wired.

I rather liked her chapter title for the look at the teen years: *Friendship in Adolescence: Confidants and Partners in Crime* ... again, there are a lot of stories fleshing this out, but there are little gems of data (or near-data) such as:

> As an adult, you still need to feel that your friends reflect your identity (or your desired identity), but that drive was probably more urgent when you were an adolescent. ... In fact, to the average thirteen-year-old, friends are just as emotionally supportive as parents, and to seventeen-year-olds, they are more so.

As this suggests, the influence of parents, while not non-existent, is, by the mid-teens sort of a "background noise" for the kids whose emotional context is far more set by their friend group. Unfortunately, this means if you've not steered your children towards a positive set of kids, you may have blown it ... as peer pressure is likely to trump anything you're going to be able to bring to the table, and this can easily (at the prodding of the worse kids) spiral into dangerous behaviors.

The author breaks down a lot of dynamics in various settings, and I found this bit of interest:

> A key difference between middle school and high school emerges as late adolescents form romantic attachments, which sometimes take precedence over friendships. Still, it's all a continuum: The skills

> *kids use to keep up their same-sex friendships are further developed through their romantic ties.*

And, of course, as the years build up, the patterns shift from assorted types of groups, into pairs, and networks of pairs.

The "perks of friendship" chapter goes into a lot of psychological/sociological (many researchers are name-checked, but most get dealt with "in passing" rather than in any particular detail) dynamics on how friendships work among adults ... including some very interesting material about the friendship of Matisse and Picasso (and later Renoir & Monet, and Gauguin & van Gogh). She examines a fairly wide array of situations (with stories which illustrate same), and breaks down the functions of friendship in these, but there isn't much that I found that would be useful to add here.

Flora is back to the "dark side of friendship" next, and she sort of frames this chapter with:

> *Since friends are powerful influences in your life, they can just as easily have negative effects as positive ones, especially if they are not right for you, or if the dynamic between the two of you is unhealthy.*

She notes some recent investigative work which suggests that van Gogh did not cut off his own ear (as is the usual story), but lost it in a sword fight with his long-time associate Gauguin, as an extreme illustration of this. Much of what she discusses in this section is gender-based, with significantly different patterns of behavior being prevalent on either side of that divide ... although there's quite a bit that's displayed universally (or, at least among the negative friend relationships) ... and brings in examples of numerous studies on the details.

This is followed by her consideration of on-line friendships ... which leads off with a heart-breaking story of a couple of gals who were both dealing with serious health issues (one with cancer, one with an immune system defect), who became best friends on line, although they lived on other sides of the planet (California and Australia). Somehow they never moved out of the on-line modality, and when one of them stopped responding (assumed dead), the remaining friend had no way of contacting anybody to get any information. It's a sad tale, but also somewhat cautionary (I must admit that I have "pixel people" who I'd be hard pressed to find "IRL" since I only know them by their on-line personas) for those who "live on-line". The author does point out some research that indicates that, despite the ability to have thousands and thousands of web "friends", most folks start to get overwhelmed if they try to keep up regular, on-going, active virtual relationships with more that the "Dunbar number" of 150 contacts. I guess biology beats out technology when it comes to our interpersonal relationships. She also looks at the generational gap, from those of us who remember pre-web communications, to those younger folks who have always been digital ... and the attitudes that these differing realities engender. She has some quotes from literary critic William Deresiewicz on the subject of on-line relations, of which I found this particularly arch (speaking of his Facebook "friends"): *"They're simulacra of my friends, little dehydrated packets of im-*

ages and information, no more my friends than a set of baseball cards is the New York Mets." She later quotes some other researchers who note the somewhat disturbing factoid that: *"the eating, drinking, and smoking of our friends who live hundreds of miles away appear to have as much influence as the habits of our friends who live next door".*

There are some interesting things in the final chapter, such as a study from Gallup that identifies eight "vital roles" that are likely to be in one's friend group. These are "Builders", Champions", "Collaborators", "Companions", "Connectors", "Energizers", "Mind Openers", and "Navigators" ... a model intriguing enough that I may have to pick up that book[3] at some point. Here the author also looks at studies and stories on loneliness, and how being friendless causes a whole raft of physical and psychological ills. At the end of this chapter she does a very nice wrap-up, with advice for nearly each stage and situation ... but it's a couple of paragraphs, and I guess I'm just going to leave it to you to find it instead of throwing in an overly big blockquote at the end of this review.

If you are interested in checking Friendfluence[4] out, as noted up top, it's still available in the paperback edition (so might be at your local bookstore), but the on-line new/used guys have "like new" copies of the hardcover (which is what I found at the dollar store) for a penny (plus shipping), which means that it is an easy option. I quite enjoyed this, and found it (despite being heavier on the "stories" than on the "research") full of educational items.

Notes:

1. http://btripp-books.livejournal.com/192473.html
2. http://amzn.to/2cLBGOT
3. http://amzn.to/2dSnDqk
4. http://amzn.to/2cLBGOT

Saturday, October 15, 2016[1]

"You can't handle the truth!", or something ...

I'm a big fan of CreateSpace, and use it for putting out annual collections[2] of print versions of these reviews, among other projects, but (as a former "real" publisher), I realize that there's a bit of a stigma about books coming out from that channel, as they're not "vetted", and pretty much anybody with a PC can put out their scribblings there. I have, generally speaking, pooh-poohed much of this, but having Brien Foerster's Lost Ancient Technology Of Peru And Bolivia[3] in hand, I can see where much of that criticism is coming from.

Now, *some* would take issue with the *subject* here, but I specifically *bought* the book (at full retail, no less) because I was interested in that ... but I'm *shocked* at the lack of editing and design exhibited here. Frankly, I wish that people like the author of this would hire people *like me* to do editing and lay-out for their books. At various points in reading this I was wondering if he was using one of those voice-to-Kindle programs (as there were a couple of places where sound-alike words appeared, such as "services" appearing instead of the clearly-intended "surfaces" - something that would not have resulted from keyboard input, even with an over-eager spellcheck program running), and at other points wondering if this had been cobbled together via cut-and-paste from a web site (as the text occasionally refers to images that weren't there, or weren't in the "location" indicated). I also suspect that this had been generated for Kindle first and then converted to print – something that would explain the otherwise mystifying (and extremely irritating) lack of page numbers. Aside from these issues, there were also at least a dozen egregious typos that *should* have been caught by a spellcheck (such as stray extra letters in the middle of common words), as well as "editorial/style" issues of apparently randomly using assorted variations of the spelling on culture or site names. Again, the vast majority of these issues would have been solved by a once-over by an actual editor.

While the subject matter here is *fascinating*, this is largely a "picture book", with nearly every page having some image from either the author's explorations at the sites in South America, or pictures obtained from the web (which the author – obviously acclimated to the habitually more "grey area" IP conventions of the Internet – assumes were copyright free because he got them from "free file sharing sites"). I will give Foerster this, however ... he's certainly not *soaking* the readers, as this 200+ page 8.5x11" book is priced at only $9.95, which means he's barely making a profit (a whopping 30¢) on "expanded distribution" bookstore sales, and only clearing two bucks and change via Amazon ... I guess if you want professional editing and lay-out you gotta pay more.

Anyway ... that bit of kvetching over ... to the book itself.

I have been fascinated by the theories of the many authors in the "vanished ancient culture" niche, John Anthony West, Graham Hancock, Robert Bauval, Robert Schoch, Charles Hapgood, Rand Flem-Ath, and others, and this is certainly in that stream – if not *theoretically* so, at least in presenting a lot of architectural artifacts as being *best explained* by it. As devoted readers of this space (there *are* some, aren't there?) know, I've been down to Peru a couple of times, and have been to a few of the sites covered here, so I've seen first-hand some of the amazing stonework that's down there, but nowhere near the extraordinary things that Foerster shows throughout this volume. A prime example is that cover picture, which is looking down a perfectly drilled-out *tube* cut through extremely hard rock. Today, we'd probably have to use a specially lubricated diamond-tipped corer to replicate this ... when the "official timeline" advocates claim these were made (i.e. by the Inca), there was *nothing* available that would have been able to make that, or any of the assorted inverted corners carved into andesite, basalt, and granite stones in the more megalithic construction phases.

One of the things I don't believe I'd encountered previously that the author injects several places through the book is the "Mohs scale", which is a ranking of hardness of materials (based on what can scratch what), and most of these megalithic stones are in the 6-7 range on that scale ... which is telling when you notice[4] that *steel* is only a 4-4.5 on that scale, with materials like copper, brass, and bronze (that were typical of Incan tools) being only around a 3 ... not likely to be able to be able to make much of an impression *at all* on these building materials, let alone carve the very complex formations clearly evident at these sites.

And, this, of course, doesn't even begin to address how some of these massive megalithic sites, such as Sachsayhuaman (which I have visited), had blocks[5], nearly the size of a house and weighing hundreds of tons, that were transported from quarries some 35 miles away to the site – at a time when there were no suitable trees in the region that could be used for rollers (if that was even possible with stones that size). One of the most fascinating things here (that I'd likewise not previously encountered) was the concept of "previous ages" of the Hanan Pacha and the Uran Pacha (leading to our current Ukan Pacha, which is when the Inca were building), which, respectively, did the carving of living rock, and the building with megalithic forms. Using these three modes, Foerster is able to analyze the building phases of most of the ruins he visits, identifying the fairly evident different construction elements that are frequently seen one on top of the other.

Of course, one has to be willing to accept the possibility that there *was* an advanced global culture that existed more that twelve thousand years ago, which left its mark in very ancient, highly precise and/or massive constructions that can still be found in places like Peru and Bolivia, as well as examples such as the Osireion at Abydos in Egypt, or the thousand-ton megaliths found at the Baalbek complex in Lebanon. This culture would have thrived before the end of the last ice age, and was destroyed in a worldwide catastrophe likely caused[6] by a major "solar proton event" with accompanying coronal mass ejection.

The author doesn't get too deep into that particular line of thought (the originators of the Hanan-Uran-Ukan Pacha model have some serious woo-woo in there – claiming that gravity was less in the distant past, etc.), but it is, in its broad strokes, quite a plausible frame for noting the different construction styles encountered. As impressive a culture that the Inca were (much of the terracing, etc. seen all over the region were indisputably Incan engineering projects), they had nothing that could produce the sort of stone work[7] that is seen all over the place (and identified as Uran Pacha construction). There is also the theory that these ancient cultures had a technology for making stone "soft"[8] so that it could be easily carved, and then re-solidified – which, as bizarre as it may sound, would go a long way to explaining the "how" of some of the amazing walls[9] in Cuzco and elsewhere.

Once setting up a basis (to varying extents) of these theories, Foerster walks the reader through a couple of dozen sites across Peru and Bolivia, most of which he has visited, some he's just reporting via others' accounts. In a number of the pictures (and, again, this is very much a "picture book", as most pages are at least a third dedicated to an image, and there are lots of pages with just a picture and caption) an engineer by the name of Chris Dunn[10] is shown measuring surfaces, checking angles, and determining geophysical alignments ... he has a couple of books out based on his research in Egypt, as this has only been out a couple of years, I wonder if he's working on a volume dealing with the "Incan" ruins.

They eventually end up at Tiwanaku and Puma Punku (familiar to all who watch the History Channel on cable), and, to their credit, don't launch into the whole "ancient alien" thing[11] about it being a spaceport or something ... but they do note that it, like many of the other sites discussed, does appear to have been violently destroyed at some point in the distant past – in a way that would be hard to explain by the technology of the past couple of thousand years being involved.

Is Lost Ancient Technology Of Peru And Bolivia[12] good book? That depends. I really love this "ancient advanced culture" genre, and do appreciate that the author only dips his toe into "the deep end" of that niche. His photos (and those he appropriates), although all B&W, are mostly quite illuminating, and he generally does a good job of putting them in context ... however, the "editing" thing comes up here as well, there's one point (I'd mention the page numbers, but there *aren't* any) where he repeats the same image on facing pages, as well as sticking in a 2/3rds-page-large image of the cover of his Machu Picchu book *twice* when discussing that site (I'm hardly one to talk about pimping out one's books, but, *really*, an "other books by the author" page in the back would have sufficed), which, needless to say, does not add *anything* to the information content.

Of course, as noted above, he has this very reasonably priced, so the deficiencies in the editing and design of the book (which would be a weekend project for somebody who "does books" to fix) are easier to let slide than if it came at a heftier cost. It's a shame, however, as most of what is *wrong* with this could easily be rectified. Of course, as a "book guy" and editor, the stuff that I found irritating here might fly totally under the radar for most readers. I suspect that (the egregious typos aside) the Kindle version reads a lot better, as I'm guessing that this project started on that side of the digital/dead-tree divide. Because of the way this was published, I'm not sure you'd have much luck finding it in bookstores (although he mentions that it's available in the gift stores near a number of the sites), so the $9.95 cover price through the on-line big boys looks like your best bet (there *are* copies kicking around the used channels, but with shipping they'd be more than free shipping "retail"). Aside from the numerous editorial caveats expressed above, I quite enjoyed reading/viewing this, but, then again, in general I've "been there, done that, got the t-shirt", so my enthusiasm for it *might* be on the high side due to familiarity/interest. As Dennis Miller would have it, "your mileage may vary", but it's something that's likely worth looking into if you share my appreciation of the subject.

Notes:

1. http://btripp-books.livejournal.com/192542.html
2. http://eschatonbooks.com/BTB/BTB.html
3. http://amzn.to/2e6S8Mz
4. https://goo.gl/Y5fJCJ
5. https://goo.gl/zVpmY3
6. http://btripp-books.livejournal.com/171713.html
7. https://goo.gl/nsXDWx
8. https://goo.gl/VWgTrN
9. https://goo.gl/duakFP
10. http://amzn.to/2eDItNN
11. https://goo.gl/5ciFvD
12. http://amzn.to/2e6S8Mz

Sunday, October 16, 2016[1]

The right side of the airwaves ...

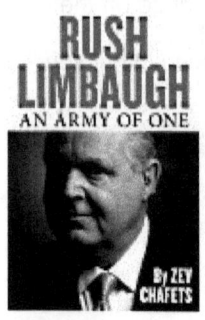

I don't "do radio", so Rush Limbaugh isn't on my radar the way he could be. I found his TV show back in the Klinton years amusing, but since he's been "audio only", I've not heard him in *ages*. I did, however, find Rush Limbaugh: An Army of One[2] on the dollar store shelves a couple of years back, and it's been sitting in my "to be read" piles since. A few weeks ago I was looking for the next book to slot into my active reading rotation, and noticed that the *author* of this was the same Zev Chafets that wrote that Roger Ailes[3] bio that I reviewed last month, which I'd enjoyed, so figured I'd have a go at this.

I have to admit, going in, that the little bookmarks that I put into what I'm reading (and are generally a good indicator of my engagement with a book) are few and far between here. As quotable as Rush may be on his show, the story of his life is considerably less so (or at least from my take on it). This volume is more a straight biography of the man than a celebration of his material, so focuses more on his trials and tribulations (and, to some extent "feet of clay"), than being a rah-rah session for "dittoheads".

There was, however, quite a lot of stuff in here that I didn't know about the man, that I might very well have were I a "regular listener", first and foremost of which is the factoid that he has been, for quite a long time, for all intents and purposes *deaf*. I'm guessing that this is something that his ongoing audience knows, but it was somewhat of a shock to read, as it hadn't filtered down to me, despite being a regular consumer of on-line conservative punditry. Go figure.

The other piece of this that I found somewhat odd was that, until late in his career, Limbaugh was not particularly political. The book describes how his *father* (and other relatives) were, but not Rush. His goal, from a quite early age, was to succeed in *radio*, and he didn't become the conservative icon that he is until that had become the key element to "his shtick" on-air ... which does lead one to wonder just how dedicated to the *doctrine* he is (a question that at least gets danced around a bit here).

It's not that he didn't have any interest in conservative political thought, there is a touching bit here regarding (one of my childhood heroes) William F. Buckley and *National Review*:

> ... Limbaugh had once read a book by Buckley that he had found in his father's library, and he sometimes watched Firing Line. Rush even did a very funny imitation of Buckley's mellifluous, multisyllabic English. But it wasn't until Limbaugh began doing political satire full-time that he actually began reading National Review on a regular basis.
> "I thought you had to be invited to read it," he said in an emotional broadcast on the day Buckley died. "I thought there was a select group of people

> *that were entitled to be a part of that. I'd never seen it on a newsstand. I had never seen it anywhere at anybody's house.*

That's a clear view of how far from the political bubble he had lived (as I'd been a subscriber to N.R. all my teen years!), and he thought the only way to get the magazine was to contact it and ask to be *allowed* to subscribe. His moving to the nationally syndicated show changed that, and he was soon invited into WFB's inner circle – Buckley was evidently a fan, and eventually he became something of a father figure to Rush.

Having at one point aspired to a career in radio myself, much of Rush's early employment arc was rather painful to read. He went from being a high-school DJ to a brief stint in college, to assorted small stations in secondary markets, and a predictable string of firings ... that just being the nature of the business. For a while he'd stepped away from radio and went to work for the marketing department of the Kansas City Royals, where he ended up forging a somewhat improbable lifetime friendship with Royals star George Brett. While with the Royals, Rush went through two marriages, and by the time he was fired, "shock radio" was starting to fill the airwaves. Larry Lujack (of WLS in Chicago), Don Imus, and Howard Stern were pioneering this niche, as well as (on the West Coast), Morton Downey Jr. ... who was caustic enough to get fired just at the right time. Rush was hired by a guy who'd worked at a station he'd previously been at to replace Downey on the Sacramento station where he'd been based ... on the theory that Rush would be edgy, but not as inflammatory. Of course, Limbaugh's new-found conservative voice made the California liberals *nuts*, and that drove his ratings. This got the attention of Ed McLaughlin, former head of ABC radio, who worked a deal to get Rush out of his Sacramento contract and on the air in New York in 1988, and two months later his syndicated national program debuted with fifty-six stations. Chafets notes what drove his success: *"His innovation was to bring top-40 radio's energy to political issues ..."* and *"A lot of what makes Limbaugh's show fun is his irreverence toward subjects that conservatives discuss, in public, with extreme reverence or not at all."*, and almost immediately Rush was making serious money. However, he remained an outsider. What he wanted most in life was to be accepted into the "media world", to be "one of them", but because of the ultra-leftist orientation of the New York media environment, he was – despite his extreme success – mocked and exiled by the foot-soldiers of the Progressive culture wars ... and on some level the acceptance he had from the likes of Bill Buckley and other conservative icons (including Ronald Regan) still wasn't enough to salve that hurt.

Like in the Ailes book, Chafets weaves his experiences in working on the book throughout. He notes that many of Rush's family and friends were quite hesitant to talk with him – with at least one being convinced that if he talked to this guy from the *New York Times*, he was sure to be depicted as some Neanderthal and/or idiot ... and at one point he mentions a question he'd put to Rush about his (massive) contract: *"... it sounded to him like a hostile question, a Democrat question ..."*, so the distrust of everything on the Left was pretty ingrained. This makes his exultation at the demise of the laughable Leftist "Air America" more understandable:

> Less than two years after {Air America's} grand launch it filed for bankruptcy protection. Limbaugh celebrated the fall, calling Air America, "an embarrassing, blithering, total bomb-out of a failure." Liberals, he said, can't compete in the open marketplace of ideas, because they don't really want to spell out what they actually believe. "There's no hiding on talk radio," he said, "When your ideas sound stupid, it's out there to be exposed for one and all ..."

Chafets has a very insightful look at the matrix in which Rush operates, in terms of the media establishments, and although it's a couple of paragraphs, I figured it was to-the-point enough to include here:

> If Limbaugh had been all bombast, his act wouldn't have lasted long. But he proved to be not just a great broadcaster but a very astute media critic. He realized that the mainstream media's greatest vulnerability was high-handed obtuseness. News organizations acted as though their biases and interests – financial, political, and personal – were invisible to the public. Limbaugh pointed out, in the clearest possible way, that the Emperor's clothes were all tailored in the same shop, according to the same specifications, and he let his listeners in on why and how.
> This was embarrassing, of course. Journalists like to think of themselves as independent thinkers and speakers of "truth to power." In fact, they work for big organizations and, like organization people everywhere, they toe the company line. To soften this reality, editors and reporters are almost uniformly recruited from a pool of like-minded people. They don't need to be explicitly told what to cover or how, any more than the Pope needs to send out memos to his cardinals about abortion. Here and there you can find editors and reporters with a certain degree of independence, but they are rare. As for editorial writers, they have all the latitude of West Point cadets.

While the lock-step march of the Leftist MSM, and their political allies, presents an often insurmountable challenge to non-"Progressive" politicians (cf. the hugely skewed moderation of the Trump-Clinton debates), it did nothing but make Rush money. In fact, the Obama regime opted to "run against Rush", all but coronating him as head of the Republican Party ... which was not happy news for the actual head of the RNC at the time. While Rush took to this with a gusto, the Leftist media was in full assault mode, trying to belittle and dismiss Rush (while still insisting that he was "the Boss" of the party). This eventually got quite ugly with attacks on Limbaugh for his addiction to pain pills (that he eventually beat), as only the Left can "do ugly".

This book came out in 2010, so it only got into the ramp-up of the last election cycle, but there is quite a bit about how Rush was playing in that (he "won" a Gallup poll of who was the most trustworthy conservative voice). There are also parts on his family life, a good deal on the above-mentioned challenges with his hearing (he has a call-taker that's a former court reporter, so she can transcribe what's being said by callers in real-time onto his monitor), and other assorted issues (his dalliance with the NFL – that got sabotaged by the usual suspects making the predictable and unjustified claims of "racism").

Rush Limbaugh: An Army of One[4] is still in print in the paperback edition, so you might be able to find it in brick-and-mortar book stores that don't discriminate against conservative voices (there *are* a lot of liberals who will throw a hissy fit at the very sight of Rush's visage on the cover, their panties suddenly twisting into sanity-reducing knots), but otherwise the on-line big boys have it … and the used guys have "like new" copies of the hardcover going for as little as a penny (plus shipping). If you're interested in Rush, the conservative movement, or in broadcasting in general, you'll likely find something worthwhile in this.

Notes:

1. http://btripp-books.livejournal.com/192923.html
2. http://amzn.to/2dwGCe1
3. http://btripp-books.livejournal.com/191534.html
4. http://amzn.to/2dwGCe1

Monday, November 14, 2016[1]

Mission Implausible ...

I had, obviously, lost track of Dick Hoagland quite a while back. I'd been following his EnterpriseMission.com web site through the 90's, but even when I reviewed his Monuments of Mars[2] six and half years ago, I was wondering "what happened" to him, and he'd sort of dropped off my radar. I'd picked up Dark Mission: The Secret History of NASA[3] by him and Mike Bara a few years back, but only got around to reading it last month (it kept getting passed over due to being nearly 600 pages). If you're unfamiliar with Hoagland, he's the guy who glommed onto "the face on Mars" and ran with it. I don't really want to re-hash a lot of the stuff from my previous review, however, but there's a lot about *this* book which has pretty much the same issues I had with the earlier one.

Getting ready to write this, I popped over to his site, and was surprised to find that he's updated it over the past couple of years (it had been static for so long, I never got over there unless I was looking to background something on "hyperdimensional physics"), plus having developed a new radio show. One interesting thing there was coverage of China's lunar lander program, which I'd, frankly, missed when it happened a couple of years back.

Now, Hoagland is "an acquired taste", and is easy for most folks to brush off as an obsessed eccentric. Honestly, he brings this on himself, "leading with his chin", as it were, with picture after picture after picture of *extremely* ambiguous stuff on the Moon or Mars which he claims "clearly" shows artificiality. I have been following this guy's material for what at this point is *decades*, and I have yet to see a picture from, for instance, the Moon where the "structures" he insists are self-evident in these grainy, digitally processed images, are even vaguely suggested. Not a single shot of the "lunar domes" which take up a lot of this (and are the focus of his info on the Chinese mission on his site) looks to me as anything other than random "noise". And, like Fox Mulder, I *do* "want to believe", but time after time what he's pitching as being in these pictures are less convincing than seeing Jimmy Durante in a cloud formation. Oh, and as an editorial note, a lot of Dark Mission[4] is set up as a 3rd person presentation with Hoagland being a character in the telling, rather than being the "speaker", and those "Hoagland found ..." bits get irritating fast – unless, of course, Mike Bara was the primary author of this.

However ...

I really *hate* that this evidently arose[5] from his measurements of angles of stuff in the "Cydonia" area on Mars. There are a couple of numbers that come out of this which keep appearing (especially the latitude of 19.5°) in various energetic phenomena across the solar system. This led him to develop/uncover a "hyperdimensional/torsion physics" which is both the subject of quite a lot of Russian research, and goes (according to this book) back to James Clerk Maxwell's original equations, which reflect his argument that *"the only way to solve certain problems in physics was to account for some phenomena as 3D 'reflections' of objects existing in higher spatial dimensions"*, but this "scalar" component was, after Maxwell's death, stripped out of his original equations by Oliver Heaviside, resulting with the "normal space" classic Maxwell equations which underlie much of modern physics. I have found this material fascinating, and I suspect that Hoagland has stumbled onto something that is quite important, but he goes back to it so frequently, it's like finding "hidden Mickeys" at Disney World ... albeit even more so.

As one might guess, a nearly-600-page book (set in fairly small type), has a massive amount of detail crammed in, and I'd *love* to go on-and-on about the physics stuff, but it would take way too much space to give it justice in even the broad strokes, so I'm just going to note my enthusiasm for that material, and suggest that if it sounds like something you might find of equal interest (check out the bits on his site to get a sense of it), pick up the books ... you can focus on those parts without having to swallow the rest.

And the rest is a *lot* to swallow. As should not be surprising given the subtitle, this book is largely a history of NASA ... but not so much in the mundane, this mission did this, that mission did that, mode, but a "way over the edge" version which tracks the space program back to the early days. Now, pretty much everybody knows that the US and USSR were in a race to see how many German rocket scientists they could sweep up in the final days of the Third Reich, and that we ended up with Wernher von Braun (and some of his assistants) who was the leading light of NASA in the post-war years. Hoagland puts forth information that suggests that not only was von Braun an *enthusiastic* Nazi (in contact with the top echelons the Reich), but he was somewhat of an *unrepentant* Nazi, even after being mainstreamed in the US. There was also a very strong *Masonic* element involved. Now, I've never quite understood the paranoia around the Masons ... while I've never been *personally* involved, both my maternal grandfather and my father-in-law were 33rd Degree Masons, and I never saw anything creepy in either family related to that (well, unless you count the very large and garish "logo" flower arrangement that the Eastern Star organization sent to my mother-in-law's funeral). Hoagland, however, does the cable-ready "oooh – Secret Society!" thing here, and notes how many NASA administrators and astronauts were quite active Masons (and, I will admit, some of the material here – astronauts posing in official photos symbolically exhibiting their Masonic rings, and having Masonic organizational flags being included in their personal effects brought with them to the Moon ... which is sort of suggested by the obviously photoshopped cover image – is awfully suggestive of more than just *individual* expressions of "Masonic pride"). And, of course there is Jack Parsons, a devotee of Aleister Crowley, and O.T.O. member, whose work with Theodore von Karman in developing rockets, is used by Hoagland to paint the senior scientist with the same occult brush (although I was unable to dig up anything more than just the JPL connection).

So, Hoagland feels that there is a Nazi/Mason/Occult (he even presents an "organizational chart" for this) theme to NASA, and constantly returns to "ritual timing" of various elements in the program. I would normally dismiss this, but the timing/orientation of key events (at least as Hoagland describes them) does seem to hew to a very specific line ... a line that seems to be rooted in ancient Egyptian religion. This goes down a rather convoluted rabbit-hole, but, like much in Hoagland's world, there's just enough "real stuff" that keeps one from totally saying he's simply nuts. In this case, there is a lot of "symbolic" elements in the naming, iconography, etc. of NASA programs that relate to the Osiris/Isis/Horus deity matrix, and Hoagland keeps pointing to "ritual alignments" time/location-wise that are quite suggestive that this sort of thing *could* be happening. He even identifies a key Egyptian scientist who was brought in for the Apollo program, and suggests that he is the one setting out the plans for those enactments. Again, there is a lot here that sounds like so much hooey, especially the "lion"/sphinx stuff (mainly on Mars), as well as the rather convoluted "evidence" of Sirius or some star of Orion's belt being above/below/on a horizon at a particular time. There's a lot in the genre of "more ancient cultures than generally accepted" that I totally believe (like the Giza Sphinx aligning to an event that happened several thousand years prior to when Zahi Hawass and the like would hold to be possible), but deciding, when less-obvious pictures of "the face" came in, that it was "half-lion, half-man" (which Hoagland enthusiastically does here) is more than a bit "out there".

The other main theme here is the "conspiracy to hide stuff" which, while certainly *plausible* given the track record that Hoagland outlines of endless promises of releases, only to be followed by evidently *intentionally degraded* images, or no images at all (or even, at one point, an order to *destroy* all existing images from a program). Why would NASA do this? I guess it goes back to the notorious "Brookings report", which noted that much turmoil could be expected were the public to hear that we had contacted or found evidence of extraterrestrial cultures/races, which included quotes such as *"How might such information, under what circumstances be presented to or withheld from the public for what ends?"* and:

> *While face-to-face meetings with it will not occur within the next twenty years (unless its technology is more advanced than ours, qualifying it to visit Earth), artifacts left at some point in time by these life forms might possibly be discovered through our space activities on the Moon, Mars, or Venus.*

Hoagland, perhaps more than *anybody*, believes that we have evidence of these sorts of artifacts (and, again, as much as I might like to see indisputable proof of this, the vast majority of the photos require a very active imagination to "see" what Hoagland and his associates "see" in them). However, the concept that the overriding "model" for both NASA and other space programs is that were evidence of ETs made public, that human society would break down into chaos, is at least a point to explain a lot of what Hoagland notes would otherwise have to be due to *massive* incompetence in the handling of space imaging.

As noted, Dark Mission[6] is a very long book in fairly small type, and ends up a quite a slog through a lot of theorizing that isn't necessarily all that "evidence based" – but that's *my* call on the evidence, the authors here certainly seem to have a much lower bar for what's "convincing proof". There is also a good deal of paranoia exhibited in these pages, again, perhaps not erroneous, as Hoagland has certainly made himself a target of at least ridicule by the "mundane explanation" forces, and if even a third of what he's raising here is true, there must be a substantial conspiracy to keep the "official line" being the only one that gets serious consideration (but, as we've seen in the 2016 election cycle, the press is perfectly capable of defending an orthodoxy in the face of overwhelming evidence against it, if stonewalling against that evidence suits their agenda).

Can I recommend this book? Probably not. I'd suggest you dig through the EnterpriseMission.com web site first to get a sense of where Hoagland is coming from, and if you want to delve deeply into the more paranoid and conspiratorially-inclined aspects of that, then this book's for you. If not, you've been spared a very long strange read. I really wish that Hoagland (or somebody) would do a solid look at the hyperdimensional/tetrahedral/torsion physics that was *separate* from all the "oh, look, it's a *pyramid* ... oh, look, it's a *robot head* ... oh, look, it's a *city*!" stuff and put that out as a sane, serious book. Needless to say, despite having some very interesting material covered, this is *not* that.

Notes:

1. http://btripp-books.livejournal.com/193065.html
2. http://btripp-books.livejournal.com/31028.html
3-4. http://amzn.to/2fPhrB1
5. http://www.enterprisemission.com/hyper1.html
6. http://amzn.to/2fPhrB1

Tuesday, November 15, 2016[1]

Saling away ...

Sometimes I'm not sure how a book got into my to-be-read piles, especially it it's been lingering in there for quite a while. This is one of those. Frankly, I'd thought, when encountering this when looking for the "next" book, that it was something that I'd picked up at an author event a few years back, but when I got into it, I noticed a barcode sticker over the actual barcode on the back, indicating that it was likely a dollar store find instead. Oh, well.

Needless to say, Philip Delves Broughton's The Art of the Sale: Learning from the Masters About the Business of Life[2] had been in that not-being-read purgatory for as long as it had for that whole "sales" thing ... I've never been good at sales, not having the sort of psyche needed to take endless rejection, so when I have read "sales books", it's been sort of a latter-day "cod liver oil" for me, something to take because I need it, not that I really want it.

However, it turns out that this is a *delightful* book ... sort of a string of mini-biographies of a wide array of people who sell, and how these examples illustrate core truths about selling. I realize that this sounds counter-intuitive, given my antipathy toward "teaching stories", but these aren't "dancing around the subject", just addressing it from real-world examples. I have to admit that I took a peek at the Amazon reviews before launching into this and there were quite a number of people who were being bitchy about this not being "sales manual" – which is, basically, what I was dreading getting into.

The genesis of this book was the author's previous (about his mid-life attending Harvard's business school) ... and how he was shocked to find there was nothing about *sales* in most MBA programs, and how his professors suggested he "take a two-week evening program somewhere" if he wanted to study sales (oddly, I got a similar response when I wanted to study typography as part of my art major in college). He notes that there are two general schools of thought on sales, on one hand the "Dale Carnegie" side which sees sales as a path to success open to all, and the "Death of a Salesman" side which holds sales to be a soul-crushing hell. The stories here don't end up on either extreme, but float around in the real-life zone between.

The book starts with a memory of the author (who was born to English expats) at age 12 in Morocco where his parents went shopping for rugs in the bazaar. Unlike many, his family was up to the process, and he fondly recalls the event. This sets up the tale of his visiting a Moroccan named Majid, who has become famous ... *"He is known to interior decorators, collectors, and antiques dealers the world over, and yet he started out a street hawker."* ... Majid grew up in a family of traders and artisans, and he learned how to size up buyers and sellers early on. There's a bit in here of him selling a carpet to a Texan, who wanted "the very best", which Majid understood meant "the most expensive" – had he interpreted that as "the finest" he would have wasted his time selling the wrong rug. The initial take-away the author presents here is: *"Accurately perceiving the motivations of a customer then, is just as important as understanding what product they want."* ... before going into a discussion of some research on "declarative knowledge" in sales.

The next chapter starts with a look at Tony Sullivan, a TV infomercial host, known for his pitches for the Smart Mop, among many other products. As a child, his father placed gambling machines in pubs, etc., and would sometimes send Sullivan out to do collections ... then one summer he was helping to sell t-shirts at a festival, and encountered a guy that was selling something called a "Washmatic", and moving unit after unit with a highly animated pitch. Sullivan was fascinated, and after a while convinced the other fellow to let him learn the business. He apparently was a natural, and began selling all sorts of products at various events around the U.K., eventually making a break into TV by moving to the U.S., and selling the Smart Mop to and then on the Home Shopping Network. Interestingly, for coming from a "hucksterism" environment, he is very adamant on only selling stuff he, essentially, believes in, saying *"if a product doesn't work, or people don't think they're getting value, they can destroy your reputation online"*. He also isn't "always on", noting that he needs to take a product home, use it, think about it, and take a considerable amount of time to come up with a pitch. Broughton says:

> Stories serve two purposes in sales. They enable a salesperson to sell to a customer, and they enable salespeople to sell themselves on the value of their work. A good story works in three stages, which resemble those of the sales process itself. ...
> These are the same stages Aristotle prescribed for tragedy in the <u>Poetics</u>: an inciting incident, a climactic struggle, and, finally, a resolution.

The chapter then switches over to discussing Las Vegas hotelier Steve Wynn, who was highly impressed with another hotel's efforts to provide over-the-top service for his family while on vacation. His enthusiasm about this, told to the other hotel chain's chairman, started his outreach to Wynn employees with a system called "storytelling" that encourages staff to create service that's worthy of being told as a story. This then moves to a bit about P.T. Barnum, and then a look at an anonymous jewelry salesman who had gone to work at Cartier (getting the job after having spent nearly all his savings on Cartier products that he subtly produced at the interview), and developed into *"a keen reader of people's underlying fears and wants"*, much like the skills exhibited by Majid.

The next chapter starts off with a look at the nature of sales, from the general elements true across all settings (*"At its most basic and technical, selling is about understanding a customer's needs and delivering a product to meet them."*), then into various types of sales, and some research that showed how fundamentally different the aspects of the sale (motivation, aptitude, etc.) were in the different sorts of settings. This is followed by the work of Robert McMurry, who *"helped establish a unique position for the study of sales, somewhere between economics and psychology"*, and listed various "levels" of sales, from the simple to the very complex, and characteristics of successful salespersons, but with the "single most important trait" being *"the wooing instinct"*, which is found in those with *"a compulsive need to win and hold the affection of others"* ... whose behaviors are unsettling close to the dynamics found in psychopaths. He then shifts to a consideration of the insurance industry, but focusing on this in Japan, and a woman (rare in the upper echelons of Japanese business), Mrs. Shibata, who is the top salesperson at Dai-ichi Life, having worked her way up from nothing. This looks at the dynamics of that industry, then flips back into some more research on the psychology of sales, then into some more examples of insurance salespeople, and thence to skipping through car sales, pharmaceutical sales (whose sales force is largely staffed by ex-cheerleaders), and funeral service sales. The chapter ends with a bit of a profile of the legendary Ron Popeil (one of whose daughters was a classmate of mine in high school) which introduces a bit on "ethical questions".

Speaking of which, the book now moves to a look at "cultish" sales environments, starting with Apple, whose devotees' blind allegiance has always irritated me (especially for grossly over-priced products), this then goes to a look at some books comparing sales and religion, a look at "utopian groups" which then leads to the world of network marketing. This then shifts to a more philosophical stance, looking at optimism and pessimism and confidence and fear ... ending up with a recommendation of a stance of "cheerful realism". There are a vast number of figures name-checked here, generally with a story that then either sets up or illustrates some piece of research, making it hard to cherry-pick items for the review.

The next chapter is "Leveling", about how sales allow people to rise up from nothing if they have the right mix of dedication and skills. The first story here is of a black lady, Madam C.J. Walker, who made a fortune in hair care products ... which leads into looks at Estée Lauder and Mary Kay Ash. There was a particularly arch bit in here, discussing the prejudices many have against salespeople:

> *Managers are dependent on them, but fear their power, which seems an uncontrollable, Dionysian force, overwhelming to those in the neater world of financial spreadsheets and strategic plans.*

The chapter concludes with an extensive description of a Mexican contractor called "Memo" who has an interesting quote: *"once you have built something from scratch, you know you can do it anywhere, anytime again"*.

What follows is a relatively brief chapter on the Art world, with several figures in assorted levels of that arena (which involves a whole other set of dynamics, skills, and psychology). Subsequent chapters relate illustrations from the author's experiences around preparing for his marriage, software and technology sales, and the business of selling jet liners. Again, there are a lot of names, companies, products, and the contexts in which those operate ... all interesting enough, but not as notable as the longer looks at key figures. Another bit, returning to the genesis of the author's look at sales, stood out here:

> *If nothing else, selling is an endless confrontation*

with truth, the truth about yourself and about others. It is raw and uncomfortable and personally exposing in a way other business functions rarely are. This hard truth may help explain why business schools, which prefer to paint a less brutal vision of business life, are so loath to teach it.

As noted up top, I quite enjoyed reading The Art of the Sale[3], although parts of it were decidedly uncomfortable for me (I'm totally the wrong personality type to succeed at this – reflected in how much I related to the line *"If they felt lost or purposeless they could not sell"*). It's not a "sales manual", but it is has a plethora of information that would help anybody "wrap their head around" the world of sales.

The paperback of this is still in print (as one might hope as it's only been out a couple of years), but the hardcover (which I guess I found at the dollar store), can be had in "like new" condition from the new/used guys online for as little as a penny plus shipping. While this won't be of interest to *everybody*, if you've ever wondered about sales, thought about sales, or been faced with the necessity of actually *doing* sales, you're likely to find something worthwhile in this. If nothing else, it's quite an enjoyable read ... especially for a "business book"!

Notes:

1. http://btripp-books.livejournal.com/193382.html
2-3. http://amzn.to/2dQ30zw

Wednesday, November 30, 2016[1]

Calls you out by name ...

This past summer I was very excited to have gotten a ticket to see Bob Mould in concert. As much as I'd gone out to see bands "back in the day", there are some glaring gaps in acts that I *really* liked that I'd never gotten to experience live (and none of us are getting *any* younger). Bob Mould was one of these, as I'd never caught Hüsker Dü when they were together and had "just missed" Mould several times over the years. It also didn't help that I had long since disconnected from any media that would let me know about upcoming shows (one year I only found out about a new years eve gig in town the week after it happened). Oddly, I'd caught his old bandmate, Grant Hart, a number of times when he was through town, but never Bob. Fortunately, things conspired to get the info in front of me in time to score a ticket (I think I bought it four months in advance!), and I got to cross that off my "bucket list". I mention this stuff here as I ended up buying Bob Mould's See a Little Light: The Trail of Rage and Melody[2] in the run-up to that show, and eventually got around to reading it about a month back.

Now, I'd been a fan for, quite literally, *decades*, but was surprised to find that a lot that I "knew" about Mould was skewed at best. I am, of course, assuming that the timeline and events put out in this book are accurate, and *my* take on this was off ... but I was somewhat chagrined to find that my mental data on him and his bands was so substantially erroneous. I've been trying to wrap my mind around this diverging, and can only come up with the fact I wasn't plugged into much "rock media" for the past couple of decades, and so what I "knew" came from bits and pieces here and there, notes on albums (I have nearly all of Mould's discography at this point), and "rumor mill" stuff (like the wife of an old drinking buddy who had supposedly lived in the same dorm as Hüsker Dü at one point).

As mentioned above, I finished reading this a month or so back (I've not been able to triage any time for getting out to write reviews for quite a while), so the details have gotten a little hazy for me, and, unfortunately, there are only a couple of little bookmarks in here, one of which flags a place where I have *no clue* what I was wanting to go back to. Bummer. This means you're only going to be getting the broad strokes here ... although with an autobiography like this, that's not necessarily a bad thing. Frankly, Mould sorts of sets it up for this approach in *his* approach to the book. In the Preface he writes (following noting *"how integrated my personal and professional lives had finally become"*):

> ... writing this book was an emotionally taxing process. Even though my life and work have been on public display for many years, I have always been a very private person. My desire for privacy has often bordered on secrecy. The thought of revealing certain aspects of my personal life was hard to reconcile. As time progressed, I found myself los-

> *ing track of certain memories. It felt like it was time to assemble the key pieces into a narrative. Instead of telling individual anecdotes (the typical memoir), I'm telling my story in order – and by doing so, I can see the patterns. In a way, I'm finally making sense of my life.*

One wonders how much of what the finished book is comes via the efforts of Mould's co-author, Michael Azerrad, a music journalist with a couple of other well-regarded books out there ... and what sort of process was involved in the *three years* it took for this to get done (coming out in 2011). Speaking of "coming out" (nice segue, eh?), one of the more surprising (to me) parts of this is "the gay stuff" ... of which there is quite a lot. One of the things he had been keeping secret for a long time was his sexual orientation ... this based on both the somewhat homophobic vibe of the early punk scene, and having grown up in a very hostile environment for gays (he tells the story of a guy he knew who had returned to their old home town and ended up being gruesomely murdered). I had recalled that he had been "outed" by a magazine at some point (in the early 1990's), but had always heard that it was a "political" outing that caught Mould by surprise, but in reading this that doesn't seem to be exactly the case (and it was in *Spin*, rather than in the gay press, as I'd previously thought). He notes that he was very focused on writing gender-neutral lyrics for most of his albums, to not have this become an issue for some listeners. He certainly got over that by 2009, when his *Life and Times* solo album featured some songs[3] which are fairly clearly written from a gay context.

Frankly, not being much familiar with gay subjects, it was *fascinating* (if in a somewhat voyeuristic mode) looking in on his various relationships, and his coming to grips with being a gay public figure. In the course of the telling, he does take the reader into a lot of places that they might not ever have had occasion to go (such as the clothing-optional resort where he and his boyfriend are getting thrown out of in the opening story).

The other thing which was surprising (and this I had *no* inkling of), was his time with WCW – the *wrestling* operation. Mould had grown up a big wrestling fan, and was somewhat involved in it in his teens (some of Hüsker Dü's tour managers were from that world). Somewhat out of the blue, he got hired as a "creative consultant" in the fall of 1999, and was pretty much 24/7 with that (traveling constantly) until the spring of 2000, when the team he was part of got replaced by the WCW management. He called this his "dream job" ... which is interesting for a rock star (whose regular job is the "dream job" of many) to say.

Another thread throughout the book is the subject of "substances". Hüsker Dü had dissolved in a booze-and-drug-induced haze, and eventually Mould got cleaned up ... primarily on his own. As I managed to get 30+ years of sobriety without A.A. (where I have since ended up trying to go for the "sanity" part that I sort of missed back when I got *physically* sober), I found his story on this of interest ... especially as it had some remarkably direct parallels with my own experience ... here's a key bit of this, about when he stopped drinking in 1986:

> It was a vivid and sudden realization: I had to catch myself and stop this addiction before it escalated any further. I was twenty-five years old and I said to myself, I've had a drink every day for twelve years. If I keep this up, I will not make it to thirty. I was a high-functioning alcoholic. I had scotch in my desk drawer, started drinking straight from the bottle at 2 PM, and could still complete a full day's work. It's great to be a high-functioning alcoholic – I could drink a fifth of scotch and drive just fine. It didn't interfere with my work, so why wouldn't I do it? No one ever pointed out the problem to me. ... There was no program, no AA, no handbook ... I did no twelve-step program and had no counseling. It was an act of sheer will-power, a testament to my ability to scare myself straight. ... That was it. I haven't had a drink since.

This is *not* a popular theme around the 12-step crowd, as it's a rare individual who can get and stay sober without the structure and support of a program, and I've even had AA folks question if I were *really* an alcoholic for getting sober without them, despite a rather indicative history (and I'm guessing they'd ask the same about Mould).

Anyway, aside from these themes, most of the book is what you'd expect ... tales from the road, tales from the recording studio, drama within bands, despicable "industry" folks, and a good deal of name-checking. Needless to say, this could have gotten *quite* ugly about the break-up of Hüsker Dü, but I think Mould deliberately pulled his punches there. He describes Grant Hart's descent into heroin addiction, and Greg Norton's fading interest in the music (and how he and Grant ended up re-recording Norton's bass parts on several songs on 1987's *Warehouse: Songs And Stories*), as well as issues with the label. If anything, the music parts reflect that *"telling my story in order"* idea here – which, while essentially *structuring* the book, somewhat makes the telling dry – with scenario after scenario being looked at, but without any *point* other than recording the facts. This is not to say that the *writing* is particularly "dry", as there are some great descriptions of places and processes involved, like this bit on the recording of one of my favorites of Mould's albums, 1990's *Black Sheets of Rain*, at The Power Station in NYC:

> I piled on so many layers of electric guitars that it felt almost claustrophobic. Then in the final mix stage, Steve Boyer and I enhanced the drums – already thick and huge from recording in Studio A, a cavernous wooden room with a churchlike peaked ceiling – with samples that made them sound colossal. Every part of the sound spectrum was saturated to maximum capacity.

While not being a substantial part of the book, in places here and there lyrics are quoted and discussed, which is probably more interesting to a long-time fan such as myself than to the casual reader. Another aspect here is how Mould acted as business manager in several phases of his career, and that is also an interesting look at dynamics of the music business that don't often get a strong light shined on them (especially when he'd hired a manager, who ended up screwing him out of his publishing rights for a couple of albums, exchanged for tour-support money from the label).

Is See A Little Light[4] a read for the non-fan? I don't know. Bob Mould's music has been "significant" in my life for over thirty years, so it's somewhat integral to who I am ... making it hard to look at this with an uninvolved eye. It is, as noted above, a window into a lot of areas that one might not be otherwise privy to, from the gay lifestyle, to the wrestling business, to the music industry details. These are all interesting, and could provide enough hook for somebody who wasn't as familiar with the author's music[5] to enjoy the book anyway.

The hardcover edition that I have has been out since 2011, with the paperback appearing a couple of years later (I don't know if there was any update between those). It appears that the hardcover is currently out of print, so is only available in the aftermarket, but you can get a "very good" copy for under two bucks (plus shipping). The on-line big boys have the paperback at only 10% off of cover, which suggests that its still selling fairly well, so you might be able to find it at your local brick-and-mortar, if you wanted to go that route. Again, this is a great read for the right fan base, but might be too narrowly-focused for the "general reader" ... but I suspect you'll know which side of that line you fall!

Notes:

1. http://btripp-books.livejournal.com/193632.html
2. http://amzn.to/2dppCEh
3. https://goo.gl/AoLOLW
4. http://amzn.to/2dppCEh
5. http://amzn.to/2gkZAUM

Saturday, December 3, 2016[1]

Learning to Stop Worrying and Love the Bomb?

Every once in a while I'll hit a book where I have *no clue* how it got into my to-be-read piles, and this is one of those. It doesn't have any of the typical marks or stickers that would indicate that it came from the dollar store, or some clearance table, but I really think I would have recalled *ordering* this, or getting it as a review copy from the publisher ... but I got *nuthin'* ... it was just *there* and it looked to fit what I felt like reading a month or so back.

Jonathan Stevenson's Thinking Beyond the Unthinkable: Harnessing Doom from the Cold War to the Age of Terror[2] is a tough one to get a fix on ... the dust jacket claims that it *"traces the recent evolution of constructive apocalyptic thinking from its zenith in the early nuclear era"*, and more-or-less on up to its 2008 release date ... but it's fairly narrowly focused on a class of think-tank and related elements than would be of significant interest to most readers. The author is a professor of strategic studies at the U.S. Naval War College, and it's tempting to chalk this up to being something of a text book for classes in that context, but it's not really structured that way.

The book starts with a question: *"What was it about the strategic thinking of the Cold War that <u>worked</u>? How did we manage not to incinerate ourselves with nuclear weapons?"* and goes into a rather grisly, if brief, run-down of the military horrors of the past century ... such as:

> the British firebombing of Hamburg in 1943 ... resulted in a fireball two kilometers high that imploded the oxygen in the air and raised windstorms strong enough to uproot trees; household sugar boiled, glass melted, and bubbling asphalt sucked people into the streets; in one night forty-five thousand civilians were killed

... along with the "feel good" sentiments of Joseph Stalin who famously remarked: *"a single death is a tragedy; a million deaths are a statistic"*. Despite being less deadly than their pre-atomic predecessor technologies, the attacks on Hiroshima and Nagasaki created a decided shift in military thinking. Using the A-bomb on Japan (and bluffing that we had a stockpile of 'em), prevented a long and massively deadly ground/air/sea war on their home islands ... *"the reaction of most of the men who would become leading nuclear strategists was profound relief"* ... and the author quotes later nuclear abolitionist Freeman Dyson (then with the RAF) as saying *"it was a fantastic relief that the killing was going to <u>stop</u>"*.

Books discussing the new realities of nuclear weapons started appearing as early as 1946, and things only got more complicated with the development of the H-bomb in 1952. Of course, the tenor of the discussion/debate was in the context of a *"titanic struggle between Western capitalism and Soviet communism"* which pushed out other considerations of conflict (which made later situations such as Vietnam and non-state terrorist actors so difficult to merge into existing frameworks). The first parts of the book look, in fairly expansive detail, at how the Truman and Eisenhower administration addressed this, the committee/commission reports generated, and the major players emerging from the various universities, government departments, and military organizations.

Of course, one of the key elements was Project RAND (which was simply R&D written differently), whose

> first hirees were mathematicians, engineers, statisticians, and physicists. By 1947 it became clear that RAND needed to be a broader church, and political scientists, historians, sociologists, psychologists, and economists were brought on.

Most notable of that crew in terms of nuclear strategy was Albert Wohlstetter[3], a key figure in the book, along with Thomas C. Schelling, Herman Khan, Bernard Brodie, William Kaufmann, and Henry Kissinger.

I need to make a bit of a snarky comment at this point. I read a lot. I have an excellent education. So, I want to ask *who* is Stevenson *writing for* when he uses words like "eviscerating", "escalatory", "lugubrious"[4], and "hortatory"[5] ... in a *single paragraph*? It's rare for me to have to look up two words out of a *dozen* books, so it sort of stands out here. Again, what audience is familiar with those last two? Students at the Naval War College (we could only hope)? Anyway ...

One of the profiles which stood out for me in the book was that of Herman Kahn[6], whose book *Thinking About the Unthinkable* was obviously the inspiration for this book's title. The author notes:

> One of Kahn's essential convictions was that an apocalyptic war could be won, and it stemmed from his refusal to divorce human fallibility from strategic calculations. For him, the scenarios that governed policy had to take account of the irrationality of people and their subsequent unpredictability.

When being accused of "icy rationality", Kahn responded *"Would you prefer a warm, human error? Do you feel better with a nice emotional mistake? We cannot expect good discussion of security problems if we are going to label every attempt at detachment as callous, every attempt at objectivity as immoral."*

The book progresses from the 40's to the 50's and into the 60's, primarily focused on the Cold War nuclear stalemate, but other conflicts were on the horizon ... unfortunately *"Nuclear strategists in general were not inclined to grapple with the vicissitudes and complexities of nationalism, religion, and ideologies other than those falling under the broad contours of communism and democracy."*, and Stevenson quotes one as saying *"Vietnam crept up on me like everyone else."*

A figure that surfaces here is the somewhat notorious Daniel Ellsberg[7], who was with RAND from 1959 to 1970.

> He embodies both thesis and antithesis of RAND's underperformance in the area of conventional war, having evolved from a hard-nosed strategic thinker, to in-country Pentagon adviser in Vietnam, to anti-war activist and revealer, in 1971, of the Pentagon Papers[8].

The debacle of Vietnam *"tainted RAND and the community of civilian strategists and knocked them from the perch to which they had ascended on the strength of the contributions to nuclear strategy"* ... and *"Over the course of the Vietnam war, RAND, on balance, promoted U.S. policy in Vietnam without informing or challenging it much."* This allowed another old RAND hand to move to the forefront of strategic thought, Henry Kissinger. Kissinger steered the Nixon administration through decoupling from the Vietnam conflict, and building detente with the Soviets.

The rise of the "neo-cons" was largely in reaction to the "cautious" Kissinger-era moves, and this was coupled with a strong anti-Western "Orientalism" emerging from the Islamic world. The Vietnam conflict had driven a wedge between camps in the U.S., and *"The absence of synergy between government and academia on strategic matters involving Islam also failed to spur the U.S. government to enhance its collective understanding of Middle East political, ethnic, and religious dynamics."* ... while *"Arab paperback apocalyptics had conjured visions of devastating attacks on New York and visiting mass destruction on the United States."*

Obviously, these are just the broad strokes. Thinking Beyond the Unthinkable[9] has a great deal of detail on the figures, the stances, the challenges, etc. I was somewhat surprised that it was as "Cold War" heavy (given that *"to the Age of Terror"* in its subtitle) as it is, but the logical arc of the telling makes sense by the time it gets to where it's going (in the last year of the GWB administration), albeit with less detail for the Vietnam, and post-Vietnam eras. I have to admit that this was a bit of a *chore* to read, and again I'm left wondering what the target audience is for the book. Needless to say, if one is a fan of military/political strategy, this will be in your wheelhouse, but it's otherwise pretty much a look at fairly rarefied zones of what could be called "cultural philosophy", and might not be particularly appealing to many. I *did* learn quite a lot about many things in reading it, so I think that was worth the effort ... but "your mileage may vary". This does appear to be currently out of print (suggesting that it's *not* a textbook), and it seems to have never had a paperback edition; but you can get "very good" copies from the online big boys' new/used vendors for as little as $4.00 (1¢ plus $3.99 shipping), so it's not going to set you back much if you want to have a go at it.

Notes:
1. http://btripp-books.livejournal.com/193982.html
2. http://amzn.to/2edsKSV
3. https://en.wikipedia.org/wiki/Albert_Wohlstetter
4. https://www.merriam-webster.com/dictionary/lugubrious
5. https://www.merriam-webster.com/dictionary/hortatory
6. https://en.wikipedia.org/wiki/Herman_Kahn
7. https://en.wikipedia.org/wiki/Daniel_Ellsberg
8. https://en.wikipedia.org/wiki/Pentagon_Papers
9. http://amzn.to/2edsKSV

Sunday, December 4, 2016

So many scammers ...

I picked this one up at a clearance table at B&N some months back ... the one by me, at least, has had very little clearance action the past couple of years, which is sad, as I used to get a number of books from them. This has the "look & feel" of one of those B&N-published books, but it doesn't have any copy to that end ... but what's really strange is that this hardcover had a $7.98 (pre-clearance) cover price, while the still-available *paperback* is going for $24.95! I'm sure there's some "story" behind this, bit it's odd having the paperback going for 3x the hardcover's price.

It is possible that there might have been international rights involved in that situation, as Beggars, Cheats, & Forgers: a History of Frauds Through the Ages' author, David Thomas, is the former Director of Technology at Britain's National Archives, and many of the characters (although hardly all) covered in the book are in the U.K. The book does have that "hobbyist" air to it, and might have been a "retirement project" for Mr. Thomas. This is not to demean the book, but it does sort of lack a "point", and has that feel of somebody organizing a bunch of information that he's been dithering with for quite a while.

As one could surmise from the title, this deals with assorted lowlifes and scammers ...which the author points out were active *long* before the internet, although many of the noted scams on the web are very much based in much older schemes. It is something to think, however, that the *same things* worked when communication was via very slow postal channels, versus more recent fax, email, and other electronic vehicles. The book is broken up into five main thematic sections, "The Greatest Con Men", "The Document Forgers", "Begging Letter Writers", "The Spanish Prisoner", and "Sturdy Beggars", with a time span going back as far as the medieval era, and as recently as Bernie Maddof (who was certainly the king of the rackets, having scammed *billions* of dollars).

While I found the book reasonably engaging, I ended up with *none* of my little bookmarks in it flagging places that I wanted to return to (primarily for doing this review), so I'm going to be having to cherry-pick at random here. Part of the problem is that these stories are frequently intertwined, with 20th century names coming before and after those operating, for instance, in the wake of the Irish Potato Famine in the late 1840's ... and frequently filled with details (how much who paid for what, where money was borrowed from, courts that heard cases, etc., etc., etc.) that would be interest to an *enthusiast* for these subjects, but not adding much for the general reader. From my perspective, it also doesn't help that the author mixes in *fictional* characters with the *historical* ones (although he does note that in some cases, many of the latter figures have a lot of fictional over-lay to their stories). In the "Con Men" chapter, one thing I found interesting were the details of the schemes of Charles Ponzi ... for someone whose name became synonymous with a particular type of fraud, his main run of it was remarkably brief (a couple of years at most – although when he got out of prison he started up some other illegal operations), and hardly original, with the author detailing similar frauds that preceded it. The book picks though how that worked, how it broke down, and how other scams (including Madoff's) resembled it.

The chapter on Forgers is somewhat murky, as the author brings in a *lot* of activities under that umbrella, from artists making fake works of old masters, to producing ephemera that would be only of interest to specific markets, even to the suggestion in H.P. Lovecraft that there existed an actual *Neconomicon* book (although you can hardly accuse HPL of *forging* that, as it's more of a literary conceit than anything) ... which is set in a discussion of other (more famous, even) works which purported to be histories rather than pieces of fiction (and even dips a toe into the "who wrote Shakespeare" morass). Regrettably, some of the forgers were in positions to be able to pass judgment on the authenticity of pieces, creating some lingering question marks in several institutions (one of these forged papers at the famed Tate Gallery to provide background for faked paintings being produced by an accomplice). There is a figure detailed here who "specialized" in creating ("discovering"?) Mormon -related documents, that he knew that LDS churchmen would have a hunger for (and if you're accepting the *canonical* Mormon materials, it's hardly a leap to be taken in by convincing forgeries that seem to have a plausible provenance). Another of these forgers had an interesting method of "discovering" materials that he'd originated ... sneaking them into otherwise-reputable antiquarian stores that had large collections of miscellanea, where he'd subsequently "find" the item and *buy* it from them, thus having a purchase receipt from a legitimate source.

The book delves into some technical discussion on forensics, and techniques for creating convincing "old" documents. Also covered are ways that these forgeries are discovered ... such as a letter between two scientists which was dated when one of them would have been only 12 (the forger later tried to "back fill" the story with a forged note supposedly from the prodigy's tutor), or significantly wrong forms of address, or even pencil marks on the materials. The psychological implications are also dealt with, as many librarians, archivists, art collectors, etc., are quite unwilling to accept that *their* hard-obtained finds are not real. In many cases the forgers and their co-conspirators are strenuously defended by those who they'd scammed, because the pallor it would cast on the collections if they were proven guilty.

The "Begging Letters" is pretty much what it sounds like, sending off letters asking for money (or other things – Charles Dickens had requests for a 12-15 pound wheel of cheese and a *donkey* come in), and was such a problem that an organization "the Mendicity Society" was formed to fight this (subscribers were able to have the writers investigated). The author notes:

> *The 1840's appear to have been the peak time for begging letter writers. The means was provided because of growing literacy – from 1833 central government began to fund schools for the poorer children. The opportunity was provided by the introduction of a nationwide penny post in 1840. Suddenly, posting a letter became affordable for almost anyone and many people, including the criminally inclined, took full advantage.*

I was at first confused, and then fascinated, with one of the punishments doled out to these miscreants ... one of them is noted as having been *"sentenced to transportation for life"*, which sounded odd (frankly, my first thought was *The M.T.A. Song*[3], although that wouldn't have been a possible punishment for a century or more), but I eventually figured out that "transportation" involved being sent off to The Colonies, to the Americas prior to 1776, and to Australia thereafter. While this letter-writing practice still continues, in recent times the targets are often Lottery winners, who names are published in the papers ... creating easy marks. The author notes that a new-tech version of this are the "fake charity" web sites that crop up after every disaster and purport to be some fund to aid the survivors, but with nearly no money ever finding its way to the stated beneficiaries.

The next section, on "The Spanish Prisoner" scam, is the direct ancestor of the Nigerian/419 scams that flood in-boxes world-wide. The author says the earliest example he's been able to find dates to 1797, where a fellow (later to found France's Sûreté Nationale) who had been imprisoned for a while in his youth, noticed that other prisoners were making money via letters while incarcerated:

> *The letters were sent to wealthy people and were allegedly from the valet of a marquis who had escaped from the dangers of the French Revolution carrying a cask filled with gold and diamonds. The marquis and his valet had found themselves pursued by revolutionaries and had been forced to throw the cask into a deep ditch. They eventually escaped abroad and the valet had come back to recover the the treasure. Unfortunately, the valet had been arrested and was in prison; he was so short of money that he would have to sell a trunk which contained a plan showing the location of the treasure-cask. However, if the recipient could send some money the valet would send him the plan and they could share the treasure. By a strange coincidence the recipients of these letters always lived close to the place where the money was hidden. ... The scam was hugely successful, about 20 per cent of the letters were answered and many people came to the prison and were supplied with treasure maps.*

By the 1870's the organized form of this scam had settled primarily into Spain (hence the "Spanish Prisoner"), and the gang operating in Barcelona was estimated to be netting, in the 1890's, what today would be 29 million dollars a year. For decades, efforts were made to entrap these scammers, but it appears that their money reached deep into the Spanish postal system and courts, leading to very few being arrested. Needless to say, the Nigerian descendants of this scam operate within a similar "friendly" governmental matrix ... but it is amazing that, a couple of hundred years later, folks are still falling for these scams, some in a big way.

The author introduces the "Sturdy Beggars" chapter with this definition: *"people who, though capable of working, choose a life of idleness and beg-*

ging and develop elaborate techniques for persuading passers-by to give them money". One might expect that this was a more realistic "career path" in earlier times, but I just found an article[4] where it estimates that one can bring in around $15/hr doing this today. Here Thomas does a fairly detailed over-view of these folks in Britain, going as far back as 1531, with a look at the "hobo"-like subcultures that arose in various times and places. He also discusses "Rogue Literature", which likewise dates from the mid-1500's, *"describing the lives of criminals and beggars and allegedly revealing the secrets of the underworld".* Again, much of the story line here is based in the U.K., with idiosyncrasies that seem to spring straight out of a Dickens novel. Oddly, the book has an appendix dealing with street performers, although they figure in some of the material on beggars. I suppose one could argue that there's just a matter of degree between "busking" and "begging", the former requiring at least a modicum of competency in a skill beyond psychological manipulation of the crowd.

Anyway, Beggars, Cheats, & Forgers[5] is an interesting enough read, if for a mixed history of the less-savory types in society. As noted, this probably makes more connections with U.K. readers, as a significant portion of it deals with settings over there (the American portions are also more recent, from Ponzi in the 1920's to Madoff in the 2000's). It's a fairly *brief* book, running only 150 pages, so I would *not* recommend getting the higher-priced paperback. The new/used guys have "very good" copies of the hardcover for as little as a penny (plus shipping), and that's probably right about where this ought to be for most folks (unless you have a passion for the subject equivalent to the author's).

Notes:

1. http://btripp-books.livejournal.com/194223.html
2. http://amzn.to/2eo5T64
3. http://www.mit.edu/~jdreed/t/charlie.html
4. https://goo.gl/OqwbQT
5. http://amzn.to/2eo5T64

Wednesday, December 28, 2016[1]

Complicated Abe ...

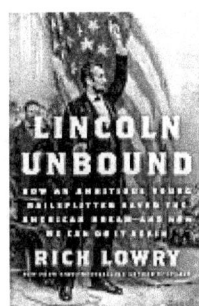

This was one of those fortuitous dollar store finds from a few months back. I *almost* didn't pick it up, because, as amenable to reading history books as I am, I am not one of those with a particular interest in the Civil War, or Mr. Lincoln. However, when I noted that Lincoln Unbound: How an Ambitious Young Railsplitter Saved the American Dream--and How We Can Do It Again[2] was penned by Rich Lowry (editor of the late, great William F. Buckley's National Review), I figured that I'd at least get some rah-rahs out of it. This just came out in 2013, so I wasn't greatly surprised to see that it's still in print, and was just lucking out from one of those Walmart shelf dumps that (thankfully) feed the dollar store channel.

Towards the end of the book, Lowry notes: *"Lincoln himself is so revered that nearly everyone wants to make a claim on him. And his tradition is capacious enough that nearly everybody can."* This, to a certain extent, points to the *raison d'être* of the book ... something of a reclaiming, or re-centering, Lincoln into the mainstream of the Republican Party. On one hand, the Statists hold Lincoln up as a justification of their incessant power grabs and extra-Constitutional pen-and-phone dictates, while on the other front (and I've read a good deal of *this* online), hard-core Libertarians hold Lincoln up as an example of how easily "tyranny" can establish itself here (decrying the very things the Left lauds him for). A lot of books are out there that drag Mr. Lincoln left, right, and even into zombie hunting ... in his book, Rich Lowry seems to be trying to return this great President to his legitimate historical setting.

While I generally enjoyed reading this, I was somewhat disappointed to find that I had dropped in only a couple of my little bookmarks pointing me to the "good stuff" to put in this review, and both of those come in the last chapter. This, of course, means that you're going to be seeing more "broad strokes" here than otherwise. One of these, though, I felt was quite good at summing up the over-all theme of the book, so forgive the multiple-paragraph quote:

> *It is altogether proper that we celebrate Lincoln the war leader and the emancipator. He transfixes us, and always will. The events stretching from Secession Winter in 1860-61 to the assassination at Ford's Theater constitute the greatest drama in American history this side of the Revolution. But they aren't all there is to Lincoln. Long before any shots were fired, he was committed to a vision that would create the predicate for modern America.*
>
> *Lincoln believed in a dynamic capitalism that dissolved old ways of life. He thought all men were created equal and deserved the opportunity to make the most of themselves. He urged them to make the effort to do so. He found in America's*

> constitutional system and its free institutions the best possible platform for the realization of this vision. This is the Lincoln that is too often lost – and must be found – to truly understand him and, really, to understand who we are as a people.

While nominally structured as a biography, with a narrative arc tracking through his history, much of the descriptive material (of which there quite a lot that I'd not previously encountered, some of which was *fascinating*) serves as a jumping-off point for discussions of what could be called Lincoln's *philosophy*, or as Lowry puts it at one point, not the "how" or "what", but the *"why"*.

In the opening pages of Lincoln Unbound[3], the author introduces a theme that works its way throughout the book … that Lincoln was no fan of his modest origins, and constantly strove to create conditions where his fellow citizens wouldn't be chained to rural subsistence for their survival:

> We might romanticize his background, the log cabins and all the rest of it. Lincoln didn't. He didn't want to be poor; he wanted to be respectable. … From his first stirrings as a politician, Lincoln committed himself to policies to enhance opportunity. He wanted to build canals and railroads to knit together the nation's markets. He wanted to encourage industry. He wanted to modernize banking. He hated isolation, backwardness, and any obstacles to the development of a cash economy of maximal openness and change. He thrilled to steam power and iron, to invention and technology, to the beneficent upward spiral of a commercial economy.

Of course, much of the flow of the book is quite familiar to anybody paying attention in school … the many jobs the young Lincoln held, his work with the Whig Party, his early attempts at public service and political office, and these are certainly all here, albeit in a lot more detail than the basic grade school (or high school) text – which on occasion floated into that TMI zone where I found myself not really *caring* about the details of so-and-so and his store, or such-and-such campaign, etc. … although I suppose their inclusion adds to the richness of the tale. I *was* interested in reading of the books that the young Lincoln felt to be fundamental to his learning, and to the relation of instances where he expressed a nearly Jain[4]-like (certainly *very* extreme for the time and culture) consideration for animals. Everybody knows of Lincoln's penchant for reading, but it is amusing to see all the quotes strewn through here of employers, associates, and relatives accusing him of being *lazy* for the large amounts of time he spent "reading & thinking" … evidently also not generally approved of in his early environment.

As one might expect, a great deal of the book traces Lincoln's political career … but here this is presented in a level of detail which digs deep into the structures of political parties at the time (and how the Whigs more-or-less transmuted into the Republican Party), how various parts of government operated (banking is a recurring issue in relation to this), and, as things moved forward to the advent of the Civil War, how the North and South differed (one factoid presented stood out to me: *"if the South were a country in 1860 ... it would have been the fourth richest in the world"*). A lot of space is dedicated to the on-going Lincoln-Douglass debates (Lincoln essentially following along behind the well-funded and "deluxe" Douglas campaign and making *his* speeches following – having "traveled coach" on standard commercial rail transport. In regards to Lincoln's rhetoric Lowry notes:

> *His truest blow against his opponents in the 1850s and 1860s were those he struck while wielding the Declaration of Independence. The purposes he identified in the Founders and their handiwork are continually relevant. ... He believed that they drew us back into the deepest principles of our republic in the Declaration. And they gave us, of course, our foundational law in the Constitution.*

Somewhat oddly, the war is only peripheral to the story arc here ... while it and Lincoln's assassination "hang over" the history, they are largely only referenced in relation to other, more *philosophical* elements. Again, the focus here is on Lincoln's "whys" throughout his life, which led up to the Civil War, and he was dead within a week of the Confederacy's surrender – not leaving much room for any "summing up" of his thoughts on the subject.

I rather enjoyed Lincoln Unbound[5], but I do need to make a note that I am politically rather in sync with its author ... and I noticed that among the generally quite positive Amazon reviews/ratings (82% 4-5 stars), the ones which were *not* positive tended to feature Statists/Leftists throwing hissy fits about the underlying framing involved here. So, if you're the type who has ever worn a Che t-shirt, you'll probably not like this *nearly* as much as I did ... although I suspect if those types could side-step their indoctrination, the charms of this telling might still engage them.

As I noted up top, this is still available at retail (despite copies floating off to the dollar stores), with the online big boys offering it for a considerable discount (41% off of cover as of this writing) ... so there is a decent chance of it being on the shelf at your local brick-and-mortar book vendor. However, no doubt due to it *having* hit the dollar stores, "very good" copies can be had online for a penny plus shipping ... making it pretty reasonable should you think this would be something you'd like to venture into!

Notes:

1. http://btripp-books.livejournal.com/194415.html
2-3. http://amzn.to/2ezRVjW
4. https://en.wikipedia.org/wiki/Ahimsa_in_Jainism
5. http://amzn.to/2ezRVjW

Thursday, December 29, 2016[1]

Awesome book ...

As folks who have been reading my reviews over the past dozen or so years will recall, I spent a chunk of the 80's and 90's studying shamanism in various cultural settings, and so have a bunch of "filters" for books on the subject that tend to lead me to somewhat caustic assessments of way too many of these. So, it's a real pleasure when I run into titles which I can wholeheartedly recommend (see this[2] and this[3] for examples), and the current book is one of this sort. Heck (and those keeping track of how many books these days come my way via the dollar store will realize how extreme this is), I actually bought a second copy at retail (well, Amazon's discounted retail) to give to a shaman[4] friend who I felt had to read this. Frankly, I'm amazed this took six years to get on my radar (it came out in 2010), but I'm glad it did.

Of course, I was quite positive about this book's predecessor[5], so I was pre-disposed to be open to don Miguel Ruiz & don Jose Ruiz' The Fifth Agreement: A Practical Guide to Self-Mastery[6]. Interestingly, this is co-authored by Jose, the son of Miguel who has been pioneering the "Toltec Wisdom" niche, and I wonder how much of this book emerges from that influence. It certainly is *different* in a lot of ways from *The Four Agreements*, the concepts of which are re-framed in the first half of this book. Here are a couple of bits setting up both the initial four and the fifth:

> ... the Four Agreements slowly help you to recover your authentic self. With practice, these four simple agreements take you to what you *really* are, not what you pretend to be, and this is exactly where you want to be: what you really are. ... The fifth agreement is ultimately about seeing your whole reality with they eyes of truth *without* words. The result of practicing the fifth agreement is the complete acceptance of yourself just the way you are, and the complete acceptance of everybody else just the way they are.

At this point I need to indulge in some mental churning ... bear with me. The comment I want to make about this volume is that it reminds me quite a bit of "Fourth Way" (Gurdjieff/Ouspensky/Bennett/etc.) material – which is a *compliment* – but this, somewhat ironically, brings to mind a bit of snark I'd read about Castaneda's writing (which seems to be the origin point of a lot of the "Toltec" concepts), that it was just "Gurdjieff in a serape". Obviously, Castaneda was presenting his vision in the context of fictionalized narratives, and not as "systems" per se (although there is a very good book[7] which attempts to extract something of a system out of Castaneda's various writings), so wasn't so much a similar thing, but *dynamically* frequently walked the same pathways. The Fifth Agreement[8], as opposed to Castaneda, *does* seem to be intended to be a "system", building from the first four, and moving into some really advanced ground.

I suppose here would be as good a place as any to "cut to the chase" as far as what the 5th is ... and this is likely to be a shocker to anyone used to "fluff bunny" new age twaddle ... it reads: *"Be Skeptical, But Learn To Listen"*, with the further commentary:

> Don't believe yourself or anybody else. Use the power of doubt to question everything you hear: Is it *really* the truth? Listen to the intent behind words, and you will understand the real message.

The book gets into some *deep* stuff ... talking about awareness and language in a way that drives all the way back to the womb, and how our perception of reality is really a perception of our *words* for reality and not reality itself. At one point the authors state: *"Toltec is a Nahuatl word meaning artist."* ... I have no way to judge the veracity of that claim (within the scope of effort I'm willing to devote to getting this review done), but it feeds into another over-arching conception here:

> All humans are artists, *all* of us. Every symbol, every word, is a little piece of art. ... thanks to our programming, our greatest masterpiece of art is the use of a language to create an entire virtual reality within our mind. The virtual reality we create could be a clear reflection of the truth, or it could be completely distorted. Either way, it's art. Our creation could be our personal heaven, or it could be our personal hell. It doesn't matter; it's art.

This is interesting, but it gets more intense:

> Humans are born with awareness; we are born to perceive the truth, but we accumulate knowledge, and we learn to deny what we perceive. We practice not being aware, and we master not being aware. The word is pure magic, and we learn to use our magic against ourselves, against creation, against our own kind.

And then it gets a bit more technical:

> If we can understand what the human mind is, and what the human mind does, we can begin to separate reality from virtual reality, or pure perception, which is truth, from symbology, which is art. Self-mastery is all about awareness, and it begins with self-awareness. First to be aware of what is real, and then to be aware of what is virtual, which means what we believe about what is real.

... and all that heavy content is sketched out in the first 25 pages!

The rest of the first half of the book (which is split into two sections, Part I – The Power of Symbols, and Part II – The Power of Doubt), then walks the reader through the original Four Agreements (plus an additional chapter), re-stated to set in the new context. I don't want to delve too deeply into this material, but figured it might be useful to at least note the chapter titles (especially if you don't recall the Four Agreements): "The Story of You – The First Agreement: Be Impeccable with Your Word", "Every Mind Is a World – The Second Agreement: Don't Take Anything Personally", "Truth or Fiction: The Third Agreement: Don't Make Assumptions", (the extra chapter, "The Power of Belief – The Symbol of Santa Claus"), and "Practice Makes the Master – The Fourth Agreement: Always Do Your

Best". Those headings give you a general idea of how the re-framing goes in relation to the first book. There are a number of terms familiar from the Castaneda material, like *form* and *dream*, along with more general terms like "belief" and "faith" that are used in specific ways here. I was really tempted to grab a few paragraphs of this (notably from pages 76-77 from the "Belief" chapter), but everything sort of builds on the surrounding info, and it would have had to have been a big honking blockquote to get across what I would have hoped to convey, so this is one point where I'm just going to say "buy the book already!".

The second half of the book was what really blew me away. It starts with the introduction of the Fifth Agreement (which is, as noted above: *"Be Skeptical, But Learn To Listen"*) which extends the preceding material into direct action, à la:

> *Once you realize that hardly anything you know through symbols is true, then <u>be skeptical</u> has a much bigger meaning. <u>Be skeptical</u> is masterful because it uses the power of doubt to discern the truth. Whenever you hear a message from yourself, or from another artist, simply ask: <u>Is it truth, or is it not truth? Is it reality or is it a virtual reality?</u> The doubt takes you <u>behind</u> the symbols, and makes you responsible for every message you deliver and receive. ... if faith is believing without a doubt, and doubt is not believing, <u>be skeptical. Don't believe.</u>*

This is all pretty heady ... and then the book makes a total jump. One of those Castaneda concepts is "attention" (I have contemplated writing a book on the various, and sometimes interpenetrating, concepts of "attention", from the "Toltec" to the "Fourth Way" to the "attention economy" contexts ... hey, in Judy Tenuta's <u>line</u>[9]: *"it could happen"*), and it suddenly is the "payoff" of the book, with three progressively more "advanced" chapters, featuring "The Dream of the {First/Second/Third} Attention". This starts off in the Eden myth:

> *The Tree of Knowledge is just a reflection of the Tree of Life. We already know that knowledge is created with symbols, and that symbols aren't real. When we eat the fruit of the Tree of Know-ledge, the symbols become a virtual reality that talks to us as the voice of knowledge, and we live in that reality believing that it's real, which means without awareness, of course.*
>   *It's obvious that humans ate the fruit of the Tree of Death. ... there are billions of humans walking around in this world who are dead, but they don't <u>know</u> they are dead. Yes, their bodies are alive, but they are dreaming without any awareness that they are dreaming, and this is what the Toltec call <u>the dream of the first attention</u>.*

This chapter continues to pretty much take apart all religious belief as *"all the lies that come with the whole Tree of Knowledge"* ... which moves to belief in general:

> *The symbols are competing for control of our attention, and in one way or another they're changing all the time; they're taking turns possessing us. There are thousands*

> *of symbols that want to take their place in our head and control us ... those symbols are alive, and that life comes from us because we <u>believe</u>.*

The way to get out of being "dead" (or be "resurrected")? Awareness ... *"When you recover awareness, you resurrect and come back to life."* ... which leads on to the dream of the second attention. Another familiar Castaneda term comes in here, *integrity*, which is the drive that launches "the war of the gods":

> *It's a war between the authentic self and what we call <u>the tyrant, the big judge, the book of law, the belief system</u>. It's a war between ideas, between opinions, between beliefs. ... We give our power to these symbols, we take them to the realm of the gods and we sacrifice our lives in the name of these gods.*

The authors talk of "human sacrifice" here, which they define as originating *"because we believe in so many superstitions and distortions in our knowledge"*, with the actual war happening inside our heads, that expresses itself outside ourselves in various lethal conflicts ... even in conflict with ourselves in endless self-punishment of past failings. The chapter goes into detail of how to use the five agreements as tools to win that war:

> *Once you recover awareness of what you are, the war in your head is over. It's obvious that you are the one who creates all the symbols. ... The war is over because your faith is not invested in lies. Even though lies still exist, you no longer <u>believe</u>.*

The next chapter, on the dream of the third attention (or that of the masters) is a bit esoteric, but the basis is:

> *In the dream of the third attention, you finally have the awareness of what you are, but not with words. ... The highest point you can reach is when you go beyond symbols and become one with life ...*

Some concepts come in here, "presence" and *intent* ...

> *Look at your own hand. Move your fingers. The force that moves your fingers is what the Toltec call <u>intent</u> ... Intent is the only living being that exists, and it's that force that is moving everything. You are not the fingers. You are the force that is moving them.*

This gets pretty far out there (arguably in an Atman/Brahman mode), connecting the individual with all motion, with light, universes within universes, and on to *soul*. Again, this is pretty extreme stuff here, and I'd probably not be doing it or you a service to try to summarize it. Also, the following chapters, being based on these "dreams", will likewise be hard to convey ... but they are *Becoming a Seer*, and *The Three Languages* (which are "1-2-3", "A-B-C", and "Do-Re-Mi") which has a key question: *"What kind of messenger are you?"*. This all may seem, in my outlining it, so much "woo-woo", but I assure you (especially from the standpoint of having studied this stuff a long time) it all works together into a very congruent whole ... and I highly recommend it.

In fact, The Fifth Agreement[10] is likely to get another behavior out of me that almost never happens with any book ... I intend to block out some time to *re-read* it, and I suspect that I may even re-re-read it at some later date. I don't know when the last time I was so taken by a book (maybe Ouspensky's *In Search of the Miraculous*), so that's high praise indeed.

Of course, there *is* a certain caveat lurking in all the above ... I've read all the Castaneda books, I've read almost all the "Fourth Way" books, I've read a *lot* of Shamanic material, and have been boots-on-the-ground (entheogens in the head?) working with assorted Shamanic teachers ... so MY context on this book is very likely to not be shared with many, and I can see where somebody without that background, coming to this cold, might be very tempted to reject it out of hand. I do think this is something that *ought to* be read by "all and sundry", however.

This is sufficiently popular that it will no doubt be available at your local book store, at its quite reasonable cover price ... the online big boys, however, have it at a substantial discount which makes getting it via that channel pretty much a wash with what used copies (when shipping's added) would set you back. This isn't just a bit of New Age fluff, but a coherent system based on a very convincing philosophical approach. Good stuff ... go get a copy!

Notes:

1. http://btripp-books.livejournal.com/194810.html
2. http://btripp-books.livejournal.com/71456.html
3. http://btripp-books.livejournal.com/44577.html
4. http://btripp-books.livejournal.com/170205.html
5. http://btripp-books.livejournal.com/33869.html
6. http://amzn.to/2fe6Rqz
7. http://btripp-books.livejournal.com/24516.html
8. http://amzn.to/2fe6Rqz
9. https://youtu.be/vknNzCtR954
10. http://amzn.to/2fe6Rqz

Friday, December 30, 2016[1]

"not mandatory"

Well, *that's* interesting ... I just took a peek at my collection[2] over on LibraryThing.com and discovered that I'd only previously read *one* of Bill O'Reilly's books ... I was under the impression I'd been through more (probably it's my familiarity with him via TV that was suggesting that). I went looking because I was trying to dig up something serve as a basis form some "compare & contrast" cogitation with his 2013 release (and fairly recent dollar store find) that I just finished, Keep It Pithy: Useful Observations in a Tough World[3]. The reason I was looking for some context is that, by the time I got done reading this, I couldn't figure out *why* this book existed. Honestly, the general impression I took away from this was that it was the text equivalent of one of those "contractual obligation" releases that bands sometimes spew out to expedite moving from one label to another. There was no indication here that O'Reilly is in the process of switching publishers, but this had that sort of "mailing it in" vibe that albums tend to have in those situations.

In the introduction, the author sort of sets the book up (and he notes *"this book is not mandatory"*, and that it is something of *"a literary highlight reel"*) with the following:

> Over the past twenty years, I have written millions of words. "Bloviating" doesn't even begin to cover it. Eleven bestsellers, thousands of newspaper columns, a daily talking points memo on television, and so on. On my tombstone I want these words inscribed: "He finally stopped talking."
> Many publishers have asked me to simply reprint my past stuff. I've always said no. That's because some of what I've written is obsolete. Dated. Not relevant to anything anymore. That happens because life passes quickly and season change, to say the least. What was fascinating five years ago may be very boring right now. ... But some of what I've put down on paper is worth another look ...

That gives you the basic sense of what's going on here ... he (or his publishing aide, Charles Flowers) cherry picked bits and pieces out of his writings (generally a paragraph or so, sometimes a couple of pages), which he then intermittently comments on (and typically only a sentence or two when he does. The book starts out with material from his book *Culture Warrior* from 2006, which he considers "prophetic" on a lot of levels in sketching out what befell this country under Obama (who was a "vote present" do-nothing Senator embarrassing the state of Illinois *{don't blame me, I voted for "the black guy",* Alan Keyes[4], *for that seat!}* at the time), with a "told ya so!" overtone. Of course, giving the timing of the book, much of what's in here focuses on the Klinton years, and the media/left dog pack that hounded the Bush administration.

The book attempts at some organization ... it's in three sections, with 3-5 chapters each, "State of the Union", "State of Yourself", and "Keeping it Pithy" ... but even with the chapters focusing on a particular group of topics, the over-all feel here is of random bits pulled together simply to get a book out (O'Reilly mentions that they'd *"selected some of my best stuff and have presented it in a way that is designed to help your life"*, and that latter point seems to be the *purpose* here, O'Reilly magnanimously seeking to *"impart some guidance"* to his readers ... although I don't quite see who would be particularly enlightened by the mish-mash of material here).

Some of the topics covered (flipping through the contents listing) are the "progressive agenda", "European socialism", minority issues, "religion under attack", terror, materialism, Hollywood, liberal control of education, activist judges, media and leftist movements in cahoots, traditional values, his interactions with the "rich and powerful", and assorted other hot buttons.

I was somewhat surprised to find that I had inserted *zero* of my little bookmarks in this, indicating that there wasn't anything that jumped out at me as being particularly, well, "pithy", which is sadly somewhat damning in a collection that purports to be his "best stuff". Frankly, this book would be *ideal* if I were setting up a Social Media program for O'Reilly, as it's chock-full of little snippets that would make swell Twitter or Facebook posts ... a walk through this, and I'd have two years worth of an "editorial calendar" good-to-go (if being somewhat "dated" – one could always sprinkle in "opinion of the day" as it came up to keep things fresh). However, that's the sort of challenge I feel that I'm facing in trying to summarize the book in a way that would produce a satisfactory "review" ... it's all so random (if amassed into "themed" sections), and none of it stood out as something that was sufficiently notable to yank out as a blockquote. Well, with at least one exception ... in the final chapter he gets into some details of his "No Spin Zone" concept, and briefly presents it as a "philosophy" of sorts. I hate to indulge in a four-paragraph grab here, but since I'm not sharing anything else, I figured that we'll all (you, me, and O'Reilly) be OK with it:

> A personal No Spin Zone will save you time, money, and frustration. It will allow you to make value judgements base upon hard facts and evidence. And – provided that you keep an open mind and examine all credible data – you'll be comfortable with your conclusions on most matters.
>
> Here's the key that unlocks the Zone: the ability to be rigorous with yourself in always challenging your initial thoughts and conclusions. The Zone is no place for zealots, lemmings, or weak-minded followers. It is a state of mind that demands the discipline of clear thinking and the flexibility to change that thinking should the evidence dictate. Summing up, the No Spin Zone is <u>not</u> an easy place to be.
>
> Why? Because it's far easier to let others form your opinions. You then don't have to exercise your brain cells and the crowd will readily accept you. Politicians, commentators, and others vying to fill

your head space are eager to supply you with particular points of view. And increasingly, many Americans are buying into viewpoints that crush independent thinking. Why think when media talking heads and newspaper columnists will do that for you? After all, aren't these people "experts"?

Well, no, they are not. At least most of them aren't. There are no experts when it comes to making personal decisions. That's your own private domain. Sure, nobody is right all the time and you won't be either. We are all occasionally defeated on the field of logic. But take your shot at forming your own personal philosophy. It's actually fun and satisfying to develop a code of behavior and clear thinking pattern. Don't let pinheads, even smart pinheads, do your thinking for you.

Speaking of a "code of behavior", O'Reilly presents what seems to be *his* (it's just in there as its own section) early on in the book:

1. Work hard.
2. Keep a clear head. ...
3. Don't compromise when you know you're right.
4. Give most people the benefit of the doubt.
5. Don't fear authority.
6. And definitely have a good time.

... not a bad list when you think about it. One thing that I *do* have a significant problem with in the book is his use of "S-P" as shorthand for the people he opposes, which stands for Secular-Progressive. As anybody who has read my blogging over the past decade and a half will know, I *strongly* identify with the label "Secular", and feel that most religion-driven people, movements, and organizations (they're *all* ISIS to some degree!) are as *dangerous* to the great enlightenment experiment that is the United States as are the Communist/Socialist/"Progressive" forces that are plainly seeking to destroy it. It is one of my great frustrations in life that folks that I would wholeheartedly agree with on *most* points (O'Reilly, Ann Coulter, etc.) end up at some point going completely off the rails and start getting their marching orders from "the fairies in the back of the garden" (or some Bronze Age middle-eastern sheep herders' equivalent delusions).

Anyway, I guess I'd be hard-pressed to give Keep It Pithy[5] much of a recommendation. I suppose if you were looking for an "O'Reilly sampler", this might be of use to you, but it's pretty much *just* that. This does appear to still be in print, despite it drifting into the dollar store channel, and the online big boys are currently offering the hardcover at 39% off of the cover price ... but you can snag a "like new" copy from the new/used guys for as little as a penny plus shipping, so if you don't stumble over this on the dollar store shelves, that would be your best bet for picking this up, were you to be so inclined.

Notes:
1. http://btripp-books.livejournal.com/194915.html
2. http://btripp-books.com/
3. http://amzn.to/2hNwoGB
4. https://en.wikipedia.org/wiki/Alan_Keyes
5. http://amzn.to/2hNwoGB

Saturday, December 31, 2016[1]

"everyday is silent and grey"

I'm not exactly sure how Morrissey's Autobiography[2] got on my radar ... it evidently took a few years (this came out in 2013, and I only ordered it this past fall), but somewhere I read something that was singing its praises, and, being a fairly long-term Morrissey fan (and having recently indulged in another rock autobiography[3] by a guy of similar vintage, which I enjoyed), I snagged a copy. While this is a remarkable book, it could well be three (or four) books, and might benefit by at least being internally divided (this runs on for 450 pages with only a rare extra space between paragraphs, let alone any chapters or clearly delineated sections) along those lines.

When I started in on this, I was blown away. Morrissey was sort of "channeling James Joyce" and producing prose of richness, complexity, art and wit that had me *raving* about it and thinking that this was going to be featured on English departments' curriculums in the very near future. The first couple of hundred pages takes the story from his family's roots, his childhood, on through the early years of The Smiths and are an enchanting piece of writing. Tellingly, all the little bookmarks I put in here are from that part of the book. To give you a sense of what was so appealing here, the following is the very start of the book, a small part of a paragraph that runs *four and half pages*:

> My childhood is streets upon streets upon streets upon streets. Streets to define you and streets to confine you, with no sign of motorway, freeway, or highway. Somewhere beyond hides the treat of the countryside, for hour-less days when rains and reins life, permitting us to be amongst people who live surrounded by space and are irked by our faces. Until then we live in forgotten Victorian knife-plunging Manchester, where everything lies where ever it was left over one hundred years ago. The safe streets are dimly lit, the others not lit at all, but both represent a danger that you're asking for should you find yourself out there once the curtains have closed for tea. ...

While telling the story of his youth and school years, it is generally like this ... perhaps having the task of recreating the past being an opening for literary flourish. Part of me wishes this went for the rest of the book. However, when the story turns to the demise of The Smiths, and into a vastly ugly court case where former band members are trying (ultimately, successfully) to essentially re-write the agreements of many years previous, the tone of the writing also changes, and those are *very* difficult parts to read. The last part of the book is also less lyrical, with a long wander through shows here, shows there, places Morrissey lived, people Morrissey hung out with, and random details on the reception of his solo albums. Now, I suppose that hard-core Morrissey fans would eat up the latter part, but it, and the claustrophobic, panic-inducing, press of the industry/court phases, makes one wish those first couple of hundred pages were a thing unto themselves.

Speaking of fan info ... I'm guessing that others knew this before it got in here, but I was surprised to read the origin of Morrissey's nickname "Moz" ... which I had sort of assumed had been something that had "organically" arose out of The Smiths' fandom or the press, but it's a bit different:

> ... My own name is by now synonymous with the word 'miserable' in the press, so Johnny {Marr} putters with 'misery' and playfully arrives at 'misery mozzery', which truncates to Moz, and I am classified ever after. ...

As I only have a small smattering of my bookmarks pointing back to particular sections, and they're all up front, I guess I'll deal with them now, and get into the rest of the book after. Now, another "comment" here (not really intended as a criticism), the flow of his early years, while having random contextifying data, are not particularly *linear*, or anchored to ages, dates, or events, so it's often fairly hard to pin down how old he was in things he's covering. In a section discussing various acts and albums of which he's enamored, he mentions *"It is considered odd that a boy so young should care so much."*, which leads into the following:

> ... Here and there my eyes and ears are caught only by the solo singers; town-crying to all people at all times, television troubadours minus jingle-jangled nodding musicians. The song bears witness, the body weaves, and there are no camera cuts to blandly smiling session-players when all we want to see is the sculpted singer – alone, carrying all, sub-plot and sub-text, the physical autobiography; simultaneously, subjectively and objectively at the same time. There is no way out for the solo singer; introduction, statement, conclusion, quick death – all conveyed in the pop sonnet, with no winking glance over to guitarists in order to ease the setting. There are visions of divine things ... I still don't know what it's all about, but like the science of signs, I am called to, because the song is the art of using language as persuasion, and with that allowance and hope, I want to cry. I am caught and I am devoted to a fault. Snobbery jumps in. If I can sing, I am free, and no legislation can stop me.
> ...

The next section is easier to pin down, as he cites the date of his first concert (T.Rex in 1972, when he would have been 13), and this bit relates to a number of acts and songs he's discussing:

> It seemed to me that it was only within British pop music that almost anything could happen. Every other mode of expression seemed fixed and pre-

> dictable and slow. ... Marc Bolan's lyrics are steeped in the quietly insane world of the gothic English novel, and are too deeply eccentric to survive any explanation. On earlier records, Bolan sounds as if singing in Olde English – incomprehensible to the modern ear. Yes, but the Bible speaks of <u>'a whole earth of one language'</u>, and this is something that only pop singers can manage. ...

At one point he gets into discussing the poetry of a number of writers (possibly idiosyncratically English, as I only recognized a few of the names), and drifts into this rather florid exposition (which is presented leading up to the purchase of an instrument ... albeit a *drum kit*):

> ... The will surrenders to the resolve and dignity of the written word, and I, the gentle self, step forward, pattering up the ramp, one half of an incomplete person, knowing with certainty that I cannot live – yet wondering if I could possibly write? Slight and weary and full of angularity, my heart is never unbroken, but I am unable to call out. I have a sudden urge to write something down, but this time they are words that must take a lead. Unless I an combine poetry with recorded noise, have I any right to be? Yet, let it begin, for who is to say what you should or shouldn't do? In fact, everyone tries to knot your desires lest your success highlight their own failure. Better, it is thought, that we all swill in the same bucket, just making do. But I have no intention of surviving for eighteen years in order that I might be strangled to death in my nineteenth. I will never be lacking if the clash of sounds collide, with refinement and logic bursting from a cone of manful blast. Here, from the weeds, the situation worsens since each abiding art-form lacks one essential ingredient – and that ingredient is the small and bowed passionate I. Since there is no living being as recipient of my whispers, and since there are no certainties that one shall ever appear, then the off-balance distortion of my everyday feeling <u>must</u> edge into the un-cooperative world <u>somehow</u>.

A somebody who has written a vast lot of poetry in certain phases of *my* life, Morrissey's phrase: *"the off-balance distortion of my everyday feeling"* certainly echoes in my core. Given the length of the above quote, I am hesitant to add another, but one of the questions that arose while reading the descriptions of the music business, and especially as it related to The Smiths, was "why is it that all bands seem to end up getting screwed?", and Morrissey has a *scathing* dissection of this (long after the fact, of course), which runs from page 170 to 172 ... far too long for this space, so let me dust off some more ellipses and at least dole out the high points:

> *We signed virtually anything without looking. ... The specifics of finance and the gluttonous snakes-and-ladders legalities were deliberately complicated snares that all pop artists are expected to understand immediately. ... The basic rule, though, is to keep the musician in the dark at all costs, so that the musician might call upon the lawyer repeatedly. ... A vast industry of music lawyers and managers and accountants therefore flourish unchecked due to the musician's lack of business grasp. ... pop stars come and go with lightning speed, while the fraternity of managers and lawyers remain in place forevermore ...*

Etc., etc., etc. ... it is quite a rant, and somewhat reminiscent of a song[4] he penned regarding the later court case. This takes me both to the last of my bookmarks, and the point where the tone changes. The Smiths were classically clueless on the business angles, and basically got ripped off at every point, including when they got lured away from their initial record company. One interesting thing in here was the later near-remorse (perhaps just bitterness) of Factory Records (home of Joy Division, etc.) head Anthony H. Wilson who seemed to rather hate The Smiths for his having not signed them early on, with at least one letter from him to Morrissey reproduced in its entirety. Unfortunately, communications with The Smiths' original label, Rough Trade, and its head Geoff Travis, were rarely much more civil, and many of these missives are quoted here.

These are hard to read, because, despite the band making some iconic albums at the time, they are evidently being bled at every turn. Plus, they seem (at least in Morrissey's telling) to be much hated in the press, and faced with radio programmers who seemingly outright refused to play their records (despite having reasonably robust sales). I guess if Morrissey wasn't depressed *before* all this, one can't fault him for being morose because of it all. However, worse stuff was on the horizon. One of the initial band members, drummer Michael Joyce, had attempted (through *"an array of legal firms"*, most of whom soon dropped his case) to try to retroactively increase his stake in the band, now nearly a decade past its end. He eventually managed to get a trial and a very sympathetic judge and prosecutor (or, perhaps, just ones *hostile* to Morrissey). Now, I have no information on this trial outside of what Morrissey writes, so it's *his* version, and he is certainly painting himself as the victim of a fraudulent claim pushed through an incompetent court, but who knows. The tale told in this part of the book (which was hardly a pleasant read), suggests that Joyce' claim had no backing, that "corporately" the band was Morrissey and Marr (the latter was only peripherally involved in the trial – although one assumes he had the same financial stake in it – lending credence to the idea that this was an effort to "get" Morrissey), and that the other band members had been operating under an agreement which were paid them a 10% cut with no interest in any additional monies. The judge invoked some rulings from *1890*, and agreed that Joyce, although having no documentation, a long string of legal firms that opted out of representing him, and a story that changed repeatedly, had been an "equal partner" in The Smiths, and so due 25% of those (long-gone) funds. On top of how the deck was stacked against Morrissey, *his* lawyers faded off and passed the case down to less-seasoned (and *informed*) representation at the last minute. The details presented in this part of the book are horrific (if what Morrissey is writing is, indeed, correct – and I have no grounds to doubt him – any sane person would have thrown Joyce's case out with even a cursory look at the specifics), and the writing is far less poetic, and seethes with the author's justified frustration.

I guess later success, however, is its best revenge, and once he gets past the trial, most of the remainder of the book deals with his solo career. While this was still not smooth sailing, it has obviously been a lot more lucrative than The Smiths ended up being. While interesting in a music-magazine sort of mode, this is full of way more information than I really needed to know: concerts, tours, festivals, events, and the famous people he interacted with. Needless to say, this latter element is in full swing when he moved to Los Angeles, even featuring a picture of Nancy Sinatra posing with a Morrissey poster (why?). I hate to say it, but that last section is more "Tiger Beat" than *Dubliners*, but that, I suspect, is "just me", and that the sort of detail in there is likely to appeal to a lot of people.

Again, I was disappointed that the *whole* of Autobiography[5] wasn't the literary delight of the first third, but it's Morrissey going through his life experiences, and the icky bits with the industry, with the media, with the lawsuits, and the rest are part of that. While the writing isn't as *special* in the latter parts of the book, it never devolves down into the "newspaper reporting" voice that frequently shows up in biographies. If the whole was like the start, I'd be telling you that you absolutely *had* to get a copy, but as it is, I'd suggest that you should at least *consider* it. Needless to say, it would help if you were a Smiths/Morrissey fan.

It appears that the hardcover is out of print at this point (although you can get "new" copies from the new/used guys for as little as the assorted grades of "used"), but there's a paperback available, which has a good likelihood of being on the shelf at your local surviving brick-and-mortar book store. This is an *interesting* read throughout, with parts of it being *brilliant* … so it could well be worth your while to make the effort (it *is* 450 pages) to give it a read!

Notes:

1. http://btripp-books.livejournal.com/195257.html
2. http://amzn.to/2gsqry8
3. http://btripp-books.livejournal.com/193632.html
4. https://goo.gl/0QTlcv
5. http://amzn.to/2gsqry8

QR code links to the on-line reviews:

The Rapture of the Nerds:
A tale of the singularity, posthumanity,
and awkward social situations
by
Cory Doctorow & Charles Stross

Marilyn & Me: A Photographer's Memories
by
Lawrence Schiller

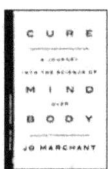

Cure: A Journey into the Science of Mind Over Body
by
Jo Marchant

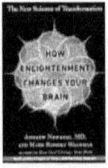

How Enlightenment Changes Your Brain:
The New Science of Transformation
by
Andrew Newberg, MD & Mark Robert Waldman

Hug Your Haters:
How to Embrace Complaints
and Keep Your Customers
by
Jay Baer

The Age of Radiance:
The Epic Rise and Dramatic Fall of the Atomic Era
by
Craig Nelson

Less Medicine, More Health:
7 Assumptions That Drive Too Much Medical Care
by
Dr. H. Gilbert Welch

The Magic of Believing
by
Claude M. Bristol

It's Not Who You Know, It's Who Knows YOU!
A Practical Business Guide to Raising Your Profits
By Raising Your Profile
by
David Avrin

Influence: The Psychology of Persuasion
by
Robert B. Cialdini

Love Is the Cure:
On Life, Loss, and the End of AIDS
by
Elton John

The Art of People:
11 Simple People Skills
That Will Get You Everything You Want
by
Dave Kerpen

The Upside:
The 7 Strategies for Turning Big Threats
into Growth Breakthroughs
by
Adrian J. Slywotzky

On Writing: A Memoir of the Craft
by
Steven King

If it Ain't Broke...Break It!:
And Other Unconventional Wisdom
for a Changing Business World
by
Robert J. Kriegel

Success is Not an Accident:
The Mental Bank Concept
by
John G. Kappas, Ph.D.

Righteous Indignation:
Excuse Me While I Save the World!
by
Andrew Brietbart

Gödel, Escher, Bach:
An Eternal Golden Braid
by
Douglas R. Hofstadter

Auguste Escoffier: Memories of My Life
by
Auguste Escoffier

Listen To This
by
Alex Ross

An Unquiet Mind:
A Memoir of Moods and Madness
by
Kay Redfield Jamison

The Invisible Sale: How to Build
a Digitally Powered Marketing and Sales System
to Better Prospect, Qualify and Close Leads
by
Tom Martin

On Killing: The Psychological Cost
of Learning to Kill in War and Society
by
Lt. Col. Dave Grossman

God Is Not Great:
How Religion Poisons Everything
by
Christopher Hitchens

We the People: The Modern-Day Figures
Who Have Reshaped and Affirmed
the Founding Fathers' Vision of America
by
Juan Williams

Arms & The Man
by
George Bernard Shaw

The Third Industrial Revolution:
How Lateral Power Is Transforming
Energy, the Economy, and the World
by
Jeremy Rifkin

The Joy of Hate:
How to Triumph over Whiners
in the Age of Phony Outrage
by
Greg Gutfeld

Talking with My Mouth Full:
My Life as a Professional Eater
by
Gail Simmons

The Simple Beauty of the Unexpected:
A Natural Philosopher's Quest for Trout
and the Meaning of Everything
by
Marcelo Gleiser

Living in Blue Sky Mind:
Basic Buddhist Teachings for a Happy Life
by
Richard Gentei Diedrichs

Beyond Reason:
Using Emotions as You Negotiate
by
Roger Fisher & Daniel Shapiro

Lyric Poems
by
John Keats

Outlaw Journalist:
The Life and Times of Hunter S. Thompson
by
William McKeen

The Conscience of a Libertarian:
Empowering the Citizen Revolution
with God, Guns, Gold and Tax Cuts
by
Wayne Allyn Root

Breaking the Spell:
Religion as a Natural Phenomenon
by
Daniel C. Dennett

 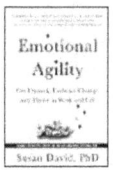

Emotional Agility:
Get Unstuck, Embrace Change,
and Thrive in Work and Life
by
Susan David, PhD.

The Decision Maker:
Unlock the Potential of Everyone
in Your Organization, One Decision at a Time
by
Dennis Bakke

Steal the Menu:
A Memoir of Forty Years in Food
by
Raymond Sokolov

Choice Point: Align Your Purpose
by
Harry Massey & David R. Hamilton, Ph.D.

Darwin's Devices:
What Evolving Robots Can Teach Us
About the History of Life and the Future of Technology
by
John Long

Love & War:
Twenty Years, Three Presidents, Two Daughters
and One Louisiana Home
by
Mary Matalin & James Carville

Pure Goldwater
by
John W. Dean & Barry M. Goldwater Jr.

Don't-Know Mind: The Spirit of Korean Zen
by
Richard Shrobe

Captive:
My Time as a Prisoner of the Taliban
by
Jere Van Dyk

JFK Jr., George, & Me: A Memoir
by
Matt Berman

Tracks in the Sea:
Matthew Fontaine Maury
and the Mapping of the Oceans
by
Chester G. Hearn

Golden Gate:
The Life and Times of America's Greatest Bridge
by
Kevin Starr

Roger Ailes: Off Camera
by
Zev Chafets

Sane New World:
A User's Guide to the Normal-Crazy Mind
by
Ruby Wax

The Power of Meaning:
Crafting a Life That Matters
by
Emily Esfahani Smith

Friendfluence:
The Surprising Ways Friends Make Us Who We Are
by
Carlin Flora

Lost Ancient Technology Of Peru And Bolivia
by
Brien Foerster

Rush Limbaugh: An Army of One
by
Zev Chafets

Dark Mission:
The Secret History of NASA
by
Richard C. Hoagland & Mike Bara

The Art of the Sale:
Learning from the Masters About the Business of Life
by
Philip Delves Broughton

See a Little Light:
The Trail of Rage and Melody
by
Bob Mould & Michael Azerrad

Thinking Beyond the Unthinkable:
Harnessing Doom from the Cold War
to the Age of Terror
by
Jonathan Stevenson

Beggars, Cheats, & Forgers:
a History of Frauds Through the Ages
by
David Thomas

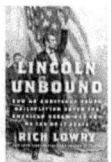

Lincoln Unbound: How an Ambitious Young Railsplitter
Saved the American Dream
- and How We Can Do It Again
by
Rich Lowry

The Fifth Agreement:
A Practical Guide to Self-Mastery
by
don Miguel Ruiz & don Jose Ruiz

Keep It Pithy:
Useful Observations in a Tough World
by
Bill O'Reilly

Autobiography
by
Morrissey

BTRIPP BOOKS - 2016   277

CONTENTS - ALPHABETICAL BY AUTHOR

David Avrin   page 31
*It's Not Who You Know, It's Who Knows YOU!
A Practical Business Guide to Raising Your Profits
By Raising Your Profile*

Jay Baer   page 15
*Hug Your Haters: How to Embrace Complaints
and Keep Your Customers*

Dennis Bakke   page 154
*The Decision Maker: Unlock the Potential of
Everyone in Your Organization, One Decision at a Time*

Matt Berman   page 185
JFK Jr., George, & Me: A Memoir

Andrew Brietbart   page 65
*Righteous Indignation:
Excuse Me While I Save the World!*

Claude M. Bristol   page 28
The Magic of Believing

Philip Delves Broughton   page 230
*The Art of the Sale: Learning from the Masters
About the Business of Life*

Zev Chafets   page 198
Roger Ailes: Off Camera

Zev Chafets   page 222
Rush Limbaugh: An Army of One

Robert B. Cialdini — page 34
Influence: The Psychology of Persuasion

Susan David, PhD. — page 149
Emotional Agility: Get Unstuck, Embrace Change, and Thrive in Work and Life

John W. Dean & Barry M. Goldwater Jr. — page 174
Pure Goldwater

Daniel C. Dennett — page 144
Breaking the Spell: Religion as a Natural Phenomenon

Richard Gentei Diedrichs — page 125
Living in Blue Sky Mind: Basic Buddhist Teachings for a Happy Life

Cory Doctorow & Charles Stross — page 1
The Rapture of the Nerds: A tale of the singularity, posthumanity, and awkward social situations

Auguste Escoffier — page 74
Auguste Escoffier: Memories of My Life

Roger Fisher & Daniel Shapiro — page 129
Beyond Reason: Using Emotions as You Negotiate

Carlin Flora — page 213
Friendfluence: The Surprising Ways Friends Make Us Who We Are

Brien Foerster — page 218
Lost Ancient Technology Of Peru And Bolivia

Marcelo Gleiser — page 120
The Simple Beauty of the Unexpected: A Natural Philosopher's Quest for Trout and the Meaning of Everything

Lt. Col. Dave Grossman — page 88
On Killing: The Psychological Cost of Learning to Kill in War and Society

Greg Gutfeld — page 111
The Joy of Hate: How to Triumph over Whiners in the Age of Phony Outrage

Chester G. Hearn — page 188
Tracks in the Sea: Matthew Fontaine Maury and the Mapping of the Oceans

Christopher Hitchens — page 93
God Is Not Great: How Religion Poisons Everything

Richard C. Hoagland & Mike Bara — page 226
Dark Mission: The Secret History of NASA

Douglas R. Hofstadter — page 70
Gödel, Escher, Bach: An Eternal Golden Braid

Kay Redfield Jamison — page 81
An Unquiet Mind: A Memoir of Moods and Madness

Elton John — page 38
Love Is the Cure: On Life, Loss, and the End of AIDS

John G. Kappas, Ph.D. — page 61
Success is Not an Accident: The Mental Bank Concept

John Keats   page 133
              Lyric Poems

Dave Kerpen   page 42
     *The Art of People: 11 Simple People Skills
     That Will Get You Everything You Want*

Steven King   page 51
          On Writing: A Memoir of the Craft

Robert J. Kriegel   page 56
     *If it Ain't Broke...Break It!: And Other Unconventional
     Wisdom for a Changing Business World*

John Long   page 165
     *Darwin's Devices: What Evolving Robots Can Teach Us
     About the History of Life and the Future of Technology*

Rich Lowry   page 245
     *Lincoln Unbound: How an Ambitious Young Railsplitter
     Saved the American Dream --and How We Can Do It Again*

Jo Marchant   page 7
     Cure: A Journey into the Science of Mind Over Body

Tom Martin   page 84
     *The Invisible Sale: How to Build a Digitally Powered Marketing
     and Sales System to Better Prospect, Qualify and Close Leads*

Harry Massey & David R. Hamilton, Ph.D.   page 162
          Choice Point: Align Your Purpose

Mary Matalin & James Carville   page 169
     *Love & War: Twenty Years, Three Presidents,
     Two Daughters and One Louisiana Home*

William McKeen	page	135
Outlaw Journalist: The Life and Times of Hunter S. Thompson		
Morrissey	page	256
Autobiography		
Bob Mould & Michael Azerrad	page	234
See a Little Light: The Trail of Rage and Melody		
Craig Nelson	page	19
The Age of Radiance: The Epic Rise and Dramatic Fall of the Atomic Era		
Andrew Newberg, MD & Mark Robert Waldman	page	11
How Enlightenment Changes Your Brain: The New Science of Transformation		
Bill O'Reilly	page	253
Keep It Pithy: Useful Observations in a Tough World		
Jeremy Rifkin	page	108
The Third Industrial Revolution: How Lateral Power Is Transforming Energy, the Economy, and the World		
Wayne Allyn Root	page	138
The Conscience of a Libertarian: Empowering the Citizen Revolution with God, Guns, Gold and Tax Cuts		
Alex Ross	page	78
Listen To This		
don Miguel Ruiz & don Jose Ruiz	page	248
The Fifth Agreement: A Practical Guide to Self-Mastery		

Lawrence Schiller *Marilyn & Me: A Photographer's Memories*	page 5
George Bernard Shaw *Arms & The Man*	page 105
Richard Shrobe *Don't-Know Mind: The Spirit of Korean Zen*	page 179
Gail Simmons *Talking with My Mouth Full: My Life as a Professional Eater*	page 116
Adrian J. Slywotzky *The Upside: The 7 Strategies for Turning Big Threats into Growth Breakthroughs*	page 46
Emily Esfahani Smith *The Power of Meaning: Crafting a Life That Matters*	page 207
Raymond Sokolov *Steal the Menu: A Memoir of Forty Years in Food*	page 157
Kevin Starr *Golden Gate: The Life and Times of America's Greatest Bridge*	page 193
Jonathan Stevenson *Thinking Beyond the Unthinkable: Harnessing Doom from the Cold War to the Age of Terror*	page 238
David Thomas *Beggars, Cheats, & Forgers: a History of Frauds Through the Ages*	page 241

Jere Van Dyk   page 182
: *Captive: My Time as a Prisoner of the Taliban*

Ruby Wax   page 203
: *Sane New World:
A User's Guide to the Normal-Crazy Mind*

Dr. H. Gilbert Welch   page 23
: *Less Medicine, More Health:
7 Assumptions That Drive Too Much Medical Care*

Juan Williams   page 99
: *We the People: The Modern-Day Figures
Who Have Reshaped and Affirmed
the Founding Fathers' Vision of America*

CONTENTS - ALPHABETICAL BY TITLE

The Age of Radiance: The Epic Rise and Dramatic Fall of the Atomic Era
Craig Nelson — page 19

Arms & The Man
George Bernard Shaw — page 105

The Art of People: 11 Simple People Skills That Will Get You Everything You Want
Dave Kerpen — page 42

The Art of the Sale: Learning from the Masters About the Business of Life
Philip Delves Broughton — page 230

Auguste Escoffier: Memories of My Life
Auguste Escoffier — page 74

Autobiography
Morrissey — page 256

Beggars, Cheats, & Forgers: a History of Frauds Through the Ages
David Thomas — page 241

Beyond Reason: Using Emotions as You Negotiate
Roger Fisher & Daniel Shapiro — page 129

Breaking the Spell: Religion as a Natural Phenomenon
Daniel C. Dennett — page 144

Captive: My Time as a Prisoner of the Taliban
Jere Van Dyk   page 182

Choice Point: Align Your Purpose
Harry Massey & David R. Hamilton, Ph.D.   page 162

The Conscience of a Libertarian: Empowering the
Citizen Revolution with God, Guns, Gold and Tax Cuts
Wayne Allyn Root   page 138

Cure: A Journey into the Science of Mind Over Body
Jo Marchant   page   7

Dark Mission: The Secret History of NASA
Richard C. Hoagland & Mike Bara   page 226

Darwin's Devices: What Evolving Robots Can Teach Us
About the History of Life and the Future of Technology
John Long   page 165

The Decision Maker: Unlock the Potential of
Everyone in Your Organization, One Decision at a Time
Dennis Bakke   page 154

Don't-Know Mind: The Spirit of Korean Zen
Richard Shrobe   page 179

Emotional Agility: Get Unstuck, Embrace Change,
and Thrive in Work and Life
Susan David, PhD.   page 149

The Fifth Agreement: A Practical Guide to Self-Mastery
don Miguel Ruiz & don Jose Ruiz   page 248

Friendfluence:
The Surprising Ways Friends Make Us Who We Are
Carlin Flora   page 213

God Is Not Great: How Religion Poisons Everything
Christopher Hitchens   page 93

Gödel, Escher, Bach: An Eternal Golden Braid
Douglas R. Hofstadter   page 70

Golden Gate:
The Life and Times of America's Greatest Bridge
Kevin Starr   page 193

How Enlightenment Changes Your Brain:
The New Science of Transformation
Andrew Newberg, MD & Mark Robert Waldman   page 11

Hug Your Haters: How to Embrace Complaints
and Keep Your Customers
Jay Baer   page 15

If it Ain't Broke...Break It!: And Other Unconventional
Wisdom for a Changing Business World
Robert J. Kriegel   page 56

Influence: The Psychology of Persuasion
Robert B. Cialdini   page 34

The Invisible Sale: How to Build a Digitally Powered Marketing
and Sales System to Better Prospect, Qualify and Close Leads
Tom Martin   page 84

It's Not Who You Know, It's Who Knows YOU!
A Practical Business Guide to Raising Your Profits By Raising Your Profile
David Avrin   page 31

JFK Jr., George, & Me: A Memoir
Matt Berman   page 185

*The Joy of Hate: How to Triumph over Whiners
in the Age of Phony Outrage*
Greg Gutfeld   page 111

Keep It Pithy: Useful Observations in a Tough World
Bill O'Reilly   page 253

*Less Medicine, More Health:
7 Assumptions That Drive Too Much Medical Care*
Dr. H. Gilbert Welch   page 23

*Lincoln Unbound: How an Ambitious Young Railsplitter
Saved the American Dream -- and How We Can Do It Again*
Rich Lowry   page 245

Listen To This
Alex Ross   page 78

*Living in Blue Sky Mind:
Basic Buddhist Teachings for a Happy Life*
Richard Gentei Diedrichs   page 125

Lost Ancient Technology Of Peru And Bolivia
Brien Foerster   page 218

*Love & War: Twenty Years, Three Presidents,
Two Daughters and One Louisiana Home*
Mary Matalin & James Carville   page 169

Love Is the Cure: On Life, Loss, and the End of AIDS
Elton John   page 38

Lyric Poems
John Keats — page 133

The Magic of Believing
Claude M. Bristol — page 28

Marilyn & Me: A Photographer's Memories
Lawrence Schiller — page 5

On Killing: The Psychological Cost of Learning to Kill in War and Society
Lt. Col. Dave Grossman — page 88

On Writing: A Memoir of the Craft
Steven King — page 51

Outlaw Journalist: The Life and Times of Hunter S. Thompson
William McKeen — page 135

The Power of Meaning: Crafting a Life That Matters
Emily Esfahani Smith — page 207

Pure Goldwater
John W. Dean & Barry M. Goldwater Jr. — page 174

The Rapture of the Nerds: A tale of the singularity, posthumanity, and awkward social situations
Cory Doctorow & Charles Stross — page 1

Righteous Indignation: Excuse Me While I Save the World!
Andrew Brietbart — page 65

Roger Ailes: Off Camera
Zev Chafets   page   198

Rush Limbaugh: An Army of One
Zev Chafets   page   222

Sane New World:
A User's Guide to the Normal-Crazy Mind
Ruby Wax   page   203

See a Little Light: The Trail of Rage and Melody
Bob Mould & Michael Azerrad   page   234

The Simple Beauty of the Unexpected: A Natural Philosopher's
Quest for Trout and the Meaning of Everything
Marcelo Gleiser   page   120

Steal the Menu: A Memoir of Forty Years in Food
Raymond Sokolov   page   157

Success is Not an Accident: The Mental Bank Concept
John G. Kappas, Ph.D.   page   61

Talking with My Mouth Full:
My Life as a Professional Eater
Gail Simmons   page   116

Thinking Beyond the Unthinkable: Harnessing Doom
from the Cold War to the Age of Terror
Jonathan Stevenson   page   238

The Third Industrial Revolution: How Lateral Power
Is Transforming Energy, the Economy, and the World
Jeremy Rifkin   page   108

*Tracks in the Sea: Matthew Fontaine Maury
and the Mapping of the Oceans*
Chester G. Hearn   page 188

An Unquiet Mind: A Memoir of Moods and Madness
Kay Redfield Jamison   page   81

*The Upside: The 7 Strategies
for Turning Big Threats into Growth Breakthroughs*
Adrian J. Slywotzky   page   46

*We the People: The Modern-Day Figures Who Have Reshaped
and Affirmed the Founding Fathers' Vision of America*
Juan Williams   page   99

www.ingramcontent.com/pod-product-compliance
Lightning Source LLC
Chambersburg PA
CBHW071302110426
42743CB00042B/1140